Catholic England

Manchester Medieval Sources series

series adviser Janet L. Nelson

This series aims to meet a growing need amongst students and teachers of medieval history for translations of key sources that are directly useable in students' own work. The series will provide texts central to medieval studies courses and will focus upon the diverse cultural, social as well as political conditions that affected the functioning of all levels of medieval society. The basic premise of the new series is that translation must be accompanied by sufficient introductory and explanatory material and each volume will therefore include a comprehensive guide to the sources' interpretation, including discussion of critical linguistic problems and an assessment of the most recent research on the topics being covered.

already published in the series

Janet L. Nelson *The Annals of St-Bertin: ninth-century histories, volume I*

Timothy Reuter *The Annals of Fulda: ninth-century histories, volume II*

forthcoming titles in the series will include

Donald Bullough *The Vikings in Paris*

John Edwards *The Jews in western Europe, 1400–1600*

Chris Given-Wilson *Chronicles of the Revolution, 1397–1400*

Rosemary Horrox *The aftermath of the Black Death*

Simon Lloyd *The impact of the crusades: the experience of England, 1095–1274*

Richard Smith *Sources for the population history of England, 1000–1540*

J. A. Watt *The origins of anti-semitism in Europe*

CATHOLIC ENGLAND

FAITH, RELIGION AND OBSERVANCE BEFORE THE REFORMATION

translated and annotated by R. N. Swanson

Manchester University Press
Manchester and New York

distributed exclusively in the USA and Canada by St. Martin's Press

Published by Manchester University Press
Oxford Road, Manchester M13 9PL, England
and Room 400, 175 Fifth Avenue, New York, NY 10010, USA

*Distributed exclusively in the USA and Canada
by St. Martin's Press, Inc.*, 175 Fifth Avenue, New York, NY 10010, USA

British Library Cataloguing-in-Publication Data
A catalogue record for this book is available from the British Library

*Library of Congress cataloging in publication data
Applied for*

ISBN 0 7190 3465-5 *paperback*

Reprinted 1995

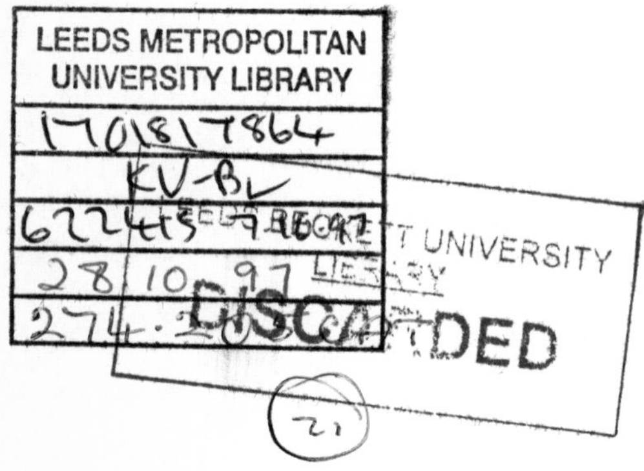

Printed in Great Britain
by Bell & Bain Ltd, Glasgow

Contents

Foreword *page* ix
Preface xi
Note on the documents xv

Introduction. In search of pre-Reformation English spirituality 1

PART ONE: THEORY

I. The Bible 46

1. The Vulgate (Latin) version 46
2. The Wycliffite Bible 47
3. A modern translation 48

II. Disseminating the faith 51

A. Instruction in the faith:
4. Lenten instruction by John Drury of Beccles 53

B. Sermons
5. From John Mirk's *Festial* 58
6. From the main Wycliffite cycle 64
7. From an anonymous compilation 67

III. The mass 78

8. Instructions in preparation for the mass 79
9. Lay action during mass: *The Lay Folks' Mass Book.* 83

IV. Designs for living and dying 92

10. *The Abbey of the Holy Ghost* 96
11. Walter Hilton, *Epistle on the Mixed Life* 104
12. *The Book of the Craft of Dying* 125

PART TWO: PRACTICE

V. Parish celebrations 150

13. Scarborough: parish accounts, 1435–6 151
14. Great Yarmouth: selected accounts, 1386–1505 157

15. King's Lynn: selected accounts, 1398–1536 159

VI. Private religion 164

16. Licences for private chapels and oratories 166
17. Vows of chastity 173

VII. Saints, shrines, miracles, and pilgrimage 175

A. Shrines and offerings by pilgrims
18. Ornaments of shrines in York Minster 179
19. Receipts from offerings at Hereford cathedral 182
20. Receipts of St Etheldreda's shrine, Ely 186
21. Small shrines and vicarious pilgrimages 195

B. Miracles
22. Miracles of St Osmund, *c.* 1453 196
23. Miracles of Henry VI 197

VIII. Security for the living 201

A. Indulgences
24. Appointment of proctors for a bridge, 1484–5 203
25. Appointment of proctors for a bridge, *c.* 1490 204
26. Appontment of proctor for St Anthony's Hospital, London, 1479 205
27. Appointment of proctor for St Anthony's Hospital, London, 1536 206
28. Indulgence granted for a chapel 207
29. Profits of indulgence: St Anthony's Hospital, London, 1513 207

B. Guilds and fraternities
30. Franciscan letter of confraternity 210
31. Mendicant letters of confraternity 211
32. Regulations of a trade fraternity: the carpenters of York, 1482 213
33. Guild membership: the Palmers of Ludlow, 1505–6 215
34. Cumulative totals of guild subscriptions: the Palmers of Ludlow, 1447-8 216
35. National membership receipts: the Palmers of Ludlow, 1538–9 217
36. Benefits of membership of the fraternity of St Chad, Lichfield 218

IX. Security for the dead 222

A. Obits and anniversaries

37. Provision of trentals, 1487 224
38. Obit arrangements: William Paston 225
39. Establishment of an obit or anniversary, 1458 227

B. Chantries and almshouses

40. Establishment of a chantry: St James's priory, Bristol, 1400 229
41. Establishment of a chantry in a friary: Bristol, 1469 231
42. Establishment of a chantry through feoffment to uses: Bridgwater, 1482 233
43. Regulations for a chantry and almshouses: Ludlow, 1486 234

X. Distributions at death: wills 242

44. The will of Thomas Kebell, 1500 244
45. The will of Lady Jane Strangweys, 1500 249
46. The wills of Sir John Port, 1528–40 252

XI. Complaint and opposition 259

A. Anticlericalism?

47. The burgesses of of Saltash complain about their vicar, *c.* 1406 261
48. Complaints at visitation: Kent, 1511–12 262

B. Heresy and Lollardy

49. The hunt for heretics: Bury St Edmunds,1428 267
50. The definition of 'Lollardy' 268
51. Lollard confessions, 1430 270

Bibliography of printed works cited 281

Index 295

Foreword

Robert Swanson's book is timely in a double sense. In contemporary historiography the Reformation debate has attained new levels of subtlety, of geographical range and social depth. Yet for British students, the playing-field has been distinctly uneven: while evidence in English has made the sixteenth century relatively accessible, non-readers of Latin or Middle English have found it hard to acquire for the fourteenth and fifteenth centuries the sense of familiarity that comes only from careful reflection on primary sources. It depends of course on which sources – and Swanson's work is path breaking precisely because it take us into areas that previous source-collections have not reached: from Part I's Theory – of sermons, liturgy and devotional literature – to Part II's Practice – of private vows, pilgrimages, confraternities and provision for the dead. Timely this book surely is in a second sense too: for it's clearer now in the 1990s than at any time since the Second World War how fundamentally important religion is in social life as in politics, in shaping local and national communities, as well as in allowing individuals self-definition. Religious history is about popular as well as learned belief and practice; and about the constant interplay (rather than contradiction) between the official and the unofficial. Swanson shows what the evidence for later medieval England looks like. He shows how to 'read' lay religious practice from parish accounts and inventories of shrine offerings, and how to probe beneath the surface of the rich material on complaint and opposition: lay criticisms of clergy could be shaped by devout expectations, and lay absence from the local church could indicate not heretical leanings but preference for another church. Swanson begins by acknowledging the 'most daunting difficulty: to penetrate minds'. Undaunted, he has made mind-reading his agenda – and enabled his readers to make it theirs.

Janet L. Nelson, King's College London

Preface

The debate on the Reformation among historians of Tudor England has continued intermittently almost since the upheaval itself.[1] In recent years, it has acquired a new twist, and something of a new vitality and virulence. In the one corner are those, such as A. G. Dickens,[2] who interpret the changes as the outgrowth of revulsion against a decadent and unsatisfactory spirituality and ecclesiastical system; opposing are those like Christopher Haigh and J. J. Scarisbrick[3] who, on re-examining the evidence on the nature of the pre-Reformation Church, have constructed a picture of a vital spirituality, one which was remarkably popular, but which was smashed from above by governmental decree.

For those historians whose courage fails as 1534 approaches, the battle among the Reformation historians has been somewhat bewildering. Their normalities have suddenly become the novelties of the 'revisionists'. At the same time, the rediscovery and reconstruction of the pre-Reformation church shows signs of going too far: there may be a danger that too rosy a picture is constructed of complete harmony, so that any manifestation of opposition to the structure becomes a precursor of Protestantism. Something of that sort seems to have occurred in a recent consideration of the religious changes in SW England.[4]

The purpose of the present collection is to present some of the evidence for the spiritual state of England before the Reformation onslaught, in part to allow readers to reach their own conclusions about which side of the fence they wish to place themselves. But it goes beyond that. Its function is not restricted to the partisanship of the Reformation debate; for there is in any case a singular shortage of collections of accessible texts illustrating the activities of the late medieval church in England. For most historians, the prime collection of historical documents is the series of *English Historical Documents*;[5] but this was

1 R. O'Day, *The Debate on the English Reformation*, London, 1986.

2 A. G. Dickens, *The English Reformation*, 2nd ed., London, 1989.

3 C. Haigh, 'Introduction', in *The English Reformation Revised*, ed. C. Haigh, Cambridge, 1987, pp. 1–17; J. J. Scarisbrick, *The Reformation and the English People*, Oxford, 1984.

4 R. Whiting, *The Blind Devotion of the People: Popular Religion and the English Reformation*, Cambridge, 1989.

5 A. R. Myers, ed., *English Historical Documents, 1327–1485*, London, 1969; C. H. Williams, ed., *English Historical Documents, 1485–1558*, London, 1963. The volume for the earlier period contains several documents concerning the Church, but mainly dealing with its institutional and administrative development. However, one section (F) contain a number of extracts relating to devotional writings, and another (G) deals with Lollardy and heresy. The later volume is distinctly biased towards the Reformation in its choice of documents.

drawn up before the outbreak of the present phase of the Reformation debate, and when the main concern among ecclesiastical historians was still essentially with administrative and organisational matters. Now that attention focuses more on the more popular aspects of spiritual activity, that collection does not fully address the current questions. Some filling of the gap is done in Christopher Harper-Bill's pamphlet on *The pre-Reformation Church in England*;[6] but shortage of space and the enormity of his total concern has rather restricted the range of examples. The present selection seeks to give a more targeted collection of documents, precisely reflecting the spiritual developments within the late medieval Church in England.

I make no claims that the documents presented here are a full reflection of the spirituality of late medieval England. For reasons which will become clear in the Introduction, I even doubt whether we can validly conceive of something to label 'pre-Reformation English spirituality'. Nevertheless, the production of a collection is justified by the increasing attention being paid to the Church prior to 1534. The gap was glaringly obvious to me when I was working more generally on the late medieval church: I see this selection as providing a companion volume for the chapters on spirituality and unorthodoxy in my *Church and Society in Late Medieval England*;[7] by the nature of the material, it also complements several other aspects of that book.

The documents reproduced here generally date from between 1350 and 1530: from the Black Death to the Reformation. There are a couple which go outside those limits, at the latter extreme because that was the only document conveying that information in the collection.[8] The material has been translated from Latin and Middle English. Translation from the former is these days self-evidently justified; with the latter it may be felt that the task is less necessary. Yet the apparent similarities between modern and medieval English are deceptive: the transformations in word usage and grammatical conventions over the past five centuries make it safer to treat them as two separate languages. For the utility of this collection, there is no advantage in bringing together documents which will remain comprehensible only with difficulty.

The choice of documents has been guided by two main concerns. Firstly, I wanted to include as representative a selection as possible, within the limits imposed by the need to produce a book which was not so large as to preclude publication. I hope that that has been achieved, although there are doubtless some areas where readers will feel that there are omissions. One in particular, relating to the devotional reading, is the absence of any of those blood-chilling descriptions of the crucified Christ which seem so common a feature of that type of material. Here my excuse is provided by the second main determinant of the contents: I have sought to include material which is not available in translation elsewhere. At least once I know that another translation is

6 London and New York, 1989.

7 Oxford, 1989.

8 No. 35.

available; but for the majority of the documents I believe that this is their first appearance in translation. For many, indeed, this is the first appearance in print.

The purpose of this series of volumes is declared to be the publication of key texts. A disparate accumulation such as this may seem to go against that aim, particularly when some of the documents are brief, and have little to make them stand out. Here, however, I would argue that that lack of distinctiveness is the demonstration of their importance, and their key feature: the collection aims not to deal with the extraordinary, but to offer an insight into the normality of pre-Reformation spirituality in an England which, while feeling the draughts of questioning and opposition to the ecclesiastical structure and prevalent spirituality through the activities of 'Lollards', was still a part of that single structure which claimed to be the one, holy, catholic, and apostolic Church.

The production of any book incurs a number of debts. I am principally grateful to Richard Purslow and Jane Carpenter of Manchester University Press for inviting me to contribute to the series, and for the latter's tolerance as a deadline was pushed further and further backwards. The collection could not have been drawn together without the assistance of numerous librarians and archivists, who allowed me access to their collections, provided copies of documents, and generously entered into correspondence on a variety of questions. As I have not given a list of manuscripts in the Bibliography, this is a convenient point at which to list the repositories which have provided the documents: the Borthwick Institute of Historical Research, York; the British Library, London; York Minster Library (archives of the Dean and Chapter of York Minster); Lichfield Joint Record Office, Lichfield; Hereford Cathedral Archives, Hereford (archives of the Dean and Chapter of Hereford Cathedral); Cambridge University Library (archives of the Dean and Chapter of Ely Cathedral); St George's Chapel, Windsor (archives of the Dean and Canons); Norfolk County Record Office, Norwich (archives of the Dean and Canons of Norwich Cathedral); Shropshire County Record Office, Shrewsbury; Shrewsbury Public Library. In addition to their assistance with collecting and checking the documents, I am most grateful to the owners and custodians who have given the appropriate permission for reproduction. For printed material, the resources of Birmingham University Library have, as usual, been invaluable. The extract from the Latin Vulgate Bible appears by permission of the Deutsche Bibelgesellschaft, Stuttgart; that from the *New English Bible* © 1970, by permission of Oxford and Cambridge University Presses. Last, but by no means least, I have to acknowledge the tolerance of my family, who in the final stages of compilation put up with more than should have been imposed on them.

Note on the documents

My main aim has been to let the documents speak for themselves. For that reason, I have not given extensive commentaries, or sought to explain every obscure reference. In each section, I have limited the commentary to a brief introduction, which along with discussion in the Introduction provides access to further literature and points out the main features of the sources. Obviously, the available literature on several aspects is immense: I have not sought to cover everything. The works referred to will generally provide a route to further reading; for a large-scale bibliography (to 1989) on the late medieval English Church, see my *Church and Society in Late Medieval England* (a bibliographical update is in the 1993 paperback version).

Translation is necessarily interpretation. I have sought in the treatises to provide a fluent translation, within the limitations of the texts. For the more administrative material, the translation is of course more formal, and more stilted. In general, I have translated complete documents, or those fragments of documents dealing with the relevant issues (accounts, in particular, are not always printed in full, given the extensive range of their contents). Where I have made cuts within a document, they are generally indicated by '…'. Minor additions to wording to clarify a text are not usually marked; others – curtailed dating clauses, or additions to clarify a reference – are incorporated in square brackets. Some of the documents, while primarily in one of the translated languages, contain odd words or phrases from another; where it seemed important to note that distinction (particularly in some of the tracts), I have printed those sections in italics. However, where there are lists which are basically bilingual, the switch has not generally been indicated. In a few instances, I have not been able to modernise placenames, which are therefore given in italics. To make some of the longer documents more 'user-friendly', I have silently added paragraphing where it seemed appropriate. For the same reason, in some instances numbers which appear in figures in the original texts have been silently converted into words; while different spellings of the same surname within a document (or entry in a run of documents) have been silently standardised. I have not corrected the arithmetic in the financial statements: usually it adds up, but there are occasionally discrepancies, and sometimes oddities in the calculations which might not seem immediately explicable but which become clear on closer inspection.

A final word is necessary about the monetary system used in some of these documents. The basic units are those which constituted the English currency until 1971: a pound (£) consisting of twenty shillings (s.), each of which contained twelve pence (d.). However, in the accounts the sums are not uniformly and neatly divided into such units: figures in pence are commonly encountered up to 40d.; sums in excess of twenty shillings are often expressed in that unit up to (sometimes beyond) 100s. Alongside this system, another accounting system dealt in terms of 'marks', equivalent to 13s. 4d., or two-thirds of a pound. Both systems may be encountered in the same document.

Introduction. In search of pre-Reformation English spirituality

Terms of reference

Attempts to understand the spirituality of any age face a number of fundamental difficulties. Of these, perhaps the most daunting is the need to try to penetrate minds. Yet to do that is to open a Pandora's box, subject to all the issues of subjectivity and reality which bedevil any search for the recreation of the past.[1] To make the attempt in areas dealing with people's faith is even more of a challenge, for it is necessary to seek precision about just what is being explored. After all, just what is this 'religion'; what is 'spirituality'? Both terms certainly existed in the medieval period, but did not carry quite (or, depending on usages, anything like) their modern connotations.[2] In his search for an acceptable definition of 'religion' for historical usage, Gavin Langmuir has recently proposed a distinction between 'religion' as a prescribed, to some extent authoritarian, structure of beliefs, and 'religiosity' – setting aside some of the pejorative overtones which more general usage of that term tends to carry – as an essentially individual construction of expressions of spiritual belief and action.[3] This is certainly an intriguing and enticing distinction, particularly for the pre-Reformation period. Then, while the Church may have proclaimed its Catholicity, it did so more in terms of its supposedly all-inclusive nature, which meant that it was impossible not to be a non-member, than in terms of fixed dogmas of 'Roman Catholicism'. The monolith apparently created by the Council of Trent, the Catholic Reformation, and the opportunities for standardisation which came with printing simply could not exist in earlier centuries. Moreover, any attempt to create it would confront the basic difficulty which arises with any approach to Christianity: it may be institutionalised,

1 For these and other problems, e.g. R. F. Atkinson, *Knowledge and Explanation in History: an Introduction to the Philosophy of History*, London and Basingstoke, 1978.

2 P. Biller, 'Words and the medieval notion of "religion"', *Journal of Ecclesiastical History*, XXXVI, 1985, pp. 351-69; P. Sheldrake, *Spirituality and History: Questions of Interpretation and Method*, London, 1991, ch. 2, esp. pp. 34–6.

3 G.I. Langmuir, *History, Religion, and Antisemitism*, Berkeley, Los Angeles and Oxford, 1990, esp. ch. 7, 9, 10.

but the faith itself is essentially atomistic, dependent on individuals creating their own relationships with the divinity, and finding a means to express that relationship in their own terms. That may include modes of expression authorised and controlled by institutional structures; but it could not preclude or exclude personal variations, choices reflected in devotion to particular saints, the adoption of particular lifestyles, even rejection and heresy. The atomism of medieval Christianity is perhaps particularly elusive, because the tendency – the temptation – is to seek the generalisation. The available sources either hide the particular in blanket considerations, at their crudest monetary totals which do not reveal individual payments, or highlight certain individuals while provoking the quest for generalisations from their particularities. While accepting the utility of Langmuir's distinction, however, it may need some qualifications. In particular, I would argue that, while the guardians of 'religion' did prescribe (and proscribe), they were to some extent led rather than leaders: they had to respond to changes in 'religiosity' and often (no matter how reluctantly) accept changes imposed by popular demand. Pre-Reformation Catholicism was, in some respects, a 'demand-led' religion.[4]

But does 'religiosity' in this fruitful sense equate with 'spirituality' in this period? Here, again, the problem is that the modern notion of spirituality reflects a usage of the word which has developed only recently, and which remains remarkably difficult to pin down.[5] If it means a mental state, involving some degree of abstraction from the world, then there was a vaguely synonymous medieval term, 'devotion'; but that seems insufficient to cover all the ways in which the people of pre-Reformation England made their religious concerns manifest. It also seems to undervalue the active element in medieval Christianity, the sense of social responsibility inherent in the doc-

4 My definition of 'religion' would thus necessitate a minor modification of Langmuir's. His is essentially prescriptive (*History, Religion, and Antisemitism*, p. 136), although this implicitly includes proscription in the reaction to heresy. I would give it rather more explicit emphasis, particularly in the attempts to control some of the minutiae of 'religiosity', as the ecclesiastical authorities sought to contain some of its manifestations (see, e.g., C. Zika, 'Hosts, processions, and pilgrimages in fifteenth-century Germany', *Past and Present*, CXVIII, Feb. 1988, pp. 28–30, 33–5, 50–9; for an English attempt at limitation, D. M. Owen, 'Bacon and eggs: Bishop Buckingham and superstition in Lincolnshire', *Studies in Church History*, VIII, 1972, pp. 140–2). The practice of prescription and proscription might be fairly localised: just as 'Christianity' was not a monolith, nor was 'the Church': we ought perhaps to envisage something like a federation of churches, forming a composite univeral Catholicism, much as political historians are now investigating early modern 'states' as composite entities.

5 See note 2.

trines, the mutuality of many of the actions.[6] The integration of the world into concepts of 'spirituality' has been emphasised in the proposal that, to give it precision, spirituality should be defined as

> not merely the techniques of prayer but, more broadly, a conscious relationship with God, in Jesus Christ, through the indwelling of the Spirit and in the context of the community of believers. Spirituality is, therefore, concerned with the conjunction of theology, prayer, and practical Christianity. ... [The] relationship with God ... is lived out, not in isolation, but in a community of believers ...[7]

This emphasis on community, on existence within a community which must necessitate action within a community, seems the appropriate usage to adopt here; reflecting as it does the integrated fulfilment of the two supreme obligations of practical Christianity, of love of God and love of neighbour.

In the search for pre-Reformation English spirituality, it has to be accepted that every overview is incomplete, and necessarily partial. The difficulties derive not just from the subject but from the sources, and it is these which require most consideration in the following pages. The Church as an institution was all-pervasive, producing massive quantities of records for its own purposes.[8] Of course, these were not produced or preserved with the enquiries of later historians in mind, and therefore pose problems of approach; but the basic fact is that there is an awful lot of material available to be sifted, perhaps for the most part still insufficiently examined. As well as the institutional, administrative material, considerable quantities of private records have to be incorporated into the quest – personal correspondence like the Paston letters; devotional and instructional tracts of varying length; prayers; private accounts; and more. The literary material may range from a few lines, little more than graffiti, through to lengthy works of spiritual guidance. Much is anonymous; some falsely foisted on to the great vernacular spiritual writers of the period, like Richard Rolle; other works are correctly attributed to named individuals. Again, this presents problems, because of the way texts were treated; and from the 1470s there is the additional complication of the impact

6 R. N. Swanson, *Church and Society in Late Medieval England*, Oxford, 1989, pp. 299, 301.

7 Sheldrake, *Spirituality and History*, pp. 52–3.

8 For brief surveys, G. R. Elton, *England, 1200-1640*, London, 1969, pp. 93–115; D. M. Owen, *The Records of the Established Church in England, Excluding Parochial Records*, British Records Association: Archives and the User, I, 1970.

of printing as it affected aspects of spirituality. But the basic reality is that, with this material taken on as well, there is a great deal of written evidence for both the theory and the practice of late medieval English religion and spirituality.[9]

The literary, the written, is necessarily the format which receives most attention in a book such as this – even if it is impossible to give total coverage to the numerous genres and forms of that evidence. Two points need to be made here. First, that although texts are widely used by modern writers and commentators, this is no guide to their original importance: the manuscript tradition on which, say, Margery Kempe's book hangs is extremely tenuous; and yet it is now one of the most discussed of later medieval religious texts. The printed form in which it became available from *c.* 1501 – a strictly edited text which gave a totally different impression of her life to provide 'a manual of practical mysticism' – only serves to emphasise that modern approaches are vastly different from those of the pre-Reformation years.[10] Other texts of the period pose similar problems.[11] Secondly, it must not be forgotten that the written, the documentary, is only a fragment of the totality of evidence available for late medieval spiritual practices and ideals. There is also the physical evidence. There is some overlap here: after all, texts do have a physical existence, and the physical form in which they survive can indicate use and impact, whether as small portable scrolls, or much-thumbed collections, or elegant presentation copies. The physical context of individual texts within compilations is a means of gaining an entree to spirituality which is now receiving increasing attention.[12] But beyond the documentary there are the

9 For assessment of spirituality in late medieval England, see also C. Harper-Bill, *The Pre-Reformation Church in England, 1400–1530*, London and New York, 1989, ch. 7; Swanson, *Church and Society*, ch. 6.

10 S. E. Holbrook, 'Margery Kempe and Wynkyn de Worde', in *The Medieval Mystical Tradition in England: Exeter Symposium IV. Papers read at Dartington Hall, July 1987*, ed. M. Glasscoe, Woodbridge, 1987, pp. 27–46, esp. 39–40, 42. Pre-Reformation access would also obviously be affected by problems of distribution and reproduction. The contrast between the 'publication' of manuscripts and of printed works is succinctly stated in A. I. Doyle, 'Publication by members of the religious orders', in *Book Production and Publishing in Britain, 1375–1475*, ed. J. Griffiths and D. Pearsall, Cambridge, 1989, p. 110.

11 C. A. Martin, 'Middle English manuals of religious instruction', in *So Meny People, Longages, and Tonges: Philological Essays in Scots and Mediaeval English Presented to Angus McIntosh*, ed. M. Benskin and M. L. Samuels, Edinburgh, 1981, pp. 285–7.

12 Martin, 'Manuals', pp. 287–92; A. Barratt, 'Works of religious instruction', in *Middle English Prose: a Critical Guide to Major Authors and Genres*, ed. A. S. G. Edwards, Brunswick, N.J., 1984, pp. 427–8. For reproductions of complete

plastic survivals: the buildings themselves (albeit in their post-Reformation survivals); the scattered remains of shrines, of statues and images, the glass, the alabasters and the wall-paintings, all of which affected understanding of the Christian message.[13] Evidence of this sort is not necessarily strictly 'ecclesiastical' in derivation: moralistic and devotional wall paintings existed in domestic settings, like those (of the early fourteenth century) at Longthorpe Tower, or in the less lavish surroundings of a cottage at Piccotts End in Hertfordshire, dating from *c.* 1500; alabasters might have been among household furnishings.[14] All this material has its uses, much of it fitting into the category of 'books for the unlearned' which was used to justify their existence and explain their utility,[15] and allows a partial recovery of attitudes. But some elements are irrecoverable, or very imperfectly recoverable: the emotional responses which were generated by participation in this continuity of celebrations, from presence at plays to attendance at services and processions, and being caught up in the drama and emotional appeal of the liturgy, to responses to the

manuscripts which ilustrate the mingling of types of text, see e.g. *Cambridge University Library MS Ff.2.38*, introduction by F. McSparran and P. R. Robinson, London, 1979 - from the late fifteenth or early sixteenth century; *The Thornton Manuscript, Lincoln Cathedral MS. 91*, introduction by D. S. Brewer and A. E. B. Owen, London, 1975 - from the mid fifteenth century; *The Vernon Manuscript; a Facsimile of Bodleian Library, Oxford, MS. Eng. Poet.a.1*, introduction by A. I. Doyle, Cambridge, 1987. For analysis of one manuscript's compilation, O. S. Pickering, 'Brotherton Collection MS. 501: a Middle English anthology reconsidered', *Leeds Studies in English*, n.s., XXI, 1990, pp. 141–65 (esp. 149–61); see also the volume edited by D. Pearsall, *Studies in the Vernon Manuscript*, Woodbridge, 1990, esp. N. F. Blake, 'Vernon manuscript: contents and organisation', at pp. 44–59.

13 Despite its terminal dates, J. Alexander and P. Binski, eds., *The Age of Chivalry: Art in Plantagenet England, 1200-1400*, London, 1987, offers an excellent introduction to such survivals. The bibliographies provide more detail, and over a longer time-span to cover most of the pre-Reformation period. See also F. Cheetham, *English Medieval Alabasters*, Oxford, 1984; A. Craiger-Smith, *English Medieval Mural Paintings*, Oxford, 1963; B. Coe, *Stained Glass in England, 1150–1500*, London, 1981. For salutary comment on the difficulties of 'artistic' material, B. Hamilton, *Religion in the Medieval West*, London, 1986, pp. 72–3. Beyond the artefacts which survive, it is also necessary to integrate material which has been destroyed since (and sometimes because of) the Reformation; see e.g. M. F. Wakelin, 'A note on preaching "roodes and othyr ymages" in mediaeval England', *Downside Review*, CIII, 1985, pp. 76–86.

14 Craiger-Smith, *Medieval Mural Paintings*, pp. 25, 65, and pl. XIII; M. Wood, *The English Mediaeval House*, London, 1981, pp. 399–401; Cheetham, *Alabasters*, pp. 28–30.

15 M. Aston, *Lollards and Reformers: Images and Literacy in Late Medieval England*, London, 1984, pp. 115–17, 183–6.

increasingly complex polyphonic music of the age.[16] Some of these emotional responses may have been the loss of self in the beauty of holiness; for others the reaction was antipathy and hostility; both are spiritual responses, of equal validity, but not necessarily equal weight in the final analysis, in so far as that can be offered.[17]

The overall impact of all this remains essentially intangible. Here, again, problems of the relationships with the source material come into play. To use it is necessarily to interpret it, but via a modern comprehension. Yet the production of an artefact does not control its reception: how contemporaries (let alone later audiences) understood these works and fitted them into their world-pictures could differ greatly from the intentions of their creators. This perhaps applies most to the 'plastic' texts, whose iconography required a cracking of the code and a reading of the images.[18] It cannot be assumed that all readings were identical. Modern readings will also vary, drawing on ambivalences and ambiguities which – equally – may not have been visible, audible or important, to the original addressees.[19] While such difficulties are insurmountable, a legitimate historical appreciation of this material does demand a deliberate rejection of modern stances: to recapture the period requires an attempt to bridge the emotional chasm introduced by the Reformation, and deepened and widened by later 'rationalism'. It is all too easy to approach the pre-Reformation laity with a patronising stance: gulls who were completely taken in by the superstition of the time – a sense of gullibility only heightened by references to forgeries of indulgences, and evidence of clerical bad behaviour and exploitation. But then, as now, only the scandalous needed to be reported – good news is bad news. In terms of gullibility, these superstitious practices made more sense than involvement in chain letters or pyramid selling. As for arguments based on 'rationality',

16 R. N. Swanson, 'Medieval liturgy as theatre: the props', *Studies in Church History*, XXIX, 1992, pp. 239-53; F. Ll. Harrison, *Music in Medieval Britain*, 4th ed., London, 1980, ch. IV (see also R. Bowers, 'Obligation, agency, and *laissez-faire*: the promotion of polyphonic composition for the church in fifteenth-century England', in *Music in Medieval and Early Modern Europe: Patronage, Sources, and Texts*, ed. I. Fenlon, Cambridge, 1981, pp. 1–19).

17 On the problems of access to 'religiosity', Langmuir, *Heresy, Religion, and Antisemitism*, pp. 199–200.

18 No English case comes immediately to mind, but see the 'reinterpretation' of a French sculpture referred to in C. Beaune, *The Birth of an Ideology: Myths and Symbols of Nation in Late-Medieval France*, Berkeley, Los Angeles and Oxford, 1991, p. 84.

19 For one such exploitation of ambiguity, in drama, see A. Gash, 'Carnival against Lent: the ambivalence of medieval drama', in *Medieval Literature: Criticism, Ideology, and History*, ed. D. Aers, New York, 1986, pp. 74–98.

they presuppose that twentieth-century rationality is necessarily better than the pre-Reformation variety. Yet, from that pre-Reformation perspective, could there be anything less rational than the denial of God; and than the assumption that death did not have to be approached without doing all in one's power to ensure a safe deliverance at the Last Judgement and as brief a period in Purgatory as possible? It all depends on premisses; and to understand the spirituality of the late Middle Ages, the premisses on which it was constructed have to be identified, and accepted as the starting point.[20]

There is another level on which modern views may have to be jettisoned: the notion of a nation-wide 'English' spirituality. Given the structures of belief, and the varieties of religious experiences, it is more appropriate to accept a fragmentation of religious and spiritual systems within the overall canopy of 'the Church', allowing local and regional devotions and practices to take on their own significance rather than being subsumed within a generalisation of questionable validity. Parishes, dioceses, towns thus acquire a certain degree of spiritual autonomy, meriting detailed investigation in their own right, and perhaps requiring differing degrees of appreciation.[21] To jump forward some way in the arguments, it is not impossible that some of the religious debates raised during the course of the period under consideration – linking in with issues of 'Lollardy' – may reflect conflicts between the relative spheres of autonomy within the englobing institution.

How then, is pre-Reformation English spirituality to be identified and analysed? There does seems to be a rough division between consideration of theory, and analysis of practices. Even more roughly, that is a division between tracts, the literary material constructed with instructional and devotional purposes, and administrative records, the accounts, charters, and other records. This is not necessarily a division

20 Here, again, I would slightly modify what I understand to be Langmuir's stance: while accepting many of his strictures about the definition of 'religion' for historians, and the need to incorporate individual 'religiosities', the fact that people did actually believe in a religion and act on its dictates cannot actually be written out of history.

21 For a stimulating assessment of a regional spirituality, G. McM. Gibson, *The Theater of Devotion: East Anglian Drama and Society in the Late Middle Ages*, Chicago and London, 1989. It is important not to overstate the unity of 'England' in the pre-Reformation period. Major linguistic divisions - including actually different languages like Cornish, and Welsh in parts of Herefordshire, and the significant dialect divisions between various forms of English which might render northern and southern forms almost mutually incomprehensible - would only tend to reinforce regional and local loyalties and spiritualities.

between public and private – many of the 'archival' records are also privately produced, none more so than the wills. It may be a division between 'elite' and 'popular' approaches to religion; but the existence of such a distinction is highly questionable, and attempts to uphold it require too rigid a break within the Christian society.[22] Clearly, however, it is a division between ideals and realities.

Theory

To varying degrees, everyone needed to know the content of the faith, and to receive instruction both about that content and about how adherence should be manifested. A full survey of this in every aspect is impossible, despite its crucial importance for the continuity of spirituality.[23] One of the most important means, but the least revealed, would be through familial activities and simple cultural continuity. Here, a vital element might be instruction within the domestic context. The most often cited text for such instruction, the 'Instructions for a devout and literate layman', envisage an almost deliberate process of instruction by a paterfamilias, tantamount to bringing the Church and its message back home to be spread among the household.[24] This model seems to be reiterated in the early sixteenth century, in Richard Whytford's *A Work for Householders*,[25] but how general the pattern was

22 See also Langmuir, *History, Religion, and Antisemitism*, pp. 236–7. He would stress the individuality of 'religiosities' within 'religion'. Here, again, I think some modification is needed, to allocate some place to group responses. It seems to me that the distinction between 'elite' and 'popular' is essentially false because in many - perhaps most - instances the former as a superstructure actually incorporates the latter. 'Elite' or 'learned' religion had to be self-consciously acquired, while everyone participated in 'popular' religion (even if not in all of its manifestations); the elite aspects were therefore adopted in addition to the popular aspects of spirituality and, while the latter were perhaps suppressed by some, could not be totally repressed and replaced by an 'elite' system. Needless to say, the distinction also presupposes an identifiable and distinct elite, self-identifying and self-perpetuating, which could share in and control this form of spirituality.

23 I will consider these issues further in *Religion and Devotion in Europe, 1215-1515*, Cambridge, forthcoming.

24 W. A. Pantin, 'Instructions for a devout and literate layman', in *Medieval Learning and Literature: Essays Presented to Richard William Hunt*, ed. J. J. G. Alexander and M. T. Gibson, Oxford, 1976, pp. 398–422, esp. 407-8.

25 M. Collins, 'A little known "Art of Dying" by a Brigittine of Syon: *A daily exercise and experience of death* by Richard Whytford', in *Dies illa: Death in the Middle Ages. Proceedings of the 1983 Manchester Colloquium*, ed. J. H. M. Taylor, Vinaver Studies in French, I, Liverpool, 1984, p. 180.

is uncertain: that familial instruction was less structured, and much more basic, seems more likely. The few references to the activities of godparents suggest the inculcation of the basic tenets of the faith through little more than rote-memory: the Creed, the Our Father, and the Ave, available for constant repetition.[26] There are hints that much of this instruction was provided by women: this was perhaps a religion which was at its most basic matrilineal (most explicitly represented in the traditional iconography of St Anne teaching the Virgin to read).[27] However, beyond the basics, and setting aside oddities like Julian of Norwich and certain female 'Lollards',[28] it is inescapably the case that most evidence for the deliberate instruction of the laity is provided by works written by men; here precisely because of the priestly function of most authors. To that extent, we are also confronted by a structure which was, unashamedly, patriarchal in its concern to control lay spirituality, and the modes of manifestation which were available to it.

As far as the processes for providing access to the faith are concerned, the fundamental text should have been the Bible. Yet, equally clearly, contact with the Bible was limited (although perhaps less so than was once thought), and was almost invariably mediated.[29] Language provided an immediate restriction on access: the authoritative Biblical

26 H. Littlehales, ed., *English Fragments from Latin Medieval Service-Books*, Early English Text Society, extra ser., XC, 1903, p. 5; G. Kristensson, ed., *John Mirk's Instructions for Parish Priests, Edited from MS Cotton Claudius A II and Six Other Manuscripts, with Introduction, Notes, and Glossary*, Lund Studies in English, XLIX, Lund, 1974, p. 76, ll.151–4; R. N. Swanson, 'Chaucer's Parson and other priests', *Studies in the Age of Chaucer*, XIII, 1991, pp. 70–1.

27 E.g. S. G. Bell, 'Medieval women book owners: arbiters of lay piety and ambassadors of culture' in *Sisters and Workers in the Middle Ages*, ed. J. M. Bennett et al., Chicago and London, 1989, pp. 142, 148–55, 160 (also in *Women and Power in the Middle Ages*, ed. M. Erler and M. Kowaleski, Athens, Ga., and London, 1988, pp. 149–87); cf. P. Sheingorn, 'Appropriating the Holy Kinship: gender and family history', in *Interpreting Cultural Symbols: Saint Anne in Late Medieval Society*, ed. K. Ashley and P. Sheingorn, Athens, Ga., and London, 1990, pp. 189-90. On a slightly different tack, but touching on the possibility of a 'gender-based' interpretation of spirituality, see also the comments on the nature of the English Reformation in C. Richmond, 'The English gentry and religion, c.1500', in *Religious Belief and Ecclesiastical Careers in Late Medieval England*, ed. C. Harper-Bill, Woodbridge, 1991, pp. 140–2.

28 G. M. Jantzen, *Julian of Norwich: Mystic and Theologian*, London, 1987; C. Cross, '"Great reasoners in scripture": the activities of women lollards, 1380–1530', in *Medieval Women*, ed. D. Baker, Studies in Church History, Subsidia I, Oxford, 1978, pp. 359–80.

29 M. Deanesly, *The Lollard Bible and Other Medieval Biblical Versions*, Cambridge, 1920, ch. 13; J. A. H. Moran, *The Growth of English Schooling, 1340–1538: Learning, Literacy, and Laicization in Pre-Reformation York Diocese*, Princeton, N.J., 1985, pp. 186–93.

text was in Latin, which necessarily required a certain educational achievement to make it accessible – a degree of education which was virtually restricted to the clergy (and, indeed, possibly beyond the lowest levels of the clergy). While the laity were undoubtedly becoming increasingly literate during the later Middle Ages,[30] no matter what criteria might be adopted for the definition of literacy, Latinity nevertheless remained a minority attribute.

To widen access to the Bible therefore required other tacks. The most obvious would be translation; the production of an English Bible. However, translation risked widening access beyond control: the Bible, as authoritative, had to be properly interpreted, within the ranges accepted by the Church. Too much freedom of access, linked to freedom of interpretation and the threat of misinterpretation, was dangerous. Therefore, although a Bible was available in English – the so-called Wycliffite translations of the later fourteenth century – access to these was meant to be strictly limited. From 1409, licences were officially required for their possession (although the effectiveness of the licensing system is unclear), and it seems inescapable that the English text was officially accorded less authority than the Latin.[31] Of course, attempts to restrict access could not be wholly successful: instances of 'Lollards' with access to texts – frequently individual gospels or epistles rather than a complete Bible – are manifold.[32] The translation itself was seemingly generated in a milieu of heresy, no matter how respectable individual owners of English Bibles might be in the fifteenth century;[33] and there seems to have been a tradition of vernacular scripture which persisted beyond the written. The impres-

30 Moran, *Growth of English Schooling*, pp. 171–82; J. Coleman, *English Literature in History, 1350–1400: Medieval Readers and Writers*, London, 1981. The process of acquiring literacy would also be a process of reinforcing the morality and basic statements of Christianity: M. Denley, 'Elementary teaching techniques and Middle English religious didactic writings', in *Langland, the Mystics, and the Medieval English Religious Tradition: Essays in Honour of S. S. Hussey*, ed. H. Phillips, Woodbridge, 1990, pp. 224–8.

31 A. Hudson, *The Premature Reformation: Wycliffite Texts and Lollard History*, Oxford, 1988, pp. 23–4 (esp. p. 23 n. 93); A. Hudson, *Lollards and their Books*, London and Ronceverte, 1986, pp. 147–9; Swanson, *Church and Society*, p. 339. While attention focuses on the Wycliffite text, it is important not to ignore the availability of other versions of translations, such as Richard Rolle's translation of the Psalter: Deanesly, *Lollard Bible*, pp. 144–6.

32 E.g. C. Cross, 'Religious and social protest among Lollards in early Tudor England', in *The Church in a Changing Society*, Publications of the Swedish Society of Church History, XXX, Uppsala, 1978, pp. 72–3; J. A. F. Thomson, *The Later Lollards, 1414–1520*, Oxford, 1965, pp. 242–3.

33 The most readily accessible discussion of the Wycliffite Bible remains Deanesly, *Lollard Bible*, ch. 10–11, but now showing signs of age (e.g., the claims for John

sive nature of medieval memorial techniques[34] allowed whole Biblical texts to be committed to memory. The Psalter was traditionally the book most thus affected – the recitation of psalters being a normal devotional practice. Other sections (not always complete books) also appear to have been memorised.[35] Here, it may be that the Church really did have to confront changing traditions: while it was happy for the basics to be committed to memory by rote (and demanded them, as they were annually tested at the confession prior to the Easter communion)[36] nevertheless it sought to control the other version of memory, which linked texts with interpretations. If people (not just 'Lollards') were absorbing texts beyond the written, beyond the controls of physical access by a commitment to memory which then allowed opportunities for rumination, reflection and reinterpretation, then a major control on definitions of spirituality had been removed. The problem that translation imposed interpretation was clearly recognised when the challenge of producing an authoritative English version was taken up in the sixteenth century: in the 1540s conservative bishops wished to retain a largely Latinate vocabulary for the more doctrinally sensitive aspects of Christianity, to prevent dilution or deviation of the traditional orthodoxies.[37]

The Bible did not have be available in massive chunks, let alone in totality. Indeed, despite the restrictions on the availability of English Bibles, it is probably too easy to understate the amount of access there was to fragments of the text in English. A notable feature of sermons and much of the instructional literature is the regular smattering of Biblical quotations, often first in the authoritative and (as far as physical considerations permitted) standardised Latin, and then in more individual English forms, whose variety makes it pointless to

Purvey as author are demolished in Hudson, *Lollards and their Books*, pp. 102–8). The extent of Wyclif's own involvement in the process remains uncertain: M. Wilks, 'Misleading manuscripts: Wyclif and the non-Wycliffite Bible', *Studies in Church History*, XI, 1975, pp. 147–61 (but his participation/instigation is reasserted by C. Lindberg, *The Middle English Bible: The Book of Judges*, Oslo, 1989, pp. 74–5).

34 M. J. Carruthers, *The Book of Memory: a Study of Memory in Medieval Culture*, Cambridge Studies in Medieval Literature, X, Cambridge, 1990.

35 Hudson, *Premature Reformation*, pp. 190–2; Thomson, *Later Lollards*, p. 114.

36 Kristensson, *Mirk's Instructions*, p. 115 ll. 805–10.

37 This concern for Latinity is usually associated with Stephen Gardiner, bishop of Winchester: S. L. Greenslade, 'English versions of the Bible, 1525–1611', in *The Cambridge History of the Bible*, [vol. III]: *The World from the Reformation to the Present Day*, ed. S. L. Greenslade, Cambridge, 1963, pp. 152–3; but see now G. Redworth, *In Defence of the Church Catholic: the Life of Stephen Gardiner*, Oxford, 1990, pp. 159-63.

postulate the 'use' of an English Bible to provide the translations.[38] Of course, this was mediated access, which controlled the interpretation; but it was nevertheless access. Similarly, pictures, plays and other art forms provided a form of access. Here, however, different problems arise: on the one hand because of the inclusion of much that was apocryphal (although it was clearly not denied authority on those grounds: the rejection and dismissal now implicit in 'apocryphal' has to be overcome); on the other, because the function of such acts of communication was generally not to convey the simple 'Biblical' text but to provide guidance to doctrinal knowledge and interpretation, thus in some ways providing a form of preaching.[39]

For most people in England the main access to the Bible, and indeed to instruction in the faith, would be through hearing priests from their pulpits. 'Sermons' were a fundamental instructional medium. Preaching as a means of communication is one of the most problematic areas of the discussion of late medieval spirituality. Sermons themselves are very much a growth area of research; and the numerous surviving texts merit extensive assessment and analysis. Yet here problems recur. While we have the texts, even full sermon cycles, consideration of preaching per se, and the impact of sermons, is extremely difficult. After all, the texts that survive are precisely that: texts, written artefacts. The extent to which they reflect sermons as preached is uncertain. Some clearly were delivered, because the conclusive evidence is available – but they may not have been preached as they survive (most obviously when they survive only in Latin). Others which survive as cycles may have had a totally different function, although not quite determinable. Some volumes seem to be presentation copies, and therefore may not actually have had much of a readership. Others seem to have been produced as meditative aids, as

38 See comment on the Bible translations in the 'Lollard sermon cycle' by Wilks, 'Misleading manuscripts', pp. 158–9.

39 For plays as a pre-interpreted form of access to the faith, see e.g. L. Lepow, *Enacting the Sacrament: Counter-Lollardy in the Towneley Cycle*, London and Toronto, 1990, although I think some of the arguments are over-stretched; M. G. Briscoe, 'Preaching and medieval English drama', in *Contexts for Early English Drama*, ed. M. G. Briscoe and J. C. Coldewey, Bloomington and Indianapolis, 1989, pp. 150–72. For the scattering of texts, Aston, *Lollards and Reformers*, pp. 111–12. The importance of the role of interpretation cannot be over-stressed: latently anything capable of interpretation, by analogy or any other means, was usable to convey a 'spiritual' message. Mendicant preachers, for instance, used lyrics in this way: S. Wenzel, *Preachers, Poets, and the Early English Lyric*, Princeton, N.J., 1986. The many layers of association which could thus be developed might, therefore, be extremely complex.

literature rather than oral/aural products, and thereby pass into the category more of devotional than instructional works. Indeed, that may explain much of the apparent unsatisfactoriness of much of this material, which seems singularly uninstructional, playing more on the emotions than the intellect. Even where use is evident, the 'sermons' may have been merely skeletons on which fully developed texts could be hung (as is suggested by statements in some of them); while others which seem excessively long may have been constructed in order to be segmented, possibly for memorising in chunks which could then be reused in other permutations as required.[40]

Nevertheless, there was obviously much more than this to sermons. That listening to them was a relatively popular activity is evident from Margery Kempe's comments on preaching at King's Lynn; but she provides little information about their content, being more concerned to show their effect on her.[41] As with the Bible, sermons provided access to the faith, but an access which it was even more difficult to control. Sermons disseminated not just the faith but interpretations and debating standpoints; and could thereby generate conflict and uncertainty as much as anything else. This may particularly have been the case with sermons by members of the religious orders, the professional preachers, but they were not the only ones to have such an effect. Successive sermons at major preaching locations, like Paul's Cross in London, could amount to the presentation of opposing sides in a debate; while other instances, such as Nicholas Hereford's sermon at Oxford on Ascension Day 1382, stirred up a hornet's nest, and suggest that preachers sometimes had watchdogs set over them lest they went too far.[42] In 1426, a York friar was hauled before a provincial council on heresy accusations when his sermon – at a chapel within the city – overstepped the mark; while in London in the 1460s the

40 The main surveys of preaching are in T. J. Heffernan, 'Sermon literature', in *Middle English Prose: a Critical Guide to Major Authors and Genres*, ed. A. S. G. Edwards, Brunswick, N.J., 1984, pp. 177–207; G. R. Owst, *Preaching in Medieval England: an Introduction to Sermon Manuscripts of the Period c.1350–1450*, Cambridge, 1926; G. R. Owst, *Literature and Pulpit in Medieval England: a Neglected Chapter in the History of English Letters and of the English People*, 2nd ed., Oxford, 1961.

41 B. L. Windeatt, ed., *The Book of Margery Kempe*, Harmondsworth, 1985, pp. 187–9, 204–7; C. W. Atkinson, *Mystic and Pilgrim: the Book and the World of Margery Kempe*, Ithaca and London, 1983, pp. 114–15, 143–4.

42 P. McNiven, *Heresy and Politics in the Reign of Henry IV: the Burning of John Badby*, Woodbridge, 1987, p. 102; F. R. H. du Boulay, 'The quarrel between the Carmelite friars and the secular clergy of London, 1464–1468', *Journal of Ecclesiastical History*, VI, 1955, pp. 158–63; S. Forde, 'Nicholas Hereford's Ascension Day sermon, 1382', *Mediaeval Studies*, LI, 1989, pp. 205–8.

Carmelite friars were giving provocative interpretations of the demands of Christian poverty as part of a battle against the secular clergy.[43] It may have been deceptively easy to go close to the limits: even John Colet, dean of St Paul's, had accusations of heresy levelled against him for some of his doctrinal expositions in sermons; and in the 1520s the pulpit offered the battleground in the first stages of what became the Reformation.[44]

Reaction to these sermons also produces difficulties: modern readers' preconceptions about what a sermon 'should' contain often produce a judgemental frame of mind on acquaintance with the text. Other difficulties arise with problems of interpretation, particularly in attempts to categorise texts as reflecting particular aspects of contemporary religious ideals. This perhaps especially applies with the hunt for heretical strands in texts, where the imposition of a title by a modern editor may seek to dictate the interpretation more than the contents perhaps justify.[45]

With all this material, it also remains likely that the dramatic sermons were in fact the oddities. Urban sermons may have differed from those of the countryside – mainly perhaps because friars and several of the major religious houses were basically urban establishments.[46] More common may have been preaching of the sort sketched in John Mirk's *Instructions for Parish Priests*, which provided a basic instructional text for the clergy throughout the fifteenth century: preaching which outlined the basic elements of the faith, a commentary on the

43 *The Records of the Northern Convocation*, Surtees Society Publications, CXIII, 1907, pp. 146–72; Thomson, *Later Lollards*, p. 197; du Boulay, 'Quarrel between the Carmelite friars', pp. 156–74.

44 J. H. Lupton, *A Life of John Colet, D.D., Dean of St Paul's and Founder of St Paul's School*, London, 1887, pp. 202–4; R. Rex, 'The English campaign against Luther in the 1520s', *Transactions of the Royal Historical Society*, 5th ser., XXXIX, 1989, pp. 86, 89–90, 101–2.

45 E.g. the title given to the volume recently edited by G. Cigman, *Lollard Sermons*, Early English Text Society, original ser., CCXCVI, 1989. I can see little in the contents of these which actually justifies their interpretation as unorthodox. Their Lollard nature is reaffirmed - but not to my mind proved - in G. Cigman, 'The preacher as performer: Lollard sermons as imaginative discourse', *Journal of Literature and Theology*, II, 1988, pp. 69–82; they are also discussed in G. Cigman, 'Luceat lux vestra: the Lollard preacher as truth and light', *Review of English Studies*, XL, 1989, pp. 479–96, again in terms of their 'evident but as yet undefined Lollardy' (p. 481), while pointing out that they are in style different from other Wycliffite sermons so far available in print (p. 493).

46 But that, of course, does not mean that mendicant preaching was solely urban: see the bequest of Sir Humphrey Stafford in Richmond, 'English gentry and religion', p. 129.

Commandments, the Creed, the seven sins, and so on.[47] This type of activity is for the most part unrecorded, at least as being preached; but it clearly has affinities with other forms of instruction in the faith, the explicitly instructional material intended to convey such elements of the faith.[48]

This programme inspired a whole genre of religious writing, from the thirteenth century through to the sixteenth.[49] To emphasise or pick out particular elements as especially characteristic of the fifteenth century would be wrong: here the eclectic nature of much of late medieval spirituality is explicit, for texts from the thirteenth century retained their validity throughout. There was continual commentary on the constitution for reform of the clergy originally issued by Archbishop John Pecham of Canterbury in 1281, the tract *Ignorantia sacerdotum*, with one such lengthy discussion of the mid fifteenth century incorporating translations of appropriate parts of a number of other penitential texts.[50] The fifteenth century also saw revisions – and indeed printing – of the so-called *Layfolks' Catechism*, originally produced in 1357 in York but subjected to considerable revision thereafter in various ways.[51] These revisions similarly demonstrate the autonomy of texts in a manuscript tradition: little was canonical, almost everything was available for adaptation, revision and plagiarism, as necessary. The basic content may have been fairly static – as in the survey of the content of Christianity produced by the priest John Drury at Beccles in the 1420s[52] – but it could be amplified and emphasised almost at will. At its most basic, the content could be reduced simply to mnemonics, like those recounted by Drury: a technique which takes things back to the rote-learning of the Creed,

47 Kristenssen, *Mirk's Instructions*, pp. 71–96; D. B. Foss, 'John *Mirk's Instructions for Parish Priests*', *Studies in Church History*, XXVI, 1989, pp. 131–40; Swanson, 'Chaucer's Parson', pp. 72-3, 75–7.

48 Swanson, 'Chaucer's Parson', pp. 74–5.

49 L. E. Boyle, 'The Fourth Lateran Council and manuals of popular theology', *The Popular Literature of Medieval England*, ed. T. J. Heffernan, Tennessee Studies in Literature, XXVIII, Knoxville, Tenn., 1985, pp. 30–44; J. Shaw, 'The influence of canonical and episcopal reform on popular books of instruction', in *ibid.*, pp. 44–60; Barratt, 'Works of religious instruction', pp. 419-24; V. Gillespie, 'Vernacular books of religion', in *Book Production and Publishing in Britain, 1375–1475*, ed. J. Griffiths and D. Pearsall, Cambridge, 1989, pp. 317–19.

50 P. Hodgson, '*Ignorancia sacerdotum*: a fifteenth century discourse on the Lambeth constitutions', *Review of English Studies*, XXIV, 1948, pp. 2–11.

51 A. Hudson, 'A new look at the *Lay folks' catechism*', *Viator*, XVI, 1985, pp. 243–58.

52 Below, no.4.

Our Father and Ave. That this was the case is perhaps confirmed by the appearance of identical mnemonics in a priest's commonplace book from the mid fifteenth century, containing a miscellany of pieces which could also serve for instruction of the laity, possibly in a less formal format than that set out by Drury.[53] Pictorial representations were also possible, like the extremely complex scheme outlining the efficacy of the sacraments as the remedy to original sin for those willing to act on their demands which is crammed on to two pages of a manuscript now in the British Library.[54]

The control over the Bible, the sermons and the instructional literature all fits within a broad category of 'official publications', a hierarchical attempt to limit and direct the material available to the laity, and to channel their intellectualisation of the demands of Christianity. However, as texts, whether as written or memorised, they could escape those channels, and some quite probably did. Nevertheless, there is a broad distinction – even if fuzzy at the boundary – between such material and the more informally produced material, made available by authors for the laity for either instructional or devotional purposes. The fuzziness is not just in the extent to which the official could be taken over by the laity; but also in the ways in which devotionally instructional material might be officially promulgated to the laity. Here the system of licensing of texts in English – scant as the evidence is for its continuation throughout the fifteenth century – may have played a part. Certainly, with something like Nicholas Love's *Mirror of the Blessed Life of Jesus Christ*, there is a suggestion of official promulgation; while the attachment of indulgences to the reading of specific texts bespeaks a similar process (although one which could also be diverted by the surreptitious transfer of indulgences to other texts in the copying process).[55]

The instructional and devotional material prepared for the laity was of

53 R. M. Haines, *Ecclesia Anglicana: Studies in the English Church of the Later Middle Ages*, London and Toronto, 1989, pp. 169–70; see Swanson, 'Chaucer's Parson', p. 75.

54 London, British Library, MS Add. 37049, ff.72v–73r, discussed and reproduced in H. Mellick, 'In defence of a fifteenth-century manuscript', *Parergon*, VIII, April, 1974, pp. 20–4.

55 Swanson, *Church and Society*, pp. 292, 339; A. I. Doyle, 'Reflections of some manuscripts of Nicholas Love's *Myrrour of the blessed lyf of Jesu Christ*', *Leeds Studies in English*, n.s., XIV, 1983, pp. 82–93.

considerable variety.[56] It would be wrong to differentiate too rigidly between the two categories, for there was obviously considerable overlap: material which was instructional also served a devotional purpose, and vice versa. The emphasis on 'meditation' in late medieval spirituality – on thinking about the implications of texts (and artefacts) for recollection of the life of Christ and man's relationship with God – would also serve to break down the distinction: something as relatively 'dry' and 'instructional' (to modern perceptions) as Chaucer's *Parson's Tale* might in fact be as legitimately a focus for meditation as an image, or an intensely emotional prayer.[57] Some works did explicitly fall into one or other category; but many fell between the two stools, although with varying emphases. The overlap is evident in the three lengthy tracts presented here: the *Abbey of the Holy Ghost*, Walter Hilton's *Epistle on the Mixed Life* and the *Book of the Craft of Dying*. Each offers a different approach to the lay experience, seeking to provide a means whereby spirituality could be encouraged and hope confirmed, without going to extremes. The lack of extremism is important: it is too easy to place too much emphasis on the 'Middle English mystics', and judge others by their yardstick.[58] Yet mysticism almost by definition is a rarity: the majority had to live more ordinary lives, perhaps influenced by the writings of the mystics but incapable for a variety of reasons of achieving their spiritual depth or appreciation. Most simply did not have the time to become mystics: the world pressed too hard. Yet emphasis on withdrawal and meditation could prove discouraging; lay experience within the world had itself to be spiritualised, to be given a spiritual legitimacy which could then provide the basis for further spiritual development. That is the aim of the first two of these three tracts. The *Abbey of the Holy Ghost* is

56 P. S. Jolliffe, *A Check-List of Middle English Prose Writings of Spiritual Guidance*, Pontifical Institute of Mediaeval Studies, Subsidia Mediaevalia, II, Toronto, 1974, esp. pp. 1–31, 36–56; M. G. Sargent, 'Minor devotional writings', in *Middle English Prose: a Critical Guide to Major Authors and Genres*, ed. A. S. G. Edwards, Brunswick, N.J., 1984, pp. 147–75; Barratt, 'Works of religious instruction', pp. 413–32. For further discussion and treatment of such material in the manuscripts, see Gillespie, 'Vernacular books of religion', pp. 317–44.

57 T. H. Bestul, 'Chaucer's Parson's Tale and the late-medieval tradition of religious meditation', *Speculum*, LXIV, 1989, pp. 600–19; see also J. C. Hirsh, 'Prayer and meditation in late medieval England: MS Bodley 789', *Medium Ævum*, XLVIII, 1979, pp. 55–66.

58 For the mystics generally, see D. Knowles, *The English Mystical Tradition*, London, 1961; J. Walsh, *Pre-Reformation English Spirituality*, London, n.d.; V. M. Lagorio and R. Bradley, *The Fourteenth Century English Mystics: a Comprehensive Annotated Bibliography*, New York and London, 1981.

avowedly aimed at those whose circumstances prevent their withdrawal from the world to achieve their spiritual quests. Instead, it offers a programme of moral development which is to be considered just as 'regular' as any monastic experience. By adopting the morality it offers, the individual is encouraged to spiritual development, and thereby to awareness of the divine.

Walter Hilton's *Epistle* equally offers a way of life, seeking to resolve the old dichotomy between the 'active' and the 'contemplative' lives.[59] The 'active' life, within the world, which could detract from spiritual development, preventing the achievement of spiritual fulfilment, was nevertheless seen as a necessary part of human existence. On the other hand, the 'contemplative' life, a life of withdrawal and meditation, was demanding and impossible for those with extensive commitments. Hilton offers a *via media*, asserting the validity of the normal, of a lay experience organised without either extremity, providing a middle way which justified and spiritualised a life lived subject to the demands of a busy world. Apart from its basic message, the text is important because it derives precisely from the milieu of the English mystics, Hilton being one of the major exponents of that group. Yet it demonstrates that those authors were well aware of the problems of their contemporaries, and sought to encourage their spiritual development without demanding or expecting too much of them. It may well be that the *Epistle on the Mixed Life*, like many of the other writings (including those of Richard Rolle) was intended to be only a preliminary stage in development for some, whose spiritual progress could be expected to lead them beyond this world to a greater appreciation of the next – given that the tract is addressed to someone with considerable social (and perhaps local governmental) responsibilities, it might not be amiss to view the readership as containing some of those non-monastic clerics and government officials who were late entrants to the Brigittine and Carthusian orders in the fifteenth and early sixteenth centuries.[60] But, again, for the majority of the readership it is likely that Hilton's programme would be the limit of their development. This might be only a staging post; but for many that happy medium which he proclaims would be the ultimate achievement.

59 For debates on the two lives in the earlier medieval period, C. Butler, *Western Mysticism: the Teaching of Augustine, Gregory, and Bernard on Contemplation and the Contemplative Life*, 3rd ed., London, 1967, part II.

60 D. Knowles, *The Religious Orders in England*, 3 vols, Cambridge, 1948–61, II, pp. 137–8, III, pp. 212–15.

The third tract in this group, *The Book of the Craft of Dying*, is different in character; but nevertheless does fit in. Like Hilton's *Epistle*, it also reflects other aspects of contemporary developments. On the one hand, it is within the tradition of translations into English, the original being a continental production (possibly associated with the Council of Constance of 1414–18) which was then translated into almost every European language in the fifteenth century.[61] On the other hand, its history in English demonstrates the problems of ensuring textual continuity, for all the manuscripts are slightly different, and indeed when a variety came to be printed, it appears that Caxton and later printers produced new translations from the French (whether this shows that they were unaware of the existence of an English version is not clear: that does, however, seem unlikely).[62] Beyond that, it also reveals some of the problems of attribution, for the text in some versions is ascribed to Richard Rolle. The desire, by contemporaries and later commentators, to father so many works on Rolle suggests that his name was considered as offering some sort of *nihil obstat* to the spirituality contained in any tract, and might also attract attention from the reading and listening public.[63]

The *Book of the Craft of Dying* falls into the genre of instructional texts of the fifteenth and sixteenth centuries whose theme was preparation for death.[64] In so far as there was a 'late medieval cult of death',[65] the point of death would be its focus: the point at which the individual lost

61 M. C. O'Connor, *The Art of Dying Well: the Development of the Ars Moriendi*, New York, 1942.

62 F. M. M. Comper, *The Book of the Craft of Dying, and Other Early English Tracts Concerning Death*, London, 1917, pp. 55–102; O'Connor, *Art of Dying Well*, pp. 164–70.

63 O'Connor, *Art of Dying Well*, p. 49. For the variety of tracts erroneously fathered on Rolle (but not mentioning the *Book of the Craft of Dying*), H. E. Allen, *Writings Ascribed to Richard Rolle, Hermit of Hampole, and Materials for his Biography*, Modern Language Association of America, Monograph Series, III, New York and London, 1927, ch. 10–13. For the continuing uncertainty about the canon of Rolle's works, J. A. Alford, 'Richard Rolle and related works', in *Middle English Prose: a Critical Guide to Major Authors and Genres*, ed. A. S. G. Edwards, Brunswick, N.J., 1984, pp. 37, 48.

64 Jolliffe, *Check-List*, pp. 122-6. Several are printed in Comper, *Book of the Craft of Dying*; see also O'Connor, *The Art of Dying Well*, pp. 179–80, 185–8, and Collins, 'A little known "Art of Dying"', pp. 181–90; Gillespie, 'Vernacular books of religion', pp. 324–5.

65 The traditionally morbid approach is exemplified in J. Huizinga, *The Waning of the Middle Ages*, London, 1968, pp. 134–46, which relies on continental evidence. Death and its occurrence were certainly important, and had to be prepared for, but precise attitudes are uncertain, see e.g. Swanson, *Church and Society*, p. 254.

whatever control there may have been over the fate of his or her soul, and became dependent on the prayers of those left behind to ensure speedy release from Purgatory, and on God's mercy to gain assured admittance to Heaven. The *Book* provides guidance in preparation for that crux, to ensure that faith did not waver through the onset of despair, and to encourage a hopeful entrance into the next world. While responding to the challenges which individuals faced at death, it also provides access to approaches to spirituality, with the process of catechising, and the portrayal of an individual death as something of a group experience as those around the deathbed share in the process of preparation, and at the moment of death become responsible for the initial commendations of the departed. The numerous prayers recorded in the tract also point to an area of spirituality which is rarely presented for consideration or assessment: the laity's access to personal intercession beyond mere repetition of the Ave, Creed and Our Father. Certain repetitions of these prayers appear to have been the fundamental spiritual exercise of the period – assisted by the development of the devotion of the Rosary – and the instructions for behaviour during the mass focus simply on such repetitions.[66] Other evidence suggests some widening of that prayer cycle: traditionally certain of the psalms (notably the *De profundis*, for the dead) had been added to the basic three recitations.[67] The development of Books of Hours assisted the process of increasing the reservoir of prayers.[68]

66 They also merged into the trafficking in indulgences: see the devotional woodcuts and the indulgences which they earned, in C. Wordsworth, ed., *Ordinale Sarum, sive directorium sacerdotum*, Henry Bradshaw Society, XX, XXII, 1901, ii, pp. 648–58; C. Dodgson, 'English devotional woodcuts of the late fifteenth century, with special reference to those in the Bodleian library', *Walpole Society*, XVII, 1928–9, pp. 97–100, 103; E. Duffy, 'Devotion to the crucifix and related images in England on the eve of the Reformation', in *Bilder und Bildersturm im Spätmittelalter und in der früher Neuzeit*, ed. R. Scribner, Wolfenbütteler Forschungen, XLVI, Wiesbaden, 1990, pp. 25–6. By encouraging the recitation of prayers in a domestic setting, woodcuts might also promote the creation of 'household shrines': for illustration of a print of St Christopher in a domestic setting (and therefore a slightly different devotional concern), D. Kunzle, *The Early Comic Strip: Narrative Strips and Picture Stories in the European Broadsheet from c.1450 to 1825*, Berkeley, Los Angeles and London, 1973, p. 11.

67 Moran, *Growth of English Schooling*, p. 53.

68 On Books of Hours and their contents, R. S. Wieck, ed., *Time Sanctified: the Book of Hours in Medieval Art and Life*, New York, 1988. M. W. Driver, 'Pictures in print: late fifteenth- and early sixteenth-century English religious books for lay readers', in *De Cella in Seculum: Religious and Secular Life and Devotion in Late Medieval England*, ed. M. G. Sargent, Woodbridge, 1989, pp. 235–8. For a fifteenth-century English rendition of the basic contents of such a compilation, H. Littlehales, ed., *The Prymer, or Lay Folks' Prayer Book*, part 1, Early English Text Society, original ser., CV, 1895.

Personal prayers are less generally recorded; but the construction of commonplace books did provide an opportunity for the creation of such collections. One set of private prayers, entered in a liturgical text linked with a nunnery at Chester, may well derive from the context of a female religious house, and so reflect a particular form of spirituality which was not widely shared; but the prayers themselves – invoking Jesus and guardian angels – are probably not too far removed from those which others recited.[69] It might, however, be necessary to impose a division between the longer vernacular prayers, which may have been deliberately 'devotional', and had to be read, and the shorter 'tags' of verse – equally prayers – which may have been more of an instinctive and rote-memory response.[70]

The existence of instructional and devotional texts – and the number available was considerable – offers testimony to the widespread desire for access to such works, and is therefore presumably indicative of the spiritual hunger of the period, and the extent to which it could be addressed. Whether it actually demonstrates the satisfaction of that hunger is less readily demonstrable. There are problems about the contemporary treatment of these texts, which have to be stated even if they cannot be resolved. On the one hand, there is the question of readership. With the increase in literacy in late medieval England,[71] there would theoretically be ever-widening access to the texts, if the texts could be made available. This would be not merely through visual reading, but also through the greater availability of people to read to an audience. The number of 'textual communities' could therefore be expanded.[72] Could be; but whether they actually were is of

69 J. W. Legg, ed., *The Processional of the Nuns of Chester*, Henry Bradshaw Society, XVIII, 1899, pp. 26–33.

70 For examples, R. H. Robbins, 'Private prayers in middle English verse', *Studies in Philology*, XXXVI, 1939, pp. 466–75; R.H. Robbins, 'Popular prayers in middle English verse', *Modern Philology*, XXXVI, 1938–9, pp. 337–50. On prayers in general, see now J. Bossy, 'Prayers', *Transactions of the Royal Historical Society*, 6th ser., I, 1991, pp. 137–48; V. Reinburg, 'Note on John Bossy, "Prayers"', *ibid.*, pp. 148–50.

71 Above, n. 30.

72 For 'textual communities', see B. Stock, *The Implications of Literacy: Written Language and Models of Interpretation in the Eleventh and Twelfth Centuries*, Princeton, N.J., 1983, esp. pp. 90–2, 522–4; B. Stock, *Listening for the Text: on the Uses of the Past*, Baltimore and London, 1990, pp. 22–4, 149–58. Stock's models mainly derive from the twelfth century and before, but are clearly applicable to later times. In England, a prime example would be the means whereby 'Lollard' groups shared their awareness of texts; but obviously any sharing of liturgical arrangements also fits into the pattern.

course unascertainable. Owners, and successions of owners, might well mark their ownerships of a text; listeners could not. Against the spread of literacy and the possible widening of access must be placed a growing uncertainty about what might licitly be read: potential listeners might be chary of those whom they knew to possess books, just in case. Some 'heresy' accusations, based on possession of books in English, may demonstrate such wariness on the part of would-be listeners – although if the charge was subsequently rejected, and the questioned texts presumably thereby legitimised, then they might well wish to become audiences.[73] The process of spiritual development via reading is well exemplified in the case of Margery Kempe, a King's Lynn woman of the early fifteenth century. She had books read to her by her local priest: that process could have been repeated countless times throughout pre-Reformation England.[74]

Mere access, however, did not guarantee comprehension; and the extent to which much of this instructional and devotional material was understood, and the manner in which it was comprehended, also needs some consideration. Here, however, the passage of time again intervenes. Without being able to identify precisely what individuals were hoping to gain from acquaintance with such works, whether they succeeded cannot be judged. Indeed, it is sometimes not clear precisely what the texts were aiming to convey. The very physical nature of some of the spiritual exercises – the detailed descriptions of the decaying and suffering body of Christ, for instance, which are in some ways as gruesome as the special effects in a horror film, jar against modern susceptibilities as aids to spiritual development. But modern reactions cannot be equated with medieval reactions; and judgement certainly cannot extend to any justified denigration of the spirituality of the time as it reacted to such descriptions. Our squeamishness, and insistence on a definition of spirituality which tends to invalidate anything which does not approach the mystical – and preferably the Dionysian version of mysticism through the penetration of the darkness surrounding an ineffable divinity, rather than that which offered an affective, emotion-centred and emotion-directed access to God[75] – places a major barrier between the twentieth century and pre-Reformation religious practices. Such qualms are perhaps most vividly

73 Hudson, *Premature Reformation*, pp. 167, 186–7, 205.

74 Windeatt, *Book of Margery Kemp*, p. 182. This is clearly something which also happened with 'Lollard' groups.

75 Butler, *Western Mysticism*, pp. 6, 124.

exemplified in the difficulties commentators face when dealing with the highly individualistic spirituality of Margery Kempe. Her *Book* provides a detailed and extremely precise autobiographical statement of her devotional experiences; but just how they should be treated is debatable. Although she is traditionally counted among the 'Middle English mystics', some would deny the reality of her mysticism; some condemn her as a mere hysteric; some make her a determined feminist; some object to the extremely physical (and at times apparently banal) descriptions of her visions and her comments on them.[76] One possibly fruitful recent interpretation seeks, however, to set her in a more general spiritual context, stressing contemporary insistence on what might be labelled 'devotional theatre' (the re-enactment, whether mental or physical, of aspects of the message and history of Christianity): certainly that reduces the extraordinariness of Margery's experiences, and while perhaps not bringing her down to earth, does seem to cut her down to size.[77]

Equally insidious as an obstacle to empathy, although perhaps less obvious a barrier to appreciation of pre-Reformation reactions to these texts, is the undeniable fact of linguistic change and development over the centuries. The technical vocabulary of theology and spirituality, even if not part of everyday language, is nevertheless now fairly readily accessible, and capable of being comprehended without too much difficulty even if via a dictionary definition. The language has been absorbed. But this may well not have applied with many of the instructional and devotional texts of the pre-Reformation period. The technical vocabulary existed in Latin, but not in English: an English language to convey the gradations of spirituality had to be created as these texts were being constructed. Of necessity, the language adopted was highly Latinate; but that poses a problem in any attempt to assess the effectiveness of the transmission of the spirituality contained in these texts. If the audience was non-Latinate, how would they actually

76 Reactions to her are surveyed in J. C. Hirsh, 'Margery Kempe', in *Middle English Prose: a Critical Guide to Major Authors and Genres*, ed. A. S. G. Edwards, Brunswick, N.J., 1984, pp. 109–10; see also S. Beckwith, 'A very material mysticism: the medieval mysticism of Margery Kempe', in *Medieval Literature: Criticism, Ideology, and History*, ed. D. Aers, New York, 1986, pp. 34–57 (especially the discussion of mysticism at pp. 38–41); U. Stargardt, 'The beguines of Belgium, the Dominican nuns of Germany, and Margery Kempe', in *The Popular Literature of Medieval England*, ed. T. J. Heffernan, Tennessee Studies in Literature, XXVIII, Knoxville, Tenn., 1985, pp. 297–313.

77 Gibson, *Theater of Devotion*, ch. 3. See also J. C. Hirsh, *The Revelations of Margery Kempe: Paramystical Practices in Late Medieval England*, Medieval and Renaissance Authors, X, Leiden, 1989.

understand this language? Would they be forced to make up meanings as they went along, and hope that they were right? Clearly the problem was appreciated by some of the authors; and there does in fact seem to be a distinction in the level of language used for varying texts. The more simple, more basically instructional, works retain a language which tends to avoid the Latinate, glossing over the theological and doctrinal obstacles, working on the basis that too much detailed knowledge was unnecessary. The more advanced texts do use a Latinate text; although even here glosses and synonyms may be incorporated as guidance to the interpretation.[78]

Such linguistic distinctions must also revive questions about the intended audience of such works (which is rather different from discussing the real audience – a problem not unknown to film censors). Does a Latinate text presuppose an audience which already had access to Latin anyway, and which was not necessarily monoglot? If so, then were the authors building into their texts presuppositions of different levels of spirituality which were appropriate for different types of audience? And were those differences based on purely educational achievement, or was there also a social element involved? This leads on again to the possibility of a distinction between elite and popular culture; but the deterministic trend of the questions must not be pushed too insistently. The realities of the fragmentation of the contemporary spiritual world have again to be dragged into the equations, as must the realities of social organisation. The immediate contact with the text was only the first point of contact – possibly mediated through a parish priest or private chaplain, who could then explain the Latinity if necessary. Beyond that, there was scope for much wider dissemination, through all the channels which might then become available: the instructing priest would also have access to pulpits; the instructed layperson would participate in a variety of social and domestic networks which provided opportunities for spreading the message (Margery Kempe's tedious tabletalk comes immediately to mind, but is by no means the only such possible instance).[79]

78 Swanson, *Church and Society*, p. 263; W. Riehle, *The Middle English Mystics*, London, Boston and Henley, 1981, pp. 4–5. The general linguistic issues are addressed in N. F. Blake, *The English Language in Medieval Literature*, London and New York, 1977, esp. ch. 2.

79 Windeatt, *Book of Margery Kempe*, pp. 97, 99–102; Atkinson, *Mystic and Pilgrim*, p. 54.

Practice

To go beyond the theory of access and availability, from ideals of the instructional and the devotional word to the reality of what people actually did to demonstrate their spirituality, is to cross a major divide in the quality of the evidence. The theory prescribes; the practice describes.

The sources from which a picture of the practice of spirituality can be reconstructed are for the most part financial in either their origins or their concerns. How people actually spent their money in the economy of salvation can provide insights into their appreciation of spiritual matters; but it would be fatuous to claim that it is a precise mirror.[80] Some of the payments were, after all, compulsory; other voluntary offerings, at marriages and other religious ceremonies, might be virtually on a tariff basis. Even so, the evasion of some compulsory payments (notably tithes and mortuary dues) may be illustrative of sentiments about the clergy even if not about religion. Real danger creeps in with other influences which affected expenditure on things supposedly spiritual: the problems of social convention in the distribution of gifts; fashion in particular types of spirituality which might be pursued precisely for fashionable purposes; and the need to maintain social status by demonstrative donation to create a memory which, while procuring prayers for a soul, would also secure a secular reputation. All of these strands may be visible, and have been identified – some were at the time. The fashion for self-abasing funerals in the late fourteenth and early fifteenth century was condemned *c.* 1405–10 by the author of *Dives and Pauper* as defrauding the poor of their rightful expectation of doles.[81] Other trends of the period have been labelled by more recent commentators. The regular giving to friars in wills has been seen as no more than a response to social pressures, something which everyone did and which therefore provides no real reflection of any attachment or commitment to mendicant morality or spirituality. In like fashion, some of the cadaver tombs of the fifteenth century have been tied in with noble fashions and political allegiance to the Lancastrians (although in this case it is likely that the fashion slowly

80 Swanson, *Church and Society*, pp. 209–28.

81 P. H. Barnum, ed., *Dives and Pauper*, Early English Text Society, original ser., CCLXXV, CCLXXX, 1976-80, i, pp. 213–17.

permeated down through the social layers).[82]

Being largely concerned with finances, the available material varies both in survival rates and particular utility: the problems of interpretation which it poses are just as great as those affecting the literary works. Indeed, they are perhaps even greater, for much of the practice of spirituality required no recording: there were no censuses of church attendance, no Gallup polls of the most popular saints, no clicking turnstiles as people circulated around shrines. The material is extremely fragmentary, and scattered. While virtually every parish was presumably maintaining churchwardens' accounts by 1500, only a small minority of those accounts survive from that date; the extremely prosaic – and incomplete – nature of their recording generally makes them an insufficient guide to what was actually going on in the churches in anything other than a structural way.[83] They may be vitally important for charting changes at the Reformation, which were reflected in changing furniture with all its connotations;[84] but for the pre-Reformation period their utility is less quantifiable. The maintenance of chantry properties and the payment of the priests certainly indicates the continued fulfilment of the original contract between donors and wardens; but says little about the real attitude to the

82 A. K. Warren, *Anchorites and their Patrons in Medieval England*, Berkeley, Los Angeles and London, 1988, p. 235; P. King, 'The English cadaver tomb in the late fifteenth century: some indications of a Lancastrian connection', in *Dies Illa: Death in the Middle Ages. Proceedings of the 1983 Manchester Colloquium*, ed. J. H. M. Taylor, Vinaver Studies in French, I, Liverpool, 1984, pp. 45–57.

83 For a general, but old, survey of churchwardens' accounts, J. C. Cox, *Churchwardens' Accounts from the Fourteenth Century to the Close of the Seventeenth Century*, London, 1913; see also comments in C. Burgess, '"A fond thing vainly invented": an essay on Purgatory and pious motive in late medieval England', in *Parish, Church, and People: Local Studies in Lay Religion, 1350–1750*, ed. S. J. Wright, London, 1988, pp. 76–8. Some parish records are more illuminating, for example those associated with some of the Bristol churches, as exploited in several articles by C. Burgess: '"For the increase of divine service": chantries in the parish in late-medieval Bristol', *Journal of Ecclesiastical History*, XXXVI, 1985, pp. 46–65; '"By quick and by dead": wills and pious provision in late medieval Bristol', *English Historical Review*, CII, 1987, pp. 837–58; 'A service for the dead: the form and function of the anniversary in late medieval Bristol', *Transactions of the Bristol and Gloucestershire Archaeological Society*, CV, 1987, pp. 183–211; 'Strategies for eternity: perpetual chantries in late medieval Bristol', in *Religious Belief and Ecclesiastical Careers in Late Medieval England*, ed. C. Harper-Bill, Woodbridge, 1991, pp. 1–32; 'Late medieval wills and pious convention: testamentary evidence reconsidered', in *Profit, Piety, and the Professions in Later Medieval England*, ed. M. A. Hicks, Gloucester, 1990, pp. 14–33.

84 R. Whiting, *The Blind Devotion of the People: Popular Religion and the English Reformation*, Cambridge, 1989, uses them extensively for this purpose (see his comments at p. 5); see also R. Hutton, 'The local impact of the Tudor Reformations', in *The English Reformation Revised*, ed. C. Haigh, Cambridge, 1987, pp. 114–38.

existence of chantries. Gifts may be recorded, expenditure on plays set out, and occasional payments for episcopal and other services noted; but they convey little about spirituality – especially when submerged in much lengthier lists of payments for nails and plaster, wages due to labourers for minor building works, lists of rents for church sheep and cattle, payments for wax and other evidence of concern with the sheer physical upkeep of the church and its properties. Churchwardens' accounts can yield evidence of spiritually-directed concerns and activities, but it must not be taken out of context and given a prominence not built into the records. Equally, when this evidence is isolated, it requires numerous small fragments over a fairly lengthy period of time to create much of an impression. (It is precisely for that reason that no churchwardens' accounts are extracted here: to convey a proper impression of their contents would require the inclusion of an unjustifiably large amount of extraneous material.)

Slightly different problems arise with much of the other surviving material: that it provides only a glimpse of what must often be assumed to be much more widespread practices. However, here the problems mentioned earlier about the cohesiveness of English religious practices again come to the fore. If the evidence is highly localised, how far can it be extrapolated to nation-wide application? How many small scraps need to be amalgamated before a statement can be applied to England, rather than be restricted to (say) Kent, the 'south-west', or an even smaller geographical area – just one town or village? Conversely, but just as importantly, how much evidence needs to be assessed (and how?) to demonstrate that there were differences in regional or more localised spiritual attitudes? Was, for instance, the spirituality of the people of Hull really so 'remarkably insular, inert, and shallow, untouched by the new devotions, perfunctory almost in the old ones, uninterested in, and showing no deep acquaintance with, doctrine' as has been concluded in one study of the available will evidence?[85]

It seems fitting to draw attention to one particular area of activity which may illustrate the problems better than most: what actually went on in a church? Given that there was a fundamental division between lay and clerical perspectives on the use of the ecclesiastical building – most blatantly revealed in the division of responsibilities for

85 P. Heath, 'Urban piety in the later middle ages: the evidence of Hull wills', in *The Church, Politics, and Patronage in the Fifteenth Century*, ed. R. B. Dobson, Gloucester, 1984, p. 229.

the fabric, with the laity liable for repairs to the nave, while the rector (whether an individual cleric or corporate entity) generally had to maintain the chancel – then there is an immediate division in the types of material to be consulted. For the lay perspective, churchwardens' accounts would clearly provide the main evidence of oversight. However, as already noted, the prime function of those accounts is to reflect the care for the fabric and for the funds devoted to that fabric, with additional oversight of chantries coming second (but nevertheless important). Churchwardens' accounts, because they are not concerned with the day-to-day services, are but poor mirrors to the spiritual activities within a church. Similar strictures may apply with the sources available from the opposing perspective, of the rectory.[86] There, again, finance was the main concern; but generally seeing the benefice as a whole as a functioning economic entity, and as a source of profit. The survival of detailed accounts is sporadic, and usually for benefices which had been appropriated to a religious house or other institution. The accounts are often summary, like those of Great Yarmouth or King's Lynn (although much can be made of those brief statements): they do not adequately reveal the amalgam of individual spiritual events which were taking place. When it comes down to it, there are very few records which do. The odd years for which detailed accounts survive for Scarborough, in the first half of the fifteenth century, seem to come the closest: the listing of receipts from devotional offerings presents almost a diary of special celebrations, of funerals, marriages, purifications, and special masses from which the rector gained some financial benefit.[87] Detailed as it is, this evidence is almost certainly an incomplete statement: there is nothing here relating to the individual chantries, nothing here for the private masses celebrated by individual chaplains, which presumably did occur (although it might be legitimately countered that the silence of the accounts is a reflection of the silence within the church: that there were no such celebrations by private chaplains).[88] The detail of the services which are listed is nevertheless impressive. But Scarborough cannot be made to stand for the whole of England: individual parishes clearly differed. The Scarborough material is to some extent paralleled by that

86 R. N. Swanson, 'Standards of livings: parochial revenues in pre-Reformation England', in *Religious Belief and Ecclesiastical Careers in Late Medieval England*, ed. C. Harper-Bill, Woodbridge, 1991, esp. pp. 153–66.

87 Below, no. 13.

88 For the chantries in Scarborough church, see N. A. H. Lawrance, *Fasti Parochiales, vol. 3: Deanery of Dickering*, Yorkshire Archaeological Society Record Series, CXXIX, 1967, pp. 110–16.

from Hornsea, also in Yorkshire. Those accounts give evidence from a rural context; but, while very detailed, are less precise in their dating than the Scarborough material.[89] Other parish accounts permit some calculation of the number of particular types of services, but little more – although they do show the variation in the demand for priestly services for some of the essential staging posts in human existence. Where runs of accounts survive, as opposed to odd years, then some statement of the ebb and flow of interests can be abstracted, as for Great Yarmouth and King's Lynn, analyses which are particularly instructive in revealing aspects of the more voluntary aspects of contemporary spirituality, especially devotion to saints.[90]

The fiscal quantification of services is, once more, only a partial, drily non-emotive, record of events. Paradoxically, it seems that the most revealing indicators of the liveliness of a parish church may derive from the purely secular sphere, from the evidence provided by witnesses being asked to testify to the age of minors laying claim to their inheritances: the 'proofs of age' demanded by the royal courts in a variety of property cases. These often contain scattered references to events on a particular day or in a particular week – a cleric saying a first mass; the busy succession of baptisms, marriages, funerals, and purifications; people setting off from the church on pilgrimage; and so on. Again, the material is scattered, and defies quantification. Moreover, the organisation of these records has produced justifiable doubt about their historical veracity; but what is important is that the depictions were clearly not considered incredible by contemporaries.[91]

89 P. Heath, *Medieval Clerical Accounts*, St Anthony's Hall Publications, XXVI, York, 1964; see also P. Heath, *The English Parish Clergy on the Eve of the Reformation*, London and Toronto, 1960, pp. 166–73 (one year's accounts are printed in translation in A.R. Myers, ed., *English Historical Documents, 1327–1485*, London, 1969, no. 449). Detailed receipts for Blunham (Beds.) in chronological order from April to October 1535 and Christmas 1538 to Michaelmas 1539 are in N. H. Bennett, 'Blunham rectory accounts, 1520–39', in *Hundreds, Manors, Parishes, and Churches: a Selection of Early Documents for Bedfordshire*, ed. J. S. Thompson, Publications of the Bedfordshire Historical Record Society, LXIX, 1990, pp. 145–6, 161–3. It is likely that rather more of this detailed material has survived than is generally appreciated, and awaits assessment. See, for instance, discussion of some Oxford city parish revenues as recorded in the accounts of Lincoln College in A. Clark, ed., *Lincoln Diocese Documents, 1450–1544*, Early English Text Society, original ser., CXLIX, 1914, pp. 23–35.

90 Swanson, 'Standards of livings', pp. 168–9; I am currently preparing work on the Lynn accounts for publication.

91 E.g. J. L. Kirby, ed., *Calendar of Inquisitions Post Mortem and Other Analogous Documents Preserved in the Public Record Office; vol. XVIII, 1–6 Henry IV, 1399–1405*, London, 1987, nos. 309–10, 314–15, 662–3, 666–7, 670–3, 675, 856 (compare with

Such evidence does indicate the regularity of visits to church, for whatever purpose, and possibly also the futility of trying to identify particularly 'spiritual' elements in individual lives: the church was there, was used, was so integral that it did not need to be thought about.[92]

Whatever picture of spirituality may be constructed from this disparate material, the fact remains that it has to be constructed from disconnected snippets, creating a generalisation by asking questions which the record was not constructed to answer, and from records which were often seen at the time as ephemeral and with no relationship to the other individual documents or evidence which has to be correlated. Similar obstacles apply to much of the other material which has to be tackled in the search for glimpses of pre-Reformation English spirituality. Numerous individual documents survive to record indulgences and pardons, attesting to the popularity of such practices; there are records galore indicating the existence of chantries and guilds; but it is often extremely difficult to get beyond the basic statement to any kernel of spirituality, to assess motives and the reality of participation. Nevertheless, some attempt must be made to break through the barriers. Perhaps the most intractable problems occur with wills, which survive in relative abundance. Yet, although such material has been treated statistically, in the hope of actually quantifying people's charitable (and synonymously spiritual) concerns, the testamentary evidence remains an elusive guide to the reality. How free was the choice exercised by the testator when drawing up the document? Sermon literature suggests that the presence of clerics could easily produce distortion. How much were people guided by social convention in their dispositions? How much is the picture obscured by focusing attention on what is, after all, the *last* will (with little indication of any changes of mind), and giving no indication of any pre-mortem arrangements for spiritual security? Indeed, how much are wills a proper reflection of deathbed dispositions anyway? Arrangements for land usually required a separate document, which

675), 857–8, 944, 953, 990, 994, 997, 1178–82. For the reliability of these records R. F. Hunnisett, 'The reliability of inquisitions as historical evidence', in *The Study of Medieval Records: Essays in Honour of Kathleen Major*, ed. D. A. Bullough and R. L. Storey, Oxford, 1971, p. 206 and refs. at n. 6. They are viewed more charitably in S. S. Walker, 'Proof of age of feudal heirs in medieval England', *Mediaeval Studies*, XXXV, 1973, pp. 306–23.

92 Here, again, I think I would disagree with some of Langmuir's formulations. While I am clearly refering to what he would define as 'religiosity', I am not sure that it can actually be treated as an independent and definable element in individual existence, to be distinguished from other aspects of medieval life.

often did not go through the same administrative procedures as the ecclesiastically-probated will (which, generally, only dealt with movable property)? And, even when we have the wills, how much can they be trusted? A will was only a statement of intent: for implementation it required the co-operation of the executors. On the one hand, executors might be allowed considerable discretion in the disposal of the (unquantified) residue of the testator's property for the good of his or her soul; on the other they notoriously were not to be trusted (and, if the visitation evidence is to be considered valid, well deserved their reputation). Effective implementation also requires the testator actually to possess the wealth so meticulously distributed. Archbishop Courtenay of Canterbury, when making his will in the 1390s, actually made arrangements for the possibility that resources would not match the demands of the will; for others there might be the embryonic bankruptcy arrangements to upset their proposals. Wills might indicate what people wanted to have done, at a particular point; but they are no guarantee that things actually were done. And, perhaps more than most other sources, other issues come to the fore: regional and social distributions are important – is the spirituality revealed (assuming that any is) dictated by the social origins of the testators, or by particular regional devotions and customs which may not now be evident but were built into the assumptions of the testators?[93] To answer all these questions adequately in this volume would require the printing of considerable numbers of wills: any selection which claimed to address them would necessarily pre-judge the issues. Most of the questions, therefore, will not be addressed here: the few wills offered here give no more than a glimpse at this sort of material, as a deliberately and somewhat arbitrarily chosen sample which indicates the variety of concerns which may be expressed in them; but each is exceptional (and chosen for that reason) in the range of concerns revealed.

Opposition

To posit a distinction between 'theory' and 'practice' to some extent presupposes a unity in which these were the complementary and

93 Swanson, *Church and Society*, pp. 265–8; Burgess, 'Late medieval wills and pious convention'. Complaints about the failures of executors abound in K. L. Wood-Legh, ed., *Kentish Visitations of Archbishop William Warham and his Deputies, 1511–1512*, Kent Records, XXIV, 1984.

competing aspects. That built-in supposition of unity requires some attention, for, stated in those terms, it falls into an obvious trap: it assumes that there was really a monolith which can be called 'pre-Reformation English spirituality'. However, it has to be repeated that that monolith did not, and could not, exist. There was neither the cultural unity nor the administrative and technical ability to create so unified a structure at that time. Printing may have helped in the process, by canonising particular variants of texts, and in some spheres the process of standardisation was obviously under way throughout. The most potent instance of this is provided by what can only be considered the spiritual imperialism of the Use of Sarum, the slow process whereby the liturgy of Salisbury became the liturgy of almost the whole of England.[94] The outcome of this was the increasing marginalisation of the other regional uses (but what was Sarum but a regional use to begin with?); although this process was still incomplete in 1530, and York for one seems to have retained considerable vitality.[95] Moreover, the piecemeal introduction of new liturgical feasts still meant that even those areas which had adopted the Use of Sarum might lack the latest variants and additions to the liturgical round.[96] And, regardless of such spiritual imperialism, there would always have to be some element of adaptation to the local calendar, to incorporate some obscure saint (or would-be saint) or other.

Perhaps more significantly, it was impossible to impose a particular definition of acceptable spirituality. The wide variety of options available meant that there would always be some degree of questioning, possibly even active opposition to prevailing definitions. Challenges had to be faced, which were in their own ways proclamations of alternative spiritualities, generally aiming either to increase spiritual awareness and receptiveness or to offer alternative definitions and explanations. The first of these two branches might be said to encompass movements of complaint and 'anticlericalism'; the second, the active search for alternatives, throws up the whole question of

94 R. W. Pfaff, *New Liturgical Feasts in Later Medieval England*, Oxford, 1970, pp. 7–8; A. A. King, *Liturgies of the Past*, London, 1959, pp. 285–6, 292–300, 208–26, 330.

95 King, *Liturgies*, pp. 293–4, 297, 327–69; W. H. Frere, 'York service books', in *Walter Howard Frere: a Collection of his Papers on Liturgical and Historical Subjects*, ed. J. H. Arnold and E. G. P. Wyatt, Alcuin Club Collections, XXXV, 1940, pp. 159–69 (listing manuscripts and editions at pp. 167–9).

96 For some of the feasts, Pfaff, *New Liturgical Feasts*, and his comments on the 'introduction' of feasts at pp. 4–5 (see also pp. 38, 48, 81). For reports at visitation of the lack of service books for the new celebrations, Wood-Legh, *Kentish Visitations*, pp. xix, 100, 110–11, 118, 220.

heresy and 'Lollardy' in late medieval England.

The problem of pre-Reformation 'anticlericalism' has been one of the foci of interest in searching for the roots of the Reformation itself. It seems to follow that, if the English were increasingly anticlerical, then that might account for their apparent indifference to the changes which were being foisted on them from 1529 onwards, as Henry VIII moved increasingly from Rome and gradually demolished the old structures of religious observance. The debate itself, however, rests on rather insecure foundations, reflecting as much on the debaters as the issues raised. After all, just what is 'anticlericalism'?[97] If it merely means dislike of the activities of clerics – individually and collectively – then it becomes a fairly meaningless generalisation. Throughout the centuries, the laity had opposed clerics who were not behaving as they ought, or as was considered appropriate. Clergy who got drunk, fornicated, demanded excessive tithes, or disturbed the peace were not likely to be popular except among their cronies: these were clerics who were not living up to their cloth, and who were therefore to an extent failing their parishioners. But it could be argued that such failure is different in character from failure to fulfil the spiritual obligations of their role – to maintain the succession of masses, provide the last rites for the dead, offer instruction and effective spiritual oversight. And that, in turn, is different from opposition to the very existence of the priestly order, which is probably the only true definition of 'anticlericalism'. There is certainly evidence for complaints about inappropriate behaviour and dereliction of duties, most frequently revealed in visitation material and Church court records. Such opposition is epitomised in the series of complaints delivered by the burgesses of Saltash against their vicar in the early fifteenth century, which is one of the most comprehensive indictments to be found. The third type of challenge to clerical power, the rejection of any need for priesthood, leaves much less evidence, although its existence is suggested in some supposedly Lollard doctrines, particularly the denial of the sacramental powers of the priesthood, and is implicit in something like Simon Fish's *Supplication of the Beggars* (although that

97 C. Haigh, 'Anticlericalism in the English Reformation', in *The English Reformation Revised*, ed. C. Haigh, Cambridge, 1987, pp. 56–74; A. G. Dickens, 'The shape of anticlericalism and the English Reformation', in *Politics and Society in Reformation Europe: Essays for Sir Geoffrey Elton on his Sixty Fifth Birthday*, ed. E. I. Kouni and T. Scott, Basingstoke and London, 1987, pp. 379–410; A. G. Dickens, *The English Reformation*, 2nd ed., London, 1989, pp. 316-25; R. N. Swanson, 'Problems of the priesthood in pre-Reformation England', *English Historical Review*, CV, 1990, pp. 845–69.

seems to be rather a nihilistic tract, a vituperative complaint about the scale of clerical financial exactions rather than a statement about the spiritual role of the clergy).[98] The complaints about actions were not limited to laypeople: fifteenth-century clerical reformers, and even more vociferously those of the early sixteenth (like John Colet, in his Convocation sermon of 1512) castigated clerics who failed to live up to their responsibilities, who were too enmeshed in the world to give sufficient attention to the spiritual aspect of their duties.[99] This reformist strand, which might almost be called a programme, despite its ineffectiveness, seems to have united both clergy and laity: after all, the visitation and court material reflects concerted action by laity and ecclesiastical hierarchs to remedy defects within the system. That unity of purpose suggests not opposition to clerical status but a concern and demand that clergy should act in accordance with their status, a desire that clerics should be more clerical – and that they should be more effective as clerics. If that is the case, then any justification for using the term 'anticlerical' simply dissolves.

This is not to underestimate the scale of revulsion against bad clerics: both in the record evidence, and in the literature, the stereotype of the unclerical cleric leaps forth, to be contrasted with the equally stereotypical clerical cleric. It is that revulsion, and the search for proper clerical activity, which is manifested in much of the complaint material, whether the Saltash missive or the complaints of the 1512 visitation of the diocese of Canterbury and the other visitation material.[100] But what is notable in this material, taking it all together, is the general lack of complaints about the theological activities of the clergy. Whether they were offering a religion which the twentieth century would consider acceptable may well be unlikely; but it does seem that they were offering observances and interpretations acceptable to their parishioners, that they were for the most part meeting the spiritual demands made of them.

Nevertheless, there were some for whom 'ordinary' Christianity clearly was in some respects, if not many, unsatisfactory. Its doctrines and observances seemed not to make sense, possibly indeed actually to be wrong. The response to such questioning might entail the creation

98 C. H. Williams, *English Historical Documents, 1485-1558*, London, 1963, pp. 669–76.

99 Heath, *English Parish Clergy*, pp. 70–2. The sermon is in Williams, *English Historical Documents*, pp. 652–60. For a judicious assessment of the validity of Colet's attack, C. Harper-Bill, 'Dean Colet's convocation sermon and the pre-Reformation church in England', *History*, LXXIII, 1988, pp. 191–210.

100 Below, nos 47–8.

of an alternative Christianity which resolved those doubts; or, more radically, actual scepticism about the validity of Christianity and the dogmas of received orthodoxy.[101] Evidence of a search for an alternative Christianity in late medieval England becomes increasingly widespread from 1380, in association with the development of the doctrines of John Wyclif and the energetic opposition which they faced from the ecclesiastical establishment, especially after his attack on accepted interpretations of the doctrine of transubstantiation, and the supposed identity of his ideas with those behind the Peasants' Revolt of 1381. Heresy-hunting became a feature of English ecclesiastical administration from then onwards, and continued, in fits and starts, right through to the Reformation (and beyond).[102]

The people so hunted are generally lumped together as 'Lollards', but Lollardy as a phenomenon poses many problems, both at the time, and for later historians. The epithet of 'Lollard' was certainly used by contemporaries; 'Lollards' were hunted in the anti-heresy drives; doctrines were ascribed to 'Lollards' in the questionnaires constructed by the authorities as guides to what constituted heresy. Unfortunately, no one actually voluntarily identifying him (or her) self as a Lollard provides a list of doctrines which actually define a Lollard, and the uncertain boundary between orthodoxy and heresy does not permit rigid distinctions between individual 'heretics' and 'orthodox' in many instances.

The trouble is that the historico-literary hunt for Lollardy has now become an industry in itself. There is no shortage of evidence which

101 On the problem of religious scepticism in Europe before the Reformation, S. Reynolds, 'Social mentalities and the case of medieval scepticism', *Transactions of the Royal Historical Society*, 6th ser., I, 1991, pp. 21–41.

102 For a brief overall survey, J. A. F. Thomson, *The Transformation of Medieval England, 1370–1529*, London, 1983, pp. 355–71; in more detail for the fifteenth and early sixteenth century, Thomson, *Later Lollards*, esp. pp. 239–50. Hudson, *Premature Reformation*, is now indispensable and a magisterial treatment; my comments on 'Lollardy' in *Church and Society*, pp. 329–45, were written before I had absorbed that work, and would need some modification. See also criticism of my approach in R. G. Davies, 'Lollardy and locality', *Transactions of the Royal Historical Society*, 6th ser., I, 1991, p. 191 n. 4; that whole article (pp. 191–212) persuades me to modify my views on continuity to some degree. See also J. A. F. Thomson, 'Orthodox religion and the origins of Lollardy', *History*, LXXIV, 1989, pp. 39–55; Hudson, *Lollards and their Books*, pp. 125–40; A. Hope, 'Lollardy: the stone the builders rejected?', in *Protestantism and the National Church in Sixteenth Century England*, ed. P. Lake and M. Dowling, London, New York and Sydney, 1987, pp. 1–35. For the lack of specificity in late fifteenth-century use of the term 'Lollard', S. Powell, 'Lollards and Lombards: late medieval bogeymen', *Medium Ævum*, LIX, 1991, pp. 134–6.

attests to the concern for the eradication of heresy; but the extent to which that evidence is evidence for a specific and identifiable sect remains debatable. Given the problems with that, alternative tacks have been adopted, most particularly the emphasis on the literary manifestations of Lollard ideas. The evidence is convincing that there was a deliberate policy of fostering Lollard writing in the later years of the fourteenth century, both in the production of standardised texts and in the appearance of new works.[103] But, predictably, not everything is straightforward. Indeed, while the record evidence presents problems for assessments of continuity and coherence, the literary evidence raises issues of definition and circularity. With these works, there is the danger of using the preconception of what Lollardy is to define a tract as 'Lollard', and then using that tract so categorised as evidence to prove the existence of 'Lollardy' as a definable construct.

That there was opposition to the Church from the late fourteenth century is undeniable: the drawing up of lists of errors, the trials, the questionnaires, and some of the literary material here all come into play. But that said, there are difficulties about the continuity of beliefs, and their derivation and coherence, to which have to be added the problems of subjective interpretation of responses to the heresy hunt, whether by contemporaries or later historians.[104] The fifteenth-century authorities may have exaggerated the scale of the threat, and by their approach to the issues made Lollardy appear more concrete and coherent than it actually was. Similarly, later commentators, equally concerned to find a national movement against Catholicism before the Reformation or beguiled by the desire to label aspects of spirituality, may have made Lollardy a greater problem than is warranted by the evidence.

To deny that Lollardy was a major problem is not to say that challenges to orthodoxy were negligible and unimportant. The anti-heresy measures, and the records of the trials, suggest that the concern

103 Hudson, *Premature Reformation* pp. 249–50, 258–60; Hudson, *Lollards and their Books*, pp. 4–6, 14–28, 184–5, 188–9; A. Hudson, ed., *English Wycliffite Sermons*, vol. I, Oxford, 1983, pp. 189–96, 199–202; see also A. Hudson, 'Wycliffite prose', in *Middle English Prose: a Critical Guide to Major Authors and Genres*, ed. A. S. G. Edwards, Brunswick, N.J., 1984, pp. 249–70; A. Hudson, 'Lollard book production', in *Book Production and Publishing in Britain, 1375–1475*, ed. J. Griffiths and D. Pearsall, Cambridge, 1989, pp. 125–42.

104 See the comments, both caustic and constructive, in Davies, 'Lollardy and locality', pp. 211–12.

was valid, even if there was over-reaction by the authorities. The mandate issued by the bishop of Norwich for the inquest at Bury St Edmunds in 1428 reveals the range of issues which were of concern, which seems to have extended beyond what might be recognised as heresy to mere suggestions of religious abnormality.[105] So widely-cast a net presents problems of interpretation for evidence which is often unspecific: to change the goalposts to incorporate all (or almost all) those accused of heresy into 'Lollardy' is in itself to admit the dubious nature of the label. That people denied a future belief in heresies (without defining what those heresies were) need not mean that they actually believed any heresies at the point of recantation. Nor can it be asserted that everyone else was necessarily orthodox. Indeed, given the variety of beliefs in circulation, which could be derived from a variety of sources (without carrying a warning label: this doctrine can threaten your soul), and which created all the individual amalgams which constituted the atomised belief-systems of Christianity, it seems quite possible that many people at some point fell into believing something which might turn out to be heretical.

Indeed, the problems of reconciling the demands of Christian doctrines with the practicalities of life made that quite probable. The evidence for opposition to orthodoxy may well reflect not coherent adherence to a set of beliefs which came packaged as 'Lollardy' but a personal rationalisation of objections to doctrines. This sometimes merely constituted a mirror image of more 'orthodox' spirituality. In some Salisbury cases of 1491 the blunt denial of the effectiveness of prayers to images seems to reflect that approach – but the documents record little explicit challenge to the notion of sainthood, or denial of the validity of praying to saints; the focus is on a challenge to the practice of directing prayers through images.[106] This is not actually proof that those charged were not members of a sect – there is no means of using any of the evidence formally to prove non-membership – but the balance of probabilities seems to suggest that. There were occasional groups which, for a variety of reasons, maintained some coherence and continuity, as elements in that collection of fragmented spiritualities which made up the pre-Reformation

105 Below, no. 49.

106 D. P. Wright, ed., *The Register of Thomas Langton, Bishop of Salisbury, 1485–93*, Canterbury and York Society, LXXIV, 1985, esp. no. 495, and see also nos 484–5, 501, 503. At no. 497 William Carpenter is explicitly sceptical of the validity of canonisation as proof of real sainthood.

English Church.[107] While in some instances similar ideas may have resurfaced simply because they were rethought, in others there was possibly more consistent continuity, through family traditions particularly (and again raising the possibility of a matrilineal religion and a patriarchal Church). Texts were still copied, but the literary vitality of Lollardy was evidently much weaker after the 1450s.[108] In this combination of circumstances, the debate about the role of Wycliffite beliefs in the pre-Reformation English Church, and the extent to which their continuity provided a basis for the new spirituality of the Reformation, becomes more uncertain.[109] As the texts had not actually disappeared, even though their location in the fifteenth century was seemingly deliberately not recorded (indications of the ownership of Wycliffite Bibles and of the Wycliffite sermon cycle are conspicuously absent from the volumes),[110] so there was always the possibility that they would be read. As many other texts included some of the ideas now identified as Wycliffite, then again the possibility for the continuity of those ideas was increased – even, perhaps unwittingly, among the orthodox.[111] But the basic problem remains: is the evidence for production of texts and trials of heretics proof of a unity of beliefs continuing over time, or merely of individuals proclaiming their own idiosyncrasies; of deeply-held convictions, or of a unified code of doctrines imposed by officials on a mass of disconnected and incoherent material and on individuals who would otherwise never have been aware that they had fallen into heresy?

107 Davies, 'Lollardy and locality', pp. 194–210; Hope, 'Lollardy', p. 17. The most obvious group is probably that centred on William White, for which see Aston, *Lollards and Reformers*, pp. 78–98 (but cf. Davies, 'Lollardy and locality', pp. 200–1). Groups such as this are almost paradigmatic 'textual communities' in the model developed by Stock.

108 Hudson, *Premature Reformation*, pp. 10–18, 451–3.

109 Aston, *Lollards and Reformers*, pp. 219–42; J. F. Davis, 'Lollardy and the Reformation in England', *Archiv für Reformationsgeschichte*, LXXIII, 1982, pp. 217–36; Hope, 'Lollardy', pp. 1–2, 21–5; Dickens, *English Reformation*, pp. 49-60.

110 Hudson, *Premature Reformation*, pp. 201, 231–4; Deanesly, *Lollard Bible*, pp. 333–6; Hudson, *English Wycliffite Sermons*, pp. 51–97, esp. 51, 60; Hudson, 'Lollard book production', pp. 136–7.

111 Hudson, 'Lollard book production', p. 135.

Conclusion

The problems of access to the faith, or awareness of what being a Christian entailed; of assessing the validity and impact of the theoretical and practical manifestations of Christianity; and of determining the nature and importance of statements suggesting opposition to prevalent orthodoxies, all have to be addressed when seeking to define the nature of spirituality in pre-Reformation England. They are problems of source material and its interpretation, problems of contemporary and later commentators and their own subjective responses – to events and to the records of those events. That there can be so many interpretations provides the basis for the continuing discussions of England's receptiveness to Reformation, and attempts to define the pre-existing mental structures to which that Reformation had itself to respond.

Because there are such problems, no judgement on the nature of English spirituality between 1350 and 1530 can be considered definitive. It is not for me to decree that the situation actually was such-and-such; but it is permissible to suggest what it may have been. That suggestion is naturally the outcome of work over several years on the evidence; it is also a reflection of personal predilections, of subjective responses and interpretations. For what it is worth, then, it seems to me that English spirituality was vibrant in this period. It was vibrant in both practical and theoretical terms.[112] There was active involvement in most aspects of devotion, from the purchase of indulgences to pilgrimage; from membership of guilds to foundations of chantries. There was a ready readership and audience for instruction in the faith, through sermons, texts, and plays (even if some of the latter were imperfect summaries of Christianity).[113] When printing came, the market could not be saturated.[114] People were willing to pay, and willing to pray. At the heart of the observances was the mass, and the repeated transformation of mere bread and wine into the body and blood of the Son of God. The focus was very much on Christ, but devotion to the saints – and, supreme among them, to the Virgin Mary – was a vital element: at times the devotion to Mary almost seems to

112 Swanson, *Church and Society*, ch. 6; Duffy, 'Devotion to the crucifix'.

113 Swanson, *Church and Society*, p. 279;

114 H.S. Bennett, *English Books and Readers, 1475 to 1557*, 2nd ed., Cambridge, 1969, pp. 57–8, 65–76. Printing is not just a matter of books: the printing of more ephemeral indulgences and woodcuts also needs to be taken into account here.

challenge the scale of devotion to her son. This was a religion – and religiosity – which was often ritualistic, often ostentatious. It also had private and personal elements which only occasionally attracted attention, or were committed to record. Of course, not all was rosy: there was hostility to clerical greed, often resentment at the cost of some of the foundations, and reluctance particularly by executors to diminish their own inheritances for the good of someone else's soul. But that cannot really contradict the evidence for full participation in the observances of Catholicism.

At the same time, this was not a 'national' religion. It remained atomised, individual. What it actually entailed, over the course of a year, varied from region to region; it also fluctuated over time, as new observances and devotions sprang up, old cults declined; as new buildings and new fashions changed the ways in which religion and devotion were portrayed and enacted. The change was part of the manifestation of vitality; as was the ability to build on old material through a continuing acceptance of the validity of old texts, while also incorporating newly-imported and newly-translated works from beyond England: in this respect, Luther was little different from the *Imitation of Christ.*

To provide an actual portrait of this spirituality in practice is, however, less easy than might be supposed. The very nature of the evidence means that the overall generalisations have to be constructed from pieces which were never intended to be fitted together; time, place and personalities all tend to dissolve, leaving a fairly amorphous statement which, at that level of generalisation, perhaps amounts to very little. To make it concrete demands that the atomisation of Christianity be recognised, and that an attempt be made to produce a portrait of an individual. Certainly something of that sort is possible, and as research continues the attitudes of individuals may become increasingly obvious. But again, they will be for the most part incomplete, because the evidence is not total.

Of those individuals for whom some sort of overall identification of spirituality is possible, a notable feature is that so many of them are women; and so many (perhaps predictably) from the upper classes. By examining things like book possession, promotion of translations, the organisation of chantry decoration, daily routines, and even the naming of children, it has been possible to suggest the nature of the individual spirituality and piety of people like Margaret, Lady Hungerford, Cicely, Duchess of York, and Lady Margaret Beaufort. This is all the result of forensic analysis: no personal statements conveniently define their spirituality in their own words. These are all, also, women in peculiar situations: two being mothers of kings, and with especially important social and political rank. Margaret Hungerford is at a slightly lower level, but would still have been affected by many of the same pressures. While it is therefore possible to postulate their spirituality, the outward manifestation of that spirituality would have been in part dictated by what was expected of them in their social, political and economic roles. It is also partly due to others' depiction of them – the picture of Lady Margaret Beaufort's piety owes much to the post-mortem eulogy by John Fisher.[115] Attempts to generalise spirituality have tended to concentrate on the use of will evidence, and to focus on the gentry.[116] However, the integration of other material into the picture, and the analysis of 'gentry spirituality' which results from that, has provoked a certain amount of debate.[117]

Below the level of the gentry, the source which is usually considered most revealing is the *Book* of Margery Kempe. Here an upper bourgeoise from a provincial town (King's Lynn) shows off her own spirituality through a work which can be considered as autobiographical as anything written by a ghost writer ever is, and also reflective of contemporary practices.[118] Margery's centrality to the record obviously affects the picture of her considerably; and reactions to her self-portrayal vary greatly: a subjective response is very difficult to avoid. Yet here we do have a picture of a piety which is acquired through

115 M. A. Hicks, 'The piety of Margaret, Lady Hungerford (d.1478)', *Journal of Ecclesiastical History*, XXXVIII, 1987, pp. 19–38; C. A. J. Armstong, *England, France, and Burgundy in the Fifteenth Century*, London, 1983, pp 140–56. Fisher's sermon for Lady Margaret Beaufort is in J. E. B. Mayor, ed., *The English Works of John Fisher, Bishop of Rochester*, Early English Text Society, extra ser., XXVII, 1876, pp. 289–310; for a fuller treatment of her piety, effectively placing it in its overall context, see now M. K. Jones and M. G. Underwood, *The King's Mother: Lady Margaret Beaufort, Countess of Richmond and Derby*, Cambridge, 1992, pp. 150, 153–4, 157–60, 167, 169, 171–201, countering to some extent 'the hagiographical treatment of her piety, which has generated its own mythology' (p. 150).

116 P. W. Fleming, 'Charity, faith, and the gentry of Kent, 1422–1529', in *Property and Politics: Essays in Later Medieval English History*, ed. T. Pollard, Gloucester, 1984, pp. 36–57; M. G. A. Vale, *Piety, Charity, and Literacy among the Yorkshire Gentry, 1370–1480*, Borthwick Papers, L, York, 1976.

117 C. Richmond, 'Religion and the fifteenth-century English gentleman', in *The Church, Politics, and Patronage in the Fifteenth Century*, ed. R. B. Dobson, Gloucester, 1984, pp. 193–208; C. Carpenter, 'The religion of the gentry of fifteenth-century England', in *England in the Fifteenth Century: Proceedings of the 1986 Harlaxton Symposium*, ed. D. Williams, Woodbridge, 1987, pp. 53–74; Richmond, 'English gentry and religion', pp. 121–50.

118 Windeatt, *Book of Margery Kempe*; Hirsh, 'Margery Kempe', pp. 113–14.

listening to sermons, consulting those with religious reputations, having devotional works read to her; which is not afraid to debate with bishops, even if she gets told off for her hyper-religiosity by her fellow pilgrims. Margery Kempe is someone who participates in many of the 'typical' contemporary devotional activities, especially pilgrimages both in England and overseas; who takes a vow of chastity; who is so individual as to be feared as a heretic; who readily believes in saints and miracles; whose piety is based on meditation which brings the focal actors of the Christian story very much to life around her. This is someone immersed in contemporary spirituality, and carrying aspects of it to extremes.

But to extrapolate from these individual depictions for the rest of England is dangerous. The case of Margery is particularly so; it may be that her self-portrait owes more to contemporary German spirituality than to a home-grown English version.[119] Yet that brings things back to the possible need to reject the monolith of 'English spirituality' for a more fragmented picture: Margery, from an east-coast town which had strong trading contacts with the Hanseatic towns (and who herself acquired a German daughter-in-law), may reflect a regional spirituality which was necessarily affected by Germanic trends to some extent. Just as the spirituality of the upper-class women reflected the cultural pressures on them, so the cultural pressures and milieu of late medieval King's Lynn created the spirituality of Margery Kempe.

Of course, the search to identify spirituality through concentration on individuals must accept the fact that these people are individuals, and with that the individuality of Christianity. To extrapolate, to generalise, must remove the individuality, and thereby blur the outlines. Yet the more the outlines are blurred, the more difficult it becomes actually to define the spirituality of the time. Just what 'a typical Englishman', if there was such a creature, actually believed is virtually unstatable. The description of the calm devotional spirituality of the English people presented by the Milanese ambassador during the reign of Henry VII is a comforting one: the English readily attending church, happily attending services, and behaving in a generally exemplary Christian fashion.[120] If placed alongside the funeral sermon for Lady Margaret Beaufort, and the strictures of the instructions for the

119 Stargardt, 'Beguines of Belgium', pp. 285–308.

120 C. A. Sneyd, *A Relation, or Rather a True Account, of the Island of England, with Sundry Particulars of these People and of the Royal Revenues under King Henry the Seventh, about the Year 1500*, Camden Society Publications, 1st ser., XXVII, 1847, p. 23.

devout and literate layperson, it is possible to construct a picture of constancy, of acceptance, of England as a truly Catholic country. Against this, there is the evidence of complaint, of deviation, of hostility; the complaints of clerics that the English were lukewarm in their devotions, prefering Robin Hood and the pub to sermons and prayers, and not giving as generously as in the past to shrines and other devotional works.[121] Some complaints were of course stereotypical – moralistic preaching has to castigate and urge to improvement, it cannot congratulate and encourage complacency; while the golden age is always in the past. Precisely where the emphasis is to be placed becomes to a large extent a subjective judgement: hence the debates about the origins of the Reformation.

For the Reformation hangs, unavoidably, over these last centuries of Catholic England. Assessments of the nature and deep-rootedness of the period's spirituality have to try either to ignore what happened after 1529 or come to terms with the rapidity of change, and the apparent ease with which this whole structure of Catholicism was overthrown. Any judgemental stance, however, would be inappropriate here, when the whole aim is to present evidence which, it is hoped, will allow for personal balancing of the scales (despite possible bias in the choice of documents). It is, though, worth recalling that any judgement cannot be restricted either to the clergy or to the laity. The reforming movement of the early sixteenth century, while laying considerable emphasis on the need for the clergy to change their ways, nevertheless saw such reformation as part of a package: reform of the laity was a necessary corollary of reform among the clergy.[122] Research suggests increasingly that there was a real movement for reformation of the English Church before 1530, one which, if anything, was diverted, possibly even deformed, by the events of later decades.[123] How things would have developed had Henry VIII not decided to rid himself of Catherine of Aragon (or if Clement VII had acquiesced in his desire) is not worth considering; but there would clearly have been major developments in spirituality, in the directing and controlling of religious practices. The reign of Henry VIII would probably have been a watershed in any event, whether England had remained Catholic or not.

121 Barnum, *Dives and Pauper*, i, p. 189; Hereford Cathedral Archives, transcript of Chapter Act Book I, p. 289.

122 Swanson, *Church and Society*, p. 314.

123 Swanson, *Church and Society*, pp. 312-29; P. Gwyn, *The King's Cardinal: the Rise and Fall of Thomas Wolsey*, London, 1990, pp. 338–40.

PART ONE: THEORY

I. The Bible

Because the Bible was so fundamental, it is appropriate to begin with an extract from it. Whereas the rest of this volume consists of translations, here I have deliberately retained the original languages, and provided a modern translation. All three passages contain the second chapter of the Epistle of St James, which provides a neat summary of the basic demands of Christianity with its insistence on obedience to the Law, assertion of the link between faith and works and the necessity for works, and its demand for fulfilment of the charitable requirements of the faith. As such it obviously connects with much else which will be represented in other documents throughout the collection. The aim of retaining the original languages is to demonstrate the problem of access in a society which was not necessarily Latinate, and the extent to which control of interpretation could be retained by those possessing the linguistic key.

1. The Vulgate (Latin) version [Text from R. Weber, ed., Biblia sacra iuxta Vulgatam versionem, 2 vols., Stuttgart, 1969, II, pp. 1860–1 (my punctuation)]

[1] Fratres mei, nolite in personarum acceptione habere fidem Domini nostri Jesu Christi gloriae. [2] Etenim si introierit in conventu vestro vir aureum anulum habens in veste candida, introierit autem et pauper in sordido habitu; [3] et intendatis in eum qui indutus est veste praeclara, et dixeritis ei: Tu sede hic bene; pauperi autem dicatis: Tu sta illic, aut sede sub scabillo pedum meorum. [4] Nonne judicatis apud vosmet ipsos, et facti estis judices cogitationum iniquarum? [5] Audite, fratres mei dilectissimi, nonne Deus elegit pauperes in hoc mundo, divites in fide, et heredes regni quod repromisit Deus diligentibus se? [6] Vos autem exhonorastis pauperem. Nonne divites per potentiam opprimunt vos, et ipsi trahunt vos ad judicia? [7] Nonne ipsi blasphemant bonum nomen, quod invocatum est super vos? [8] Si tamen legem perficitis regalem secundum scripturas: Diliges proximum tuum sicut teipsum, bene facitis. [9] Si autem personas accipitis, peccatum operamini, redarguti a lege quasi transgressores. [10] Quicumque autem totam legem servaverit,

offendat autem in uno, factus est omnium reus. [11] Qui enim dixit: Non moechaberis, dixit et: Non occides; quod si non moechaberis, occides autem, factus es transgressor legis. [12] Sic loquimini, et sic facite, sicut per legem libertatis incipientes judicari. [13] Judicium enim sine misericordia illi qui non fecit misericordiam; superexultat autem misericordia judicio. [14] Quid proderit, fratres mei, si fidem quis dicat se habere, opera autem non habeat? Numquid poterit fides salvare eum? [15] Si autem frater aut soror nudi sunt, et indigent victu cotidiano, [16] dicat autem aliquis de vobis illis: Ite in pace, calefacimini et saturamini, non dederitis autem eis quae necessaria sunt corporis, quid proderit? [17] Sic et fides, si non habeat opera, mortus est in semet ipsam. [18] Sed dicet quis: Tu fidem habes, et ego opera habeo; ostende mihi fidem tuam sine operibus, et ego ostendam tibi ex operibus fidem meam. [19] Tu credis quoniam unus est Deus, bene facis; et daemones credunt, et contremescunt. [20] Vis autem scire, o homo inanis, quoniam fides sine operibus otiosa est? [21] Abraham, pater noster, nonne ex operibus justificatus est, offerens Isaac, filium suum, super altare? [22] Vides quoniam fides cooperabatur operibus illius, et ex operibus fides comsummata est? [23] Et suppleta est Scriptura, dicens: Credidit Abraham Deo, et reputatum est illi ad justitiam, et amicus Dei appellatus est. [24] Videtis quoniam ex operibus justificatur homo, et non ex fide tantum? [25] Similiter autem et Raab, meretrix, nonne ex operibus justificata est, suscipiens nuntios, et alia via eiciens? [26] Sicut enim corpus sine spiritu emortuum est, ita et fides sine operibus mortua est.

2. The Lollard Bible [From J. Forshall and F. Maiden, eds., *The New Testament in English, According to the Version by John Wycliffe, about A.D. 1380, and Revised by John Purvey about A.D. 1388*, Oxford, 1879, pp. 453–4]

[1] Mi britheren, nyle ȝe haue the feith of oure Lord Jhesu Crist of glorie, in accepcioun of persoones. [2] For if a man that hath a goldun ring, and in a feire clothing, cometh in ȝoure cumpany, and a pore man entrith in foul clothing, [3] and if ȝe biholden in to hym that is clothid with clere clothing, and if ȝe seie to hym, Sitte thou here well, but to the pore man ȝe seien, Stonde thou there, ether sitte vndur the stool of my feet; [4] whether ȝe demen not anentis ȝou silf, and ben maad domesmen of wickid thouȝtis? [5] Heere ȝe, my moost dereworthe britheren, whethir God chees not pore men in this world, riche in feith, and eiris of the kyngdom, that God bihiȝte to men that louen him?

[6] But ȝe han dispisid the pore man. Whether riche men oppressen not ȝou bi power, and thei drawen ȝou to domes? [7] Whether thei blasfemen not the good name, that is clepid to help on ȝou? [8] Netheles if ȝe performen the kingis lawe, bi scripturis, Thou schalt loue thi neiȝbour as thi self, ȝe don wel. [9] But if ȝe taken persones, ȝe worchen synne, and ben repreued of the lawe, as trespasseris. [10] And who euere kepith al the lawe, but offendith in oon, he is maad gilti of alle. [11] For he that seide, Thou schalt do no letcherie, seide also, Thou schalt not sle; that if thou doist not letcherie, but thou sleest, thou art maad trespassour of the lawe. [12] Thus speke ȝe, and thus do ȝe, as bigynnynge to be demyd bi the lawe of fredom. [13] For whi dom with out merci [is] to hym, that doith no mercy; but merci aboue reiseth dom. [14] Mi bretherin, what schal it profite, if ony man seie that he hath feith, but he hath not the werkis? whether feith schal mowe saue hym? [15] And if a brother ethir sister be nakid, and han nede of ech daies lyuelode, [16] and if ony of ȝou seie to hem, Go ȝe in pees, be ȝe maad hoot, and be ȝe fillid; but if ȝe ȝyuen not to hem tho thingis that ben necessarie to bodi, what schal it profite? [17] So also feith, if it hath not werkis, is deed in it silf. [18] But summan schal seie, Thou hast feith, and Y haue werkis; schewe thou to me thi feith with out werkis, and Y schal schewe to thee my feith of werkis. [19] Thou bileuest, that o God is; thou doist wel; and deuelis bileuen, and tremblen. [20] But wolt thou wite, thou veyn man, that feith with out werkis is idul? [21] Whether Abraham, oure fadir, was not iustified of werkis, offringe Ysaac, his sone, on the auter? [22] Therfore thou seest, that feith wrouȝte with hise werkis, and his feith was fillid of werkis. [23] And the scripture was fillid, seiynge, Abraham bileuede to God, and it was arettid to hym to riȝtwisnesse, and he was clepid the freend of God. [24] ȝe seen that a man is iustified of werkis, and not of feith oneli. [25] In lijk maner, and whether also Raab, the hoore, was not iustified of werkis, and resseyuede the messangeris, and sente hem out bi anothir weie? [26] For as the bodi with out spirit is deed, so also feith with out werkis is deed.

3. A modern translation [From *The New English Bible*, Oxford and Cambridge, 1970, pp. 293–4 (verse numbers added)]

[1] My brothers, believing as you do in our Lord Jesus Christ, who reigns in glory, you must never show snobbery. [2] For instance, two visitors may enter your place of worship, one a well-dressed man with

gold rings, and the other a poor man in shabby clothes. [3] Suppose you pay special attention to the well-dressed man and say to him, 'Please take this seat', while to the poor man you say, 'You can stand; or you may sit here on the floor by my footstool', [4] do you not see that you are inconsistent and judge by false standards?

[5] Listen, my friends. Has not God chosen those who are poor in the eyes of the world to be rich in faith and to inherit the kingdom he has promised to those who love him? [6] And yet you have insulted the poor man. Moreover, are not the rich your oppressors? Is it not they who drag you into court [7] and pour contempt on the honoured name by which God has claimed you?

[8] If, however, you are observing the sovereign law laid down in scripture, 'Love your neighbour as yourself', that is excellent. [9] But if you show snobbery, you are committing a sin and you stand convicted by that law as transgressors. [10] For if a man keeps the whole law apart from one single point, he is guilty of breaking all of it. [11] For the One who said, 'Thou shalt not commit adultery', said also, 'Thou shalt not commit murder'. You may not be an adulterer, but if you commit murder you are a law-breaker all the same. [12] Always speak and act as men who are to be judged under a law of freedom. [13] In that judgement there will be no mercy for the man who has shown no mercy. Mercy triumphs over judgement.

[14] My brothers, what use is it for a man to say he has faith when he does nothing to show it? Can that faith save him? [15] Suppose a brother or a sister is in rags with not enough food for the day, [16] and one of you says, 'Good luck to you, keep yourselves warm, and have plenty to eat', but does nothing to supply their bodily needs, what is the good of that? [17] So with faith; if it does not lead to action, it is in itself a lifeless thing.

[18] But someone may object: 'Here is one who claims to have faith and another who points to his deeds'. To which I reply: 'Prove to me that this faith you speak of is real though not accompanied by deeds, and by my deeds I will prove to you my faith.' [19] You have faith enough to believe that there is one God. Excellent! The devils have faith like that, and it makes them tremble. [20] But can you not see, you quibbler, that faith divorced from deeds is barren? [21] Was it not by his action, in offering his son Isaac upon the altar, that our father Abraham was justified? [22] Surely you can see that faith was at work in his actions, and that by these actions the integrity of his faith was

fully proved. [23] Here was fulfilment of the words of Scripture: 'Abraham put his faith in God, and that faith was counted to him as righteousness'; and elsewhere he is called 'God's friend'. [24] You see then that a man is justified by deeds and not by faith in itself. [25] The same is true of the prostitute Rahab also. Was she not justified by her action in welcoming the messengers into her house and sending them away by a different route? [26] As the body is dead when there is no breath left in it, so faith divorced from deeds is lifeless as a corpse.

II. Disseminating the faith

Instruction in the details of the faith was chiefly received from priests, either through a detailed syllabus of points which had to be covered, or through discussion of particular aspects via sermons.

The short list of the contents of the faith compiled by John Drury as part of his task of parochial instruction at Beccles is reasonably typical of a wide range of similar materials: although in this particular version it is known from only one manuscript, which contains an incomplete Latin version as well as that in English, it is produced here because it is a succinct – almost skeletal – statement which gives a good indication of the range and nature of this material. The tract dates from the first quarter of the fifteenth century; but the widespread distribution of similar material makes it virtually timeless.[1]

Choosing representative sermons is rather more difficult. The three given here are taken from compilations. They are all based on the same text, the parable of the vineyard in St Matthew's Gospel, 20. 1–16, and were constructed to be delivered on the same Sunday, Septuagesima (the date varies according to the occurrence of Easter, from 19 January to 22 February). They show the differences in treatment between preachers and sermon compilers, giving differing layers of penetration of the meaning of the text. Despite the links with Lollardy which are well attested for one, and have been suggested for another, there is little in the texts which can actually be considered heretical.

John Mirk's Festial *was a lengthy collection of sermons which remained extremely popular throughout the period. Its date of compilation is not certain – it used to be placed in the late fourteenth or early fifteenth century, but recent*

1 For similarly brief (and briefer) collections, see G. H. Russell, 'Vernacular instruction of the laity in the later middle ages in England: some texts and notes', *Journal of Religious History*, II, 1962, pp. 114–17. Individual elements in the teaching process, such as the meaning of the Ten Commandments, or the analysis of the Creed, might themselves be the the focus of specific tracts (*ibid.*, pp. 104–14). One of the longest, and most important, analyses of the requirements of the Ten Commandments is provided in P. H. Barnum, ed., *Dives and Pauper*, Early English Text Society, original ser., CCXXV, CCLXXX, 1976–80. With such tracts, the 'pick-and-mix' approach allowed the compilation of collections covering the full range, either in long works like *The Pore Caitif*, or through transcription into personal manuscripts like the Thornton manuscript. See also V. Gillespie, 'Vernacular books of religion', in *Book Production and Publishing in Britain, 1375–1475*, ed. J. Griffiths and D. Pearsall, Cambridge, 1989, p. 325.

suggestions date it probably to the 1380s.[2] *Once constructed, it provided a store from which others drew: individual sermons from the collection turn up in other assemblages, while in the fifteenth century new users amended and reworked the text, sometimes substantially.*[3] *However, it retained its utility: some twenty printed editions are known from between 1483 and 1532. Intellectually, the cycle is not especially demanding: the moralistic approach, reinforcing the morality with stories, is well illustrated by the sermon here reproduced, with its inclusion of material from the apocryphal life of Adam and Eve after the expulsion from Paradise. Nevertheless, it may reflect the reality of some preaching: internal evidence suggests that at least some of the sermons were actually delivered.*[4]

It has been suggested that the Festial *was conceived as part of the attempt to counter Lollard activity.*[5] *The second sermon here is from one of the major Lollard texts, the sermon cycle. Like the* Festial *this survives in several versions, but with evidence of considerable care in the construction and reproduction of the compilation.*[6] *It may be indicative of the interests of those who have studied this period that, whilst the Lollard sermon cycle has received extensive consideration, Mirk's* Festial, *despite its evident popularity and importance, has not received the treatment in print that it merits, with the only available edition of that cycle being a rather deficient one from the nineteenth century. The tone of the Lollard cycle is rather more aloof than Mirk's, but the level of instruction is not strikingly higher. What is notable is that the author eschews the story-telling for analysis and social comment.*

The third sermon here is the longest of the triad. It occurs in a number of manuscripts, in association with others which suggest that they may be the remnants of a much larger compilation which may have covered the whole year.[7] *If so, it illustrates the treatment to which other sermons – like those of*

2 S. Powell, 'A new dating of John Mirk's *Festial*', *Notes and Queries*, CCXXVII, 1982, pp. 487–9; A. J. Fletcher, 'John Mirk and the Lollards', *Medium Ævum*, LVI, 1987, pp. 217–24.

3 S. Powell, ed., *The Advent and Nativity Sermons from a Fifteenth-Century Revision of John Mirk's Festial*, Middle English Texts, XIII, Heidelberg, 1981, pp. 7–39; A. J. Fletcher, 'Unnoticed sermons from John Mirk's *Festial*', *Speculum*, LV, 1980, pp. 514–22.

4 Fletcher, 'Mirk and the Lollards', pp. 220–1.

5 Fletcher, 'Mirk and the Lollards', pp. 217–20.

6 The text is being made available in a four-volume edition, of which the first three have so far appeared: A. Hudson and P. Gradon, eds, *English Wycliffite Sermons*, Oxford, 1983–.

7 G. Cigman, ed., *Lollard Sermons*, Early English Text Society, original ser., CCXCVI, 1989, pp. xliii–xliv.

the Festial – *were being subjected, being taken out of one context for use in another. The editor of the collection has suggested Lollard links, but I am not convinced.*[8] *What is notable about the sermon here is the amount of social comment which it contains (especially the continued application of the notion of the three estates and their responsibilities), and the way in which it could obviously be adapted for particular occasions (a trait evident in other sermons with which it appears).*[9] *This is also the most 'educated' of these sermon texts, with its citation of various authorities alongside the Bible, and the use of lengthy analogies to bring out the message.*

A. Instruction in the faith

4. Lenten instruction in the content of the faith by John Drury, priest of Beccles [From S. B. Meech, 'John Drury and his English writings', *Speculum*, IX, 1934, pp. 76–9; in English with some Latin]

HERE BEGINS THE TRACT ON THE MANNER OF CONFESSION GIVEN BY THE MASTER OF BECCLES IN LENT, IN THE ORDER OF MATTERS

In the heart of every man dwelling in this wretched vale of tears it is necessary that there be set spiritual labour and travail in examining his conscience at this holy time of Lent, set aside and ordered for the reformation of the soul. For, according to the proverb of old men, whoever is not holy in Lent or busy at harvest is unlikely to prosper. Everyone, therefore, beating his breast in compunction, shall rise up strongly to spiritual works. And you, dear child, should do the same.

Begin with the sacrament of penance, which consists of three parts; that is to say, contrition, confession and satisfaction. First be contrite, that is to say repentant and sorry for all the sins you have committed. After that, be shriven pure orally. And the third: do your penance well, making acquittance with that and other good deeds for all your sins. Start your shriving in this way. First, call to mind the Ten Commandments of Our Lord which you have sinfully broken and not kept as you should. And so that you can the better hold them in your mind in order, good son, learn well the verse that follows, which I your master give you at this point for your better instruction. *Hence the verse:*

8 Above, p. 14 n. 45.

9 Cigman, *Lollard Sermons*, p. xlvi.

Learn to fear God and revere the name of God;
Sanctify the Sabbath; hold your parents in honour;
Do not commit adultery; do not be noted for killing;
Beware of committing theft; do not be a witness unless true;
Do not covet wives; nor covet other people's goods.

Furthermore, dear child, having declared the Ten Commandments, and admitted your guilt in breaking them (or at least some of them), then recollect the seven deadly sins, which are destroyers of the seven principal virtues. And for this reason they are called the seven chief sins; that is to say, *capital or mortal vices*. And why *capital*? Child, in truth, because as I have taught you, *the head, that is the beginning*. The seven virtues that they destroy are these: humility, charity, patience, spiritual activity, chastity, generosity and abstinence. See, child, pride destroys humility; envy destroys charity; wrath, patience; sloth, spiritual activity; lechery, chastity; covetousness, generosity; and gluttony destroys abstinence. Take heed, child, and confess yourself absolutely how you forgo these seven virtues and carry out to the full these seven deadly sins. And truly, child, I could recite to you how many aspects each deadly sin has, but you could not imagine it. And therefore I teach you nothing more than the names of the seven deadly sins, which I bid you to know well first, so that you can the better avoid them. And see, child, they are contained in this verse. *Hence the verse*:

pride, covetousness, sloth, envy, wrath
haughtiness, avarice, torpidity, malice, and ire
gluttony, lechery
And gormandising, luxury, are the seven first to beware of.

See, child, in this way you can know precisely the names of the seven deadly sins. And after this, bring to mind the five senses which you have badly used. For if you had used them well, they would have kept you well. And why? Truly, because the five senses are like five towers or five gates to preserve or lose your soul. If they are well used, your soul is secure; if badly, insecure. But, good son, why should I call these five senses 'gates'? Truly, because just as nothing can enter a city except through the gates, just so may nothing enter your soul, good or bad, except through one of them. And therefore by my advice admit virtue and shut out vice. And in order to know them the better, son, and to keep them in mind more securely, I give them to you here, see, in this verse which follows:

tasting, smelling, hearing, seeing, touching.
Taste and smell, hearing, sight, touch;
By all these five senses everything is known to man

Having set out the five senses in this manner, see then, which are the seven acts of mercy. For at the Judgement Day that righteous judge shall reveal his grace to all those who fulfil them, and also his indignation to all their transgressors. For, as the gospel records, he shall say to the damned on his left side: 'I hungered and you gave me no meat; I thirsted and you gave me no drink; I was sick, you did not visit me; naked and you did not clothe me; in prison, you did not relieve me; homeless, you did not house me. Go, you cursed wretches, into the fire that shall never be quenched, which is established for the devil and his angels.' And to those who are at his right side he shall say thus: 'O dear souls, I hungered and you gave me meat; I thirsted and you gave me drink; I was sick, you visited me; naked, and you clothed me; in prison, you relieved me; homeless, and you housed me. Come, you blessed children of my father, receive the kingdom that was set aside for you from the beginning of the world.' But, child, because I list here only six works of mercy, and spoke first of seven, you are wondering. But know well that these six listed above are found in the gospel as it was told before; but the seventh is extracted from the story of holy Tobit, that is to say concerning burial of the dead, for which deed of charity that same holy Tobit pleased Our Lord very well. So, then, dear child, in order to know all seven of them together, I give you them here, glossed in a little verse. *Hence the verse:*

The infirm, the thirsty, the hungry, the imprisoned, the naked,
visit, drink, feed, redeem, clothe,
the vagrant, the dead
bring in, bury.

The seven deeds of mercy are so set out as you see, my child. But in so far as these seven pertain to those who have abundant possessions, and there are many members of Holy Church (that is to say, various ranks of men and women together of the Christian faith, who have no administration of temporal goods, such as men and women in religious orders, well-meaning people who have only their bare living, young men and women under the authority of their fathers and mothers, and simply all those people who do not have temporal possessions in hand), who ought not to lose the great merit set out for the performance of the seven temporal acts of mercy; therefore there are another seven acts of spiritual charity from which no creature can excuse himself, be he never so poor. So, then, if you perform these spiritual acts, if you do not have an abundance of temporal possessions or the opportunity to carry out the others, the same reward and the same joyous words shall be said at the Judgement Day to those performing these as shall be said to the others, that is to say, 'Come, you blessed children of my father', and so forth as said above. And therefore, child, as I know well that you do not have temporal goods in plenty to carry out the others, learn these seven spiritual works which are contained in the following verse: *Verse*:

Counsel, correct, console, relieve, forbear, pray
instruct, as you are able, if you would be held dear to Christ

When you have thus set out your conscience concerning the seven acts of mercy (both spiritual and corporal), then attend to the thirteen articles of your faith and belief. For, as St Augustine says, without faith it is impossible to please God. Therefore you must keep your faith uncontaminated and unbesmirched. For whoever is out of the faith, he is a renegade, a Lollard, an idler, as many have been of late, the more the pity. Some of these thirteen articles concern the Godhead, some the manhood and some the sacraments of Holy Church. All these you should actively grasp, and investigate through the ... creeds of Holy Church; and through the verse which follows, which I give you here for the same purpose. *Hence the verse*:

These are the articles: There is God who is three and one.
Christ made man, born, dead and buried
He descended, rose, who ascended, judges, and who
Gives rewards. All shall rise who offer holy things to the holy.

I told you, child, that some of the articles of the faith as remembered concern the sacraments of Holy Church; and for this and other reasons it is necessary to know them well, and they are seven in number. For whoever does not delight in them duly as Holy Church teaches, he is a heretic.

Therefore, so that you may delight in them perfectly, know them properly, for they are these: the sacrament of baptism, the sacrament of orders, the sacrament of confirmation, the sacrament of matrimony, the sacrament of the altar, the sacrament of penance, the sacrament of extreme unction. You must hold, trust, and believe that the sacrament of baptism purifies the child or adult receiving it from original and actual sin, and gives him the Holy Ghost. The sacrament of confirmation administered at the hands of a bishop confirms the Holy Ghost in the baptised person, through which he has an inflowing of grace, and is enabled to receive all virtue. The sacrament of the altar is the true food of the soul, and as offered by the hands of the priest leads to ineffable remission of sins. The sacrament of orders given to a clerk gives him power to administer and effect other sacraments through the mediation of God's word and the working of the Holy Spirit. The sacrament of matrimony removes deadly sin from the reproductive act between man and woman, so that that which would otherwise be deadly is merely venial when it is appropriately carried out. The sacrament of penance I explained to you before, it is not necessary to go into it further. Extreme unction alleviates both spiritual and bodily sickness, and strengthens the soul in its passing ... and greatly advances it towards bliss. See, child, in order to tell you quickly the number of these sacraments, and which can be repeated and which not (that is to say, which ought to be performed once only, and which more than once) pay good attention to the following verse. *Hence the verse*

B[aptism] O[rdination] C[onfirmation] M[atrimony] E[ucharist]
P[enance] E[xtreme unction] raise you from the muck of the old
B O C cannot be given twice, but M E P E can often be vowed.

See, child, after all this there yet remains one other matter to be treated, and that shall be the last that I shall teach you. And it is this: there are fourteen virtues, child, which you are required to know, and to which you ought greatly to give spiritual hearing. First, then, there are those virtues which are called divine virtues, that is to say, theological virtues, of which the first is faith, the second hope, the third charity. These are supreme virtues pertaining to God and heavenly bliss. First, faith that you should have correct faith and true awareness according to the order of the Creed. Second, that you have sure hope. For as you well know, everything that a Christian man does that is meritorious in this world is in order to gain something spiritual, which is not seen with the eye but only perceived by hope. The third is that you have perfect charity, that is to say, the due love of God, who has made you from nothing in his image, not according to your deserts, but out of his great and untellable charity. These are the divine virtues, called theological, as I said before. There are also another four virtues, and they are called cardinal virtues, and are of a different sort, for they concern the governance of human life. And they are called cardinal virtues. *Cardo*, child, is the hinge of a door, or else the socket that the bottom end of the hinge-beam is set into, and just as the hinge-beam by moving properly controls the door or gate appropriately, just so these fourteen [*sic*] virtues, as used and employed, justly govern a man's life. The first is righteousness, *justicia* in Latin. See, righteousness gives every man his own, and does wrong to no man. The second is prudence, *prudencia* in Latin. This virtue causes a man to know and avoid all vice and all dangers than might befall him, both spiritual and physical. The third is stength, *fortitudo* in Latin. This virtue makes a man mighty, agreed, but how mighty? Neither to bend [*lystyn*] nor to carry, but to be strong in the soul to withstand the fiend, the fiend's temptations, and all spiritual dangers which are likely to occur. The fourth is temperance, *temperancia* in Latin. This virtue causes a man to restrain himself from all excess, spiritual or carnal, and preserve himself in pure rule and virtuous disposition. Here are these four virtues, child: do not forget them.

There are another seven virtues, which are called moral virtues, because they refer to good manners, that is, *mores* in Latin. You know well the seven virtues mentioned when I spoke of the seven deadly sins, for those seven are opposites to the deadly sins. I will not list them again now; bring them in here, and learn them well.

And thus, child, by these things which I, the simple and unworthy John Drury, your master at this time, have given you at this Lent here in the school at Beccles, you shall the better know how you should be confessed another year. For by God's grace you will find more edification in these lessons than I will have the time to demonstrate, and so organise your life for God's delight, whose grace and mercy be with us ever more. Amen.

B. Sermons

5. From John Mirk's *Festial* [T. Erbe, ed., *Mirk's Festial: a Collection of Homilies by Johannes Mirkus (John Mirk)*, Early English Text Society, extra ser. XCVI, 1905, pp. 62–9; in English]

OF SUNDAY IN SEPTUAGESIMA: A SHORT SERMON

Good men and women, you should all know well that this day is called the Sunday of Septuagesima. And, for the reason that Holy Church is the mother of all Christian people, she takes care of her children as a good mother ought to, and sees them all deeply sick with the sickness of sin, and many of them fatally wounded by the sword of sin; which sickness they have caught throughout the past year, but especially on the Christmas days that were established in Holy Church as great solemnities. For every man ought on those occasions to act with greater solemnity, and more actively, and more humbly, and more devoutly serve God than at any other time of the year, because on those days God showed all mankind the great sweetness of his love, that he would so demean himself in order to be born in the same flesh and blood as one of us, and was laid in a cradle more meanly than any of us, and afterwards was baptised in water as one of us, and came to a wedding, he himself with his mother and his disciples, in order to sanctify marriage and cleanse it of sin, all in order to make us holy and brethren to him, and heirs of the bliss of Heaven.

For these reasons, men and women in former times were full of gladness in their souls at this time, and behaved with great solemnity, making themselves clean in body and soul from all filth and uncleanness of sin, and rooted themselves in the sober love of God and their fellow Christians, offering great alms, each man according to his possessions, to those that were in need. But now it is more harmful that solemnity and holiness have been transformed into the filth of sin and sickness of soul; into pride by the varied deceits of clothing; into covetous desire for honour, one before another unreasonably; into envy, since one is arrayed better than another; into gluttony by a surfeit of varieties of meat and drink; into lechery (which always follows gluttony); into laziness with regard to God's service by lying long abed in the morning time as a result of outrageous staying up at night; in rioting, in revelling and vain plays, in making pranks out of ribaldry and harlotry, so that he who can make the most of ribaldry and spendthriftiness is held most honoured. Thus the holy days of that feast which were established for the high worship of God and his saints, are now turned into high offence to God and great hindrance and loss of men's souls. Therefore Holy Church, seeing her children behave so, as a mother full of compassion for the great revulsion that she feels in her heart for them, on this day she sets aside Alleluias and other melodious songs, and brings out tractus, which are songs of mourning, and searching, and longing.

And also, since the holy sacrament of marriage is much befouled by such vanities, she [the Church] sets it aside for the coming days, and in Advent, and also because the newly-wed abandon themselves to desire and bodily lust, and ever think of life, and not about death. But, as a holy clerk says, it is much more beneficial to a man's soul to go to a house where a corpse is, where all weep, than to a house where all revel and laugh, for such worldly mirth causes a man to forget his God and himself as well. But where there is the sight of corpses and weeping, that makes a man dwell on his own death, which is the main aid to abandoning sin and the vanity of the world. For so Solomon taught his son, and bade him have his final ending in mind, and then he should never commit mortal sin. Then Holy Church, having great compassion of her children, has established three types of ointments with which to heal her children. They are: to meditate on death inwardly, to work actively, and to chastise the body reasonably.

Concerning the first, to meditate on death inwardly, Holy Church provides an example thus in the office of the Mass. There it says thus: '*Circumdederunt me gemitus mortis*', which is in English: 'The lamentations of death have embraced me.' So she says in teaching her good children, in order to bear in mind how hard they are encircled by death on each side, so much so that they cannot escape away, as death forever follows them with bow drawn, and an arrow therein ready to shoot at them, they never knowing where nor when. This is a major salve for each man who takes it to heart, to shun all manner of worldly vanity, and vain mirth and revelry. But in order to understand this better, I demonstrate it by an example:

STORY

I read of a king who was a man always of heavy cheer, who would never laugh nor be cheerful, but was always in mourning and despondency. Then, as his household and everyone else were grieved by this, they went to the king's brother asking him to speak to the king so that he should be of good cheer, to the comfort of his household and everyone else. Then his brother went to the king and said that he saddened everyone around him by his heavy cheer, and advised him to set aside that sad countenance and adopt a merrier approach in the coming times. Then the king was cunning, and decided to chastise his brother by a trick, and angrily ordered him to go home and meddle with matters of his own concern, and not with him. It was then the custom of that country that if any man was to be executed, trumpeters should come and trumpet before his gate. Then the king sent trumpeters, ordering them to trumpet before his brother's gate, and men with them in order to arrest him and bring him to him. But, in the meantime, the king called to himself seven men whom he trusted, and ordered them, when his brother came, to draw their swords and stand around him, with all their points about his heart. So, when the brother came, these seven men immediately did as the king had ordered. Then the king commanded everyone to dance and make all the revelry that they could, on every side; and so they did. Then the king said to his brother: 'Brother, why are you of such heavy cheer? Lift up your heart, and make merry. See, all this merriment is done to comfort you!' Then he answered and said, 'How can I be happy, when see, here I have seven swords set at my heart, and do not know which of them shall first be the death of me!' Then the king said: 'Put up your swords!', and spoke thus to his brother: 'It happens with me that, wherever I am, the seven deadly sins are always ready to stab me to the heart, and this causes me to make no happier cheer, but always to be fearful for the death of my soul.' Then said his brother: 'Sire, I beg you for mercy! I never knew this until now; and now I shall be wiser whilst I live.' Wherefore I am bold to say: he who will take this to heart, he shall have more delight to be sad than to laugh, to sigh than to sing, to cry out than to rhyme, to grieve than to dance; so that he shall find awareness of death the chief help against all manner of sin.

The other ointment is to work actively. About this labour St Paul teaches, in his epistle for this day, and says thus: ... 'Run, in order to seize the prize.' By this prize and running you should understand active labour. For he who runs for the prize, he forces himself with all his might to run swiftly. So must each good servant strengthen himself to labour in the state that God has set him in. Men of Holy Church should work actively by praying and studying in order to teach God's people; lords and other men of property should work actively to keep Holy Church in peace and quiet, as should all the common people; the commons should work busily to gain the livelihoods for themselves and everyone else. Then so that no man or woman should excuse him or herself from this labour, God in the gospel of this day gives an example, saying thus: 'A husbandman went in the morning at prime, and later in the morning, and lastly at midday, and afterwards at the ninth hour of the day, and at evening, and hired men to work in his vineyard.' So, by all the stages of the day, all the ages and orders [of mankind] should be understood, and are hired by God in order to labour whilst they are in this world. For, as Job says, a man is born to labour; and St Bernard says, 'A man who will not work here with men, shall labour in hell with devils.' For that is the bequest that Adam left to all his offspring: labour and sorrow.

Of this labour Holy Church offers an example when, on this day, it sets out how God made Adam and Eve, in order to labour and take care of Paradise, and told them to eat of all the trees in Paradise except one tree which he kept specially for himself. Then, as often as they saw that tree, they were to think of him, and know him to be their God; and so that they should not be forgetful in their happiness, he forbade them to eat of it on pain of death. Then, because the devil saw them there in so much happiness and himself in so much pain, he was envious of them, and went to Eve, and asked Eve why they did not eat of that tree. Then she said, 'Because God has forbidden that tree to us, on pain of death.' Then said the devil: 'He knows full well that, at the time you eat from it, you shall become like gods, with the knowledge of both good and evil. And if you want to test whether I am telling the truth, eat from the tree, and see.' Then Eve ate of the tree, and gave some to Adam; and because Adam loved Eve, and did not wish to anger her, he took an apple. And soon, on account of this, each saw the other's form, and was ashamed of it, and took leaves from a fig tree and hid it. Then came God soon after, and because they could not die in Paradise, nor suffer pain there, he drove them naked out of Paradise into the wretched world, weeping and bitterly lamenting. There they would endure woe and sorrow, and gain their food with labour and sweat, and die at the end. Then Adam, bitterly crying, prayed to God that he should not take strong vengeance against him, but have mercy on him, and take account of how he had sinned through ignorance, and not out of malice, and was deceived by the devil's envy. Then God took compassion on him, and because they were naked, he clothed them with skins, and ordered Adam to work and eat his food with sweat, and Eve to give birth in sorrow and pain; and he gave Adam various tools to work with, and left them there. By this example you should take care to work actively, for if Adam and Eve had occupied themselves in labour, the devil would not have overcome them so soon. For the devil is aware that he is no more able to tempt a man than when he finds him idle. Therefore you should know well that it is a precious ointment for healing sin: work actively.

The third [ointment] is to chastise your body discreetly. On this St Paul teaches us in the epistle for this day, where he says this: ... 'I chastise my body and arrange it in submission to the soul'. For human flesh is so uncontrolled and delights in sin, that it will in no way abandon its lusts and submit to the soul until it is chastised through penance; so that, by the sharpness of the penance the liking for sin shall be slain in the flesh which commits the sin.

Thus did Adam and Eve as a model for all who descend from them. For, many years before their deaths, each of them stood in a lake, at no great distance from each other, up to their chins, as penance. Then, when their flesh was as green as grass on account of the cold, the devil came to Eve, as bright as an angel, and told her that God had sent him from Heaven, and ordered her: 'Go to Adam and tell him that God instructs him to cease this penance; for he has done enough for his guilt, and you have for yours as well.' Then Eve went to Adam and told him this. But, because Adam was well aware that this came from the devil, and not from God's sending, he said to her: 'When God drove us out of Paradise for our sin, and took compassion on us when we wept at him and humbly begged him for mercy, he placed us here to do penance until our lives' ends. But then, since such a great sin may not be compensated except through great penance, the more penance we do, the greater is our reward with God. Therefore go once more to your penance, in God's name.' Later he [the devil] came once more to Eve and said; 'God has taken note of the great penance you are enduring, and has forgiven your sin: therefore tell Adam to be happy and give up his penance, lest God be angry with him for paying no regard to his message.' Then, when Eve had thus spoken to Adam, he replied and said: 'I am well aware that our penance grieves him much more than us, and he is as active as he can be to make us abandon it, and thereby lose our reward with God. But because God takes into account the good ending, and not the start, therefore let us not lose our reward, but continue our penance until our lives' end.' Yet a third time he [the devil] came again to her and said: 'Go to Adam and say to him that he started badly, and will finish even fouler. For you were beguiled first in innocence and through the fault of the devil, and now you sin on account of good deliberation and know that you do wrong; for which your guilt is now worse, with double the damnation that there was before.' Then Eve was frightened, and went to Adam, and told him this. Then Adam lamented bitterly, and said to her: 'Wretched woman, whom God in his goodness made from one of my ribs in order to help me; and now you are acting on the instructions of the devil always to entrap me. But think on this: because our former sin stank so much in God's nostrils, all our offspring shall be infected and poisoned by it until the end of the world. Therefore, although we might do as much penance as all our offspring, it would be too little to acquit us with our God. But because God in his great grace accepts a good intention even if the ability is lacking, therefore we should do our penance with a good intent, even though it is little while we are here; and then I hope that God will give us the oil of mercy when the time for mercy comes.' Then Eve went again and did her penance humbly until her life's end. And when they had lived nine hundred and thirty winters, and had thirty sons and thirty daughters, they died, and were buried together.

So, good people, know that Adam and Eve were both holy before they died, and thought of death inwardly, and both worked actively, and chastised their bodies reasonably; and so must all who descend from them, who hope to attain the joy of Paradise, and everlasting life. As a symbol for this, this Sunday is called 'Septuagesima', which is a number of sixty days plus ten. That number starts with this day and ends on the Saturday in Easter week; so that Holy Church is in mourning for her children from this day until the Saturday of Easter eve. Then she takes comfort in part, and sings Alleluia with a tract, because she is not yet in full happiness until the following Saturday, which is called *in albis* Saturday. Then she sets aside tracts, and graduals, and sings a double Alleluia, teaching each good child of God to do penance and labour with longing, until he gets to Easter Saturday – that is, until his soul passes to rest. But even then the soul is not in full joy until *in albis* Saturday, that is, until the Day of Judgement, when the body and soul shall come together, and be clothed in albs (that is, in white), seven times brighter than the sun. And then shall they sing together a double Alleluia in the joy which shall last for ever. To which joy may God bring you and me, if it be his will. Amen.

6. From the Wycliffite collection of sermons on the Sunday gospels

[From A. Hudson, ed., *English Wycliffite Sermons*, vol. 1, Oxford, 1983 pp. 378–83; in English]

THE KINGDOM OF HEAVEN IS LIKE A HEAD OF A HOUSEHOLD: MATTHEW 20

This gospel tells through a parable how God has arranged for his Church from the beginning of the world for as long as it remains here. 'The kingdom of Heaven', says Christ, 'is like a good husbandman who first went out early to hire workmen for his vineyard.' This husbandman is God, and his vineyard is his Church, and at the beginning of this world he hired men to work in it; for all those people who get to Heaven work well in his Church, and their payment is a penny, which they take for the day of their lives, and this penny is gained for men by the Godhead and manhood of Christ. 'And, after this agreement was made, he sent these workmen into his Church. And this husbandman went out at the third hour of the day, and saw others standing idle in the marketplace' to be hired. 'And this father said to them: "Go into my vineyard, and I shall give you what is right".' These workmen are the saints whom God had ordained to labour in his Church after the first age; and they stood idle on the road towards Heaven before the time that God moved them to labour in his Church. God agreed that he would give them what it was rightful for them to have, and that is the bliss of Heaven which pertains to this generous lord; but, as it is unclear to them where they should carry out this labour, on that account he promised to give them what is rightful. 'And they went out and worked well' the work of the vineyard. 'And he did the same at the sixth hour, and at the ninth hour as well', for God hired labourers according to his Church's needs; and so he waited first one hour, and then two, to hire servants. 'He went out around the eleventh hour, and found other men standing, and said to them: "Why do you stand here all day, not employed in the work in this vineyard?" And they said to him that no man had hired them. And he said to them: "Then you go into my vineyard".' He made no other agreement with them, for the two before were enough. These five hours signify both the age of the Church from the beginning until Christ came, and the true men who laboured therein. For it is generally said that the world has six ages: the first was from Adam to Noah, the second from Noah to Abraham, the third from Abraham to David, the fourth from David's time until the journey into Babylon, and the fifth from that time until Christ's nativity; the sixth age is understood as from then until the Day of Judgement. Then shall the light of Christ go down from dwelling in this world, and shine in the other world by means of the Day of Judgement. And because of the pre-eminence of Christ, he does not speak of hiring for this hour. And, as this time is to come, and God's law will be fulfilled in it, he does not speak of this sixth hiring, but takes it as included in the others. Nor should we know now the extent of this age which lasts from Christ's ascension until the Day of Judgement.

The labour in this vineyard consists of three things: first, dig around the vine roots and manure them well, and then bank them up; the second task in this vineyard is to prune the branches wisely; and the third labour is to cordon these growing vines. Some of this pertains to God, and some is done by man's labour. God himself makes these vines and plants them in his yard, for God creates true men, and gives them the sense to bear good fruit. And preachers are the assistants of God, and work on belief, but God gives the growth, even if men plant and water; for so did Jerome in the Old Testament, and so also did Paul in the time of grace. And so these labourers need to dig about these roots, lest evil weeds grow there, and suckers which lack belief. They are manured with five words which St Paul would teach the people, by which some men understand Heaven and earth and the ways to them; but the first word and the fifth are the Holy Trinity. When these five sentences have been preached and set out in a good way, then are these vines manured and well banked up with earth. But wise men prune these branches when they withdraw from accursed men, who are too numerous in the Church, and hinder it from bringing forth wine. And in this assist powerful men, who withdraw worldly goods from clerics, which they have contrary to God's law and do harm to his Church. But those who martyr God's servants, be they knights, be they priests, they are foxes which are around to destroy this vineyard. The cordons stand for the prelates and other vicars of God, who cause the classes of men to stay within the bounds that God has decreed; and if winds or other weather buffet these ranks down to the ground, by the virtue and strength of the prelates these estates should be upheld. And so each Christian man should aid this vineyard, for the growing of coleworts and other weeds causes melancholy and other sins, and does not make men happy so that they go to Heaven, but makes them sad so that they fall to Hell.

'And when evening had come, the lord of this vineyard spoke to his proctor, and ordered him to call these workmen, and give them their hire, starting with the last workmen through to the first labourers.' The lord of this vineyard is the Godhead of Christ, and the proctor of it may be called his manhood. This evening is the Day of Judgement, which is sometimes called midnight, and sometimes a clear day to various people therein, just as the same time is called here day and there night, here a fair and hot time, there foul weather and cold. The calling of these workmen is the summoning to God's judgement, that is the last trumpet, of which St Paul speaks. Christ shall begin with the people of this last period, for the people of the last age shall be more blessed and be first in worthiness compared to men of other ages, since the manhood of Christ is in the sixth age, and his mother with the apostles shall surpass all others in bliss. And similarly in other ages, the later ones have more grace, since Christ is the ruler who goes forward with constant increase. The seventh age is identified by the people who sleep in Purgatory, and the eighth age is of the blessed people in Heaven; and with these eight ages ends all the world.

'And so all the labourers took, each one, his penny. But the men of the first hour considered that they should have more' than the men of the eleventh hour, for they laboured first, and longer. And so 'they grumbled against the husbandman, and said to him: "These came at the last hour, and you made them equal to us, who bore the burden and heat of the day in labour". But he replied to one of them, and said this to him: "Friend, I do you no wrong; for you agreed with me for a penny. Take what is yours, and go"' fully paid, '"for I will give these last as much as I gave you. Should it not be lawful for me to do what I want with my own things? Should your eye be wicked because I am good?" So shall the last be first, and the first be last. For many are called, but few of them are chosen.' This grumbling by the saints is not opposition from them, but wondering in the soul, as St Gregory says. And so this judging and grumbling which this gospel talks of is wondering in the soul, and thanking God's grace that he gave so much joy to men for so little labour, for greater joy they cannot have but fully as much as they desire. And so should all well know that God does them no wrong; but that what he promised them in grace, he has fully given to them. Nor should any of them grumble against the goodness of this just father, for he may give from his own more than any man may deserve according to human justice, or the fairness of any bargaining. And so God tells each saint that he should take his reward in grace, and enter into the bliss of Heaven, where the saints shall ever dwell in peace.

7. From an anonymous late-fourteenth or early-fifteenth-century compilation [From G. Cigman, ed., *Lollard Sermons*, Early English Text Society, original ser. CCXCIV, 1989, pp. 80–92; in English. Despite the title given to this collection by its editor, I am sceptical about whether this can actually be considered a 'Lollard' collection]

... 'The kingdom of Heaven is like a householder who went out early in the morning to hire workmen for his vineyard', etc.

This gospel teaches us to work hard and not be idle while we are here wandering on this road, for the hire of the high bliss of Heaven that God has ordained for all such; and also to have a trusting hope: although we have misspent our time, yet nevertheless if we are found to be his true servants in our old age, we shall have the same reward of everlasting bliss.

This householder that the gospel speaks of is Our Lord God, who has a household of three levels – that is, Heaven, Earth, and Hell. And his following are the heavenly and earthly rational creatures that, as St Paul says ... should bow their knees to this worshipful Lord.

In Heaven there are those who have overcome, like angels and holy souls. In Hell are those who have been overcome, like devils and souls that have been overcome by them. And we are established here on earth, in the middle, to fight against our enemies and to strive to ascend to those who are in Heaven above and not descend to those who are in Hell beneath.

Although St Gregory understood by this vineyard Holy Church, and by these hours the various ages of the world from the first man until the last: from Adam to Noah, from Noah to Abraham, from Abraham to Moses, from David to the Transmigration, from the Transmigration to Christ, from Christ to Doomsday, and in all these ages God called workers into his vineyard (patriarchs, and prophets and preachers of his law); nevertheless, according to the statement of Chrisostom, this vineyard here may not properly be understood as men, 'for the workers therein are men, and therefore this vineyard is righteousness, in which are placed various sorts of righteousness as vines: that is, meekness, charity and patience, and other goods without number, which are all in general called righteousness'.

God made this vineyard in Man's soul when he made him like the Trinity, which is true righteousness, on account of his reason, mind, and will, by which he has knowledge of both good and evil.

And God has called men to work in this vineyard at various points in their lives, as though at various hours of the day, standing in the market or business-centre of this world, in which there is much buying and selling and cheating of their brothers, as customarily occurs in such places, as St John says: *The whole world is placed in the bad.*

Some he called in childhood, like St John the Baptist, St Nicholas and various others, and some in their young growing age, and some in manly adulthood, and some in old age, and some at the final stage of their lives, into this vineyard of righteousness, to work therein by true maintenance of God's commandments.

The wages that this Lord has promised them for their day's work (that is, for the true travail of this life) is a penny; that is, the everlasting bliss of Heaven, which may well be likened to a penny for the roundness which indicates everlastingness, and for the blessed sight of the king's face that is on that penny, and also for the writing that is thereon: the book of life, in which all those who are to see that sight are written for ever.

Then in the eleventh hour this householder found some standing idle in the market, to whom he said: 'Why are you standing here all day?' They answered him: 'Because no one has hired us.' By these whom God finds standing idle at the eleventh hour should be understood old men in their last age, who have stood idle all their lives, and never worked in God's vineyard.

'Sinful men', says Crisostom, 'are not idle, but dead; for he is idle who does not carry out the work of God. If you take away other men's goods, you are not idle, but dead; but if you do not take away other men's goods, but none the less do not give of your goods to powerless men, then you are idle. Would you prefer not to be idle? Do not take away other men's goods, and give of your own to poor men, and then you are cultivating the vine of mercy in the vineyard of God.

'If you are drunk and in luxury, you are not idle, but dead, as the apostle says; but if you eat and drink moderately, you do not sin, for you do not eat evilly; none the less you are idle, for you do not perform the virtue of fasting (that is, alms). Would you prefer not to be idle? Fast, and whatever you would eat during the day, give it to the powerless man, and so you will have tilled the vine of fasting.

'Also, if you commit lechery, you are dead and not idle. If you have your own wife, you do not sin; none the less you are not fulfilling the virtue of chastity. Would you prefer not to be idle? If you have no wife, do not look for one; if you are a widow, do not look for a second marriage; and so you cultivate the vine of chastity. Otherwise, if you have a wife, I will show how you can cultivate the vine of chastity: stay away from your wife in her private illness, and when she is pregnant, also when it is a great feast day, and on proclaimed fasting days, according to the commandments of the apostle.

'Also, if you are envious of your betters, you are not idle, but dead. If you do not envy, but none the less are not happy, then you are idle; therefore, not only should you not envy, but you should be happy for your betters, and then you will have tilled the vine of goodwill', or of charity.

The reason why such sorts of men have stood so often idle in the market of this world is that no man had hired them (that is, their prelates and curates, who should be God's bailiffs to hire his workmen for his vineyard), neither by the good example of their lives, which are often much worse than that of the common people, nor by proper teaching of God's law, of which they had no knowledge, or else very little, and of that little they were often stopped by the lump of tallow (that is, worldly filth) that was thrown into their mouths, so that they were like hounds that could not bark the law of Our Lord to their subjects, by which they should have been comforted to work in the vineyard of righteousness in the hope of the reward of the bliss of Heaven.

But what the householder said to them – 'Go into my vineyard' – may be understood to mean that although the prelates and curates, on account of their ignorance and negligence, or evil will, fail to fulfil their duties, nevertheless God, of his great courteousness and merciful grace, does not fail to give his people private inspiration to seek, before they pass out of this world, even at the least at their last hour, to cultivate his vines and so have the penny.

O, you merciful Lord, who so tenderly loves your people that you bought them with your blood, who, although all men fail you, you do not fail them in their need!

'When the evening came, the householder said to the overseer of the vineyard: "Call the workmen, and give to them their due, beginning with the last through to the first".'

The evening may be understood as the general day of judgement, for that shall be the last day, like the evening of this world.

The overseer of the vineyard may well be understood as he who calls the workmen together and gives them their wages, Our Lord Jesus Christ, God's heavenly Son, who for ever more seeks our profit before his Father's face. To him the Father has granted in full the judgement in that day *(He gave all judgement to the Son,* John 5.22), and power to reward the workmen who labour in his vineyard.

That he starts to give the reward with the last may be understood to mean that some of those who first began to work in the vineyard in their old age mourn and weep so completely because they had wasted their time in idleness, and working against the time with good deeds as St Paul orders, they increase so much in love in that short time that they overtake many others who began in their childhoods, like Mary Magdalene, St Paul, Matthew, and many others. And of them St Gregory understood this gospel text that says: ... To such God gives the reward of bliss as soon or sooner than some others who laboured from their youth.

Or else it may be understood thus: that God says these words to comfort those who began to serve God in their last days, so that they should not despair of being rewarded for their short labour, for that would have the penny paid to them as well as the first.

Otherwise it may be understood thus: to show how great is the mercy of God above all his works; for it is only out of the great grace and mercy of God to reward so fully such short and little labour, and so no one has reason to despair, but it is a thing of great hope since, whatever hour he comes, God with receive him.

The complaining of these first workmen against the last may not be understood here as an envious will or indignation that men would have in the Day of Judgement against the gracious reward of their brethren. For there can be no such will amongst those who are to be saved, for then they would be out of charity, which is the wedding clothing that every man must have who would come to the feast, but each of them shall be joyful, and glad at the others' good.

St Gregory says that this complaining is none other than a wondering amazement in man's soul or man's thought at the great mercy, bounty, and grace of Our Lord, who rewards each man alike, both the first and the last, with the penny of everlasting bliss.

But here you should understand that not every man has equally as much bliss, but in ratio to their love here, so shall their bliss there be more or less proportioned.

Concerning the everlastingness of bliss, which is understood by this penny on account of its roundness which has no end, each man shall have as much alike, both he who comes aged and he who comes in youth. And all this other debating which is related here in this gospel between the lord and his workmen is nothing other than the privy speaking of God in men's souls.

Or else it may be understood thus, as another gloss says: suppose that they would complain, or might complain (which they might not, since they had no cause, for the householder had dealt unjustly with them in nothing). For to him who came first, he dealt with him according to the covenant, and he might not ask for more by law nor by reason; and he who came last, he rewarded him out of his grace. And that which is graciously granted no man ought to begrudge, nor take any sort of offence from another man's goodness, for it is lawful for a man to do what he likes with his own. And thus otherwise: those who are the later called to grace shall be rather rewarded in bliss, for often those who are called in the last hour depart sooner from hence than those who come in youth, and are so sooner rewarded.

But here some might say: 'I hear by this parable that both first and last, they all had the penny; and so it appears that all men shall be saved.' But the last words of this gospel answers to that: 'Many men are called, but few are chosen.' For many men in childhood, many in their young growing age, many in manly estate, and many in old age and many at the last end 'are called'; some by preaching, some by reading, some by good counselling, some by private inspiration, some by prosperity, some by adversity, to the bliss of Heaven; but 'few are chosen'. That is: few labour thereafter to ensure that they will be chosen. And so the default is not in God, in whom is all goodness, for if he did not wish them to come, he would never call them, as that would be nothing but a fraud, and he has never done that.

Concerning this gospel, a man might consider that just as in a real vineyard there are three types of workers with various occupations, so it is the same with this spiritual vineyard.

The first are those who remove the old earth and expose the roots, and afterwards spread on them dung and new earth, so that it may grow better, and bear fruit in greater abundance. And these should be interpreted as the lowest estate of Holy Church, that is: the common people, whose occupations consist in grubbing about in the earth, like ploughing, and manuring, and sowing, and harrowing, and other occupations that belong to the earth. And these should be done justly, and to a good purpose, without deceit, or falsehood, or complaining about their estate. And this may be the root, for this was the first status that belonged to all men; and thus by their true labour they bear up and sustain the other two parts of the Church, that is, knights and clerks

Or else, thus, this exposing of the root and putting away of the old earth may well be understood as opening of your heart, in which should stand the root of righteous deeds, with true confession of your sins and putting aside the old behaviour of the earthly and sinful life, and set thereon the dung of sharp penance, like fasting, wearing hair shirts [*wolward gooing*], sleeping rough, harsh beatings, and other deeds of penance

Or else set thereto another form of manure, that is, a complete recollection of your misdeeds and wretched estate. Consider your body: how vilely, how weakly, how full of care you come into this world, weeping and wailing, and without any mirth. Afterwards, what you are, and what you shall be at the end: you are but a sackful of dirt, covered by clothing, and if what was within were to be turned outwards, he who makes the most of himself would be treated as nothing by the world. Afterwards, look all over your body: what filth comes out of each orifice in it, what at the eyes, what at the nose, what at the mouth, also at the ears, and beneath in other privy places. This is no reason for pride, if it is considered properly!

And think also of your end: how painful it will be, groaning, and gnawing, and gnashing of teeth, and smelling horrible to those who sit around. When you are dead, you shall be deftly dug and wasted by worms, be you never so worthy!

With your mind on this matter, you will make good manure to make the root of righteous works grow all the better, so that you put to it the new earth which it also needs, that is: the good will to labour well, for that should not be lacking.

The second type of workers in the vineyard are those who take up the vine from the ground, so that briars and weeds should not stifle it and stop it growing and bearing its fruit; but with great stiff trees forked above, and with other long trees laid on it, strongly support it so that it can grow and bear its grapes without hindrance. These should be seen as the second part of the Church, that is, the knighthood which, by the mightier power that they have received from God (as St Paul says, ... *All power is from the Lord God*; that is, the great and forked stiff trees which I spoke of, of which one is the love of God, the other [love of] their brethren), and by the aid of the long tree which is laid above (that is, for the hope of the bliss of Heaven), should bear up the vine of righteousness so that it should not be overgrown and oppressed with briars and weeds of wayward and worldly tyrants. For so Crisostom understands by 'briar bushes'. For, he says, just as under briar bushes there is no refreshing shadow for animals to rest under, as under other trees, but only for snakes and adders and such other worms, 'so besides a good man both good and evil may take their rest'; but beside such tyrants none might rest except for such venomous creatures as they are, or else 'adders (that is: demons) which have their bedchambers in their hearts'. And if a naive good man, who could be likened to a sheep on account of his simplicity, should dwell alongside them, they treat him as a briar bush deals with a sheep, for if he rests besides it, it grabs him and takes from him while he has anything.

The duty of the third [type of] workmen who work in this vineyard consists in pruning this vine in due time, so that it does not grow out into wild branches and bear worse fruit. And by these should be understood the third degree within the Church, which are: prelates and priests, to whom it behoves, if any wantonness or wildness of sin which grows in men's hearts should spread so far into deeds which prevent righteousness bearing its fruit, in himself or else in his brethren, by giving evil example, to prune him off with sharp biting sentences of holy writ, of if the need requires, with censures of Holy Church (that is: with sharp punishments), and then afterwards to bring forth the vine of righteous works in their subjects by their own example, and then bind them together to the hope of bliss with the bond of peace in charity.

These, then, are the three kinds of roles that pertain to the keeping and maintenance of this vineyard, if it is to be well kept to the worship of God and profit of his people. But as quickly as these three act to keep this vine, there are another three around night and day to destroy this vine, which are the world, the flesh, and the devil, of which three David speaks in the Psalter, where he speaks thus of the vine, and says: ... 'All who had gone alongside the road have plucked the grapes. The wild boar of the wood has rooted it up, or thrown it out of its place, and the individual wild beast has eaten it up.'

By those who go alongside the road should be understood worldly and covetous people, for the way towards the bliss of Heaven is the commandments of God, and all such go alongside the way, for they make a God of their goods, and thus commit idolatry, as St Paul says: *Greed, which is the slave of idols, etc.*, which is totally contrary to the first commandment, and in consequence against all the others. And all such pluck off the grapes of their good works of nature, which they carry out before they are ripe: for without good belief, which they lack, they shall never ripen into any benefit for them, as St Paul says to the Hebrews ... 'Without faith it is impossible to please God.'

Also, such worldly covetous men pluck away the grapes of their brethren, as when fatherless children, or widows, or any other people, are separated from their due inheritances, their land, or their goods. The grapes of this vine of righteousness would be that they should be fully restored thereto. Then, if any truly conscientious man busies himself about them, then these grapes begin to grow a little. But these worldly men, as I said, who go alongside the way with their bodily muck (which is their God, which helps them and speaks for them to justices, lawyers, supporters in the country, and assizers), sell their souls for silver to pluck the grape before it is ripe, so that they may never develop or come to their proper ripening.

The same applies to others who are wrongfully put into prison for theft, or manslaughter, or any other trespass: the true tillers of this vine would have them released; but they who go alongside the way pluck the grapes, and kill such people with their subtle activities, and say that it is right.

The same situation occurs in the Church, if men look well. If a prelacy or parsonage is devoid of a pastor, or there is any other cure which needs a head, it would be God's will (and the law also says it) that those who were the meekest and most set apart from the world should have such cures to save men's souls, by free election by the Church, or by the patron's presentation. Then, if any such are chosen freely by the Church, or if the patron wants to present such a perfect parson, then this grape first starts to grow. But they who go alongside the way, as I said before, pluck away the grape of right so that it shall never be ripe, with simony of silver, or the seals of lords, and in place of a good man set a shrew on the bench. And thus, as I have somewhat shown, the world is the first enemy which seeks to destroy this vineyard.

The second enemy is the boar from the wood, that is: man's flesh. The boar from the wood is wilder than the boar in the field; so man's flesh, unless it is ruled by the reason of God's law, is wilder than any other irrational animal.

Man's flesh may well be compared to this boar, for there are three properties belonging to the boar which can be likened to the three sins which derive from the flesh: first, a boar strikes hard with the tusks that are in his mouth; second, he will happily rest himself in foul bogs, or miry places; third, he has a foul stinking smell wherever he goes. And by these might be understood gluttony, sloth and stinking lechery.

First, I say, the boar strikes with the tusks that are in his mouth. So the glutton, when he is drunk, is then bold to strike hard with his accursed words against both God and man. First God, with great and horrible oaths which are then rife enough in his mouth; and then he smites his brethren, with foul shrewish and slandrous words, lying and cursing, and spares not. And thus with the wrath of his mouth he pulls up the vine, both in himself and also in his brethren.

The second condition of this boar is that he will happily take his rest in bogs. And by this may be understood the second sin that derives from the flesh, that is, sloth. For whoever will not carry out the duties that are his in the vineyard, the briars and thorns will overgrow the vine so that wine shall never come from it, but it will wither all away. Therefore the wise man says … 'I went by the lazy man's field, and found it full of briars and thorns' – that is, of wicked thoughts which destroy all the vine.

The third property of this boar is his stinking smell. And by this may be understood the third sin derived from the flesh, that is, lechery, which stinks very foully in God's sight; and with this the wild boar (that is, man's flesh) uproots the vine of all righteous works. For such a one is both proud and impatient to all who reprove him for his sin, and anxious to avenge himself, when he sees the opportunity; and he is covetous, also, to keep up his lusts; and slothful and gluttonous to maintain his appearance. And where such sins are, virtues are uprooted so that no profit may be derived from them while they lie like that. And thus this boar of man's flesh is the second enemy that goes about to destroy this vineyard.

The third enemy of this vineyard is the singular wild beast; that is, the devil. He is singular, in that there is no power upon earth which may be likened to him, as Job says in the 41st chapter ... And also, he is a wild beast, for St Peter likened him to a roaring lion.

And this singular wild beast gnaws up all the grapes and greenery that grows on this vine with the three sins that pertain to him, that is, great pride, wrath, and envy. For, as the common proverb says: ...'Even if you have plenty of worldly goods, and wisdom, and a good-looking body; if pride is a partner, it is not worth anything.' And St Gregory says: 'Whoever gathers virtues without meekness' – which is opposite to pride – 'behaves like the man who carries dust in the wind, which blows everything away.'

Also, he eats up this vine with vainglory. For if you take pride in your deeds, your reward is here among men, for you will not get more.

Also, he gnaws up this vine of all righteous works with wrath and envy, so that they may not flourish in the absence of charity, which is the chief of virtues. For this St Paul testifies, and warns us all: ... 'Though I speak', he says, 'with the tongues of both angels and men, and have prophesies and privities and proved wisdom, and also a true belief that I can move hills, and even if I give all my goods to feed poor men, and even my naked body to be burned in the fire, everything that I have done throughout my lifetime is lost, [if it is] without charity' – which is the chief of all virtues.

Thus the wicked wild beast labours night and day to make the vine of virtues empty of all grace, and by his secretions prevents it from being pleasing to the Lord. And this is the third envious enemy which eats up the vine.

Thus these three enemies of this vineyard which I have spoken of before, that is, the world, the flesh and the devil, have long laboured to destroy the vine of righteousness; and the three aforesaid workmen are so idle in their labour, each according to his status, that it is all gone awry. And therefore the lord of this vineyard may now complain about this vine, and say the words of Isaiah, in the 5th chapter: ... 'I have waited for it to produce grapes; truly it produced wild grapes which are not fit for men.'

What these wild grapes are is explained by Hosea the prophet in this way: 'There is no truth, there is no mercy, there is no knowledge of God on earth, which should be the true grapes of the vine of righteousness; but accursedness, and theft, and lying, manslaughter, and adultery have increased, and blood touched blood' – that is, sin upon sin. These are the wild grapes that grow on this vine. Alas for the time that ever they were committed!

God, in his great goodness, grant us through his grace that we may work so wisely in this world our work on this vine, each man in the estate in which he stands, that we may please the Lord therewith and be allowed the penny.

III. The mass

The mass was the central ceremony of the Church: the consecration of the bread and wine to become the body and blood of Christ.[1] *Communion was not essential more than once a year – at Easter, following Lenten confession and penance – yet presence at mass was more regular. The centrality of the mass was emphasised by its utility: masses could be said for a variety of purposes, ranging from securing good weather to assisting in the release of souls from Purgatory.*[2] *Attendance, or paying for the celebration of a mass, might also secure an indulgence or other spiritual (and sometimes, it was hoped, corporeal) benefits.*[3] *The increasing eucharistic emphasis of the pre-Reformation centuries was also assisted by the development of the cult of the Host as Corpus Christi, the embodiment of Christ, which provided a focus for a whole range of devotional celebrations, including plays.*[4]

Although they were eager to attend masses, the role of the laity was more that of spectators than participants, in a ceremony conducted in Latin, and cordoned off in the sacred space beyond the chancel arch. Awareness of events was conducted by the cues provided by the choreography in the chancel, with the climax at the elevation of the Host.

Nevertheless, although spectators to the priestly rite, the laity did have a part to play. They should show the proper reverence, and treat the ceremony seriously. Several works were therefore constructed for their edification to understand the nature of what was happening in the chancel, and to ensure that they were spiritually prepared for the ceremony. One such preparatory text is given here, dating from c.*1400.*[5]

1 On the mass in general, see J. Bossy, 'The mass as a social institution', *Past and Present*, C, August 1983, pp. 29–61; M. Rubin, *Corpus Christi: the Eucharist in Late Medieval Culture*, Cambridge, 1991, ch. 2; S. Brigden, *London and the Reformation*, Oxford, 1989, pp. 12–19.

2 For votive masses, see F. E. Warren, ed., *The Sarum Missal in English*, Alcuin Club Collections, XI, 2 vols, London, 1913, ii. pp. 99–143, 202–7 (also 64–5, 208–12, 222–4). See also Bossy, 'Mass as a social institution', pp. 39–43, 45–6.

3 E.g. R. W. Pfaff, *New Liturgical Feasts in Late Medieval England*, Oxford, 1970, pp. 63–5, 85.

4 On Corpus Christi see now Rubin, *Corpus Christi*, ch. 3–5.

5 Several other tracts were available. That formerly ascribed to 'B. Langforde' (J. W. Legg, ed., *Tracts on the Mass*, Henry Bradshaw Society, XXVII, London, 1904, pp. 19–29) appears in fact to derive from work by a Syon monk, William Bonde, in the

While generally excluded from the chancel rite, the laity were not inactive, and developed their own involvement and participation in the *proceedings through parallel series of prayers and intercessions. The* Lay Folks' Mass Book *was an early text (probably dating from the late twelfth or early thirteenth century) constructed to give guidance to action during the ceremony, instructing in the choreography and the appropriate prayers to be said by the laity as a counterpoint to the clerical actions. Originally written in French (although addressed to an English audience), it was later translated into English, and survives in a number of versions which seem to reflect actual variations in practices during the mass. The text provides some insight into the lay reaction, even if a prescription rather than description.*[6]

8. Instructions for the laity in preparation for the mass [From T. F. Simmons, ed., *The Lay Folks' Mass Book*, Early English Text Society, original ser., LXXI 1879, pp. 122-7; in English]

HERE FOLLOWS A PRECIOUS CONSIDERATION, HOW A MAN SHALL MAKE HIMSELF PURE AND PERFECTLY CLEANSED BEFORE RECEIVING THE SACRAMENT OF THE ALTAR.

Before receiving Christ's body there are six things to be considered:

The first is that a man should know by discretion what he is to receive, and what he is who receives it. See! See! What is he to receive? Assuredly Jesus Christ – truly God and man, who made everything out of nothing; and truly the man who died for us on the cross – in the form of bread. What is he who receives it? Assuredly a man and no beast, nor devil; and therefore he ought to cast off from himself all devilish malice and all beastliness of sin.

The second is heart-felt devotion; for he should consider, that

early sixteenth century (J. Bossy, 'Prayers', *Transactions of the Royal Historical Society*, 6th ser., I, 1991, pp. 145–6), although that does not detract from its message. Even in the 1530s other expositions of the mass were appearing in English, for example the lengthy *The Interpretacyon and Sygnyfycacyon of the Masse*, London, 1532. From the late fourteenth and fifteenth centuries, a number of poetic treatments were also available: T. F. Simmons, ed., *The Lay Folks' Mass Book*, Early English Text Society, original ser., LXXI, 1879, pp. 128–54; Rubin, *Corpus Christi*, pp. 103–8.

6 The text offered here is the 'B' text from the edition, which appears in fact to be the earliest, rather than one of the later fifteenth century adaptations. In terms of this collection, that may seem anachronistic; but may be justified on a number of grounds. First, the manuscripts in which that version existed had obviously survived, and therefore were still available to be used. Secondly, this text is the fullest, and gives the most instruction for the recitation of the lay prayers: the later versions may well have taken those recitations for granted, as the process of lay participation became customary rather than requiring definition.

whatever he receives he should receive it with as much holiness as he may; and take care that he therewith rejects from himself bitterness and blindness of the heart, with tearful compassion and through the activity of prayers.

The third is with heart-felt reverence, that such a vile creature and wretched sinner should be afraid to approach such a Lord. For if a man were immersed in a stench, he would be unfit to stand in the presence of the king. I ask you then: how much more unworthy is any man, in his own right, to receive Christ in the precious sacrament? For if all our good deeds are as uncleanness in his sight, what then are our sins? Truly, nothing. But notwithstanding all that, his goodness and his pity are more than all our wretchedness; and therefore we should do what we can, and trusting in him with reverent fear we should go to him, so that his worthiness shall make us fit to do him service.

The fourth is love and heart-felt desire. On account of which a man ought to take care that he does not go unthinkingly to the sacrament, nor with heaviness or irksomeness of heart, but should make sure that he does it devoutly and happily, and with great desire, on account of which it seems quite amazing to me that every person when receiving this worthy sacrament does not melt all into love.

The consideration of Christ's Passion and of his love towards us is a sovereign means whereby to turn a man's affections towards the devout reception of this holy and most blessed sacrament.

The fifth is a humble devout prayer. For it was for that purpose among others that the sacrament was established, so that a person through the offering and taking of it should ask forgiveness of sins and the grace of a good life.

The sixth is that he who ministers the sacrament is to be a priest, so that he should be most diligent about it in so far as he is able. For as much as a man is active in serving an earthly man or lord with all his diligence about him, so much more should he be active in serving Our Lord God. And therefore all types of men of greatest honesty and sobriety and of good countenance and the ability to take good counsel are then most needed to minister this most worshipful sacrament. And in order that a priest may the better undertake this worthy occupation, I counsel him to abstain from all temporal things that might defile his soul, which is the dwelling-place of Christ, the heavenly king, so that he may be much more securely grounded in God's service. Yes, yes, much more than any other secular man, and particularly at the time when he shall go to mass, so that he easily prosper himself.

The seventh [*sic*; the text originally promised only six points] is that he withdraw his mind from all external things, and gather himself completely into himself, if he may, so completely that he shall be confused neither by bodily wisdom nor by vainglory; and then ransack his own conscience, and the things that he finds to be unclean, take care that he wash them away with tears of compunction. Then it is necessary for him to go to his confessor, and cast out with humble confession all the poison of sin.

And when he has done thus, then he must lift up his heart with all sorts of the greatest humility, and consider the mercy of God, and the wretched frailty of his own flesh: how great and how worthy God is, and how little and how unworthy he is himself; and so he shall reduce himself to nothing and magnify God, in order that he shall be turned towards God so that he should see or feel no other thing but God. Then, if he suffer this humbly and patiently at all times, he may much the more lightly, and the more surely, think of the great love of our Lord Jesus Christ, who though he is so worthy himself would give his life to destroy the sinful life of mankind. Then he may well think about the stages of Christ's Passion, and beyond that to wonder at his wonderful love, that he would not only offer himself to us on the cross, but that he does offer himself to us in the sacrament of the altar so that he can be fully with us. Yes, yes, and yet even more thereto, for he gives himself to us to be most surely set in our hearts. Ah! good and gracious sweet Lord, who is capable of considering the least sparkle of your wonderful sweet love – truly, no man.

Therefore, before the reception of this worthy and most holy sacrament, a priest may say thus full perfectly in his heart: I have a theme, Lord. I know well that for all the works and deserts of men, be they never so holy, they are unworthy to receive you, Lord, so worthy, so mighty, so benign, so merciful as you are in every need. Ah! ah! truly merciful Lord; how much the more, then, am I unworthy who sin every day, and as an incorrigible human still live therein. Ah! good Lord, why do I do such despite to you, to cast you, my Lord God so precious, into so foul a pit as my conscience; for truly my sweet and gracious sovereign Lord, I acknowledge to you there is no place more stinking than my soul. Ah! Lord, Lord, so humble and so meek, what shall I do with you, kindly Lord? Why; what; shall I lay you, Lord, in that foul place? Truly Lord I dare not, except that I trust in your mercy. But sovereign Lord, full of might, I know that your mercy is more limitless than all my horrible, foul and wretched sin; therefore I entirely trust in your goodness, merciful Lord. I put myself forward to receive you, sweet Lord, as a sick man receives a medicine. You are a sure curer, Lord, and truly I am sick; therefore I take you in order to be made whole through you. And the sicker I am, by that much would I be made whole by you, my sweet Lord; and the greater the need I have of you, the more intently and earnestly should I have it in mind to call upon you, so that, Lord, in the healing of my deadly sickness the greatness of your goodness shall be well shown and commended.

And then, after this, when he has received that most powerful and blessed sacrament, he may then think thus: I do not wish after this most worthy meal to feed myself on much of the world's vanity, nor will I after such spiritual taste take fleshly delight in any creature. Nevertheless, should it be so, that a man does not feel spiritual emotions, not even devout stirrings through spiritual uplifting of the heart at the time of the reception, it is good that he should then think that this is a sign of great sickness of sin, or else of great death, or else it is a punishment of God to humble a man. For a man should always be aware in his own conscience that he is continually in default against that most mighty Lord, and therefore he should most humbly and obediently say to him thus: Ah! Lord, Lord, most merciful Lord, what shall I do now? I have put fire in my bosom, but feel no heat from it. See, see! oh Lord ever merciful to sinful wretches: I have put honey in my mouth, and I taste no kind of sweetness from it. Ah! good Lord Jesus Christ, have pity on me, a most unnatural and froward wretch, for I have received a sovereign medicine, and yet I do not at all feel any the more healthy.

Thus shall a man humbly and with good heart humble himself with the fear and love that he should have, and always ought to have, towards that worthy Lord in the sacrament of the altar in the form of bread, which is Christ Jesus. And then, thereafter, on account of his devout fear and love, he shall amend his life and turn to better things. For even if a man may not at once feel sweetness and spiritual delight in this worthy sacrament, he shall not despair on account of it, but meekly and patiently await the grace of God, and do whatever he can to acquire it. For when a sick man takes a medicine he is not made whole at once, even though he hopes to become whole because of it; and therefore he keeps himself carefully from all things that counteract his medicine, and patiently suffers the discomfort until the time that the medicine has worked in him, and restored him to well-being again.

Thus should we who are sick in sin receive the health-giving medicine of this precious sacrament.

Nevertheless, if a man through any spiritual experience should feel himself to be well, it is good for him not to think that it comes from himself, but from the goodness of God, who feeds with his grace both the good man and the bad, and then may he well think thus: Lo! lo! every sinful creature: our merciful and gracious Lord has done this to me in order to show me my wickedness, and to overcome my wretchedness with the fullness of his goodness. Lo! lo! well might I be joyful, for he has caused me, a dead man, to feel alive, and made me, a stinking worm, to taste heavenly delights. Ah! ah! since our Lord is so courteous to me, who always lives in sin, what might I believe that he would do to me if I were to offer myself fully to him; surely much better than I can say, or any heart can think.

Let us pray to God with a good intent that we might receive the sacrament to his delight. Amen.

9. Lay action during the mass [From T. F. Simmons, ed., *The Lay Folks' Mass Book*, Early English Texts Society, original ser., LXXI, 1874, pp. 2–60, text B; in English. An incomplete modern version of the same text, in verse, is in M. W. Baldwin, ed., *Christianity Through the Thirteenth Century*, London, 1970, pp. 400–12. NB: The original is in rhyme, but rather than attempt artificially to match the rhyming scheme, I have converted the text into prose. I have deliberately not modernised the version of the Our Father contained in the text, to provide an example of the many vernacular versions which were available at the time]

The worthiest thing, of most goodness in all this world, is the mass. In all the books of Holy Church that holy men have written over time, the mass is praised many times over; its benefits may never be totalled. For if a thousand clerics did nothing else, as the book tells, but list the virtues of singing the mass, and the benefits from hearing the mass, yet they could never tell more than a fifth part (for all their understanding and all their ability) of the benefit, rewards, and pardon for he who with devotion, in purity and with good intent pays honour to this sacrament. I find in a book written by someone (Dom Jerome was his name – a devout and religious man) who speaks thus in his writing. He says, you shall have a good mind not to create any commotion at the mass; he sets a great example with this why it is bad to do that; also he explains the way in which you should hear your mass. When the priest speaks, he says, or if he sings, you should listen well to him: when he prays privately, that is a time for you to pray. When I open the book, and know it, I translate it thus into English: When the altar is all prepared, and the priest is properly vested, then he takes in both hands a cloth which is upon the end of the altar, and comes back down a litte, and puts it on himself. Everyone kneels, but he stands and holds up both his hands to God: there, before he begins the mass, he humbles himself for all his sins; he confesses himself to all the people there for all his sins, both small and great. So does the clerk likewise to him, confessing himself for all his sins, and asks God's forgiveness. Before they begin to hear the mass the priest absolves them in faith, for the learned and lewd who wish to confess and acknowledge to God that they are bad, whether it be out loud or quietly. Therefore, kneeling on your knees, as you see others beside you doing, confess yourself there for all your sins, starting thus when he begins as is set out immediately beneath this rubric; and for that hold your hands together; and, so that it may turn out, also add Our Father and Ave; and before you rise, say your Creed, all the better you may proceed. Many say the confession; it is as good to say this in its place:

> I acknowledge to God almighty, and to his mother, the bright virgin, and to all the saints here, and to you, spiritual father, that I have sinned greatly, in many different sins, of thought, of speech, and of delight, in word and in action, I am in torment, and worthy of blame. Therefore I beg St Mary and all the holy saints in God's name, and you, priest, to pray for me, that God should have mercy and pity on account of his manhood for my wretched sinfulness, and give me the grace of forgiveness for all my misdeeds. Our Father, Ave, Creed.

When you have thus said your Creed, stand up quickly on your feet, for by this time, I suppose, the priest will have started the office of the mass, or else will be standing looking at his book at the south corner of the altar. Then, when you are standing, I would have you say:

> God, in your goodness, at the start of this mass, grant that all those who shall hear it may be of good and clear conscience. Lord, keep the priest who shall say it from temptation today, so that he can be pure in deed and thought, and that evil spirits do not annoy him, so that he can complete this sacrament with a pure heart and good intention, first greatly to your honour, who are sovereign of all succour, and to your mother, a pure virgin, and to your saints all together; and for all who hear it health of the soul, help and grace, and all manner of benefit. And for all whom we have in mind, relative or stranger of any sort, may God grant them on account

> of this mass forgiveness of all their sins; and everlasting rest and peace to departed Christian souls. And send us all your succour, and bring us to joy without end. Amen.

On high feasts, or on holy days, whenever people sing or say *Glory [to God] in the highest* in their mass, then say what is written here:

> Joy be to God in Heaven, with all kinds of happiness that men can name; and peace on earth to all men who are righteous and of good will. We love you, Lord God almighty, and we bless you actively; we worship you, as is fitting, and offer happiness to you, great and little; we thank you, God, for all your grace, for the great bliss that you have; Our Lord, Our God, Our heavenly King, Our God, Our Father almighty, Our Lord, the Son of God in Heaven, Jesus Christ, pleasant to name, Our Lord, Lamb of God, we name you, and Son of God, free of your father. You who defeat the sin of the world, have mercy on us, great and small; you who defeat the wrath of the world, receive our prayer at this time; you who sit at the right hand of your father, in mercy hear us living here; for you are holy, made by no one other than yourself, and only Lord. You are the Most High, of greatest wisdom, Jesus Christ, with the Holy Ghost, dwelling with your heavenly father, in more bliss than men can name. Jesus, bring us into that bliss, through the prayers of your mother. Amen.

And when you have done all this, kneel down on your knees shortly after. If they are singing or saying mass, say your Our Father throughout, until the deacon or priest reads the gospel. Then stand up, and pay attention; for then the priest carries his book north, to the other corner of the altar, and makes a cross on the writing with his thumb, he makes more progress. Then he next makes another on his face; for he has great need of grace, for then an earthly man shall speak the words of Jesus Christ, Son of the heavenly God. Both the readers and the hearers have great need, I think, of teachers how they should read and should hear the words of God, so beloved and dear. People ought to have great dread when they come to hear or read it; and also have love for that sweetness which with these words would relieve our suffering; but as our concern is with hearing, that now shall be our lesson. Clerks hear in one way, but lewd people need a different lesson.

At the beginning, take care to make a large cross on yourself. Stand, and say in this manner as you see it written here:

> In the name of the Father, and Son, and the Holy Ghost, a secure God of greatest power; may God's word be welcome to me; bliss and loving, Lord, be to you.

Whilst it is read, do not speak, but think about he who bought you dearly, saying in your mind thus, as you find it written after:

> My Jesus, grant me your grace, and power and room for amendment, to keep your word and do your will, to choose the good and leave the bad, and that it may be so, good Jesus, grant it to me. Amen.

Repeat this often in your thoughts, and until the gospel is finished do not let up; somewhere besides, when it is over, make a cross, and kiss it shortly after. People ought to say their Creed at some point; when others say theirs, make sure you say yours; I would have you say what follows in English words, for the best. Whatever they say, do nothing else, but carry on afterwards as this book sets out. Make sure you pay careful attention to this, for here is written your English Creed:

> I believe in God, the powerful Father, who has made everything: Heaven and earth, day and night, and all from nothing. And in Jesus, who is God's only son, both God and man, endlessly Lord. I believe in him, who through the meekness of the Holy Ghost, that was so mild, settled in Mary, the chaste maiden, and became a child. Under Pontius Pilate he suffered pain in order to save us, he was put on the cross, and died, laid in his grave. His soul went into Hell, to tell the truth; he rose up in flesh and feeling on the third day; he went up to Heaven with open wounds, through his power. Now he sits at his Father's right side in majesty; from thence he shall come to judge us all in his manhood, the living and the dead, all who have been of Adam's seed. I believe well in the Holy Ghost, and the Holy Church which is so good; and so I believe that the eucharist is both flesh and blood, in the forgiveness of my sins if I repent, also the resurrection of my flesh, and life everlasting.

After that, quickly following, comes the time for the offering; offer or not, as you wish. How you should pray, I would have you know: while you are standing, I advise you to say what is written next, to satisfy God:

> Jesus, you were born in Bethlehem, and three kings appeared before you. They offered gold, incense and myrrh, and you did not reject any of them, but wished them well, all three, home again, to their countries. Just so with our offerings which we offer, and our prayers which we proffer, take them, Lord, for love of you, and be our help in all things, so that all perils may be avoided. Grant us soon our good desires, amend us from all our ills, send us succour in all our needs. Amen.

Say Our Father while standing, throughout the time the priest is washing, until after having washed, the priest will bow to the altar, and then turn around. Then he asks, with a calm voice, for each man's prayers to the God of Heaven. Pay good attention to the priest: when he turns around, beat your breast, and then think that, because of your sins, you are unworthy to pray for him. But when you pray, God looks into your will, if it is good, he ignores your badness; therefore, with trust in his mercy, respond to the priest with this out loud:

> May the Holy Ghost settle in you, and give you righteousness, and govern your heart and your speaking to the honour and love of God.

Then the priest goes to his book to go through his private prayers. You should kneel down, and then say this which is next written in black: it will greatly improve your prayers if you hold up both your hands to God with good devotion, when you say this prayer:

> God, receive your service and this solemn sacrifice, for the priest and for all of us who are here now, or shall be here, to hear this Mass or pay worship, to see the sacring, or pray to it. And for all who live in God's name, that they may receive help from sin and shame; and for the souls who have passed from here, that they may have everlasting rest. Amen. Our Father; Ave Maria; Creed.

Take care that you are saying the Our Father whilst the priest is privately praying; afterwards the priest will move himself a little distance in that place, until he comes to the middle of the altar. Stand up, when he summons men in heart and body and every part; take good care and hear him well. Then he begins: *Per omnia*; and next, *Lift up your hearts.* At the end he says *Sanctus* three times, *In excelsis* he recites twice. Immediately he has done this, ensure that you are quickly ready, and say these words with a calm voice privately to God in heaven:

> In the world of worlds without end, may Jesus, my king, be thanked. I give you all of my heart, it is very right that it should be so. With all my will I worship you: Jesus, may you be blessed. With all my heart I thank you for the good that you have done for me. Sweet Jesus, now grant me this, that I may come into your bliss, to sing there with angels this sweet song of love for you: *Holy, holy, holy.* Jesus, grant that it may be so. Amen.

When this is said, kneel down, and do it with good devotion. Thank God then for all good things, and pray also for every man of every state and every rank, as the law of charity requires. Thereafter, without delaying, your speaking should be in this manner:

> Lord, you should be honoured: with all my heart I worship you. I thank you, Lord, as I well ought, for more good than I can know which I have received from you since the time I was conceived. My life, my limbs, have been lent to me by you; my true wits have been sent to me by you; you have

> preserved me through your grace from various perils in many places. All my life, and all my living, I have totally from your gift. You bought me dearly with your blood, and died for me upon the rood. Against your will I have committed many sins, great and evil; you are prepared, in your goodness, to grant me forgiveness. For these benefits, and many others, I thank you, Lord; I pray also that you forgive me all my guilt, and be my aid while I live; and give me grace to avoid doing those things which I would regret; and give me the will always to do good. Lord, consider the state of Holy Church, and the bishops, priests and clerks, so that they be kept in all good works; the king, the queen, the lords of the land, that they be well maintained in their positions in all goodness, and rule the people with justice; our kinsmen, and well-wishers, our friends, tenants, and servants, old men, children, and all women, merchants, craftsmen and tillers [of the soil], rich men and poor, great and small, I pray you, Lord, for them all, that they be preserved especially in good health, and holy life. For those who experience a hard life, with slander, discomfort, or strife, [who are] sick or imprisoned, or on the sea, poor, exiled, dispossessed, if there are any, to all such send your succour, to your worship and your honour. All those who have a good life today, and who live purely to your satisfaction, keep them, Lord, from all folly, and from all sin, for your mercy, and give them grace to stay and remain in your service, to their last ends. This world that turns in many ways, make it good for us for all our days; Lord, make the weather good and seasonable when it is hard and unstable; make the fruits of the earth plentiful; as you consider best, arrange it for us, send us such grace that in our last days, at our end, when this world and we shall part, [you] bring us to joy everlasting. Amen.

Make sure you are saying Our Father until he is making a cross over the chalice: then the time of sacring is near. People usually ring a little bell; then you shall pay reverence to Jesus Christ's own presence, which may loose all baleful bonds. Kneeling, hold up both your hands, and so behold the elevation: for that is he whom Judas kissed, and who thereafter was scourged and put on the rood, and there shed his blood for mankind, and died, and rose, and went to Heaven, and yet shall come to judge us all – each man according to his deeds: the same is he whom you look upon. This is the truth of Holy Church; who does not believe this must be filled with darkness. Therefore I counsel that you behold this sacrament with good intention. Then should you offer such prayers as you are best inspired to do. Different people, different prayers, each man in his best manner. Short prayer should be without fear, and with it Our Father and the Creed. If you are ignorant of one, I put here one which could be said; although I have set it down here in writing, you may exchange it for a better one.

> May you be loved, king; and may you be blessed, king; and may you be

> thanked, king, for all your good gifts. Jesus, all my delight, who spilt your blood for me, and died upon the rood, you give me grace to sing the song of love for you. Our Father; Ave Maria; Creed.

When you have said all your Creed, I advise you to read this short prayer which is written next in black letters; much more shall you fare the better.

> Lord, as you can and as you will, have mercy on me, who has done ill; whatever you wish to do with me, I consider myself satisfied to stick by it. Your mercy, Jesus, I would have; and out of fear I dare to beg for it. But you said, ask, and we shall receive. Sweet Jesus, make me safe, and give me the wit and proper wisdom to love you, Lord, with all my might.

When you have offered this prayer, then with devotion you should offer your prayers at that point for all your friends who have died, and for the sake of all Christian souls. You should offer a prayer such as this:

> Lord, in your holy grace hear our prayers in this place. Grant now, Lord, according to our prayer, to the Christian souls that have passed on from this life, which is sinful, that each may have a share in this mass. For their souls I pray dearly, which I shall name individually, that this mass shall be for their reward, help, and protection from all sorts of dread: father's soul, mother's soul, dear brothers, sisters' souls, kinsmen, and others individually, who wish us well, or did us good, or offered us any kindness; and may this mass be reward and medicine to all in the pains of Purgatory. Grant your grace and your mercy to all holy Christian souls; forgive them all their sins; loose their bonds, and let them pass from all manner of pain and from all care into the joy that lasts evermore. Amen.

Take care that you are saying Our Father until you hear the priest saying *'Throughout all ages'* out loud; then I would have you stand upright, for he will say in a loud voice *Our Father* to God in Heaven. Listen to him with a good will, and while he is speaking, keep quiet yourself – but answer at *'temptation'*, *'but deliver us from evil. Amen'*. There should be no need to instruct you on this, for those who do not know it are ignorant people. When this is done, say privately another prayer together with it. *Our Father*, first in Latin, and then in English as it is written here:

> Fader oure, þat is in heuen,
> blessid be þi name to neuen.
> Come to vs þi kyngdome.
> In heuen & erthe þi wille be done.
> oure ilk day bred graunt vs to day.

and oure mysdedes forgyue vs ay,
als we do hom þat trespas us,
right so haue merci vp-on vs.
and lede vs in no foundynge,
bot shild vs fro al wicked þinge. Amen.

Then shortly after the priest will speak, stand still, and always listen to him. He says '*agnus*' three times before he stops; the last words he says are about peace. You may not be in that peace if you are out of charity. Then it is good to beg of God that you may have charity. Then, when the priest kisses the pax, kneel down, and pray this:

Lamb of God, that may best take away the sins of the world, have mercy and pity on us, and grant us peace and charity. For in charity there are three types of love, which are necessary requisites for perfect peace. The first love is certainly to love the Lord above all else. Therefore I pray you, powerful God, that you make my love both day and night to be securely set in every way above all else to love you well, so that by your power and governance I shall ever be in your desire, above all to satisfy you in all that I ever can or may; and may I be ready, early and late, according to my rank and estate, to undertake all good deeds, and eschew all that are bad. The second is a private love, which is necessary for my benefit, which love is properly between my soul and my body. Therefore, good Lord, make my body and soul as one in accord, that each part with one assent should serve you with good intent. Never let my body do something bad so that it can destroy my soul. The third love is external, to love every neighbour about me, and that that love should not stop for anything. Therefore I pray you, prince of peace, that you would (as you best may) cause my heart to be in peace and rest, and prepared to love all manner of people, particularly my kinsmen, then neighbours, servants, and every subject; fellows, friends, [and] to forget none, but love every one, both far and near, like myself, with a pure heart; and so turn their hearts towards me that we may fully be friends, that I in their good, and they in mine, should ever have joy, with a glad heart. As I pray you for myself, here, grant similarly to others in like manner, so that every man may love others as well as though they were his own brothers. Let there be such love among us that we may be well loved by you; so that by this holy sacrament, which is now here present, and by the virtue of this mass, we may have forgiveness of all our guilt and all our faults, and with your help come to this bliss. Amen.

Take care that you are saying Our Father whilst the priest is washing. When the priest has finished washing, then quickly stand up on your feet. Then the clerk carries the book again to the south corner of the altar; the priest turns to his service, and proceeds to say more of his office. Then, without delaying, your speech should be in this manner:

> Jesus, my king, I pray to you, bow down your ears in pity and hear my prayer in this place. Good Lord, for your holy grace towards me and all who are here, so preserve us from all kinds of misfortune which may befall in any way in our deeds done today; whether we ride, or are walking, lie, or sit, or if we stand; whatever sudden chance occurs to us in a way other than we would wish, we pray that this mass will stand for us as a substitute for confession and also of communion. And Jesus, for your five wounds let us know the way to righteous living. Amen.

When this is said, kneel down quickly; say Our Father until the mass is over, for the mass is not ended until the time of '*Go forth, it has been done*'. Then, when you hear said '*Go forth*', or perhaps '*We bless*', then is the mass completed; but yet offer this prayer fairly quickly; after it you may well go on your way, in God's name:

> God be thanked for all his works; God be thanked by priests and clerks; God be thanked by every man; and I thank God as [well as] I can. I thank God for his goodness, and particularly now for this mass, and for all the prayers that are prayed here; I pray to God that he is satisfied. In recollection of God I bless myself here; with my blessing may God send me hence. *In the name of the Father, and of the Son, and of the Holy Spirit. Amen. Our Father. Hail Mary. Creed.*

I have told how you should spend your time at the mass: now I will end. It is good to look at the rubric from time to time, and to know the prayers without the book. It is worthwhile, without doubt, that everyone should love and honour the mass; for of all things in the world, the mass is the worthiest thing, of most goodness.

End. Amen. So be it.

IV. Designs for living and dying

As hinted in the introduction, the choice of the devotional literature for inclusion in this collection has not been easy.[1] *The three texts here printed are by no means among the most spiritually demanding; but their lack of demand is perhaps the important element. These are texts which could be accessible to a wide range of people; that they were so is evidenced by the fact that two –* The Abbey of the Holy Ghost, *and Hilton's* Epistle on the Mixed Life *– actually went into print.* The Book of the Craft of Dying *did not achieve that in the form given here; but what was seemingly a retranslation did appear.*

Both The Abbey of the Holy Ghost *and* The Book of the Craft of Dying *share other characteristics. Although now anonymous, they were both said (in at least one manuscript each) to have been written by Richard Rolle, the chief instructional writer of the fourteenth century.*[2] *(*The Abbey of the Holy Ghost *was also in the sixteenth century fathered on John Alcock, a fifteenth-century bishop of Ely who appears to have been considered saintly for a while after his death; but that was clearly an anachronistic attribution.)*[3] *Both texts are also translations, the former made* c. *1350–70 from a French original (which seems to have continued to circulate in England in the fifteenth century);*[4] *the latter presumably from the Latin, or possibly French. The considerable number of translations produced in England in the fifteenth and sixteenth centuries clearly made a major contribution to the development in English spirituality during that period; but raise problems of their own. The speed of the translation process, and the distribution of the texts, are obviously important factors: it may be that the majority of the imported texts did not begin to circulate greatly in their English forms until only just before the onset of the Reformation. Again, there is a danger that texts which are of interest to modern scholars are given an undue prominence: the lesser instructional texts may have been of much greater significance.*

1 Above, pp. 16–24.

2 H. E. Allen, *Writings Ascribed to Richard Rolle, Hermit of Hampole, and Materials for his Biography*, Modern Language Association of America, Monograph Series, III, New York and London, 1927, pp. 335–42; M. C. O'Connor, *The Art of Dying Well: the Development of the Ars Moriendi*, New York, 1942, p. 49.

3 Allen, *Writings of Richard Rolle*, p. 336. For evidence of devotion to Alcock, R. N. Swanson, *Church and Society in Late Medieval England*, Oxford, 1989, p. 227.

4 Allen, *Writings of Richard Rolle*, pp. 335–42; N. F. Blake, ed., *Middle English Religious Prose*, London, 1972, p. 88.

The level of instruction provided by the texts produced here varies considerably. The Abbey of the Holy Ghost *operates at a very general level of analogy, providing essentially moralistic advice which at times may seem platitudinous. Hilton's* Epistle *appears a more intense piece, certainly more directly addressed to the reader, and also more advanced in its demands. It is definitely instructional, backing up its argument by references to a variety of authorities. Even more well-endowed with references is* The Book of the Craft of Dying, *which ties in a whole range of authorities, ranging from the Bible, through Augustine and Gregory, to Jean Gerson, the chancellor of the University of Paris at the turn of the fourteenth and fifteenth centuries.*

While the moralistic teaching of The Abbey of the Holy Ghost *offers a fairly straightforward exhortation to an improved spiritual life, the other two texts are to an extent attempts to remove doubts and offer real advice.*[5] *Hilton's work is also important because of its author, he being one of that select group of English writers of the late fourteenth and early fifteenth centuries generally labelled 'the Middle English mystics'.*[6] *He entered the Augustinian house of Thurgarton in Yorkshire in 1384, and died in 1396. His writings, in Latin and English, are extensive, although there are some doubts about precisely which texts should be ascribed to him.*[7]

Much of Hilton's writing is concerned with spiritual direction, his major work in this realm being The Scale of Perfection.[8] *His tract on* The Mixed Life, *probably written even before he entered Thurgarton, shares some of the devotional and spiritual characteristics of the* Scale, *but operates as an 'eminently practical manual'.*[9] *to assist the laity in achieving spiritual fulfilment. A noted feature is the recommendation to the lettered to read the Bible as a preliminary to meditation – although without explicitly urging that it be read in English.*[10]

5 Above, pp. 17–20.

6 D. Knowles, *The English Mystical Tradition*, London, 1961, ch. 6 . On Hilton and his works see also A. Minnis, 'The *Cloud of Unknowing* and Walter Hilton's *Scale of Perfection*', in *Middle English Prose: a Critical Guide to Major Authors and Genres*, ed. A. S. G. Edwards, Brunswick, N.J., 1984, pp. 61–3, 69–73; D. G. Kennedy, *Incarnational Element in Hilton's Spirituality*, Salzburg Studies in English Literature: Elizabethan and Renaissance Studies, XCII:iii, Salzburg, 1982, pp. 29–39.

7 S. J. Ogilvie-Thomson, ed., *Walter Hilton's Mixed Life, Edited from Lambeth Palace MS 472*, Salzburg Studies in English Literature: Elizabethan and Renaissance Studies, XCII:xv, Salzburg, 1986, p. viii.

8 Modern English translation in Walter Hilton, *The Scale of Perfection*, trans. G. Sitwell, London, 1953.

9 Kennedy, *Incarnational Element*, p. 167 (on the work in general, pp. 167–71); Ogilvie-Thomson, *Hilton's Mixed Life*, p. x.

10 M. Deanesly, *The Lollard Bible and Other Medieval Biblical Versions*, Cambridge, 1920, pp. 217–20.

The tract demonstrates many of the problems of dealing with late medieval spiritual works. While it appears in several manuscripts (including two of the major compilations of Middle English devotional tracts, the 'Vernon' and 'Thornton' manuscripts), there are major differences between them, with the text surviving in both a long and a short version. The differences between the manuscripts testify to the artificiality of identifying a 'definitive' text, and to the equally artificial creation of a previously unknown version by processes of modern editing.[11] *Continued appreciation of the validity of Hilton's message is attested by the datable ownership marks of the manuscripts, one of which was treated as a 'common profit' volume, with others being owned by monks and nuns.*[12] *That the message did not date was acknowledged by its appearance between 1494 and 1535 in at least seven printed versions , one of which is associated with the Lady Margaret Beaufort and her circle.*[13]

The Book of the Craft of Dying *is equally didactic in purpose, focusing on what, for Christians, was the crucial point of the terrestrial existence: the point at which the individual lost control over his or her fate and became totally dependent on God and other Christians. At that point it became necessary to weigh up one brief life, while preparing for an everlasting future, and judgement. The idea of death as the last battle is given added force by the frequent appearance of this text in conjunction with the* Treatise of Ghostly

11 For the manuscripts, Ogilvie-Thomson, *Hilton's Mixed Life*, pp. xii–xxi, xxxiii–xli. (The postulation in Deanesly, *Lollard Bible*, pp. 346–7, that the tract is also included in manuscripts of the compilation known as *The Pore Caitif* is apparently incorrect: the section in question is in fact drawn from various sources, among them Richard Rolle's *Form of living*: M. T. Brady, 'The Pore Caitif: an introductory study', Traditio, X, 1954, p. 542.) See also N. F. Blake, *The English Language in Medieval Literature*, London and New York, 1977, ch. 3, esp. p. 55, on problems of editing of texts.

12 Ogilvie-Thomson, *Hilton's Mixed Life*, pp. xii–xv, xx. The arrangements for the transmission of the 'common profit' text (Lambeth Palace Library, MS 472) merit reproduction: 'This book was produced from the goods of John Killum for the common profit, so that that person who has this book entrusted to him by the person who has the power to entrust it shall have the use thereof for the term of his life, praying for the soul of the same John; and so that he who has the aforesaid use by commission, when he is not using it, shall lend it for a while to some other person. Also, that person to whom it was entrusted for the term of his life shall, under the aforesaid condition, hand it on to another person for the term of his life. And thus may it be handed on and entrusted from person to person, man or woman, for as long as the book endures' (Ogilvie-Thomson, *Hilton's Mixed Life*, p. xii).

13 Ogilvie-Thomson, *Hilton's Mixed Life*, p. xxii. The text given here, based on Horstman's edition, uses material from the printed versions, with the main body being derived from the version of the Thornton manuscript, occasionally amended in the light of the reading of the Vernon manuscript. Ogilvie-Thompson offers a new edition, but I gained access to that too late, and too briefly, to amend my version.

Battle.[14] *Despite the fact that the* Book *was not printed, it was evidently relatively popular, to judge from its manuscript tradition.*[15] *It is, also, worth re-emphasising the fact that this tract is at base a translation, one of the many which influenced English spirituality during the pre-Reformation years, and which thereby integrated the English tradition with general European developments.*[16]

Of the particular aspects of spirituality demonstrated in the text, especially noteworthy is the inclusion of several prayers, and the catechistical framework of parts of it. This last (which can be mirrored from other writings, such as John Mirk's Instructions for Parish Priests*) makes the text more than a straightforwardly devotional piece, integrating it into a tradition of practical guidance for those approaching death.*[17]

Beyond the focus on the individual about to die, the Book *clearly brings out the way in which any good death was a group experience, emphasising the responsibility of those around the deathbed to initiate the process of the soul's release from Purgatory. Here, to transfer from the text to reality, is a deathbed similar to that from which Julian of Norwich revived to embark on her own spiritual quest.*[18]

Death, however, is a highly subjective experience; and modern reactions to this tract demonstrate the problems of getting to grips with material of this sort. While some see the work as offering positive and encouraging assistance in confronting that transitional point between this world and the next, another reading has found it rather negative in its impact.[19]

14 Gillespie, 'Vernacular books of religion', p. 327.

15 Gillespie, 'Vernacular books of religion', p. 327; for manuscripts see P. S. Jolliffe, *A Check-list of Middle English Prose Writings of Spiritual Guidance*, Pontifical Institute of Mediaeval Studies, Subsidia Mediaevalia, II, Toronto, 1974, p. 123.

16 On translations, see Swanson, *Church and Society*, pp. 263–4.

17 Gillespie, 'Vernacular books of religion', pp. 324–5; G. Kristensson, ed., *John Mirk's Instructions for Parish Priests, Edited from MS Cotton Claudius A II and Six Other Manuscripts, with Introduction, Notes, and Glossary*, Lund Studies in English, XLIX, Lund, 1974, pp. 164–5; H. Littlehales, ed., *English Fragments from Latin Medieval Service Books*, Early English Text Society, extra ser., XC, 1903, pp. 6–9.

18 C. Wolters, ed., *Julian of Norwich, Revelations of Divine Love*, Harmondsworth, 1966, pp. 64–5, 181–3, 185–6.

19 O'Connor, *Art of Dying Well*, pp. 4–5; N. L. Beaty, *The Craft of Dying: a Study in the Literary Tradition of the Ars Moriendi in England*, Yale Studies in English, CLXXV, New Haven, 1970, ch. 1, esp. pp. 48–53; R. G. Twombly, 'Remembering death and dismembering the self; 1418, 1440 and after', *Journal of Literature and Theology*, II, 1989, pp. 194–8.

10. The Abbey of the Holy Ghost [From N. F. Blake, ed., *Middle English Religious Prose*, London, 1972, pp. 88–102; in English]

This is the abbey of the Holy Ghost, which is established in a place which is called conscience.

My dear brothers and sisters, I can well see that many wish to enter religion, but may not do so on account of poverty, or out of dread, or for fear of their relatives, or because of the tie of marriage. Therefore I here draw up a book of religion of the heart, that is, of the Abbey of the Holy Ghost, so that all those who may not physically enter religion may do so spiritually.

A Jesus, mercy! Where may this abbey and this order best be established? Surely, never better or more fittingly than in a place which is called conscience. It is now, then, necessary at the start that the place of conscience be cleaned by wise cleaning. The Holy Ghost shall send two well-qualified maidens: one is called Righteousness, the other is called Love-of-cleanness. These two shall cast out from the conscience and from the heart all kinds of filth of foul thoughts and foul yearnings. When the place of conscience is well cleaned, then shall the foundation be dug, large and deep. And this shall be done by two maidens: one is called Humility, who shall make the foundation deep by her self-abasement; the other is called Poverty, who makes it long and wide, by casting out from the heart everything connected with earthly things and worldly thoughts, so that although they have earthly possessions, they do not fasten their hearts on them with love. And such be called poor in spirit; of whom God speaks in the gospel and says that theirs is the kingdom of Heaven ... Blessed, then, is the religion established in poverty and humility, which is in contrast with many religious who are covetous and proud. This abbey shall also be sited on a good river, which is more restful and delightful. On such a river was the Magdalene placed and established; for which reason grace and richness of works came fully to her will. Therefore St David says ... 'the good river that makes the city pleasing to God', for it is clean and secure and rich in all goods and merchandise. Just so the river of tears cleans God's city, that is man's soul which is God's city, as the holy men say that the filth of sin subtracts from the riches of virtues and all good qualities.

When this foundation is made, then shall come Lady Obedience on one side, and Lady Mercy on the other, to raise the walls high and make them stalwart with a free heart that gives readily to the poor and disadvantaged. For when we do any good deed of charity through the grace of good intent, we set so many good stones to our mansion in the bliss of Heaven, joined together with the love of God and of our fellow Christians. We read that Solomon made his mansion of great precious stones. These precious stones are alms-deeds and holy works which shall be fastened together with the mortar of love and steadfast belief. Therefore David says: ... 'All his works are done in steadfast belief.' And as a wall may not last without cement or mortar, just so no works that we do are worth anything to God or noteworthy for our souls, unless they are done in the love of God and in true belief. Therefore, all that we do in sin is lost until we amend ourselves.

Then Lady Patience and Lady Fortitude shall raise up the pillars and underpin them so steadfastly and stalwartly that no wind of words or of anger or of spiritual temptations or of bodily lust, either inner or outer, may cast them down. After this it is necessary that the cloister be made with four corners, which is why it is called 'cloister', for it closes and shuts and shall carefully be locked. My dear brothers and sisters, if you wish to keep yourselves in spiritual religion and be at peace of soul and sweetness of heart, keep yourselves within, and guard your gates, and so carefully keep watch over your cloister that no outer or inner temptations can gain entrance to cause you to break silence or incite you to sin. Guard your eyes from foul sights, your ears from foul hearings, your mouth from foul speech and from unclean laughter, and your heart from foul thoughts.

Penance shall make the chapter-house, Preaching the frater, Prayer the chapel, Contemplation the dormitory, which shall be raised high up with high yearnings and with the prompting of love for God. Contemplation is a devout elevation of the heart: burning to dwell with God in love, and with his delights to enhance the soul, and have a partial taste of the sweetness that God's chosen shall have in Heaven. Pity shall be the infirmarer, Devotion the cellarer, Meditation shall construct the granary. And when the domestic offices have been built, then it falls to the Holy Ghost to establish the convent in grace and virtues. Then the Holy Ghost shall come, which is warden and visitor of this order, which God the Father founded by his power. As David says ... 'The high God has made it.' The Son rules it, the Holy Ghost guards it and visits it; and so we sing in church … 'Come, O God, Holy Ghost, visit the hearts of your people and fill them with your grace.'

The good Lady Charity, because she is the most worthy above all others, shall be abbess of this holy abbey. And just as those who are in religion may do or say nothing, nor go into any place, nor take nor give without permission of the abbess, just so none of these things shall be done spiritually without permission of Charity. For so commands St Paul: ... 'Whatever you do or say or think in your heart, you should do it out of love.' Ah, dear brothers and sisters, what a hard commandment this is: but it is noteworthy for our souls that our thoughts and our words and our works should only be done for love and in the love of God. Alas, if I dare say, for there are many who are in religion, yet too few religious, who do not follow St Paul's commandment or the counsel of the good Lady Charity, who is the abbess of this blissful religion. And on account of this they lose a lot of time from their reward, and add greatly to their pain, unless they amend themselves.

Therefore, dear brothers and sisters, be always wakeful and wary in your works, always actively thinking, whatever you do, that it be done in the love of God and for his love. The Lady Wisdom shall be prioress, for she is worthy ... 'At the first was wisdom created.' And we should do all that we do according to the learning and advice of this prioress. And thus says David: ... 'All that you have created, you have created it wisely.' The good Lady Humility, who always abases herself and puts herself below all others, shall be sub-prioress; you shall honour and worship her with obedience.

Ah, Jesus, blessed is that abbey and happy is that religion which has so holy an abbess as Charity, Wisdom as prioress, Humility as sub-prioress. Ah, dear brothers and sisters, blessed and happy are they – that is to say, their souls are happy – who keep the commands of the abbess, Lady Charity, the teaching of the prioress, Lady Wisdom, and counsel of the sub-prioress, Lady Humility. For whoever is obedient to these three ladies, and regulates his life by their teachings, the Father, the Son and the Holy Ghost shall comfort them with many spiritual joys, and aid and succour them in all their temptations and angers so that they shall not be defeated; nor shall they fear any deceits or wiles of the devil, for God is with him, and stands by as a true and strong warrior. And thus says David ... 'God, my stalwart and true champion, who has undertaken to fight against my enemies for me (who am so feeble and powerless), whom then should I fear? Truly, no one.' We read in the Book of Daniel that there was a mighty king whom he called Nebuchadnezzar, who appointed three men in his kingdom to act and order and arrange matters as bailiffs of the realm, so that the king should hear no unpleasantness or complaint, so that he might have peace and quiet in his kingdom. Similarly in the kingdom which has these three bailiffs in it, and the religion that has these three prelates in it, that is Charity, Wisdom and Humility, there is peace, quiet, and delight in the soul and comfort in life.

Lady Discretion, who is thoughtful and cautious, shall be treasurer. She shall have everything in her charge and actively ensure that all goes well.

Prayer shall be chantress, who with heart-felt prayers shall labour day and night. The holy man says what Prayer is: ... 'Orison is a holy prayer to God, solace and delight to angels, and torment to the devils.' It is attested in the *Life of St Bartholomew* that it is torment to the devil, when the devil cried out and said to him: ... 'Bartholomew, your prayers are burning me.' That it is delight to angels St Augustine testifies, and says: 'When we pray with devotion of the heart to God, the angels stand before us dancing and playing, and carrying up our prayers, and bringing them into the presence of the Father of Heaven. Our Lord commanded those prayers to be written in the book of life.' Because it is a sacrifice to God – yes, and one of those which pleases him most – he demands it of us and says: ... 'You shall worship me with the sacrifice of love.' Jubilation, her companion, shall help. St Gregory tells what jubilation is, and says that jubilation is a great joy which is conceived in tears through burning spiritual love which cannot be completely shown outwardly nor completely hidden. It sometimes happens with those who love God heartily: indeed, after they have been at prayer, they are so delighting in God that wherever they are their hearts sing passionate songs of longing love for their beloved, as if they yearn to clasp with the arms of love and to kiss sweetly with spiritual mournings of his gladness – and sometimes so intensely that they lack words; for the longing of love ravishes their hearts to the extent that sometimes they do not know what they are doing.

Devotion is cellaress, who keeps the wines, both white and red, with deep thoughts of the goodness of God and of the pains and anguishes he suffered and of the joy and the delights of Paradise which he has prepared for his chosen.

Penance shall be kitchener, with great activity and labour and toil both day and night to satisfy everyone, and often shall sweat with bitter tears in anger for her sins. She prepares good food, that is, many bitter regrets, all for her guilt; and these foods feed the soul. But she stints herself with abstinence, and eats but little. For even if she does ever so many and manifold good works, she always considers herself unworthy and sinful.

And Temperance serves in the fratry, so that every one takes care that moderation is in all things, so that neither too much nor too little is eaten or drunk. Sobriety reads at the table the lives of the holy fathers, and reads to them the life they led here on earth, so that they may have a good example to do as they did, and thereby win as much reward as they had.

Pity is the pittancer, who does all the good she can; and Mercy, her sister, is almoner, who gives all and can keep nothing back for herself.

The Lady Fear is porter, who actively guards the gate and the cloister of the heart and conscience, who chases out all vices, and keeps in all good virtues, and so shuts the gates of the cloister and the windows that no evil can enter into the heart through the gates of the mouth, nor through the windows of the eyes or of the ears.

Honesty is master of the nuns to teach them all courteousness: how they should speak and act, sit or stand, how they should carry themselves outwardly, how inwardly, how before God, and how with men, so that all who see them may take them as a model of all goodness.

Lady Courtesy shall be hosteller, who shall graciously receive those coming and going, so that everyone may speak well of her. And for as much as none should be on her own among the guests, for it might happen that Lady Courtesy would be too forward and too rash, she shall have Lady Innocence as her companion. For these two allied together in fellowship are secure and fitting, since one without the other is sometimes worth little, for too much innocence may result in too much simplicity or too little, and too much courtesy may result in a too agreeable appearance, either too happy or too forward to gratify the guests. But together they may fairly, well and without blame do their duties.

Lady Reason shall be purveyor, who shall arrange matters without and within so skilfully that there shall be no shortages.

Lady Loyalty shall be infirmarer, who shall work around and actively serve the sick. And since in the infirmary of this order there are more sick than well, more weak than strong, and too many for her to be able to care for alone, she shall therefore have Lady Largesse as her companion, who shall do as much as possible for each one according to his needs.

The knowing and wise lady who is called Meditation is garnerer. She shall gather and collect together good wheat and other good corn, so fully and so plentifully, that all the ladies of the house may have their sustenance from it. Meditation is good thoughts of God and of his works, of his words, and of his creation, of the pains he suffered, and of the heart-felt love that he had and has for us for whom he endured death. The good King David had this granary, for he was always rich and lived in plenty. Therefore he says in the Psalter ... 'I always have my thoughts deeply in your works.' And in another place he says: ... 'Lord, I think of your law night and day.' This is the beginning of all perfection, that a man should firmly set his heart to think deeply of God and his works; for a good thought in holy meditation is often better than many words said in prayer. It often happens that the heart is so overcome and ravished in holy meditation that it is not aware what it is doing, hearing, or seeing; so firmly is the heart set and fastened on God and his works that they lack words. And the quieter he is in such meditation, the louder he cries in God's ears. So ... David, ... as though he said: 'Lord, whilst my heart was deep in thought of you and of your works and cried to you in holy meditation, I was quiet as a dumb thing.' And at that point the gloss says: 'The great cries that we cry to God are our great desires and our great yearnings.' And thus says St Denis, that when the heart is lifted up and ravished in the love of God with jealous yearning, he cannot share in words what the heart thinks. This holy meditation which is a granary that guards the wheat, which is red outside and white within and has a split side, from which men make good bread, that is Jesus Christ who was red on the outside from his own blood, and white within through humility and patience and all kinds of cleanness of life, and had his side split with a spear's thrust. This is the bread which we receive and see in the sacrament of the altar.

And well we know that the granary should be above the cellar, and so shall meditation be above devotion, and therefore Meditation shall be granarian and Devotion cellarer, and Pity shall be pittancer. And of these three speaks the prophet David, who says ... 'They are established from the fruit of the wheat and wine and oil.' In many places in the old law God promised these three to his chosen. 'Serve me well', he says, 'and I shall give you plenty of wheat, of wine, and of oil.' Plenty of wheat means to think of the cross and of the Passion of Jesus Christ, and that is meditation. Plenty of wine, that is a well of tears which it is well to weep; and that is devotion. Plenty of oil, that means to have delight and a taste of God; and that is comfort, for the oil gives flavour to food and drink, and lights lamps in Holy Church. Also, when God's servants have thought deeply with their hearts on God and his works, with a longing love for him, then God takes pity on them and sends them the pittance of comfort and spiritual joy. At first this resembles meditation, which is the wheat which God promises us, and afterwards devotion which men acquire through meditation. Then God's son afterwards sends the wine of sweet tears. Then he sent the oil of comfort which gives flavour and enlightens their knowledge and reveals to them his mysteries in Heaven, which he hides and keeps from those who follow fleshly yearnings and give themselves up to the wisdom of this world and its fantasies. And those who are God's true servants, he so enflames with the blaze of his love that they somehow taste and feel how sweet, how good, how loving it is; but not completely, for I trust that no one can fully feel it, lest his heart should burst for delight in that bliss.

St Augustine tells of a priest who, when he heard anything enthralling about God, would be so ravished with bliss that he would fall down and lie as though he were dead; so that if at that time I placed burning fire against his naked form, he felt it no more than would a dead corpse. St Bernard enlarges upon these words of Job, where he says ... that God has light in his hands. You well know that one who holds a lighted candle between his hands may hide it and reveal it at will. So does Our Lord God to his chosen: when he wishes he opens his hands and enlightens those who love him with Heavenly delights; and when he wishes he closes his hands and withdraws that pleasure and that comfort, because he does not wish them to feel it then. But here he gives it to him so that he may taste and in part savour how sweet he is. As David said, '*Taste and see how sweet is the Lord*', as if God said to us: 'By this comfort and pleasure you, who have so short a time, might taste and feel from me how good and how sweet I am to my chosen in my world of bliss without end.' And he does this to draw us from worldly business and pleasures, and to enflame our hearts with the yearnings of love in order to win and have delight in that joy to be with him all completely in body and soul for ever, without end.

A wise and well-taught lady, whom men call Carefulness, who is ever watchful and busy always alike to do well, shall keep the clock and wake these other ladies and cause them to rise early and promptly to serve God. There is a clock in the town which wakes men to get up for physical labour, and that is the cock; and there is the clock in the city which wakes merchants to go about their trading, and that is the watchman who trumpets the day; and there is the clock in religion which wakens the convent for mattins; and there is the clock of contemplation, and that is for this holy religion which is founded by the Holy Ghost, and this is Carefulness and has a scent of perfection. It often happens in religion that in advance, even before the clock rings out, God's spiritual servants have been long awake before and have wept before God and washed themselves with their tears, and their spirits have been stirred by devout prayers and spiritual solace. And why do they rise so early? Truly, for the clock of love and Carefulness has awoken them before the clock falls due.

Ah, dear brothers and sisters, blessed are the souls whose love and longing for God makes them wake up, so that they do not slumber or sleep in the slough of fleshly lust. Therefore it says in the canticle: ... 'While I sleep physically in order to ease and rest my flesh, my soul is always awake in carefulness and longing of love for God.' Concerning the soul which is thus awake to God, I think with a full conscience as worldly men think, which is ... 'My heart has run from me, awakened by love.' What is it that causes the heart to run from the flesh, and forget it as though it were a stranger to it? Truly, carefulness with tears of love, and mourning with longing of love, conceived in the devout uplifting of the heart.

When this abbey had been well-ordered in all things, and God well served in calm and pleasure and peace of the soul, then came the tyrant of the land in his might, and put into this holy abbey four daughters of his who were loathsome and of evil behaviour. The devil was father to these four daughters. The first of this foul brood was called Envy, the second Pride, the third Complaint, and the fourth False-witness. This tyrant, the fiend of Hell, had put these four into this holy abbey out of ill-will and malice, so that they might disturb and harm the whole convent by their wickedness, so that they might have no rest or peace, night or day, nor pleasure in their souls.

When the good Lady Wisdom, the prioress, and Lady Humility, the sub-prioress, and the other good ladies of the holy abbey saw that the whole abbey was at the point of collapsing into nothing through the wickedness of these four daughters, they rang the chapter bell and gathered themselves together, and sought advice on what was the best thing to do. And the Lady Discretion counselled them that they should all fall into prayer to the Holy Ghost, who is visitor of this abbey, that he should hurry to come, as they had great need, to help them and visit them with his grace. And they all, by her advice, sang to the Holy Ghost with great devotion of the heart and with a sweet tone: '*Come, creator spirit, visit the minds of your people, fill.*' And swiftly the Holy Ghost came at their petition, and comforted them all with his grace, and chased out all the foul senses, the loathsome daughters of the fiend, and cleansed the abbey of all their filth and ordered and restored it better than it had been before.

Now I pray you all, through the charity of God, that all who read or hear of this religion be obedient with all their power and allow all the good ladies named before to do their duties spiritually each day within your hearts. And let everyone actively take care that you do no offence against the rule or obedience of this religion, particularly the superiors. And if through any mischance it should happen that any of these four daughters seek in any kind of way to gain entry to dwell within your hearts, follow the example of the good Lady Discretion, and give yourself to devotion with hearty prayers in the hope of God's help and succour, and you shall be delivered by the mercy and grace of almighty God. May he grant it to you through the intercession of his dear mother, St Mary. Amen.

Here ends concerning the Holy Ghost.

11. **Walter Hilton,** *Epistle on the Mixed Life* [From C. Horstman, ed., *Yorkshire Writers: Richard Rolle of Hampole and his Followers*, 2 vols., London, 1895–6, I, pp. 264–92; in English (on the form of the text given here, see above, p. 94 n. 13)]

THIS IS A DEVOUT BOOK COMPILED BY MASTER WALTER HILTON FOR A DEVOUT MAN OF SECULAR STATUS, ABOUT HOW HE SHOULD GOVERN HIMSELF.

HOW A MAN WHO WISHES TO BE SPIRITUAL MUST FIRST UNDERTAKE CONSIDERABLE PHYSICAL ACTIVITY IN PENANCE AND THE DESTRUCTION OF SIN.

Dear brother in Christ, there are two categories of status in Holy Church by which Christian souls please God and gain for themselves the bliss of Heaven; one is physical, the other spiritual. Physical work pertains chiefly to secular men and women who lawfully use worldly goods and willingly engage in worldly activity. It also pertains to young men starting out, who come new from the world's sins to the service of God; in order to make them capable of spiritual labour and to break down the disobedience of the body by discretion and such physical activity, so that it may be malleable and prepared, and not too contrary to the spirit in spiritual work. For as St Paul says, as woman was made for man, and not man for woman, just so bodily work was made for the spiritual, and not the spiritual for the bodily. Bodily labour precedes, and spiritual follows; as St Paul says. ... And this is a reason why it ought to be so: for we are born in sin and fleshly corruption, by which we are so blinded and so suffocated that we have neither the spiritual knowledge of God through the enlightenment of understanding nor spiritual contact with him by the pure desire of loving. And therefore we may not suddenly emerge from this dark night of fleshly corruption into that spiritual light; for we cannot endure it or bear it because of our sickness with ourselves, no more than we can behold the light of the sun with our bodily eyes when they are sore. And therefore we must wait and work through the process of time. First by physical works, actively, until we are released from this heavy burden of sin which hinders us from spiritual labour; and until our souls be somewhat cleansed of great external sins and are capable of spiritual works.

By this physical labour which I speak of you should understand all kinds of good works which your soul does by the agency of the senses and the limbs of your body, to yourself (like fasting, watching and restraining fleshly lusts by doing penance), or to your fellow Christians by fulfilment of the corporal or spiritual acts of mercy, or to God by enduring all physical discomforts for the love of righteousness. All these works truly done in charity are pleasing to God; without it they are nothing. Then whoever wishes to be spiritually engaged, it is surer and profitable for him first to be tested for a long time by this physical activity, for these bodily deeds are a sign and demonstration of moral virtues, without which a soul is incapable of spiritual labours. First break down pride in physical appearance, and also within your heart from thinking, boasting, and praising yourself and your deeds, being presumptuous about yourself, and vain pleasure in yourself for anything which God has sent you, physical or spiritual. Also break down envy and anger against your fellow Christians, whether they are rich or poor, good or bad, so that you do not hate them or wilfully disdain them either in word or deed. Also break down covetousness of worldly goods, so that by holding or getting or saving of them you do not offend your conscience, nor breach charity towards God and your fellow Christians for love of any worldly goods; but whatever you acquire, care for it and expend it without delight and vain pleasure in it, as reason requires, to the worship of God and the aid of your fellow Christians. Break down also, as much as you can, fleshly pleasures, either of slothfulness or bodily ease, gluttony, or lechery; and then when you have been well belaboured and well tested in all such bodily labours, then you may by grace dispose yourself for spiritual labour. The grace and the goodness of Our Lord Jesus, that he has shown to you by withdrawing your heart from love and delight in worldly vanity and involvement in fleshly sins, and in turning your will entirely to his service and pleasure, brings into my heart a great concern to love him in his mercy, and also greatly stirs me to strengthen you in your good purpose and in the good working which you have begun, in order to bring it to a good end if I am able, chiefly for God, and also because of the tender loving affection which you have towards me, even though I am a wretch and unworthy.

WHY GOOD DESIRE NEEDS TO BE GOVERNED BY DISCRETION, AND WORKS DESERVING REWARD PERFORMED IN THE ORDER OF CHARITY. *CHAPTER 1*

I well know the desire of your heart, that you greatly covet to serve Our Lord by holy spiritual activity, without being hindered or disturbed by worldly business, so that you might by grace come to greater knowledge and spiritual contact with God and spiritual things. This desire is good, I trust, and from God, for it is charity especially directed towards him. Nevertheless it must be controlled and governed by discretion concerning outward action, according to the position you are in, for ungoverned charity sometimes turns into vice. And therefore it is said in holy writ: ... 'Our Lord God gave me charity established in an order and rule, so that it should not be lost through my indiscretion.' In the same way, how you should follow this charity and this desire, which Our Lord in his mercy has given you, is to be regulated and ordained, as your status requires, and according to the way of life you had previously, and according to the grace of virtue which you now have. You shall not totally follow your desire to abandon the activities and business of the world which it is necessary to undertake in governing yourself and all others in your charge, and give yourself fully to spiritual occupation in prayers and meditations as though you were a monk or friar or any other man not bound to the world by children and servants as you are: for that is not for you; if you do so, you do not maintain the requirement of charity. Also, if you would totally abandon spiritual activity, especially after the grace which God has given you, and involve yourself fully in business of the world to fulfil an active life, as fully as another who never felt devotion, you desert the order of charity: for your status requires you to do both, at different times.

THAT THE LIFE OF MARY AND MARTHA, MIXED TOGETHER, IS APPROPRIATE TO THOSE WHO ARE OF HIGH STATUS. *CHAPTER 2*

You should mix the works of the active life with spiritual works of the contemplative life, and then you do well. For you shall sometimes be busy with Martha to regulate and govern your household, your children, your servants, your neighbours, and your tenants: if they do well, encourage them and help them; if they do badly, teach them to better themselves, and chastise them. And you shall also check and wisely ensure that your possessions and worldly goods are rightly cared for by your servants, organised and properly spent, so that you can use them more plenteously to perform the acts of mercy to your fellow Christians. At other times you shall, with Mary, leave the bustle of the world and sit down at the feet of Our Lord in humility in prayers and holy thoughts and in contemplation of him, as he gives you grace. And so shall you profitably go from the one to the other, deserving reward, and fulfil both: and then you keep the order of charity well. Nevertheless, so that you are not amazed by what I say, I shall therefore tell and declare to you a little of this matter more directly.

TO WHOM THE ACTIVE LIFE IS APPROPRIATE, AND TO WHOM THE CONTEMPLATIVE. *CHAPTER 3*

You should understand that there are three ways of living: one is active, another contemplative, the third consists of both and is the mixed life. Active life on its own pertains to worldly men and women who are uncouth, fleshly, and boisterous in their involvement in spiritual activity, for they feel no delight or devotion by the fervour of love as other men do, they know none of the art of it. And yet, nevertheless, they dread God and the pains of Hell, and therefore they avoid sin. They also have a desire to please God and get to Heaven, and goodwill towards their fellow Christians. For these people it is necessary and expedient to engage in works of the active life as busily as they can, to help themselves and their fellow Christians, for they can do nothing else. Contemplative life on its own pertains to such men and women who for the love of God forsake all overt sins of the world and of their flesh, and all business, duties and oversight of worldly goods, and make themselves poor and naked, down to the bare necessities of bodily nature, and flee from authority over other men into the service of God. It pertains to these people to labour and occupy themselves inwardly to obtain (through the grace of Our Lord) cleanness of heart and a peaceful conscience, by the destruction of sin and the receipt of virtues, and thereby come to contemplation. That cleanness cannot be obtained without considerable physical activity and continual spiritual labour in devout prayers, fervent longing and spiritual meditation.

HOW THE MIXED LIFE ESPECIALLY PERTAINS TO PRELATES OF HOLY CHURCH, AND ALSO TO SECULAR LORDS WHO RULE OTHER MEN. *CHAPTER 4*

The third life, that is, mixed, pertains especially to men of Holy Church, like prelates and other holders of cures, who have care and authority over other men to care for and govern them, both their bodies and (chiefly) their souls, by fulfilment of the acts of mercy, both corporal and spiritual. To these men it sometimes pertains to employ works of the active life, to assist and sustain themselves and their subjects and others as well, and sometimes to leave all external business and give themselves up for a time to prayers, meditations, readings of holy writ and other spiritual activities, as they feel inclined. Also it generally pertains to some secular men who have authority, with considerable ownership of worldly goods, and who also have (as it were) a lordship over other men, to govern and sustain them (such as a father has over his children, a master over his servants, and a lord over his tenants). These men have also received by the gift of Our Lord the grace of devotion, and a partial taste of spiritual occupation. To such also pertains this mixed life, which is both active and contemplative. For if these men, deserting the duty and obligation that they have taken on, would completely renounce the world's business (which ought to be used wisely in fulfilling their duties) and totally abandon themselves to the contemplative life, they do not do well, for they do not keep the requirement of charity. For charity, as you know, consists of love both of God and of your fellow Christians, and therefore it is reasonable that he who has charity should employ both in his works, now the one and now the other. For he who, for the love of God, through contemplation forsakes the love of his fellow Christians and does not behave towards them as he ought, when he is obliged to do so, does not fulfil charity. Also, contrariwise, he who has such concern for the works of the active life and the bustle of the world that for love of his fellow Christians he totally abandons spiritual activity, after God had inclined him thereto, he does not fully fulfil charity. This is the saying of St Gregory.

HOW OUR LORD JESUS CHRIST AND HOLY MEN OF HIGH STATUS PROVIDED MODELS OF LIVING A MIXED LIFE. *CHAPTER 5*

Our Lord, to incite some men to engage in the mixed life, took upon himself the characters of such types of men, both prelates and holders of cures in Holy Church, and of others who are inclined as I have said, and provided for them a model by his own behaviour that they should use the mixed life as he did. Sometimes he shared and mixed with men, showing them his acts of mercy; for he taught the ignorant by his preaching, he visited the sick and healed them of their sores, he fed the hungry and comforted those who were sad. At other times he abandoned the company of all worldly men, and of his disciples as well, and went alone into the desert up into the hills, and remained all night in prayer, as the gospel says. This mixed life Our Lord demonstrated himself, as an example to those who have taken on the standing and duties of this mixed life, so that they should sometimes give themselves up to the business of worldly things as reason requires, and to works of the active life to the profit of their fellow Christians for whom they are responsible; at other times give themselves fully to contemplation by devotion, prayer and meditation. This life was led and employed before now by those holy bishops who had cure of men's souls and the administration of temporal goods. For these holy men did not utterly abandon the administration, nor the oversight and expenditure of worldly goods, nor gave themselves wholly to contemplation, even though they had much grace of contemplation; but they quite frequently left the calm of their contemplation, when they would rather still be at it, for love of their fellow Christians, and involved themselves in worldly business to help their subjects; and assuredly that was charity. For wisely and discreetly they divided their lives into two: sometimes they fulfilled the lesser part of charity by works of the active life, for they were obliged to do that by taking on their prelacies: at other times they fulfilled the higher part of charity in contemplation of God and spiritual things by prayers and meditations – and so they had complete charity towards God and their fellow Christians, both in the affections of their souls inwardly, and externally in the demonstration of physical acts. Other men who were only contemplatives, and were free from all such responsibilities and prelacies, also had full charity towards God and their fellow Christians, but that was only in the affection of their souls, but never by outward demonstration, and in so far as it was the more full internally because it was not hindered by external acts; for such they might not do, nor were they necessary, nor did they fall to them.

TO WHOM THE MIXED LIFE IS MOST APPROPRIATE, AND TO WHOM THE CONTEMPLATIVE LIFE IS MOST REWARDING. *CHAPTER 6*

But these men who had prelacies, and others as well who were wholly secular men, had full charity in internal affection and also in external works: and that is properly this mixed life, which consists of both the active life and the contemplative life. And assuredly, for such a man who has the spiritual authority of a prelacy, with care and government over others as prelates and holders of cures have, or in temporal authority like worldly lords and masters are, I consider this mixed life best and most appropriate for them, as long as they are obliged thereto. But for others, who are free and not bound to temporal or spiritual administration, I trust that the contemplative life alone, if they can truly achieve it, is the best and most rewarding, fairest and most expedient, and most fitting for them to undertake and engage in, and not to be left wilfully or for any external acts of the active life, except for great necessity and great relieving and comforting of other men, whether in their bodies or their souls. Then, if need requires, at the prayer and insistence of others, or else at the command of their superiors, I trust that it is good for them to demonstrate outward works of the active life for a time, in assistance of their fellow Christians.

HERE IT IS SHOWN WHICH LIFE IS MOST APPROPRIATE FOR HIM FOR WHOM THIS BOOK WAS MADE. *CHAPTER 7*

By what I have said you may partly understand which is one life and which the other, and which fits best with your status in life. And surely, it seems to me, this mixed life suits you best. For since Our Lord has appointed you and set you in a position of superiority over other men, such as it is, and loaned you an abundance of worldly goods to govern and sustain in particular all those who are under your governance and lordship in your power and your wisdom; and also, additionally, as you have received grace by the mercy of Our Lord to have some knowledge of yourself and of spiritual desire and taste of his love, I trust that this mixed life is the best and most appropriate for you to labour in. And that would be to split your life wisely into two: sometimes for the one, and sometimes for the other. For, know you well, if you abandon the necessary business of the active life, and are reckless and do not look after your worldly goods, how they are cared for and spent, and having no concern for your subjects and your fellow Christians, because of the desire and will that you have to give yourself exclusively to spiritual occupations (believing that you are on that account let off), if you do so, you do not act wisely. What are all your works worth, whether corporal or spiritual, unless they are done justly and rationally, to the honour of God and at his bidding? Assuredly, absolutely nothing.

THAT MEN SHOULD ENGAGE IN THE MIXED LIFE AS A MAN WOULD BEHAVE WITH REGARD TO CHRIST AND HIS LIMBS. *CHAPTER 8*

Then, if you abandon that thing to which you are bound by way of charity, by right and reason, and would wholly give yourself to something else wilfully, as it were, for greater pleasure in God, which you are not fully obligated to, you do not honour him discreetly. You are active to worship his head and face, and dress it fairly and marvelously, but you ignore his body, his arms and his feet, all ragged and torn, and take no care of them. And then you do not honour him: for it is an offence for a man to be wondrously dressed on his head with pearls and precious stones, while all his body is naked and bare as though he were a beggar. Just so it is, spiritually, no honour to God that his head be covered, and his body left bare.

You should understand that Our Lord Jesus Christ as man is head of a spiritual body, which is Holy Church. The limbs of this body are all Christian men. Some are arms, and some are feet, and some are other limbs, according to the various activities they undertake in their lives. Then, if you are busy with all your power to dress his head (that is, to worship him by thinking of his Passion and of his other actions in his manhood by devotion and meditation on him), and forget his feet (which are your children, your servants, your tenants and all your fellow Christians), and allow them to be destroyed for lack of oversight – unclothed, not cared for, and not looked after as they ought to be – you do not please him, you do him no honour. You make yourself kiss his mouth by the devotion of holy prayer, but you tread on his feet and befoul them, in so far as you do not look after them, by your own negligence of that for which you have responsibility. So it seems to me. Nevertheless, if you think this is not the case, because it is a nicer duty to honour his head, by being occupied all day in meditation on his manhood, than to go lower to other works and cleanse his feet (which is to be active both in thought and deed concerning the timely aid of your fellow Christians), I do not think as you do. For assuredly he will give you greater thanks for humble washing of his feet when they are truly foul and stinking to you, than for all the precious painting and decorating that you can produce around his head by thinking of his manhood. For that is beautiful enough, and has not much need to be dressed by you. But his feet and other limbs, which are your subjects and your fellow Christians, are sometimes badly dressed, and have a need to be looked after and aided by you, particularly as you are obligated to do it; and on their behalf he will give you many thanks, if you will humbly and tenderly take care of them. For the more lowly service you do to your Lord for love of him or any of his limbs when need and justice requires it, with a happy and humble heart, the more you please him; thinking that it was sufficient for you to have the least rank and lowest status, since it is his will that it be so. For it seems to me, since he has put you in that position to labour and serve other men, that it is his will that you should fulfil it according to your ability.

THAT SOMETIMES A LORD SHOULD QUIT SPIRITUAL ACTIVITY AND HAPPILY INVOLVE HIMSELF IN REWARDING WORLDLY ACTIVITY. *CHAPTER 9*

I tell you this exemplum, not because you are not doing what I say (for I trust that you do so, and better), but I want you to do this gladly, and not be reluctant sometimes to abandon spiritual occupations and involve yourself with worldly business, by wise preservation and expenditure of your worldly goods, in good governance of your servants and your tenants, and in doing other good deeds to all your fellow Christians according to your power. You should do both types of works at different times with a good will, the one and the other, as you are able. So, if you were at prayer and spiritually occupied, you should after a certain time break off from that, and busily and happily get involved in some physical activity for your fellow Christians. Also, when you have been profitably active outside for a while with your servants or other men, you should break off and return to your prayers and devotion as God gives you grace. And so, by the grace of Our Lord, you shall set aside sloth, idleness and vain relaxation of yourself, which comes in the guise of contemplation and sometimes hinders you from rewarding and expedient involvement in external activity, and you shall always be well occupied, either physically or spiritually.

HOW BY THE EXAMPLE OF JACOB AND HIS TWO WIVES MEN SHOULD REGULATE THEMSELVES PROPERLY IN THE MIXED LIFE. *CHAPTER 10*

If you wish to do well, you should do spiritually as Jacob did physically. Holy writ says that Jacob, when he began to serve his master Laban, coveted to have Rachel, his master's daughter, as his wife, on account of her beauty, and he served to have her. But when he had meant to have her for his wife, he took Leah first, the other daughter, in place of Rachel; and later he took Rachel, and so he had both in the end. By Jacob in holy writ is understood a surmounter of sins. By these two women are understood, as St Gregory says, the two lives in Holy Church: active life and contemplative life. Leah is equivalent to saying 'labouring', and stands for active life; Rachel stands for 'sight of the beginning', that is, God, and symbolises contemplative life. Leah was fruitful, but she had inflamed eyes. Rachel was barren, but she was fair and lovely. So, just as Jacob coveted Rachel for her beauty, but nevertheless did not have her when he intended, but took Leah first, and her afterwards; just so each man, assuredly turned by the grace of compunction from the sins of the world and the flesh towards the service of God and cleanliness of good living, has a great desire and sweet longing to have Rachel (that is, to have calm and spiritual sweetness in devotion and contemplation, for it is so fair and lovely); and in the hope of achieving that life alone, he prepares himself to serve Our Lord God with all his powers. Yet often, when he intended to have had Rachel (that is, quiet in devotion), Our Lord God first caused him to be well tested and belaboured with Leah (that is, either with great temptations of the world or the devil, or else with other worldly business, physical or spiritual, to assist his fellow Christians). And when he is well belaboured by them, and almost overcome, then Our Lord God gives him Rachel (that is, grace of devotion and calm in conscience); and so he has both Rachel and Leah. So you should follow the example of Jacob, take for yourself both of these two lives, active and contemplative, since God has sent both to you, engage in them both, the one and the other. From the life that is active you shall bring forth the fruit of many good deeds by helping your fellow Christians. And by the other life you shall be made fair and bright and clean in beholding supreme brightness (that is, God, the origin of all that is made). And then you shall surely be Jacob, and surmounter and defeater of all sins. And after that, by the grace of God, your name shall be changed, as Jacob's name was changed to Israel. Israel is equivalent to 'a man seeing God'. Then, if you are first

Jacob and engage in these two lives discreetly as time allows, you shall afterwards be Israel, that is, a true contemplative. For either in this life he will deliver you and make you free of the duties and activities to which you are bound, or else after this life do it fully in the bliss of Heaven when you get there.

THAT CONTEMPLATION SHOULD BE ACHIEVED THROUGH DESIRE, AND THE WORKS OF ACTIVE LIFE ENGAGED IN WITHOUT ANGER AND IGNORANT FEAR. *CHAPTER 11*

Contemplative life is fair and rewarding, and therefore you should always desire it. But you shall mostly engage in the active life, for that is necessary and expedient. And therefore, if you are taken from your calm in devotion when you most wanted to be engaged in it, by your children, your servants, or by any of your fellow Christians, do not be angry with them, or cross, or fearful as though God would be angry with you because you abandoned him for something else – for that is not so. But leave your devotion lightly, whether it is prayer or meditation, and go do your duty and service to your fellow Christians, as readily as if Our Lord himself instructed you to do so. And endure humbly for his love without grumbling, if you can, or any unease or worry in your heart because of involvement in such business.

THAT NECESSARY WORLDLY WORKS KINDLE SPIRITUAL DESIRES, PROVED BY REAL EXAMPLE. *CHAPTER 12*

It may sometimes happen that the more troubled you have been outwardly by active works, the greater burning desire you shall have for God, and the clearer perception of spiritual things by grace of Our Lord in devotion when you get to it. For what happens then is as if you had a lighted coal and wished to make a fire with it and make it burn. First you would put sticks to it, and cover the coal, and though it might appear for a time that you would extinguish the coal with sticks, nevertheless when you have waited a while, and after that blown on it a while, there soon springs out a great flame of fire, for the sticks are turned into fire. It is just like that spiritually, with the will and desire you have for God: it is as though they are a little coal of fire in your soul, for they give you something of spiritual heat and spiritual light; but it is very little, for often it grows cold and turns into bodily rest, and sometimes to idleness. Therefore it is good that you put sticks around it, which are the good works of the active life. And if it should appear for a while that these works inhibit your desire so that it is neither as pure or fervent as you would like, do not be overly fearful about it, but wait a while and endure, and go and blow at the fire (that is, first do your deeds), and then go alone to your prayers and meditations, and lift up your heart to God and pray to him of his goodness to accept the deeds you do for his pleasure.

HOW BY HUMILITY AND VARIOUS GOOD WORKS THE LOVE OF GOD IS NOURISHED IN MANY MEN'S HEARTS. *CHAPTER 13*

Consider your works as nothing in your own opinion, but only through his mercy. Humbly know your wretchedness and frailty, and attribute with certainty all your good deeds to him in as much as they are good, and so far as they are bad and not done with all the conditions which are necessary for a good deed for lack of discretion, attribute that to yourself. And because of this humility all your deeds shall change into a flame of fire, like sticks laid on the coal. And so shall the external good deeds not hinder your devotion but rather increase it. Our Lord says thus in holy writ ... 'Fire shall always burn on my altar, and the priest who rises in the morning shall put sticks under it, so that it does not go out.' This fire is love and desire for God in the soul, which love needs to be nourished and preserved by adding sticks to it so that it does not go out. These sticks are of various kinds: some from one tree, some from another. A man who is educated and has understanding of holy writ, if he has this fire of devotion in his heart, it is good for him to gather for himself sticks of holy examples and sayings of Our Lord from reading of holy writ, and feed the fire with them. Another, uneducated, man may not so readily have to hand holy writ and doctors' sayings, and therefore it is necessary for him to do many external good deeds to his fellow Christians and kindle the fire of love through them. And so it is good that each man according to his status does as he is inclined, so that he obtains sticks from one thing or another, whether prayers or good meditations or reading in holy writ, or good physical activity, to feed the desire of love in his soul, so that it is not extinguished. For the emotion of love is fragile, and will lightly vanish away, unless it is well cared for and continually fed by physical or spiritual good deeds.

HOW THE FIRE OF LOVE CONSUMES ALL SIN AND IS A GREAT CRYING IN THE EARS OF GOD. *CHAPTER 14*

Now then, since Our Lord has sent into your heart a little spark of that blessed fire which is himself, as holy writ says – ... 'Our Lord is a consuming fire' – just as physical fire consumes all physical things that may be consumed, even so spiritual fire (which is God) consumes all types of sin wherever it touches (and therefore Our Lord is likened to a consuming fire) – I urge you to feed this fire, which is nothing other than love and charity. This he has sent to earth, as he says in the gospel ... 'I have come to put fire into the earth, and what for, other than that it should burn?' That is: God has sent the fire of love, which is a good desire and a great will to please him, into a man's soul, and for this purpose, that a man should know it and care for it, feed it and strengthen it, and be saved thereby. The greater the desire you have for him, the greater is the fire of love within you. The less this desire, the less the fire. The measure of this desire – how much it is in yourself or in any other – neither you nor any other man knows of himself, but God alone who gives it. And therefore do not prepare yourself to battle with yourself as if you might know how great your desire is, but be active to desire as much as you can, but not to know the amount of your desire. St Augustine says that the life of each good Christian man is a continual desire for God. And that is a great virtue, for it is a great crying in the ears of God; the more you desire, the louder you cry, the better you pray, the wiser you think.

WHAT DESIRE IS, AND SURE SWEETNESS. *CHAPTER 15*

And what is this desire? Assuredly nothing but a loathing in your heart for all this worldly bliss and fleshly delight, and a longing full of pleasure with a trusting yearning for Heavenly joy and endless bliss. This, I think, may be called a desire for God. If you have this desire, as I surely hope you have, I urge you to preserve it well and nourish it wisely; and when you pray or think, make this desire the beginning and end of all your activity. And in order to increase it, care for no other feelings in your senses, nor seek after any other physical sweetness, whether of hearing or taste, or wondrous light, or sight of angels, and even if Our Lord himself should appear physically to you in your sight, count it but little. But that all your activity should be so that you might feel with certainty in your thoughts a loathing and total forsaking of all kinds of sin and impurity, with a spiritual perception of how foul, how ugly and how painful it is; and that you may have a powerful desire for virtues, humility, charity and the bliss of Heaven. This, I think, would be spiritual comfort and spiritual sweetness to a man's soul, like having purity of conscience from the wickedness of all worldly vanities with firm faith, humble hope and complete desire for God. However it may be with other comforts and sweetness, I think that sweetness certain and assured that is felt in purity of conscience by powerful forsaking and loathing of all sin and by inward perception, with fervent desire of spiritual desires. All other comforts or sweetness, or any other type of sensation, unless they help and lead towards this end (that is, purity of conscience and spiritual desire for God) are not sufficiently certain to depend on.

WHAT THE DIFFERENCE IS BETWEEN DESIRE AND LOVE OF GOD. *CHAPTER 16*

But now you ask whether this desire is love of God. On this, I say that this desire is not properly love, but it is a start and taste of love. For love is, properly, the complete joining of the lover and the loved together as God and a soul in one. This coupling may not take place completely in this life, but only in desire and longing for it: just as, when a man loves another who is absent, he greatly desires his presence, to experience his love and affection. In the same way, spiritually, as long as we are in this life, Our Lord is absent from us, so that we can neither see him nor feel him as he is, and therefore we cannot have experience of his love to our full desire. But we may have a desire and great yearning to be present with him, in order to see him in his bliss, and fully to be united with him in love. This desire we may have by his gift in this life, by which we shall be saved, for it is love for him as it may be achieved here. ... St Paul says that 'as long as we are in this body we are pilgrims from Our Lord', that is, we are absent from Heaven in this exile; 'we proceed by faith and not by sight', that is we believe by faith, not by physical sensation; 'we dare, and have a good will to be absent from the body and be present with God', that is, out of purity in conscience and sure faith in salvation we dare desire to be absent from our bodies in physical act and to be present with Our Lord. 'Nevertheless, as we may not yet do it, we strive to please him, whether we are present or absent', and that is, we struggle against sins of the world and delights of the flesh with desire for him, in order to burn in this desire everything that keeps us from him.

HOW OUTWARD WORKS SHOW THIS DESIRE. *CHAPTER 17*

Yet you ask, 'Can a man have this desire continually in his heart?' You think not. On this, I say as I think, that this desire may be attained as far as the virtue and benefit goes as a continual habit, but not in action or experience, as by this example. If you were ill, whatever you did you would have (as each man has) a natural desire for physical health continually in your heart, whether you slept or were awake, but it would not always be the same. For if you sleep, or else when awake think of some worldly things, then you have this desire by habit but not in action. But when you think of your illness and your physical health, then you have it in experience. It is just so spiritually with the desire for God. He who has this desire by the gift of God, though he sleeps or else does not think of God but of worldly things, yet he has this desire in the habit of his soul, until he commits deadly sin. But when he thinks of God or purity of life or the joys of Heaven, then his desire for God is working, as long as he keeps his thought and intention to please God, either in prayer or meditation, or in any good deed of the active life. Then it is good that all our activity should be to encourage this desire and engage in it by discretion, now in one deed and now in another, as we are inclined and have grace to do it.

This desire is the root of all your actions; for know well, whatever the good deed is that you do for God, physical or spiritual, it is a utilisation of this desire; and therefore when you do a good deed, or pray or think of God, do not think in your heart, questioning whether you desire or not, for your deed reveals your desire. Some are ignorant and believe that they do not desire God unless they are always calling on God with words from their mouths, or else by desirous words in their hearts, as if I were to say thus: 'Ah, Lord, bring me to your bliss', 'Lord, make me safe', or suchlike. These words are good whether they are sounded in the mouth or formed in the heart, for they stir a man's heart to desire for God. But nevertheless, without any such words a pure thought of God or of any spiritual thing (like virtues, or the manhood of Christ, or the joys of Heaven), or the understanding of holy writ, with love, may be better than such words. For a pure thought of God is a sure desire for him, and the more spiritual that thought is, the greater is your desire; and therefore do not question or be uncertain when you pray or think of God or else do any external deed for your fellow Christians, whether you desire him or not: for the deed reveals it. Nevertheless, if it should be that all your bodily or spiritual good deeds are demonstrations of your desire for God, there is still a difference between bodily and spiritual deeds. For the acts of the contemplative life are really and by nature the working of this desire, but external deeds are not so, and therefore when you pray or think of God, your desire is more complete, more fervent, and more spiritual, than when you do other deeds for your fellow Christians.

HOW AFTER YOUR SLEEP YOU SHOULD ENLIVEN YOUR HEART WITH PRAYERS AND GOOD THOUGHTS, AND SET ASIDE BAD THOUGHTS WHICH OBSTRUCT DEVOTION. *CHAPTER 18*

Now, if you ask how you can preserve this desire and nourish it, I shall tell you a little, not so that you should always use the format I say, but so that through it you can have, if necessary, some knowledge in order to govern you in your activity. For I may not, and cannot, tell you fully what is always best for you. But I shall tell you something of what I think. At night, after your sleep, if you wish to rise to serve your Lord, you will feel yourself heavy in body at first, and sometimes lustful: then you should prepare yourself to pray and think some good thoughts to enliven your heart towards God, and arrange all your business first so as to draw your thoughts up from worldly vanities and from the vain picturings which fall into your mind, so that you can feel some devotion in speaking, or else, if you want to think of spiritual things, so that you shall not be much obstructed by such vain thoughts of the world and the flesh in your thinking. There are many ways of thinking; which is best for you I cannot say; but I trust that the thought in which you feel most pleasure and most peace at the time is the best for you.

HOW ORGANISED THOUGHT OF YOUR OWN SIN AND OTHER MEN'S NOURISHES YOUR DESIRE FOR GOD. *CHAPTER 19*

You may, if you wish, sometimes think of your sins previously committed, and of the frailty into which you fall every day, and ask for mercy and forgiveness for them. Also, after this, you may think of the sins and wretchedness in body and in spirit of your fellow Christians, having pity and compassion for them, and cry for mercy and forgiveness for them as tenderly as if they were your own. And that is a good thought, for I tell you for sure that you can make other men's sins a precious ointment with which to heal your own soul, when you have them in mind. This ointment is precious in itself, although the ingredients are not pure in themselves, for it is a syrup made of venom in order to destroy venom (that is to say your own sins and other men's brought to your mind as well); if you grind them with the sorrow of your heart and pity and compassion, they turn into a syrup which makes your soul whole against pride and envy, and brings love and charity to your fellow Christians. This is a good thought to have sometimes.

THAT MANY THOUGHTS OF THE MANHOOD OF OUR LORD, DISCREETLY UNDERTAKEN, NOURISH THE DESIRE FOR GOD. *CHAPTER 20*

Also you should have in mind the manhood of Our Lord, at his birth, or at his Passion, or in any of his works, and feed your thoughts with spiritual depiction of it, in order to incite your emotions to greater love of him. Such thought is good, and particularly when it comes freely of God's gift with devotion and fervour of the spirit. For if a man cannot easily have delight or devotion in it, I do not consider it expedient then for a man to exert himself too much about it so that he might obtain it by mastery; for he shall the more break his head, but never be the nearer. Therefore I think that for you it is good to have his manhood in mind sometimes, and if delight and devotion come as well, maintain it and follow it through for a while, but leave off soon, and do not hold on to it for too long. Also, if devotion does not come with thinking of the Passion, do not strive too much after it; take easily what comes, and move on to some other thought.

THAT THOUGHTS OF MANY VIRTUES NOURISH YOUR DESIRE FOR GOD. *CHAPTER 21*

Also, there are other thoughts which are more spiritual, like thinking of virtues, and seeing by the light of understanding what the virtue of humility is, and how a man should be humble; and also what are patience and purity, righteousness, chastity and sobriety, and suchlike, and how a man may obtain these virtues; and by such thoughts to have great desire and longing for these virtues in order to achieve them; and also to have a spiritual vision of the three principal virtues of faith, hope and charity. By the sight of and desire for these virtues a soul would feel even greater comfort if he had grace from Our Lord, without which grace a man's thought is half blind, lacking the taste of spiritual sweetness.

THAT THOUGHT OF VARIOUS SAINTS AND THEIR VIRTUES NOURISHES YOUR LOVE FOR GOD. *CHAPTER 22*

Also, think of the saints of Our Lord, such as apostles, martyrs, confessors, and holy virgins; inwardly behold their holy living, the grace and the virtues that Our Lord gave them while living here; and by this recollection stir your own heart to take them as examples for better living. And also have recollection of Our Lady St Mary above all other saints; in order to see with spiritual eyes the abundance of grace in her holy soul when she was living here, which Our Lord gave to her alone, surpassing all other creatures; for in her was the fullness of all virtues without stain of sin. She had complete humility and perfect charity, and with these the beauty of all other virtues in full, so completely that there could be no incitement of pride, envy, wrath or fleshly delight, nor could any kind of sin enter into her heart or defoul her soul in any part. The beholding of the fairness of this blessed soul should greatly stir a man's heart towards spiritual comfort; and much more, then, in excess of this the thought of the soul of Our Lord Jesus, which was fully united to the Godhead, incomparably surpassing Our Lady and all other creatures. For in the person of Our Lord Jesus there are two natures: that is, God and man, fully united together. By virtue of this blessed union, which may not be described or conceived by human intelligence, the soul of Jesus received the fullness of wisdom and love and all goodness. As the apostle says, ... the Godhead was fully united to the manhood in the soul of Jesus, just as the soul dwells in the body. To have the recollection of the manhood of Our Lord in this manner is to behold the virtues and surpassing grace of the soul of Jesus, and that would be comforting to a man's soul. So also the recollection of the power, the wisdom, and the goodness of Our Lord to all his creatures; for in as much as we cannot see God fully as himself while living here, therefore we should behold him, love him and fear him, and be amazed at his power, his wisdom and his goodness, in his acts and in his creations.

THAT THE THOUGHT OF THE MERCY OF OUR LORD, SHOWED TO SINFUL MEN, NOURISHES YOUR DESIRE FOR GOD. *CHAPTER 23*

Also, think of the mercy of Our Lord, which he has shown to you and me and all sinful knaves who are burdened with sin, locked so long in the devil's prison; how Our Lord endured us patiently in our sin and took no vengeance against us, as he might justly have done and thrown us into hell, if his mercy had not prevented him. But out of love he spared us, he took pity on us, and sent his grace into our hearts and called us out of our sin, and by his grace has turned our wills wholly to him, for love of him to forsake all types of sin. The remembrance of his mercy and his goodness, with other considerations more than I can or may recite now, brings into the soul great trust in Our Lord and full hope of salvation, and powerfully kindles the desire of love for the joys of heaven.

THAT THOUGHT OF THE WRETCHEDNESS OF MEN AND THE JOYS OF HEAVEN NOURISHES YOUR DESIRE FOR GOD. *CHAPTER 24*

Also, think of the wretchedness, the misfortunes, and the physical and spiritual dangers which occur in this life; and after that think of the joys of Heaven, how much bliss there is, and how much joy. For there is no sin, nor sorrow, nor passion, nor pain, nor hunger, nor thirst, sores or sickness, doubt or fear, shame or disgrace, no failing of strength, no lack of light, no want of will-power; but there is supreme beauty, lightness, strength, freedom, health, delight everlasting, wisdom, love, peace, honour, security, calm, joy and bliss enough without end. The more you think of and feel the wretchedness of this life, the more fervently you shall desire the joy and the calm of the bliss of Heaven.

HOW THE DESIRE FOR WORLDLY HONOUR AND THE DESIRE FOR HEAVEN IS REWARDED AT THE FINAL END. *CHAPTER 25*

Many men are covetous for worldly honour and earthly riches, and think night and day, sleeping and waking, how and by what means they might achieve them, and forget to consider themselves, and the pains of Hell and the joys of Heaven. Surely they are not wise, they are like the children who run after a butterfly, and because they do not watch their feet, sometimes fall and break their legs. What is all the pomp of this world, its richness and enjoyment, but a butterfly? Surely, nothing more, and much less. Therefore I urge you, be covetous of the joys of Heaven, and you shall have honour and riches which shall last for ever. For at the last end, when worldly covetous men weaken, they bring nothing in their hands, for all their honours and riches are transformed into nothing but sorrow and pain. Then all men covetous for Heaven who have truly forsaken all vain honours of this world (or else, if they have honours and riches, they do not put their delight and their love in them, but in fear, humility, hope, and sometimes sorrow, they patiently await the mercy of God), shall have in full that which they coveted, for they shall then be crowned like kings and established with Our Lord Jesus in the bliss of Heaven.

HOW DISCRETION IS NECESSARY IN THINKING AND PRAYING, AND HOW SOMETIMES ONE SHOULD PASS FROM ONE TO THE OTHER. *CHAPTER 26*

Also, there are many other meditations, more than I can say, which Our Lord places in a man's mind in order to incite the emotions and reasoning of the soul to loathe the vanities of this world and desire the joys of Heaven. I do not say these words to you as though I had fully revealed the types of meditation as they are in a man's soul; but I touch on them a little so that you may by this little understand the more. I do not think it is good for you if, when you incline yourself to think of God as I have said before or in any other way, your heart is dark and murky, and you feel neither in mind, nor delight, nor devotion in order to think, but only a rude desire and weak wish that you would like to think of God but cannot. Then I think that it is not good for you to battle too much with yourself, as if you could overcome yourself by your own power, for you might thereby easily fall into greater darkness, unless you were prudent in your actions. And therefore I consider it then most secure for you to say your *Our Father* or *Ave*, or else your mattins, or to read your Psalter, for that is an even more secure standard and will not fail: whoever will stick by it will not err. And if you can by praying obtain devotion, then, if this devotion is only in the emotions (that is in a great desire for God with spiritual delight), carry on with your speaking. Do not break off lightly, for it often happens that praying with the mouth produces and maintains the fervour of devotion, and if a man stops speaking devotion vanishes away. Nevertheless, if devotion in prayer brings a spiritual thought into your heart of the manhood of Our Lord, or of anything else described before, and this thought would be hindered by your speaking, they you may stop speaking and occupy yourself in meditation, until it passes away.

HOW A MAN SHALL COMPORT HIMSELF IN THINKING OF THE PASSION OF OUR LORD JESUS; WHILE DEVOTION LASTS AND WHEN IT PASSES AWAY. *CHAPTER 27*

But it is incumbent on you to be cautious about certain things in your meditation. I will tell you some of them. One is: when you have had a spiritual thought (either in picturing the manhood of Our Lord, or such other physical things) and your soul has been fed and comforted with it, and it passes away by itself, do not be over-anxious to keep hold of it by control, for then it shall convert you into pain and bitterness. Also, if it does not pass away, but stays in your mind with belabouring of yourself, and because of the comfort you get from it you will not abandon it, so that because of this it keeps you from sleep at night or else from other good deeds during the day, this is not good, and you should consciously break away when the time requires.

Indeed, sometimes when you have most devotion and are most reluctant to quit it (like when it lasts beyond a reasonable time, or else if it turns into any discomfort for your fellow Christians), unless you do do so you do not act wisely, or so I think. For a secular man or woman who, as it happens, feels devotion but twice in a year, if they feel by the grace of Our Lord great compunction for their sins, or else have recollection of the passion of Our Lord, even if it keeps them from their sleep and rest a night or two or three until their head aches, that is of no importance, because it occurs to them but rarely. But to you, or to another man who customarily has this kind of experience, as it were every other day, it is expedient to have discretion in your actions, not to pursue it fully as often as it may come. And I hold that it is good for you to employ this approach whatever devotion you are in, so that you do not stick with it so long that it either keeps you from your food or your sleep when due, or discomforts anyone else unwisely. ... Everything has its time.

HOW A MAN SHALL BEAR HIMSELF CAREFULLY IN THOUGHT AND DESIRE, AND WISELY USE THE GRACE WHICH GOD HAS GIVEN HIM. *CHAPTER 28*

There is something else which it is incumbent on you to be cautious about. If your thought is occupied in picturing the manhood of Our Lord or anything like it, and after that you are busy with all the desire in your heart to seek greater spiritual awareness and contact with the Godhead, do not press after it too much, nor allow your heart to fail from the desire as if you were waiting or eager for some unusual incitement, or some amazing feeling beyond what you had had. You shall not do so. It is enough for you, and for me, to have desire and longing for Our Lord, and if he will of his grace or his desire send us his spiritual enlightenment and open our spiritual eyes to see and know more of him than we have had previously by our usual labours, we should thank him for it; and if he will not do so, because we are not humble enough, or else are not prepared by purity of living on other accounts to receive his grace, then we should meekly acknowledge our own sins and our wretchedness, and consider ourselves satisfied with the desire which we have for him, and with our usual thoughts which easily come into our imaginations, such as our sins, Christ's Passion, or suchlike; or else with prayers from the Psalter, or something else, and love him with all our hearts because he gives us that. If you do otherwise, you may easily be beguiled by the spirit of error, for it is presumption that a man should by his own wit press too much towards knowledge of spiritual things, unless he is filled full of grace. For the wise man says ... 'He who investigates the power and the majesty without great purity and humility shall be suffocated and oppressed by himself.'

And therefore the wise man says in another place in this manner: ... 'Do not seek high things that are beyond your wits and your reasoning, and do not look into great things that are beyond your power.' By these words the wise man does not utterly forbid seeking for and investigating spiritual and Heavenly things, but he does forbid us that as long as we are fleshly and not cleansed from vain love of the world, we should not take it upon ourselves by our own labours or by our own intelligence to look into or feel spiritual things. For even though we feel spiritual things and great fervour of the love of God, so much so that we treat all earthly things as nothing and think that we would, for God's sake, abandon all the joys and all the wealth of this world, yet we are still not able and prepared to seek and behold spiritual things which are beyond us, until our souls are made supple, and until they are made sober and fixed in virtues by the process of time and the increase of grace. For as St Gregory says, no man is suddenly made supreme in grace, but he starts with a little and by progression increases until he becomes perfect. Amen.

HERE ENDS *THE MIXED LIFE*

12. *The Book of the Craft of Dying* [From C. Horstman, ed., *Yorkshire Writers: Richard Rolle of Hampole and his Followers*, 2 vols., London, 1895–6, II, pp. 406–20; in English]

HERE BEGINS THE BOOK OF THE CRAFT OF DYING

Because the passage of death out of the wretchedness of the exile of this world seems extremely hard and very perilous and also very terrifying and horrible not only to ordinary people but also to those in religion and devout people, on account of their lack of knowledge of death; therefore, in this present work and treatise, which deals with the art of dying, there is set out and contained a short form of exhortation to instruct and comfort those who are on the point of death. This form of exhortation ought to be considered subtly, noted and understood to the eyes of men's souls, for doubtless it is and may be profitable to all Christian men and women in general to have the art and knowledge of how to die well.

This work and treatise contains six parts: The first deals with the commendation of death, and knowing how to die well. The second contains the temptations of dying men. The third contains the questions to be asked of those on their deathbeds, while they may speak and understand. The fourth contains a statement with certain warnings for those who are dying. The fifth contains instructions for those who are dying. The sixth contains prayers to be said for those who are dying by those people who are about them.

CHAPTER 1. ... OF THE COMMENDATION OF DEATH, AND OF KNOWLEDGE HOW TO DIE WELL

Though bodily death is the most dreadful of all terrifying things, as the philosopher [Aristotle] says in the 3rd book of Ethics, yet spiritual death of the soul is as much more horrible and detestable as the soul is more worthy and precious than the body. As the prophet David says ... 'The death of a sinful man is the worst of all deaths.' But as the same prophet testifies: ... 'The death of good men is always precious in the sight of God, regardless of the manner of their bodily deaths.' And you should understand as well that not merely the deaths of holy martyrs are so precious, but also the deaths of all other righteous and good Christian men. And furthermore, without doubt the deaths of all sinful men, no matter how long, how wicked and how accursed they may have been during their lives before their last ends, if they die in a state of true repentance and contrition, and in the true faith and unity and charity of Holy Church, are acceptable and precious in the sight of God, as St John says in the Apocalypse: ... 'Blessed be all dead men that die in God.' And therefore God says in the 4th chapter of the Book of Wisdom: ... 'A righteous man, even if he be hurriedly' or quickly and suddenly 'dead, shall receive a place of refreshment.' And so shall every man who dies, if he manages to keep himself firm, and govern himself wisely in the temptations he shall have in the agony (or strife) of his death, as shall be recounted later. And therefore, for the commendation of the deaths of good men only, a wise man says thus: 'Death is nothing other than a release from prison, and the ending of exile, the discharging of a heavy burden (that is, the body), the termination of all infirmities, escape from all perils, destruction of all evil things, breaking of all bonds, payment of the debt of natural duty, return to the homeland, and entrance into bliss and joy.' And therefore it is said in the 7th chapter of Ecclesiastes: ... 'The day of a man's death is better than the day of his birth' – but this should be understood to apply only to the good men and the chosen people of God, for to evil and reprobate men neither the day of their birth nor the day of their death may be called good. And therefore every good, perfect Christian man, as well as every other man, even if imperfect and lately converted from sin, as long as he is truly contrite and believes in God, should not be saddened or troubled, nor dread the death of his body, no matter what form it takes and whatever the reason he shall suffer it, but he should take his death gladly and willingly, with the reasoning in his mind that rules his sensualities, and suffer it patiently, conforming and submitting his will to God's will and disposition alone, if he wishes to depart from here and die well and safely, as the wise man testifies, saying thus: ... 'To die well is to die gladly and willingly.' And therefore he adds to that and says ... 'It is not many days nor many years which cause me to say and feel that I have lived long enough, but only the rational will of my heart and soul.' Since, beyond that, by duty and by natural right all men must surely die, and almighty God wills when, how, and where. And God's will is above all good in all things, good, just, and righteous (for as John Cassian says in his collations: 'Almighty God of his wisdom and goodness disposes all things that happen, both profit and adversity, for our profit and for what is best for us, and is more careful and concerned about the health and salvation of his chosen children than we ourselves can or may be').

And since (as is aforesaid) we cannot in any manner either flee, escape or change the inevitable (or unavoidable) necessity and journey of death, therefore we ought to accept our deaths when God wills, willingly and gladly, without grumbling or fighting against it, by having the power and strength of our soul's will, virtuously disposed and ruled by reason and true discretion, even though the lewd sensuality and the frailty of our flesh will naturally complain or fight against it. Of this Seneca speaks thus: ... 'Suffer calmly, and do not complain about what you cannot change or avoid'; and the same clerk adds, saying: ... 'If you would escape that in which you are tightly trapped, you would need not to be in another place, but to be another person.'

Furthermore, in order for a Christian man to die well and soundly, he must know how to die; and as a wise man says, ... 'To know how to die is to have a heart and soul always ready to go up towards God, so that whenever death comes, he may be found prepared, and without any drawing back or withdrawing receive him ⌜death⌝ as a man would receive his well beloved and trusted friend and fellow whom he had long awaited and looked out for.' This knowledge is the most profitable knowledge of all; and for that knowledge men in religion (more especially than all others, and every day continually) should study more diligently than other men so that they might learn it, precisely because the state of religion demands and requires it more of them than of others, notwithstanding that every secular man, whether cleric or layman, whether ready to die or not, must nevertheless die when God wills. Therefore every man (and not only the religious, but every good and devout Christian man who desires to die well and soundly) ought to live in that manner, and so comport himself all the time that he may safely die at whatever hour God wills, and so he should pass his life in patience, and his death in desire, as St Paul put it when he said: ... 'I desire and covet to be dead and be with Christ.' And this much is sufficient at this time to be said shortly on the craft of dying.

THE SECOND CHAPTER DEALS WITH THE TEMPTATIONS OF DYING MEN. *CHAPTER 2*

Everyone should know without doubting that dying men in their last sickness and end experience the greatest and most grievous temptations, the like of which they never had before in all their lives; and of these temptations there are five main ones.

The first is of the faith; for as much as faith is the foundation of the well-being of a man's soul. So testifies the apostle who says ... 'No man may lay any other foundation.' And therefore St Augustine says: ... 'Faith is the foundation of all goodness, and the beginning of man's health'; and therefore St Paul says: ... 'It is impossible to please God without faith'; and St John says: ... 'He who does not believe is already judged.' And in so far as there is so much and so great strength in faith that without it no man may be saved, on this account the devil with all his might is busy to turn a man totally away from the faith in his last end, or if he may not do that, he labours busily to make him doubt it or draw him somewhat out of the way, or deceive him with some kind of superstitious and false errors or heresies. But every good Christian man is bound by nature – that is to say, as a habit, although he may not in fact and in the intellect understand them – to believe and give full faith and credence not only to the principal articles of the faith but also to all holy writ in all kinds of things, and fully to obey the statutes of the Roman Church, and firmly live and die in them. For as soon as he begins to err and doubt in any of them, at that point he departs from the way of life and his soul's health. But know well, without doubt, that in this temptation, and all others that follow after, the devil may not annoy you or prevail against any man in any way as long as he has the use of his free will and a well-disposed reason, unless he willingly consents to that temptation. And therefore no true Christian man ought to fear any of his illusions, or his false persuasions, or his feigned frights or terrors, for Christ himself said in the gospel: ... 'The devil is a liar and father of all lies'; but therefore live uprightly, and strongly, and steadfastly, and persevere and die in the true faith and unity and obedience of our Holy Mother Church. And it is highly profitable and good, as is the custom in some religious orders, when a man is in his agony or struggle of death, often to say the Creed before him in a loud voice, so that he who is sick may be fortified in the firmness of the faith, and that the demons who cannot bear to hear it may be expelled and driven away from him. And so the stability of the true faith should strengthen a sick man, especially the stable faith of our holy fathers Abraham, Isaac and Jacob, the continuously abiding faith of Job, of the woman Rachab, and Achior and suchlike, and also the faith of the apostles, and of innumerable martyrs, confessors and virgins. For by the faith all those who lived in earlier times before ours, and all those who are now, and who shall be hereafter, all please and did and shall please God by faith; for as was said before, without faith it is impossible to please God. Also, the double benefits should induce every sick man to be firm in faith. The first is, because faith may do all things (as Our Lord himself witnesses in the gospel when he says: ... 'All things are possible to him who believes steadfastly'). The second is, because true faith gains all things for a person, as Our Lord says ... 'Whatever thing you wish to pray and ask for, believe in truth that you shall receive it and you shall have it, even if you should say to a hill that it should lift itself up and fall into the sea' – as the hills of Caspia were closed together by the prayer and petition of King Alexander, the great conqueror.

The second temptation is despair, which is contrary to hope and the confidence that every good man ought to have in God. For when a sick man is sorely tormented, and vexed with sorrow and bodily sickness, then the devil is at his most active to add (or stack up) sorrow on sorrow, putting forward his sins as objections against him in all the ways he can so as to lead him into despair. Furthermore, as Pope Innocent says in his 3rd book of *The Misery of Human Nature*: 'Every man, both good and evil, before his soul passes out of his body, sees Christ put on the cross to the consolation of the good man and the confusion of the evil, making him ashamed that he has lost the fruit of his redemption.' Also, the devil particularly recalls to the mind of a man on the point of death those sins which he had committed and had not been absolved of, thereby to draw him into despair. But no one ought to despair because of that in any way; for even though any one man or woman might have done as many thefts or manslaughters or as many other sins as there are drops of water in the sea or gravel stones on the shore, and even if he had never done penance for them before and never been shriven of them, and at that point would have no opportunity to be shriven of them on account of sickness or speechlessness or lack of time, yet he should never despair; for in that case true internal contrition of the heart, with the determination to be shriven if there was enough time, is sufficient and acceptable to God to save him everlastingly; as the prophet testifies in the psalm: ... 'Lord God, you will never despise a contrite and humble heart.' And Ezekiel says also: ... 'At whatever hour the sinful man is inwardly sorry and turned away from his sin, he shall be saved.' And therefore St Bernard says: 'The pity and the mercy of God is greater than any wickedness'; and Augustine upon John says: 'We should never lose hope for any man as long as he is physically alive, for there is no sin so great that it may not be healed, except for despair alone.' And St Augustine says also: 'All the sins that a man has done before may not accuse or damn a man, if he has offered proper satisfaction in his heart for having done them'. Therefore no man ought to despair even if it was like that, and it was possible that he alone had committed all the types of sins that might be committed in this world; for by despairing a man achieves no more than to offend God much more by it, and all his other sins become the more grievous in God's sight, and everlasting pain is thereby infinitely increased for him who so despairs. Therefore, against despair, and to lead him who is sick and approaching death towards the true trust and confidence that he ought chiefly to have in God at that time, the arrangement of Christ on the cross ought greatly to attract him, concerning which St Bernard says thus: 'What man is there who could not be ravished and drawn to hope and have full confidence in God, if he diligently takes note of the arrangement of Christ's body on the cross? Take note and see his head bowed to greet you, his mouth to kiss you, his arms spread to clasp you, his hands trembling to hold you, his side open to love you, his body stretched taut to give himself wholly to you.' Therefore no one should lose hope of forgiveness, but have complete trust and confidence in God; for the virtue of trust is greatly to be commended, and of great merit with

God, as the apostle says in exhorting us: ... 'Do not lose your trust and confidence in God, which gains great reward from God.' Furthermore, we have a clear illustration that no sinful man should lose hope in any way (regardless of how greatly he had sinned, or how wickedly, or how frequently, or how long he had continued in it) in Peter who denied Christ, in Paul who persecuted Holy Church, in Matthew and Zacharias the publicans, in the sinful woman Mary Magdalene, in the woman who was taken in adultery, in the thief who hung on the cross alongside Christ, in Mary the Egyptian, and innumerable other grievous and great sinners.

The third temptation is lack of patience, which is contrary to the charity by which we are required to love God above all things. For those who are in sickness on their deathbeds suffer exceedingly great pain, sorrow and sadness, particularly those who do not die naturally and as a result of age (which happens quite rarely as clear experience shows every day to everyone), but who often die from accidental sickness such as a fever, a tumour and such other grievous, painful and long illnesses. These make men (and especially those who are not prepared to die, and die unwillingly, and lack true charity) so impatient and complaining that sometimes on account of their sorrow and impatience they become mad and witless, as has often been seen in many men. And it is clear and certain that those who die in this way fail, and lack true charity, as testifies St Jerome, who says thus: ... 'Whoever accepts sickness or death with sorrow and displeasure of heart, it is an overt sign that he does not love God enough.' Therefore, if a man wishes to die well, it is necessary for him not to complain in any way of the sickness that assails him before his death or at his dying, be it never so painful or grievous, of long or short duration. For, as St Gregory testifies in his *Moralia*: ... 'All things that we suffer we suffer justly', and therefore we would be unjust to complain about what we justly suffer. So everyone should be patient, for as St Luke says, ... 'In your patience you should possess your souls', for as by patience many men's souls are truly won and preserved, so by impatience and murmuring they are lost and damned, as witness St Gregory in his homily that says this: ... 'None shall receive the kingdom of Heaven who grumbles and is impatient, and none who have it shall grumble.' But as the great clerk Albert says, speaking of true contrition: 'If a truly contrite man submits himself gladly to all sorts of afflictions of illness and punishment of his sins, so that he may thereby worthily satisfy God for his offences'; much more, then, should every sick man suffer patiently and gladly his own sickness on his own, which is incomparably lighter than many illnesses that other men suffer; especially as the sickness before a man's death is like Purgatory to him when it is endured as it ought to be (by which should be understood, if it be endured patiently and gladly, with a free natural will of the heart). For as the same clerk, Albert, says: 'We need to have a free natural will towards God not only in those things which are for our consolation, but also in those things which are for our affliction.' And St Gregory says: ... 'It is arranged by the dispensation and just ordinance of God that the longer sickness is ordained for the longer sin.' And therefore let every sick man (and particularly he who is dying) say as St Augustine did to God: ... 'Cut here, burn here, so that you spare me everlastingly.' And St Gregory says: ... 'The merciful God gives temporal punishment to his chosen children here, lest he take everlasting vengeance elsewhere.' This temptation of impatience fights against charity, and without charity no one can be saved. And therefore, as St Paul says: ... 'True charity is patient and endures all things.' And in these words it should particularly be noted that he spoke of enduring all things, and excluded nothing: so, logically, all bodily sickness ought to be endured patiently without murmuring or difficulty. And therefore St Augustine says: ... 'To him who loves, nothing is hard, nothing impossible.'

The fourth temptation is complacency, or the delight that a man takes in himself, which is spiritual pride, with which the devil tempts and vexes most religious, and devout and perfect men. For when the devil sees that he cannot draw a man out of the faith, nor lead him into despair, nor into impatience, then he assails him with self-complacency, putting this kind of temptation into his heart: 'O, how firm you are in the faith, how strong in hope, how steady in patience!'; 'O, how many good deeds you have done!'; and other such thoughts. But against these temptations Isidore speaks thus: ... 'Do not boast, or bear yourself proudly, or make much of yourself wantonly, or attribute any goodness to yourself.' For a man may have so much delight in this kind of self-complacency that he might be damned everlastingly for it. And therefore St Gregory says: ... 'A man who considers the good deeds he has done, and on account of them is proud of himself, he shortly falls down for that before him who is the author of humility.' And therefore he who is dying must take care when he feels himself tempted by pride, so that he then abases and humbles himself, thinking of his sins, and that he never knows whether he merits love or hate (that is to say, salvation or damnation). Nevertheless, lest he despair, he should lift up his heart to God in trust, thinking and firmly recalling that the mercy of God surpasses all things and all his works; and that God, who is true in all his words, and is the truth and righteousness which neither beguiles nor is beguiled, vowed and swore by himself, and said by the prophet, ... 'God almighty says: By my life, I do not desire the death or damnation of any sinner or any sinful man, but rather that he turn himself to me, and be saved.' Everyone ought to copy St Anthony, to whom the devil said: 'Anthony, you have defeated me, for when I would raise you up with pride, you keep yourself abased with humility; and when I would drag you down in desperation, you keep yourself up by hope' – so should everyone do, both sick and healthy; and then the devil is defeated.

The fifth temptation that tempts and grieves most carnal men and secular men is excessive concern and anxiety about external temporal things, such as their wives, their children, their friends and worldly riches and other things that they have earlier loved inordinately. For he who will die well and soundly must totally and completely put all temporal and external things out of his mind, and fully commit himself to God. And therefore the great clerk Duns Scotus says this, in the 4th book of Sentences: 'Any sick man, when he sees that he shall die, if he sets his mind to it to die willingly and consents to his death as completely as if he had voluntarily chosen the pain of the death for himself and so endures death patiently, offers satisfaction to God for all his venial sins; and furthermore he removes some of the satisfaction that he owes for his deadly sins.' And therefore it is very profitable and necessary in such a time of need that a man should conform his will to God's will in all things, as everyone ought, both sick and well. But it seldom happens that a secular or carnal man (or man of religion either) will dispose himself for death, or beyond that (which is worse) hear anything about the fact of death (even though he is indeed moving quickly towards his end), hoping that he shall escape death – and that is the most dangerous and inconsistent thing that any Christian person can do, as the worthy clerk the Chanter of Paris [i.e. Peter the Chanter, d. 1197] says.

But it should be noted well that in all the above temptations the devil can compel no one, nor in any wise prevail on him to consent to them, as long as the man retains the use of his reason, unless he willingly consents to them – and that every good Christian man, and every sinful man as well (be he never so great a sinner) ought to beware of all the above things. For the apostle says: ... 'God ... is true, and will not allow you to be tempted more than you can bear; but he will give you such support in your temptations that you can withstand them.' On this the gloss says: 'God is true in his promises, and gives us grace to overcome powerfully, uprightly and with perseverance: giving us strength so that we shall not be defeated, grace to gain merit, steadfastness to overcome.' With those he gives such an increase in virtue that we may endure, and neither falter nor fall. And that is through humility; for as St Augustine says: 'They do not break in the furnace who do not have the wind of pride.' Therefore every man, the just and the sinful, should submit himself completely into the mighty hand of God; and so with his aid he shall surely obtain and gain the victory against all forms of temptations, sickness and tribulations, evils and sorrows, and death as well.

THE THIRD CHAPTER CONTAINS THE QUESTIONS TO BE ASKED OF THOSE ON THEIR DEATHBEDS WHILE THEY MAY SPEAK AND UNDERSTAND. *CHAPTER 3*

Now follow the questions to be asked of those approaching death while they retain their reason and ability to speak, so that if anyone is not fully reconciled to dying, he may be the better informed and comforted about it. And as Anselm the bishop teaches, these questions should be put to those in that situation.

First ask him this: 'Brother, are you glad that you will die in the faith of Christ?' The sick man says: 'Yes.'

'Do you acknowledge that you have not done as well as you might have done?' He answers: 'Yes.'

'Do you repent of that?' He answers: 'Yes.'

'Have you a will to amend, if you had the time and the life?' He answers: 'Yes.'

'Do you fully believe that Our Lord Jesus Christ, God's son, died for you?' He answers: 'Yes.'

'Do you thank him for that with all your heart?' He answers: 'Yes.'

'Do you truly believe that you cannot be saved, except through Christ's death and Passion?' He answers: 'Yes.'

'Then thank him always for that while the soul is in the body, and put all your trust in his Passion and in his death alone, placing trust in nothing else; commit yourself fully to this death, clothe yourself completely with this death, wrap yourself totally in this death; and if it enters your mind, or be put into your mind by your enemy, that God will condemn you, say thus: "Lord, I lay the death of Our Lord Jesus Christ between me and my evil deeds, between me and your judgment; I will not struggle against you in any way." If he says that you have deserved damnation, then say again: "I lay the death of Our Lord Jesus Christ between me and all my evil deserts, and offer the merit of his worthy passion in place of the merit which I would like to have had, but which alas I do not have." Say also: "Lord, place the death of Our Lord Jesus Christ between me and your righteousness."'

Then let him say this three times: ... 'Into your hands I commend my soul'; and let the convent say the same; and if he cannot speak let the convent or bystanders say this: ... 'Into your hands, Lord, we commend his spirit (or his soul).' And so he will surely die, but he shall not die everlastingly.

Yet although the above questions are appropriate and sufficient for the religious, and for devout people, nevertheless all Christian men (both seculars and religious) ought, according to that doctor and noble clerk the Chancellor of Paris [i.e. Jean Gerson, d. 1429] to be examined, questioned and taught at their last end more certainly and clearly regarding the state and well-being of their souls; and first thus: 'Do you believe first of all and fully in the articles of the faith; and also all holy scripture in all matters according to the exposition of the holy and true doctors of Holy Church; and do you forsake all heresies, errors and opinions condemned by the Church, and are you happy to die in the faith of Christ and in the unity and obedience of Holy Church?'

The second question shall be this: 'Do you acknowledge that you have often and in many and varied ways grievously offended your Lord God who made you out of nothing?' (For St Bernard says thus on the Song of Songs: 'I know well that there is no man who can be saved unless he knows himself, from which knowledge there grows in a man the mother of his health, which is humility, and also the fear of God; and that fear, just as it is the beginning of wisdom, so it is the beginning of the health of man's soul.')

The third question shall be this: 'Are you repentant at heart for all the types of sin which you have committed against the high majesty and the love and goodness of God, and for all the goodness which you might have done but did not, and for all the graces that you have forgone; not just on account of fear of death or any other pain but rather more out of the love for God and righteousness and because you have displeased his great goodness and kindness, and on account of the due order of charity by which we are obliged to love god above all things; and for all these things do you ask God for forgiveness? Do you desire in your heart also to have true knowledge of all the offences you have done against God, and forgotten, to have special repentance for them all?'

The fourth question shall be this: 'Do you truly intend and actually have a full will to amend yourself, and (if you should live longer) never knowingly and with your will commit deadly sin any more but, rather than offend God in a mortal manner any more, willingly abandon and lose all earthly things (regardless of how dear they are to you), and even the life of your body as well; and furthermore do you pray God to give you grace to continue in this intention?'

The fifth question shall be this: 'Do you forgive all those men who have ever done you any wrong or grievance up to this point, either in word or in deed, for the love of Our Lord Jesus Christ from who you trust to receive forgiveness for yourself; and do you ask forgiveness for yourself from all those whom you have offended in any kind of way?'

The sixth question shall be this: 'Will you have whatever kind of thing that you have wrongly acquired in any way whatsoever returned in full, as much as you are able and are obliged to, in accordance with the value of your possessions, and rather leave and abandon all your worldly goods, if you can make due satisfaction in no other way?'

The seventh question shall be this: 'Do you fully believe that Christ died for you, and that you can never be saved but by the merit of Christ's passion; and do you thank God for that in your heart as much as you can or are able?'

Whoever can truly, with a truly good conscience and in truth without any dissembling, answer you on these aforesaid seven questions, he shall truly be saved, and has a clear enough indication of the health of his soul, so that, if he dies soon after, he shall be among the number of those who are to be saved. Because there are very few who have knowledge of this art of dying, whoever is not asked these seven questions by another person when he is in peril of death, must recollect himself in his soul and ask himself, and subtly feel and consider whether he is so disposed as is set out above or not; for unless a man be ultimately reconciled in that manner, then without doubt no man may be saved everlastingly. And any man who is disposed as set out above, should commend and commit himself altogether completely to the Passion of Christ. And let him constantly recollect himself, as much as he can and as his sickness will permit, and think of the Passion of Christ; for by that most of all are the devil's temptations and wiles overcome and expelled.

THE FOURTH CHAPTER CONTAINS AN INSTRUCTION, WITH CERTAIN OBSERVATIONS, FOR THOSE WHO ARE DYING. *CHAPTER 4*

Furthermore, for as much as St Gregory says: 'every action of Christ is for our instruction and teaching', therefore, every man according to his knowledge and abilities should do the same things as Christ did whilst dying on the cross. And Christ did five things on the cross: he prayed (for he prayed these psalms: *God, my God, have mercy,* and all the psalms thereafter up to the verse *Into your hands,* as well as that verse); and he cried out on the cross (as the apostle testifies); also he wept on the cross; also he committed his soul to the Father on the cross; also he willingly gave up his spirit on the cross.

First, he prayed on the cross. Likewise a sick man on point of death should pray, particularly in his heart if he cannot with his mouth; for St Isidore says that it is better to pray silently in the heart without any external sound of the voice than to pray with words alone without any devotion of the heart. The second was, he cried. Likewise should every dying man cry out strongly with the heart, not with the mouth; for God takes more notice of the desire of the heart than of the crying of the voice. The crying of the heart to God is nothing other than a man's great desire to have forgiveness for his sins and everlasting life. The third was, he wept. Likewise, every dying man should weep, not with his bodily eyes but with the tears of his heart; that is to say, truly repenting of all his misdeeds. The fourth was, he commended his soul to God. Every man at his end should do likewise, saying thus with heart and mouth if he can (and otherwise in his heart): 'Lord God, into your hands I commend my spirit; for truly you yourself bought me dear.' The fifth was, he willingly gave up his spirit. Every man should do likewise at his death; that is to say, he should die willingly, fully conforming his own will in this to God's will, as he is bound to.

Therefore, as long as he who is at the point of death may speak, and retains the use of reason, let him say the following prayers.

Prayer: 'O, you high Godhead and endless goodness, most merciful and glorious Trinity, you are highest love and charity. Have mercy on me, a wretched sinful man, for to you I fully commend my soul.'

Prayer: 'My Lord God, most benign Father, Father of mercy, have mercy on me, your poor creature. Lord, help now my needy and desolate soul in its last necessity, that the hounds of Hell do not devour me.'

Prayer: 'Sweetest and most loving lord, my Lord Jesus Christ, God's own dear son. For the honour and virtue of your blessed Passion admit and receive me among the number of your chosen people. My saviour and redeemer, I surrender all of myself fully to your grace and mercy, do not forsake me. To you, Lord, I come; do not reject me. Lord Jesus Christ, I ask for paradise and bliss from you, not on account of the worthiness of my merits, since I am but dust and ashes and a sinful wretch, but through the virtue and effect of your holy Passion, by which you have vouchsafed and would buy me, sinful wretch, with your precious blood, and bring me into Paradise.'

Let him also often say this verse: ... 'Lord, you have broken my bonds, and therefore I thank you with the sacrifice of the offering of worship'; for this verse, as Cassiodorus says, has such great virtue that a man's sins are forgiven, if it is said three times with true good faith at a man's last end.

Prayer: 'Lord Jesus Christ, for the agony that you suffered for me on the cross, and especially at that hour when your most blessed soul passed out of your body, have mercy on my soul at its mean passing.'

Also, afterwards, with all the intensity and devotion that he can, with heart and mouth let him cry out to our blessed Lady, St Mary, who is the most effective and most willing mediator and help for all sinful men with God, saying thus: *Prayer*: 'O glorious Lady, queen of Heaven, mother of mercy and refuge of all sinful men, reconcile me to your sweet son my Lord Jesus, and intercede for me, sinful wretch, to his great mercy, that for love of you, sweet Lady, he will forgive me my sins.'

Then let him pray to the angels, and say thus: *Prayer*: 'Holy angels of Heaven, I beg you to assist me who am about to pass out of this world, and strongly preserve and keep me from all my enemies, and receive my soul into your blessed company; and particularly you, the good blessed angel which has been my continual guardian, appointed by God.'

Then let him pray in the same manner devoutly to all the apostles, martyrs, confessors and virgins, and especially to those saints whom he loved and honoured most particularly when healthy; that they will help him then in his last and greatest need.

Then, afterwards, let him say three times or more these words, or similar in meaning, which have been ascribed to St Augustine: *Prayer*: 'The peace of Our Lord Jesus Christ, and the virtue of his Passion, and the sign of the holy cross, and the virginity of our blessed Lady St Mary, and the blessings of all the saints, and the protection of all the angels, and the prayers of all the chosen people of God, be between me and all my enemies, visible and invisible, in this hour of my death. Amen.'

Afterwards, let him say this verse three times: ... 'Grant me, Lord, a clear end, that my soul shall never fall downwards; but give me everlasting bliss, which is the reward of a holy death.'

And if he who is sick does not know all these prayers, or cannot say them because of the grievousness of his illness, let someone standing by say them in front of him so that he can clearly hear him say them, changing the words which need to be changed in his speech; and he who is dying, whilst he retains use of his reason, should pray devoutly internally with his heart and desire as he can and is able; and so give up his spirit to God, and he shall be saved.

THE FIFTH CHAPTER CONTAINS AN INSTRUCTION FOR THE DYING. *CHAPTER 5*

But it is much to be noted and attended to that very seldom does any man, even among religious and devout men, prepare himself for death in advance as he ought, for every man thinks that he will live long, and does not believe that he will die soon. Without doubt that urging comes from the devil's subtle temptation, and it is often clearly seen that many men, by such idle hope and trust, have been neglectfully slothful, and have suddenly died either intestate or unexpectedly and unprepared. Therefore every man who loves and fears God and is concerned for the well-being of men's souls, should actively urge and warn each of his fellow Christians who is sick or in any peril of body or soul, that chiefly and first above all other things (and without any other delays or lengthy waiting) he should diligently provide and arrange for the spiritual medicine and curing of his soul. For often, as a certain decretal says, bodily sickness derives from sickness of the soul; and therefore the Pope in the same decretal strictly charges every physician that he should give no sick person any medicine for the body until he has charged and urged him to seek out his spiritual doctor. But this advice is now ignored by almost all men, and is turned inside out;

for people search the sooner and more readily for medicines for the body than for the soul.

Also, other evils and adversities, by the just judgment of God, shall evermore come to men on account of sin, as the prophet testifies who says thus: ... 'There is no evil in the city, unless God does it.' You should not understand that God commits the evil of sin; but he gives the punishment for sin. On account of this every ill man, and any other person who is in any danger, should be diligently urged and exhorted that before everything else he should make his peace with God, receiving spiritual medicines (that is to say, taking the sacraments of Holy Church, setting out and making his testament, and lawfully arranging for his household and other needs if he has any to arrange for).

And so, firstly, no man should hope too much for bodily health. But the opposite of that is now often done by many men, to the great peril of souls, and particularly for those who are actually and clearly approaching and near the point of death; for none of them will hear anything of death. And so, as that great clerk the Chancellor of Paris [Jean Gerson] says, often on account of such vain and false cheering and encouragement, and feigned prophecy of bodily health, and by trusting thereon, men run and fall in to everlasting certain damnation. And therefore a sick man should be counselled and exhorted to look to and obtain his soul's health for himself by true contrition and confession; and if it is expedient for him that shall greatly assist his physical health; and so he shall be the more peaceful and secure. And given that (witnessing St Gregory) a man seldom has true contrition (and, as St Augustine says in the 4th book of Sentences, the twelfth distinction, and other doctors as well, repentance that is delayed, and done at a man's last end, is rarely true repentance or penance which is sufficient for everlasting health – and especially in those who previously did not keep either the commandments of God or their voluntary vows either effectively or truly, but only feigningly and to outward appearance), on that account every sick man who is in that situation and has come to his last end is to be actively counselled to labour with the reason of his mind according to his strength to have appropriate and true repentance. That means to say that, notwithstanding the sorrow and grievousness of his illness, and the fear which he has of sudden death, he should use his reason as much as he can, and strengthen himself to have a real dislike for all sins for the due purpose and perfect intent, which is for God, and to withstand his evil natural inclination to sin, even though he might live longer, and also the delight in his previous sins, and labour as hard as he can to have a real dislike for them, even though it be never so short.

And lest he should fall into despair, instruct him and strengthen him with the things said above in the second part concerning the temptation of despair. Exhort him also to be strong in his soul against the other temptations that are listed and described there as well, to withstand them all strongly and uprightly; for he cannot be compelled by the devil to consent to any of them at all. Also, let him be warned and counselled to die as a proper and true Christian man, in full belief. Also, it has to be considered whether he is affected by any of the Church's censures, and if he is, let him be instructed that he must submit himself with all his power to the direction of Holy Church, so that he can be absolved. Also, if he who is dying has a long time and opportunity to think of himself, and is not taken with a sudden death, then devout stories and devout prayers may be read before him by those around him, in which he took most pleasure when he was healthy; or else recite before him the commandments of God, so that he may consider more deeply whether he can discover within himself any that he has negligently trespassed against. And if the sick man has lost speech, but retains whole and full awareness of the questions that are put to him, or the prayers which are recited before him, let him answer thereto with some outward sign, or merely with consent of the heart. Nevertheless it is greatly to be urged and asserted that the questions be put to him before he loses his speech; for if his answers are inappropriate, or do not seem in all respects sufficient for the full health and perpetual remedy of his soul, then remedy and counsel must be added thereto in the best manner possible. The peril that he would clearly fall into should then be explained to him, even though he should and may be greatly frightened by it. It is better and more just that he be compunctious and repentant with wholesome fear and dread, and so be saved, than that he should be damned through flattering and false dissimulation; for it is too inconsistent and contrary to Christian religion, and diabolical, that the danger of the death of the soul should be hidden from any dying Christian man or woman because of someone's vain fear that he might be greatly disturbed by it. For Isaiah the prophet did the opposite; for when King Hezekiah lay sick and close to death, he did not gloss over things or use any dissimulation towards him, but plainly and wholesomely terrified him, saying that he would die; and yet nevertheless he did not die at that time. And St Gregory similarly wholesomely terrified the monk who held private property, as may be read in the 4th book of his *Dialogues.* Also, show to the sick person the image of the crucifix, which should be always near sick people, or else the image of our Lady, or of a saint whom he loved or honoured when healthy. Also, let there be holy water about the sick person, and sprinkle it often upon him and others around him, so that devils will be driven away from them by it.

If all the things set out above cannot be done on account of urgency and lack of time, then say prayers, and particularly those which are especially directed to our saviour, Lord Jesus Christ. When a man is on the point of death, and hurries quickly to his end, then no bodily friends, nor wife, nor children, nor riches, nor any temporal possessions should be summoned into his mind or discussed before him, except in so far as the spiritual health and profit of the sick man demands and requires. In this thing which is our last and greatest necessity, all varieties of aspects and meanings of it, with the explanations [*adverbs*] which can be added to them, should be most subtly and diligently advanced and considered by each person, given that no man shall be rewarded for his words alone, but for his deeds as well, joined with and measured against his words (as is said in the book called *The Compendium of the Truth of Divinity*, the 10th chapter of the 2nd book).

And if any man desires, and will happily die well and soundly and meritoriously without peril, he must actively take notice and study and learn diligently this art of dying and the preparations for it set out above, while he is well, and not wait until death comes to him. For in truth, dear brother or sister, I tell you truthfully – believe me about it – that when death or great sickness comes upon you, devotion leaves you, and the more straitly they take you and grasp you, the further devotion flies from you. Therefore, if you would not be deceived or err, if you wish to be safe, actively do what you can while you are here in health, and have the use and freedom of your wits and well-disposed reason, and while you can be master of yourself and your deeds. O Lord God, how many (indeed, without number) of those who have so waited until their last ends have been neglectfully lazy, and deceived themselves everlastingly? Take note, brother and sister, and take care if you will, lest it happen to you in the same way. But let no man suppose or think that it is unfitting that such great care and diligence and wise preparation and foresight and active exhortation should be given and administered to those who are on the point of death and at their last ends as is said above: for they are in such danger and so great need at that time that, if it were possible, a whole city ought to gather together with all speed to the dying man; as the practice is in some religious orders, in which it is ordered that when a sick man is near death, then all of the brethren, when they hear the board being beaten, whatever the hour, and wherever they are, should speedily leave everything to come to him who is dying; and therefore it is read that religious men and women, for the dignity of their position, should not run, except to a dying man, or for fear.

THE SIXTH CHAPTER CONTAINS PRAYERS WHICH SHOULD BE SAID FOR THOSE WHO ARE DYING BY SOMEONE ABOUT THEM. *CHAPTER 6*

The last thing of all to be known is that the following prayers might be fittingly said for a sick man who approaches his end. And if he is a person in religion, then when the convent is gathered together by the beating of the board, as the custom is, then the litany with the psalms and prayers that are used with it shall be said first; afterwards, if he is still alive, let someone from the bystanders say the following prayers as time and opportunity allow, and they can be often repeated to encourage the devotion of the sick man if he retains his reason and understanding; but none the less this should not be done as a necessity, as though he could not be saved unless it were done, but for the benefit and devotion of the sick who approach their end it may be done; and it is well done if it is done. But among seculars who are ill, let these prayers be said as devotion, and disposition, and the profit of them and those around them demand and require, and as the time will allow. But, alas, there are very few (not only among seculars, but also among the religious) who have knowledge of this art and will be near and aid those who are at the point of death and departing from this world, asking them and exhorting and instructing and praying for them as is said above, especially when those who are dying do not wish or trust not to die yet, and so the sick men's souls stand in great danger.

Prayer: 'For the love that caused you to be wounded and die for the well-being and salvation of mankind, which was the most worthy and sweet love of God, your blessed father of Heaven, and for our sake made man, sweet Lord Jesus, full of mercy, forgive your servant all his trespasses in thought, word, and deed, in all the affections, desires, movements, strengths and senses of his soul and body; and in true remission of them all give him that most sufficient amendment by which you wash away the sins of the world; and in recompense for all his omissions add and give to him that holy demeanour that you had from the hour of your conception until the hour of your death; and above that the fruit of all good deeds which have pleased and shall please you in all your chosen people from the beginning of the world until its end, sweet Lord Jesus who lives and reigns with the Father and the Holy Spirit, one true God without end, Amen.'

Prayer: 'For the union of the most fervent love that stirred and made you, the life of all living things, to be incarnate of our Lady, and with great sorrow of the spirit to die for charity and love of us, we cry out to the root of your most benign heart that you forgive the soul of your servant [me] all his [my] sins, and with your most holy demeanour and the most worthy merit of your Passion make up for all his [my] negligence and omissions, and make him [me] feel by experience the most superabundant greatness of your mercies, and cause all of us (and especially this [my] person our brother, whom you have prepared to be called quickly before your glorious majesty) in the manner most pleasing to you and most profitable to him [me] and us all to be presented to you with sweet patience, true repentance and full remission, with true faith, sure hope, and perfect charity, so that he may die blessedly in a perfect state between your most sweet embracing and most sweet kissing, to your everlasting glory and praise, Amen.'

Prayer: 'Into the hands of your endless and unquenchable mercy, Holy Father, just and most beloved Father, we commend the spirit of our brother your servant, in the greatness of the love with which the holy soul of your blessed son commended itself to you on the cross; entirely praying that, for that inestimable charity by which your holy Godhead and fatherhood fully drew to yourself that blessed soul of your son, so now in his last hour you sweetly receive the spirit of our brother your servant, in the same love. Amen.'

Prayer: 'St Michael, the archangel of Our Lord Jesus Christ, help us at our great judgment. O you most worthy giant and protector, who may never be defeated, be near to our brother [me] your servant, labouring now bitterly at his [my] end, and defend him [me] strongly from the dragon of Hell and from all sorts of trickery of evil spirits. Furthermore, we pray you (who are so clear and worthy a minister of God), that in this final end or hour of life of our brother [me], you will receive his soul easily and benignly into your bosom, and bring it to a place of refreshment, peace and rest. Amen.'

Prayer: 'Immaculate and blessed Virgin Mary, singular help and succour in every anguish and necessity, help us sweetly, and show your gracious face to our brother [me] your servant, now in his [my] last end, and expel all his [my] enemies from him [me] through the virtue of your dearly beloved son Our Lord Jesus Christ, and of the holy cross, and deliver him [me] from all kinds of discomfort of body and soul, so that he [I] may thank and worship God without end. Amen.'

Prayer: 'My most sweet redeemer, more merciful Jesus, and most benign Lord; for that sorrowful voice which you had in your manhood when you were dying for us and were so consumed with sorrows and cares in your great Passion that you cried out that you had been abandoned by your father, be not far from our brother [me] your servant, but give him [me] the aid of your mercy in the hour of his [my] death, and bear in mind the grievous affliction and pain of his [my] soul which in his final moment of passing, because of the weakening and exhaustion of his spirits, has no strength to call upon you for help. But by the victory of the cross and by the virtue of your holy Passion, and by your loving death, think of it with thoughts of peace, not of affliction but of mercy, and comfort and deliver it fully from all kinds of anguish. With the same hands that you permitted to be nailed upon the cross for its sake with sharp nails, good Jesus, sweet father and Lord, deliver it from all the torments set down for it, and bring it to everlasting rest with a voice exulting in and acknowledging your mercy. Amen.'

Prayer: 'Most merciful Lord Jesus Christ, God's son, in unison with that recommendation by which you commended your holy soul to your Heavenly father while dying on the cross, we commend to your inestimable pity the soul of our brother [me] your servant, praying your most merciful goodness that, for all the honour and merits of your holy soul (by which all souls are saved and delivered from the debt of death), you would have mercy on the soul of our dear brother your servant, mercifully delivering it from all miseries and penalties, and through the love and mediation of your sweet mother bring it to the everlasting contemplation of the joy of your most sweet and delightful sight. Amen.'

Prayer: 'Merciful and benign God, who for the greatness of your mercies takes away the sins of those who are truly repentant, and removes the blame for sins which are past and done previously by the grace of forgiveness, we beseech you to look mercifully upon our brother [me] your servant, and graciously hear him [me] requesting with all the confession of his [my] heart the remission of all his [my] sins. Most merciful father, renew in him [me] all things which have been corrupted in him by bodily weakness, or befouled by the fraud of the devil, and gather him into the unity of the body of Holy Church, and make him a participant in your redemption. Have mercy, Lord, upon his actions, have mercy on his tears, and admit him to the sacrament of your reconciliation, who has no hope other than in your mercy, by Our Lord Jesus Christ. Amen.'

Prayer: 'Dear brother, I commend you to almighty God, and commit you to him, whose creation you are; so that when your humanity has paid its debt by the way of death, you may return again to God your creator, who made you from the slime of the earth. When your soul passes out of your body, may the glorious company of angels come to you; the victorious host of worthy judges and senators, of holy apostles meet you; the fair shining company of holy confessors with the victorious numbers of glorious martyrs surround you; and that worthy fellowship, the joyful company of holy virgins, receive you; and the worthy fellowship of holy patriarchs open to you the place of their joy and rest, and judge you to be among those whom they are among everlastingly. May you never know that which is horrible in darkness, which grinds its teeth and burns with fire, which punishes through torments. May foul Satan with all his servants let you pass and not aggrieve you; when he advances towards you may he be terrified by the presence of holy angels, and flee into the darkness of everlasting night, into the great troubled sea of Hell. May Our Lord arise and his enemies be scattered about, and let those who hate him flee before his face; may they weaken as smoke weakens, as wax melts before the fire so may sinners perish before the face of God; and let just men enter and rejoice at the sight of God. Let none of the opposing legions and ministers of Satan be so bold as to impede your journey. Christ deliver you from torment, who vouchsafed to die for you; Christ, God's son, bring you to the joys of happy Paradise, and may the true shepherd know you among his sheep. May he absolve you from all sins, and put you at his right side in the sorting of his chosen children, so that you may see your redeemer face to face, and being present in assisting him, clearly see with your eyes that blessed everlasting truth, and among the blessed company of the children of God have and rejoice in the joy of the contemplation of God without end. Amen.'

Prayer: 'Go, Christian soul, out of this world, in the name of the almighty Father who made you from nothing; in the name of Jesus Christ his son who suffered his passion for you; and in the name of the Holy Ghost that was established within you. May holy angels and archangels, thrones and dominations, principalities, powers and virtues, cherubim and seraphim, greet you; patriarchs and prophets, apostles and evangelists, martyrs and confessors, monks and hermits, virgins and widows, children and innocents, help you; the prayers of all the priests and deacons and all the ranks of Holy Church assist you; so that your place shall be in peace, and your dwelling everlastingly in that Heavenly Jerusalem, by the mediation of Our Lord Jesus Christ who is the highest mediator between God and man. Amen.'

PART TWO: PRACTICE

V. Parish Celebrations

The vitality of parish celebrations is only imperfectly conveyed by the financial records which they generated. Nevertheless, the round at Scarborough does indicate something of the number of celebrations, especially those for the major rites of passage: the purification of mothers after childbirth, solemnisation of marriages (although marriages did not have to be held in church), and funerals. Post-mortem commemoration is also indicated by the celebration of obits (the masses and other celebrations held on the anniversary of a death). Among the other aspects worth noting are the levels of offerings at major feast days and the few payments for special masses for individual guilds.

The accounts for Yarmouth and King's Lynn, although much more summary, give a better indication of the totality of the demands made by the local church as a benefice (as against the demands made by the churchwardens). Here there are compulsory payments: the personal tithes (equivalent to a form of income tax), and the payments of mortuaries as death duties. Other compulsory payments are hidden in block totals, such as the payment for the Holy Loaf. Beyond the compulsory there were the voluntary payments, which are perhaps more revealing. Here, the main sums are those equivalent to the Scarborough payments for the major social rites. Equally notable are the sums received in donations to shrines, especially as new devotions rose and fell: Henry VI in Yarmouth, and in King's Lynn the offerings to St Mary on the Red Mount, and later to the Good Cross in St Margaret's churchyard. These particularly emphasise the ubiquity of pilgrimages within a highly local context: it was not necessary to go to a cathedral like Ely or Hereford (see nos. 19–20). Over the years the totals received in the churches fluctuated, as did the distribution between the various categories of receipts. One particularly striking feature of the King's Lynn accounts is the way in which receipts rocketed upwards in plague years, one of which (giving the highest total in the whole recorded run of accounts) is given here.

13. Parochial religious celebrations: a year's round of special ceremonies at Scarborough, 1435–6 [From London, Public Record Office, E101/514/32, ff.2v–7r; in Latin. NB: this series records only the special celebrations and those which produced finance for the accounts; the normal daily celebrations of masses do not appear]

Month of February

4th from 1 funeral	3d.	wax: 4d.
5th from 1 funeral	31d.	wax: 8d.
6th from 1 espousal	8d.	
7th from 1 obit	11d.	wax: 8d.
22nd from 1 anniversary	9d.	wax: 8d.
Same day, from 2 funerals	6d.	wax: 4d.
Checked total: 8s. 4d.		

Month of March

7th from 1 funeral	5d.	wax: 2d.
9th from 1 funeral	4d.	wax: 2d.
13th from 1 funeral and 1 purification	5 1/2d.	wax: 2d.
20th from 1 purification	2d.	
24th from 1 purification	2 1/2d.	
26th from 1 funeral	2d.	wax: 2d.
27th from 1 anniversary	6d.	wax: 2d.
28th from 1 funeral and 1 purification	9d.	wax: 2d.
Checked total: 4s.		

Month of April

5th from 1 purification	2d.	
7th from 1 purification	2 1/2d.	
10th from 1 funeral	7 1/2d.	wax: 8d.
Same day, from 1 anniversary	5d.	wax: 8d.
12th from 1 funeral	4 1/2d.	wax: 8d.
Oblations at the feast of Easter, both in the church and in chapels, and in other small oblations	58s.	
18th from 2 funerals	9d.	wax: 8d.
19th from 1 obit	11d.	wax: 8d.
20th from 1 obit	3d.	wax: 4d.
23rd from 1 funeral	4d.	wax: 2d.
Same day, from 1 obit	1/2d.	wax: 8d.
24th from 1 funeral	3d.	wax: 2d.
Checked total: £3 6s. 8d.		

Month of May

2nd from 1 purification	4½d.	
4th from 1 funeral	2d.	wax: 2d.
Same day, from 1 purification	1d.	
6th from 2 purifications	7d.	
8th from 1 funeral	2½d.	wax: 2d.
9th from 2 funerals	8½d.	wax: 4d.
10th from 1 obit	2d.	wax: 8d.
14th from 1 funeral	3d.	wax: 4d.
15th from 1 obit	5d.	wax: 2d.
Same day, from 1 obit	5d.	wax: their own
16th from 2 purifications	5d.	
18th from 1 funeral	5d.	wax: 2d.
Same day, from 1 obit	2d.	wax: 2d.
20th, from 1 obit at Falsgrave	3d.	wax: their own
22nd from funeral of Robert Lygeman	16d.	wax: their own
Same day, from 1 funeral	3s. 2½d.	wax: their own
25th from 2 purifications	3d.	
26th from 1 obit	5d.	wax: 4d.
28th from 1 obit and 1 purification	4d.	wax: 2d.

Checked total: 12s. 6d.

Month of June

1st from 1 obit	7d.	wax: 4d.
6th from 1 obit	22d.	wax: 12d.
7th from 1 purification	2d.	
8th from 1 funeral	14½d.	wax: 6d.
12th from 1 funeral	2½d.	wax: 4d.
13th from 1 purification	3½d.	
14th from 1 funeral	14d.	wax: 8d.
Same day, from 1 wedding	12d.	
15th from 1 anniversary		wax: 8d.
17th from 1 obit	9½d.	wax: 8d.
20th from 2 purifications	6d.	
21st from 1 purification	2½d.	
22nd from 1 purification	3d.	
23rd, from guild of St John the Baptist	12½d.	
27th from 1 purification	3½d.	
Same day, from 1 funeral	2½d.	wax: 2d.

Checked total: 14s. 1d.

Month of July

4th from 2 spousals	3s.	
5th from 1 purification	$2^1/2$d.	
6th from 1 purification	2d.	
7th from 1 spousal	$6^1/2$d.	
Same day, in oblations in the chapel of St Thomas:	$5^1/2$d.	
11th from 1 purification	3d.	
13th from 1 funeral	$2^1/2$d.	wax: 2d.
14th from 1 funeral	2d.	
15th from 1 funeral	1d.	wax: 2d.
17th from 1 obit	11d.	wax: 8d.
Same day, from 1 spousal	22d.	
18th from 1 purification	$2^1/2$d.	
19th from 1 obit	4d.	wax: 8d.
Same day, from 1 funeral	$5^1/2$d.	wax: 8d.
20th from guild mass of Mary Magdalene	5d.	
22nd from guild mass of St Clement	$4^1/2$d.	
23rd from 1 purification	2d.	
Same day, from 1 purification	4d.	
24th from 2 obits	3s. 4d.	wax: 12d.
28th from 1 funeral	12d.	wax: 12d.
Same day, from 1 spousal	$15^1/2$d.	
30th from 1 spousal	$19^1/2$d.	

Checked total: 21s. 11d.

Month of August

1st from 1 obit	$6^1/2$d.	wax: 6d.
Same day, from 2 spousals and 2 purifications	2s. $6^1/2$d.	
2nd from 1 purification	2d.	
3rd from 1 obit	$3^1/2$d.	wax: 8d.
7th from 1 funeral and 1 purification	$11^1/2$d.	
8th from 2 spousals	$19^1/2$d.	
Same day, from 2 purifications	$6^1/2$d.	
10th from 1 funeral	$2^1/2$d.	wax: 2d.
11th from 1 purification	$1^1/2$d.	
12th from anniversary		wax: 8d.
Same day, from 1 funeral	9d.	
15th oblations in the church, that is for the Assumption of the Blessed Mary	12s. $2^1/2$d. [MS: 12d. $2^1/2$d.]	

Same day, chapel of St Thomas	14d.	
Same day, chapel of the holy sepulchre	7d.	
Same day, guild mass of St John the Baptist	3d.	
16th from 2 purifications	6d.	
17th from 1 purification	2d.	
18th from 1 obit	4d.	wax: 4d.
19th from 1 obit	4d.	wax: 8d.
Same day, from 1 funeral	5 1/2d.	wax: 8d.
20th from guild mass of Mary Magdalene	5d.	
22nd from guild mass of St Clement	4 1/2d.	
24th from 1 purification	2d.	
Same day, from 1 purification	4d.	
24th from 2 obits	3s. 4d.	wax: 12d.
28th from 1 funeral	12d.	wax: 12d.
Same day, from 1 spousal	15 1/2d.	
30th from 1 spousal	19 1/2d.	
[27s. 1/2d.] Checked total: 36s. 10d.		

Month of September

1st from 1 funeral	4d.	wax: 8d.
2nd from 1 obit	10d.	wax: 3s. 4d.
4th from 1 funeral	9d.	wax: 4d.
5th from 1 spousal	19d.	
Same day, from 1 purification	5 1/2d.	
8th from 1 spousal	12d.	
Same day, from 1 purification	6 1/2d.	
13th from 1 obit	10d.	wax: 8d.
18th from 1 obit	10 1/2d.	wax: 8d.
21st from 1 obit	9d.	wax: 8d.
24th from 1 obit	11 1/2d.	wax: 8d.
25th from 1 purification	2d.	
26th from 1 obit	4d.	wax: 8d.
29th from 1 purification	3d.	
[17s. 4d.] Checked total: 17s. 6d.		

Month of October

3rd from 1 funeral	4d.	wax: 2d.
5th from 1 funeral	2d.	wax: 8d.
9th from 1 funeral	5 1/2d.	wax: 6d.
Same day, from 1 spousal	13 1/2d.	
10th from 1 funeral	9 1/2d.	wax: 16d.

12th from 1 funeral	8d.	wax: 4d.
Same day, from 1 purification	3d.	
13th from 1 spousal	5d.	
16th from 1 funeral	10½d.	wax: their own
Same day, from 1 obit	9d.	wax: 6d.
17th from 1 funeral	3d.	wax: 2d.
Same day, from 2 purifications	6d.	
19th oblations at relics in the church of St Mary	13½d.	
20th from 1 purification	3d.	
21st from 1 funeral	2s. 5d.	
Same day, from 1 obit	9d.	wax: 16d.
23rd. from 1 purification	1½d.	
25th from 2 purifications	6d.	
27th from 1 obit	5½d.	wax: 2s.
29th from 1 funeral	2d.	wax: 2d.
30th from 1 obit	9d.	wax: 8d.
Same day, from 2 purifications	8½d.	

[21s. 8½d.] Checked total: 21s. 10½d.

Month of November

2nd guild mass of All Saints	13d.	
4th from 1 funeral	6½d.	wax: 4d.
6th from 1 funeral	10½d.	wax: 8d.
7th from 1 spousal	13½d.	
9th from 1 obit	5½d.	wax: 6d.
Same day, from 1 purification	4½d.	
10th from 1 funeral	4½d.	wax: 2d.
11th from 1 obit	7½d.	wax: 6d.
14th from 1 obit	5d.	wax: 4d.
Same day, from 2 purifications	6d.	
15th from 1 funeral	3d.	wax: 2d.
17th from 1 obit	12½d.	wax: 12d.
Same day, from 1 purification	4½d.	
19th from 1 funeral	6½d.	wax: 2d.
21st from 1 spousal	9½d.	
Same day, from 1 purification	2½d.	
23rd from 1 spousal	11d.	
Same day, from oblations in the chapel of St Clement at Falsgrave	18½d.	
24th from 1 funeral	3d.	wax: 2d.

25th from 1 funeral	3d.	
Same day, from 1 purification	2 1/2d.	
28th from 1 purification	2d.	
29th from 1 funeral	11d.	wax: 8d.
Checked total: 18s. 6d.		

Month of December

1st from 1 purification	3d.	
5th from 1 obit	4d.	wax: 6d.
Same day, from 1 funeral	2d.	wax: 2d.
13th from 1 funeral	6 1/2d.	wax: 8d.
14th from 1 purification	2d.	
20th from 1 obit	4d.	wax: 8d.
25th [MS: 20th] oblations in the church of St Mary at the feast day, that is the Lord's Nativity	14s. 4d.	
Same day, in the chapel of St Thomas	2s. 2 1/2d.	
Same day, in the chapel of the holy sepulchre	22 1/2d.	
26th from 1 funeral	3 1/2d.	wax: 2d.
Same day, oblations at the altar of St Stephen	19d.	
28th from 1 obit	12d.	wax: 8d.
29th oblations in the chapel of St Thomas	2 1/2d.	
Checked total: 26s. 1 1/2d.		

Month of January

2dn from 1 purification	3d.	
3rd from 1 funeral	3 1/2d.	wax: 2d.
5th from 1 purification	4d.	
10th from 1 funeral	3 1/2d.	wax: 2d.
16th from 1 purification	3d.	
23rd from 1 spousal	8 1/2d.	
25th from 1 funeral	13 1/2d.	wax: 8d.
Same day, from 1 spousal	11d.	
28th from 1 anniversary		wax: 8d.
Checked total: 5s. 10d.		

Month of February

1st from anniversary		wax: 8d.
Same day, from 1 spousal and 1 purification	10d.	
2nd, that is, day of the Purification		

of St Mary, both in the church and
in its chapels 21s.
Checked total: 22s. 6d.

Total of general oblations and wax charges this year: £13 16s. 7½d.
Item, from oblations found in the boxes this year: £5 2s. 4d.
The total stands.

14. Parish receipts from offerings and spiritual dues, I: Great Yarmouth, 1385–1505 [A selection from the accounts preserved in the Norfolk Record Office, Norwich, DCN 2/4/1–21; in Latin]

(i) *1386–7* [DCN.2/4/2]

Receipts

From personal tithes	£43 9s. 2d.
From oblations and all receipts of the altar	£75 13s. 8d.
From wax and testaments	£22 5s. 4d.
From the chapel of St Mary in the west	£20 4s. 8d.
From the great cross at the south door	44s. 5d.
From the trunk of St Nicholas and other trunks in the church	56s. 6¾d.
From profits of the house	34s.
From fisheries and Christ's part	£6 15s. 2d.

(ii) *1452–3* [DCN.2/4/13]

Receipts

From personal tithes	£22 5s. 4½d.
From oblations of the four principal feasts with many others at which the parishioners are accustomed to offer out of devotion, with the collection at the Easter candle	£14 3s. 6d.
From oblations at masses of the dead during the year	£10 11s. 11½d.
From oblations at marriages	£4 12½d.
From oblations at purifications	34s. 2½d.
From fees for masses	100s.
From bequests of the dead	34s. 6d.
From mortuaries	7s. 8d.
From trunks in the church	22d.
From the chapel of St Mary	£8 3s. 2d.
From profits of the house, with wool and lambs	18s. 8d.
From fisheries and Christ's part	113s. 7½d.

(iii) *1485–6* [DCN.2/4/16; the first year that offerings to Henry VI are mentioned]

Income of the church

From personal tithes, £20 11s. From oblations of the four principal feasts, with others at which the parishioners are accustomed to offer, with the collection of the Easter candle: £11 10s. 5d. From all masses for the dead during the year: £4 12s. 1d. From rent charges offered by the bell men at the anniversaries of various dead people, as appears by the rental: 8s. 2$^1/_2$d. From oblations at marriages during the year: 54s. 6d. From oblations at purifications, 29s. 5d. Item, for 67 chrismals, of which 30 were sold for 5s., and the rest were used for surplices and as gifts to preachers, confreres and others. From fees for masses, 72s. 2$^1/_2$d

Sum: £45 2s. 10d.

Perquisites

From bequests of the dead, 8s. 6d. From mortuaries sold, 30s. From the chapel of St Mary of Arneburgh, that is, from its box, £10 5s. 7$^1/_4$d. From the box of St Anne, 3s. ... From the trunk of St Nicholas, and other trunks and boxes in the church, 2s. 8d. From fishing and Christ's part, £9 4s. 10$^1/_2$d. ... Item, from 7 tithe piglets, and 13 goslings, 7 ducks, 80 young chickens, and 8 young doves as tithes: nothing, because used in the household. From wax sold, 50s. ...

From the chapel of St John the Baptist, newly built at the eastern corner of the cemetery of the church of St Nicholas in Great Yarmouth aforesaid – From the box of St Wandrille and from the trunk of King Henry: £15 12s. 9$^1/_2$d. Item, from 2800 herring offered to St Mary and the aforesaid King Henry, 16s. 4d. ...

(iv) *1504–5* [DCN.2/4/20]

Receipts of the church

From personal tithes, £19 7s. 6d. From oblations at the five feasts, that is All Saints' Day (38s. 1d.), St Nicholas's Day (43s. 11d.), Christmas (46s. 8d.), Purification of St Mary (4s. 10$^1/_2$d.), and Easter (68s. 4d.) – £10 22$^1/_2$d. For 44 lb. of wax offered at the feast of the Purification of St Mary, nothing here because it was used and sold in the church and chapel; however, that wax which was sold is accounted for and charged afterwards in such a heading. From the Easter candle, 18s. 11d. From the other feasts at which the parishioners are accustomed to offer out of devotion – 46s. 10d. From seven guilds of that town, 21s. 2$^1/_2$d. From all masses for the dead in the whole year

– £6 7s. 10½d. From marriages – 60s. 7d. From purifications, 32s. 5½d. From fees paid [for special masses], 42s. From bequests of the dead, 32s. 7d. From mortuaries sold, 17s. 6d. From fishing and Christ's part, £6 3s. 8d. From oblations in boats, 11s. 7d. From the chapel of St Mary, 105s. 8d. From wax sold in that chapel and the church, 67s. 2d. From the chapel of good King Henry, 22s. 8d. From boxes in the church for two years, 4s. 9d. From rents offered by the bellmen, 4s. 6d.

15. Parish receipts from offerings and spiritual dues, II: King's Lynn [A selection from the accounts preserved in Norwich, Norfolk Record Office, DCN 2/1/1–92; in Latin]

(i) *1398–9* [DCN 2/1/21]

… From oblations and obventions of the church and chapels:	£107 11s. 2½d.
From tithes and testaments:	£111 11s. 7d.

(ii) *1399–1400* [DCN 2/1/21]

… From tithes and testaments:	£105 6s.
From oblations and obventions of the church and chapels, with oblations at the pestilence time:	£198 12s. 6d.

(iii) *1400–1* [DCN 2/1/21]

… From oblations of the church and chapels:	£105 11d.
From tithes and testaments:	£119 15s. 11d.
Item, from a certain parishioner for tithes, being in arrears for many years:	£20

(iv) *1429–30* [DCN 2/1/25: the first year in which the receipts of the parish church and chapels are separated].

… From oblations and obventions of the parish church of St Margaret:	£42 7s. 2d.
From oblations and obventions of the chapel of St Nicholas:	£11 10s. 4d.
From oblations and obventions of the chapel of St James:	£13 9s. 9d.
From tithes:	£78 11s. 7d.
From testaments and mortuaries:	£7 19d.
… From masses by compact:	£3 8s. 6d.

(v) *1437–8* [DCN 2/1/32: the first year to separate out the major individual elements]

... From oblations and obventions of the parish church of St Margaret:	£44
From oblations and obventions of the chapel of St Nicholas:	£10 10s. 8½d.
From oblations and obventions of the chapel of St James:	£13 9s. 6d.
From tithes:	£60 12s. 3d.
From bequests of the dead:	£7 11s. 10d.
From mortuaries:	5s. 2d.
From masses by compact:	£6 7s. 1d.
From oblations at images in the church and chapels:	£3 2s. ½d.
For wax sold:	£4
From the friars for the canonical quarter:	2s. 6d.

(vi) *1454–5* [DCN 2/1/50: the only year to mention an indulgence]

... From oblations and obventions of the parish church of St Margaret:	£33 10s. 2d.
From oblations and obventions of the chapel of St Nicholas:	£9 5s. 1d.
From oblations and obventions of the chapel of St James:	£7 11s. 2d.
From tithes:	£21 15s. 3d.
From bequests of the dead:	67s.
From mortuaries:	11s.
From masses by compact:	£4 8d.
From oblations at images:	28s. 6d.
From the Augustinian friars for the fourth part of oblations:	22d.
For wax sold: nothing, because for use in the church.	
... From oblations at images at the time of indulgence:	107s.

(vii) *1487–8* [DCN 2/1/72: the first detailed breakdown of the receipts of St Margaret's].

... *Receipts of the church of St Margaret:* From the church of St Margaret, from £4 16s. 8d. from masses of requiem and from guilds held at St Margaret's; and from 54s. 8d. for purifications there; and from 101s. 6½d. for blessed bread there; and for 115s. 4d. for the principal feasts town; and from 25s. 4d. for bequests of the dead for the whole town; and from 18d. for one mortuary sold; and from 74s. 1$^{3}/_{4}$d. for spousals there; and from 15s. 6d. from boxes of saints in the churches and chapel of St Mary on the bridge; and from £26 11s. 4d. for personal tithes for the whole town ...

Chapel of St Nicholas: From the chapel of St Nicholas from £6 3$^{1}/_{4}$d. from the principal feasts, guilds, and oblations of the dead ...

Chapel of St James: From the chapel of St James from 109s. 2d. from the principal feasts, guilds, and oblations of the dead ...

Chapel of St Mary on the mount: From the chapel of St Mary on the mount, from £16 15s. 5$^{1}/_{2}$d. ...

(viii) *1498–9* [DCN 2/1/77]

... *Income of churches:* From the church of St Margaret, in oblations at the principal feasts (£6 6s. 4d.), masses for the dead (£8 15s. 10$^{1}/_{2}$d.), guilds (41s. 3d.), purifications (£4 5s. 9d.), and marriages (£6 14s. 4$^{1}/_{2}$d.), together with oblations of blessed bread (£4 6s.) and oblations of boats (8s. 6d.) – £32 18s. From obventions and oblations at the chapel of St Nicholas – £9 12s. 7d. From the chapel of St James – £6 14s. 6d. From personal tithes for the whole town of Lynn, £23 17s. 4d. From bequests of the dead, 15s. 10d. From mortuaries sold, 7s. 10d. From agreed payments for masses, together with a payment from the guild of the Holy Trinity, £4 2s. 4d. From the boxes of all the saints in the church of St Margaret and the chapels together with the chapel of St Mary on the bridge, 12s. 2d. From the gifts of various of Christ's faithful for the glazing of windows in the chancel of St Margaret's this year, 31s.

Receipts of the chapel of St Mary on the mount:
From oblations there this year: £26 14s.

(ix) *1507–8* [DCN 2/1/82: the first appearance of the 'good cross']

... *From the church:* From the church of St Margaret, that is to say from oblations at the principal feasts, and masses of requiem, with guilds, purifications, and marriages, together with blessed bread – £19 11s. 2d. From the chapel of St Nicholas, in oblations at the principal feasts and masses of requiem, with guilds – 107s. From the chapel of St James, in oblations at the principal feasts and masses of requiem, with guilds – 48s. 9d. From personal tithes for the whole town of Lynn,

£27 5s. 7d. From bequests of the dead, 40s. From the boxes of all the saints in the said church and chapels together with the chapel of St Mary on the bridge, 11s. 5d. From the chapel of St Mary on the mount, £21 5s. 7d. From oblations at the good cross in the cemetery of St Margaret's, £6 15s. 7d. From mortuaries sold, 5s. From agreed payments for masses, together with a payment from the guild of the Holy Trinity, 40s. ...

(x) *1510–11* [DCN 2/1/82]

... *From the Church*: From the church of St Margaret, that is to say from oblations at the principal feasts, and masses of requiem, with guilds, purifications, and marriages, together with blessed bread – £18. From the chapel of St Nicholas, in oblations at the principal feasts and masses of requiem, with guilds – 55s. 2d. From the chapel of St James, in oblations at the principal feasts and masses of requiem, with guilds – 28s. 6d. From personal tithes for the whole town of Lynn, £17 2s. From bequests of the dead, that is to say, from Thomas Thursby, £6 13s. 4d., and from the other bequests of the dead this year, 23s. From the boxes of all the saints in the said church and chapels, 4s. 5d. From the chapel of St Mary on the mount, £17 10s. From oblations at the good cross in the cemetery of St Margaret's, 21s. 6d. From mortuaries sold, 4s. From agreed payments for masses, together with a payment from the guild of the Holy Trinity, 40s. ...

(xi) *1528–9* [DCN 2/1/82: the last year to include all the headings]

... *From the church:* From the church of St Margaret, from oblations at the principal feasts and masses for the dead, with guilds, purifications, and marriages, together with blessed bread – £18 11s. 10d. From the chapel of St Nicholas, that is to say in oblations at the principal feasts and masses for the dead, with guilds – 35s. From the chapel of St James, that is to say in oblations at the principal feasts and masses for the dead, with guilds – 42s. From mortuaries sold, 30s. From the boxes of all the saints in the said church and chapels, 11s. From the chapel of St Mary on the mount, £9 8s. 6d. From oblations at the good cross in the cemetery of St Margaret's, 6s. From agreed payments for masses, together with a payment from the guild of the Holy Trinity, 40s. From personal tithes for the whole town of Lynn, £25 6d. From bequests of the dead, 12s.

(xii) *1531–2* [DCN 2/1/90]

... *The church:* From the church of St Margaret, from oblations at the principal feasts, and masses for the dead, with guilds, purifications, and nuptials, together with blessed bread – £18 4d. From the chapel of St Nicholas, in oblations at the principal feasts and masses for the dead, with guilds – 31s. From the chapel of St James, in oblations at the principal feasts and masses for the dead, with guilds – 37s. From personal tithes for the whole town of Lynn, £23 5d. From the boxes of all the saints in the said church and chapels, 4s. 8d. From the chapel of St Mary on the mount, £11. From oblations at the good cross in the cemetery of St Margaret's, 7s. From agreed payments for masses, together with a payment from the guild of the Holy Trinity, 40s.

(xiii) *1535–6* [DCN 2/1/91: the last of the extant accounts]

... *Receipts from the church:* From the church of St Margaret, that is to say from oblations at the principal feasts, and masses for the dead, with guilds, purifications, and nuptials, together with blessed bread – £14 5s. 4d. From the chapel of St Nicholas, in oblations at the principal feasts and masses for the dead – £4. From the chapel of St James, in oblations in like manner – £3 4s. From personal tithes for the whole town of Lynn, £23. From agreed payments for masses, together with a payment from the guild of the Holy Trinity, 24s.

VI. Private religion

While domestic spirituality is sometimes revealed in instructional works,[1] *and the widespread distribution of relics, images and (later) woodcuts offered opportunities for creating foci for prayer within a household, such evidence is by its nature insubstantial and difficult to pin down precisely – possessions can be traced, but not how they were used. For those who sought advanced domestic spiritual satisfaction, an episcopal licence for the celebration of divine offices within a private chapel or oratory was necessary. Information on such licences is widely spread across the country, although rarely is there any record as systematic as that for the diocese of Lichfield and Coventry in the fourteenth century.*[2] *These lists of licences reveal the distribution of the chapels across the diocese (one of the largest in England, extending from the Ribble to south Warwickshire, over Cheshire, Derbyshire, Staffordshire, and north Shropshire), and offer some insight into the range of appeal of such spiritual satisfaction. Although this run of licences is from relatively early in the period covered by this volume, it is indicative of the regularity of such grants. Some of these were repeated short-term concessions; others (indicated by mention of the 'for as long' clause) were to last during the bishop's pleasure – potentially therefore throughout the pontificate or life of the recipient. The Lichfield registers prior to 1413 contain quires which collect together such licences; elsewhere the records are scattered more widely among the administrative miscellanea, assuming that their essentially ephemeral nature has not meant that records have been discarded over the years. The activities within such private oratories have led one commentator to refer to the household itself as a 'religious community'.*[3]

Evidence from the side of the recipients of such licences – or those who should

1 W. A. Pantin, 'Instructions for a devout and literate layman', in *Medieval Learning and Literature: Essays Presented to Richard William Hunt*, ed. J. J. G. Alexander and M. T. Gibson, Oxford, 1976, pp. 399–400, 405–10.

2 The recording in the fifteenth century is much less systematic.

3 R. G. K. A. Mertes, 'The household as a religious community', in *People, Politics, and Community in the Fifteenth Century*, ed. J. T. Rosenthal and C. Richmond, Gloucester, 1987, pp. 123–39; effectively duplicated in K. Mertes, *The English Noble Household, 1250–1600: Good Governance and Politic Rule*, Oxford, 1988, pp. 139–60. Some of these private chapels developed into full-scale chapelries serving a local population: G. Rosser, 'Parochial conformity and popular religion in late medieval England', *Transactions of the Royal Historical Society*, 6th ser., I, 1991, pp. 181–2.

have received them, even if there is no record of the licence – is equally fragmentary. The correspondence of Margaret Paston as she sought the renewal of her licence offers some insights; but this is a rare survival.[4] *Other indications are provided by the physical survivals themselves, or lists of chapel possessions, such as that for the chapel in the house of Thomas Kebell, the fifteenth-century lawyer, which survives in the inventory which accompanied his will.*[5] *Other such inventories offer similar insights into the furnishing of such private sacred spaces,*[6] *although what they actually reveal about the owners of the property is perhaps less easily discernible.*

To turn from the creation of such officially sanctioned oratorical spaces to the acceptance of some degree of practical regulation is a major shift in direction, but nevertheless remains within the sphere of private religion. Generally speaking, there was no official need to record the extent of individual commitment to a spiritual life which remained within the world. The wide variety of religious commitments which were available generally required an individual to set him or herself aside from 'normality', either through commitment to a religious order, the life of a hermit (although hermits could be very worldly) or the extreme of total seclusion in an anchorage.[7] *For men, it was the fairly regulated life of the hermit – which might well involve physical labour on road building or bridge maintenance (see no. 25) – under*

4 N. Davis, ed., *Paston Letters and Papers of the Fifteenth Century*, 2 vols., Oxford, 1970. The comments, although brief, are suggestive, and merit reproduction.

(i) John Paston III to John Paston II, November 1472 (*ibid.*, I, p. 575): 'My mother sends you God's blessing and her's, and urges you to get a new licence from my lord of Norwich so that she may have the sacrament in her chapel. I got a licence from him for a year, and it has almost expired. You should get it for the bishop's life if you can.'

(ii) Margaret Paston to John Paston III, 28 January, 1475 (*ibid.*, I, p. 374): 'I would like you to speak to my lord of Norwich, and try to get a licence from him so that I may have the sacrament here [i.e. Mautby, Norfolk], because it is a long way to the church and I am sickly, and the parson is often away.'

(ii) Margaret Paston to John Paston II, 5 March 1475 (*ibid.*, I, p. 375): 'As you may recall ... about the licence which I spoke to you about, to have the sacrament in my chapel. If you cannot obtain it from the bishop of Norwich, get it from the [arch]bishop of Canterbury, for that is the safest for all places ...'

5 E. W. Ives, *The Common Lawyers of Pre-Reformation England*, Cambridge, 1983, pp. 444–5, also 436, 443,

6 E.g. the inventory of Framlingham Castle, made on the death of the Duke of Norfolk in 1524, in J. Ridgard, ed., *Medieval Framlingham, Select Documents, 1270–1524*, Suffolk Record Society, XXVII, 1985, pp. 148–53 (with other scattered goods at pp. 134, 155).

7 R. N. Swanson, *Church and Society in Late Medieval England*, Oxford, 1989, pp. 268–75; A. Clark, ed., *Lincoln Diocese Documents, 1450–1544*, Early English Text Society, original ser., CXLIX, 1914, pp. 19–21 (the volume contains a number of vows).

the 'Rule of St Paul' which was most commonly adopted.[8] *The majority of these hermits retained an officially lay status, but the adoption of the habit may be treated as reflecting a crossing of the border between a secular and regular (= religious) life. For women, the options retained the secularity. Their commitment to a life of chastity, through the taking of the appropriate vows, is something which is fairly regularly encountered, in notes recording their formal oaths. However, these documents raise a variety of questions about the rationale behind the action and the degree of free will involved. The recorded instances generally relate to widows, or those whose marriage was to be superseded for some reason; but it is clear that such vows could be taken jointly by married couples,*[9] *and therefore presumably (although I know of no recorded instance) by men alone. The question of the degree of freedom is an important one. A joint vow – especially if the husband was assuming a more strictly regular or clerical life – might reflect a degree of imposition on the wife. Equally, if the woman was the dominant partner (as appears to have been the case with Margery Kempe), it could reflect imposition on the husband. The reasons for a woman to take on the obligations of the vow could be complex: the status of a perpetual widow clearly had economic and personal advantages in a patriarchal world; it is therefore possible that (as has been suggested in the case of the Lady Margaret Beaufort) such considerations were sometimes a determining factor.*[10]

16. Licences for private chapels and oratories: grants made by Richard le Scrope as bishop of Coventry and Lichfield, 1386–8 [From Lichfield Joint Record Office, B/A/1/6 (Register of Bishop Richard Scrope), ff.122r–4v; in Latin. Other licences are also entered on these folios, but I have not indicated where such material intervenes among the grants of chapel and oratory licences]

HERE BEGINS THE YEAR OF THE LORD, 1386

Item, on 2 kal. April [31 March] ... a licence was granted to Roger Hillari, knight, so that he could have divine offices celebrated in all his oratories throughout the diocese of Coventry and Lichfield, for one year.

Item, on 4 ides [10] April ... a licence was granted to Sir Hamo Waghan, knight, that he could have divine offices celebrated in his

8 V. Davis, 'The rule of Saint Paul, the first hermit, in late medieval England', *Studies in Church History*, XXII, 1985, pp. 203–14.

9 Swanson, *Church and Society*, p. 271.

10 C. W. Atkinson, *Mystic and Pilgrim: the Book and the World of Margery Kempe*, Ithaca and London, 1983, pp. 16–17; M. K. Jones and M. G. Underwood, *The King's Mother: Lady Margaret Beaufort, Countess of Richmond and Derby*, Cambridge, 1992, pp. 153–4.

manor of *Linches* for one year, etc.

Item, on 3 ides [11] April ... a licence was granted to Sir Laurence Dotton, knight, that he could have divine offices celebrated in all his oratories throughout the diocese of Coventry and Lichfield.

Item, on 7 kal. May [25 April] ... a licence was granted to John Haydok that he could have divine offices celebrated in the manor of Bradley for one year.

Item, on 4 nones [3] July ... a licence was granted for the oratories of Thomas Sleyne in the manors of Sproston and *Northegg*.

Item, on 20 December ... a licence was granted to Matilda Gleye for her oratory at [blank] for one year.

Item, on 15 January ... a licence was granted ... to Ralph atte Wode of Houghton that he could have divine offices celebrated in an oratory within his manor of Houghton for one year.

Item, on 8 February ... a licence was granted to William Hulme for his oratory at *Gotesbyght* for one year.

Item, on ... 20 December ... a licence was granted ... to Anker Frechevyll [for an oratory] at [blank] for one year.

Item, on 12 February ... a licence was granted ... to Baldwin Frevill, knight, for an oratory at Middleton for one year.

Item, on the same date ... a licence was granted to Ralph de Brayllesford ... for his oratory at Mercaston for one year.

Item, on 17 February ... a licence was granted ... to *dominus* Richard Cochet, chaplain, that he could celebrate divine offices in the chapel at the end of the bridge of the town of Congleton for one year.

THE YEAR OF THE LORD, 1387

Item, on 6 kal. April [27 March] ... a licence was granted to John de Holand and Margaret his wife for an oratory within the manor of Dalbury for one year.

Item, on 17 June ... a licence was granted to Matilda, widow of Sir T. de Marchyngton, knight, deceased, that she could have divine offices celebrated in her manor of Rodsley, with the clause 'for as long as we', etc.

Item, on the last day of June ... a licence was granted to Elena de Eccleston, widow of John de E., deceased, for her oratories at Eccleston and Walton, for two years.

Item, on 1 July ... a licence was granted to John de Haydok for the oratories of Haydock and Bradley, with the clause, 'for as long as it pleases us', etc.

Item, on ... [10 July] a licence was granted to John de Delves that he could have divine offices celebrated in all his oratories throughout the diocese, with the clause, 'for as long', etc.

Item, on 14 July ... a licence was granted to David de Malpas that he could have divine offices celebrated in his manor of Hampton for two years.

Item, on the same date ... a licence was granted to Roger Hillary, knight, that he could have divine offices celebrated in his manor of Bescot, for two years.

Item, on 16 July ... a licence was granted to Lady Philippa, lady of Thornton, that she could, etc. in her manor of Thornton, for two years.

Item, on 19 July ... a licence was granted to Sir John de Gresleye, that he could have divine offices celebrated in his manor of Drakelow, with the clause, 'for as long', etc.

Item, on 25 July ... a licence was granted for Roger de Bradburne for his oratory at Hough, with the clause, 'for as long', etc.

Item, on 6 August ... a licence was granted for Richard de Wynyngton in his manor of Winnington, for two years.

Item, on 8 August ... a licence was granted for Sir Hamond Waghan, knight, in his manor of *Lynches*, for three years.

Item, on 9 August ... a licence was granted to Anker Frechevyll that he could have divine offices celebrated in his manor of Stanley, with the clause 'for as long as we', etc.

Item, on ... [18 August], a licence was granted to Roger Baxter of Wigan for his oratories at Wigan and Liverpool, with the clause, 'for as long'.

Item, on the same date ... a licence was granted to William Barton of Stoke on Trent for his oratory at Stoke for two years.

Item, on 23 August ... a licence was granted to Henry de Trafford for his manor of Trafford for two years.

Item, on the same date ... a licence was granted to Anabilla de Barlaston for her oratories within the diocese, for two years.

Item, on 20 August ... a licence was granted to Sir John de la Pole of

Hartington, knight, for his oratories of *Wynardesley* and Poole for two years.

Item, on 11 September a licence was granted to Richard de Gratteford for his oratory at *Gratteford*, with the clause 'for as long'.

Item, on 12 September ... a licence was granted to Roger de Eldeston within oratories throughout the diocese, for three years.

Item, on 13 September ... a licence was granted to John Mossy of Tatton, knight, for each of his oratories throughout the diocese, for three years.

Item, on 10 kal. October [22 September] ... a licence was granted to Thomas Lescath' for his oratory at *Mertholme*, with the clause, 'for as long'.

Item, on 9 kal. October [23 September] ... a licence was granted to Hugh de Ince for each of his oratories throughout the diocese, with the clause 'for as long'.

Item, on 8 kal. October [24 September] ... a licence was granted to William de Chorley, senior, for his oratory at Chorley, for two years.

Item, on the same date ... for the oratory of Roger de Hulton at Ince, for two years.

Item, on 7 kal. October [25 September] ... a licence was granted to Sir Laurence de Sutton, knight, so that within his own oratories and those whatsoever of other honest men of the diocese of Lichfield which are set up within the diocese of Lichfield, whenever he or his consort shall happen in person to come to them or any of them in person, he may licitly have divine offices celebrated for him or his free household, provided, etc., with the clause, 'for as long', etc.

Item, on 6 kal. October [26 September] ... a licence was granted to Roger Hulfeld for his oratory at Duddon, with the clause, 'for as long'.

Item, on the same date ... a licence was granted to Richard de Manley for his oratories at Manley and Whettenhall, for three years.

Item, on ... [2 October] a licence was granted to Dame Alice de Bromwych, nun of the monastery of Polesworth, that she could have divine offices celebrated within her house within the enclosure of the said monastery, with the clause 'for as long as we', etc.

Item, on 2 October ... a licence was granted to Cecilia, widow of John Downne, that she could have divine offices celebrated in her house at Chester for 2 years.

Item, on the same date ... a licence was granted to Sir Walter Blount, knight, and the Lady Sanchia his wife, for each of their oratories within each of their manors and other decent places throughout the diocese of Lichfield, with the clause 'for as long as it pleases us'.

Item, on 6 October ... a licence was granted to Robert de Fouleshurst, for his oratory at Edlaston, with the clause, 'for as long', etc.

Item, on 9 October ... a licence was granted to Sir William, lord of Astley, for his manor of Astley, with the clause, 'for as long'.

Item, on the same date ... a licence was granted to Robert Fox, citizen of Chester, for his oratory at Chester for three years.

Item, on the same date ... a licence was granted to Ralph le Vernon of Hatton for his oratories of Hatton and Chester for three years.

Item, on 10 October ... a licence was granted to Elena, widow of Robert de Faryngton, for her oratory at Farington, with the clause 'for as long'.

Item, on the same date ... a licence was granted to Lady Margaret, widow of Sir John de Shirburne, for her oratory at Longton, for two years.

Item, on 18 kal. September [15 August] ... a licence was granted to John Pulle, knight, for his oratories at Burton, Poole and Tarvin, for two years.

Item, on 2 November ... a licence was granted to Henry Blundell for his oratory at Crosby, for two years.

Item, on 6 November ... a licence was granted to John de Leycestre for his oratory at Tabley, for one year.

Item, on 8 November ... a licence was granted to John Nedeham for his oratory at High Needham, with the clause 'for as long'.

Item, on 9 November ... a licence was granted to Sir William de Legh, knight, for his oratories of Baguley and Davenport, with the clause 'for as long'.

Item, on the same date ... a licence was granted to Elizabeth, lady of Sandbach, for her oratories at Sandbach and Sproston, for two years.

Item, on 11 November ... a licence was granted to Robert Grenenore, knight, for each of his oratories throughout the diocese, etc., with the clause 'for as long'.

Item, on 20 November ... a licence was granted to J. de Knyveton, for his oratory at Woodthorpe, with the clause 'for as long'.

Item, on 22 November ... a licence was granted to *dominus* Nicholas Kynchale, canon of Tamworth, for his oratory there, for two years.

Item, on the penultimate day of November a licence was granted to Richard de Bould, knight, for his oratories of Bold and *Chynacherul*, for three years.

Item, on 5 December a licence was granted to Geoffrey Reynold for his oratory at *Eduinscote* for three years.

Item, on 7 December ... a licence was granted to Robert Leversegge for each of his oratories throughout the diocese, etc., with the clause 'for as long'.

Item, on the same date a licence was granted to the parishioners of the church of Glossop for the chapel of Mellor, with the clause 'for as long'.

Item, on 6 December a licence was granted to Hugh de Hulse for each of his oratories throughout the diocese of Lichfield, with the clause 'for as long'.

Item, on 11 December a licence was granted to John de Longford for each of his oratories throughout the diocese, with the clause 'for as long'.

Item, on 23 December a licence was granted to John de Catesby for his oratory at Coventry for two years.

Item, on 23 December a licence was granted to Gilbert de Heydok for his oratories of Haydock and Bradley, with the clause 'for as long'.

[Licence granted to John Botyler, knight, and Alice his wife, that they (jointly, individually, and with their free households) could have divine offices celebrated by suitable chaplains, in each of their oratories in each of their manors, and in the manors or houses of other honest and condign people within the diocese whenever they personally go to them, provided that the oratories are decent and no prejudice arises from this, during the bishop's pleasure. Haywood, 29 December 1387.]

Item, on the same date ... a similar licence was granted to Joan, widow of Thomas Molyneux, deceased, on the same conditions.

Item, on 24 February ... a licence was granted to Sir Richard Venables, knight, and Margery his wife for the oratories of Kinderton, Marston, and Eccleston, with the clause 'for as long'.

Item, on 24 September ... a licence was granted to James and the dwellers or inhabitants of the vill of Bridgemere, in the parish of

Wibbenbury, that they could have divine offices celebrated within the chapel on the high street there, with the clause 'for as long'.

Item, on the last day of December ... a licence was granted to Maiorie Comwyle for her oratory at *Astaston* for three years.

Item, on the same date a licence was granted to Thomas Fiton for each of [his oratories] within each of his manors or houses, and those of other decent people throughout the diocese of Lichfield, with the clause 'for as long', etc.

Item, on 8 January ... a licence was granted to *dominus* Thomas de Clayton, chaplain, that he could celebrate divine offices or have them celebrated in the chapel at the end of the bridge of Ribble beyond the shore of Ribble, and in his oratory within his house at Claughton, with the clause 'for as long'.

Item, on 11 January ... a licence was granted to Thomas de Worthyngton for his oratory at *Blaynsclogh*, with the clause 'for as long as it pleases us', etc.

Item, on the same date ... a licence was granted to Thomas de Stones for his oratory at Colton, with the clause for as long as Margery his wife was suffering from infirmity and was unable to go to the parish church.

Item, on 13 January ... a licence was granted to Robert de Craston for his oratory at Shrewsbury for two years.

Item, on 15 January ... a licence was granted to was granted to Thomas de Stafford, knight, and [illegible] his wife, etc., in the form granted to John Botiler with the clause 'for as long'.

Item, on the same date ... a licence was granted to Robert Swynson, for his oratories within the diocese, with the clause 'for as long'.

Item, on 22 January ... a licence was granted to Thomas Maistreson for the oratory at Nantwich, with the clause 'for as long'.

Item, on the same date ... a licence was granted to *dominus* Roger Salehall, vicar of Acton, for his house there, with the clause 'for as long', etc.

Item, on the same date ... a licence was granted to David de Crwe for his oratory at *Sconde*, with the clause 'for as long'.

Item, on 23 January ... a licence was granted to *dominus* Thomas Beek for each of his oratories throughout the diocese, with the clause 'for as long'.

Item, on 26 January, ... a licence was granted to Adam de Scarburgh for an oratory at Coventry for two years.

Item, on the same date ... a licence was granted ... to John Odams of Napton for his oratory at Napton for three years.

Item, on 20 February ... a licence was granted to Ralph de Egginton for his oratory at Caldecote for three years.

Item, on 21 February ... a licence was granted to Sir John Maleny, knight, for his oratory at *Newbold Ryvel*, with the clause 'for as long'.

Item, on 25 February ... a licence was granted to Hugh de Wynstanley for his oratory there, for two years, etc.

Item, on 27 February ... a licence was granted to Sir William de Hugford, knight, for his manor of Apley, with the clause 'for as long', etc.

[It is possible that there were further such licences granted in March 1387/8, but which have not been registered: there is a gap in business until May, 1388.]

17. **Vows of chastity** [Taken from entries in the York archiepiscopal registers, as printed in *Testamenta Eboracensia*, III, Surtees Society Publications, XLV, 1865; in English, French and Latin]

(i) *Elizabeth Musgrave (1383)* [p. 313]

In the name of God, Amen. I, Elizabeth de Musgrave, widow, to the honour of God and his sweet mother the Virgin Mary, and all the saints of Heaven, promise and vow to God in your holy hands, reverend father in God Alexander, by the grace of God archbishop of York, primate of England, and legate of the Roman court, that my body shall be kept in chastity, with the aid of God, throughout my life. In testimony of which thing, I have made this sign with my own hand. +

And be it remembered, that on the 17th day of October [1383] ... the aforesaid reverend father in God ... blessed the aforesaid Elizabeth, and clad and decorated her with the mantle, veil and ring of chastity, and that Elizabeth solemnly issued the above-written vow in the hands of the said reverend father ...

(ii) *Agnes Overton (1471)* [p. 341]

In the name of God, Amen. I, Agnes Overton, widow, in the presence of you, reverend father, William, by the grace of God bishop of

Dromore, by the authority of my most reverend father in God George, by the grace of God archbishop of York, primate of England, and legate of the Roman court, vow and promise to live chaste from this time forward. So God help me, and these holy evangelists. And in token hereof, I here make this cross with my hand: +

(iii) *Henry Andrew and Alice his wife (1479)* [p. 344]

In the name of God, Amen. I, Henry Andrew, vow to God and to Our Lady, and to all the saints, to be chaste from this time forward, and to live in fasting, prayer and works of piety, and that I shall never quit this habit while I live: in the presence of you, Laurence, by the grace of God archbishop of York, primate of England, and legate of the Roman court; and promise to live stably in this vow in accordance with the order of hermits during my life. In witness whereof with my own hand I make here this +. ...

In the name of God, Amen. I, Alice Andrew, wife of Henry Andrew, vow to God and to Our Lady and to all saints, in the presence of you, Laurence, by the grace of God archbishop of York, primate of England, and legate of the Roman court, to be chaste from this time forward; and promise to live stably in this vow during my life: and, in witness thereof, with my own hand I make here this + ...

VII. Saints, shrines, miracles, and pilgrimages

Within Christianity, the principal focus of devotion was necessarily the divinity, in particular Christ, the second person of the Trinity. A striking feature of late medieval England is the Christ- and crucifix-centred nature of the spirituality, expressed in small-scale daily devotions, in visionary and devotional literature, in the integration of new feasts into the liturgical round and in the multiplication of pilgrimage crosses scattered across the country, complementing the physical relics of Christ, such as the holy blood at Hailes.[1]

Alongside Christ, the saints also attracted considerable devotion. The Virgin Mary was supreme among the saints, devotion to her being expressed in the inclusion of the Ave in the triad of basic recitations alongside the Our Father and Creed; while Marian prayers were a major component of the Books of Hours.[2] *As for the multitude of other saints, official and unofficial, commemorations of them were ubiquitous; their integration into the normality of spiritual practices fundamental. Saints' lives were a major genre of vernacular literature, being constantly added to throughout the period.*[3] *Cults might be encouraged and exploited for a variety of reasons, not all spiritual: under Henry V, the encouragement of the commemoration of Anglo-Saxon saints has obvious links with contemporary activity against France and the creation of English national identity.*[4] *Here, and elsewhere, the spiritual side cannot be discounted; but it is difficult to disentangle.*

1 E. Duffy, 'Devotion to the crucifix and related images in England on the eve of the Reformation' in *Bilder und Bildersturm im Spätmittelalter und in der früher Neuzeit*, ed. R. Scribner, Wolfenbütteler Forschungen, XLVI, Wiesbaden, 1990, pp. 21–36; for one wayside cross, D. M. Owen, 'Bacon and eggs: Bishop Buckingham and superstition in Lincolnshire', *Studies in Church History*, VIII, 1972, pp. 140–1.

2 R. S. Wieck, ed., *Time Sanctified: the Book of Hours in Medieval Art and Life*, New York, 1988, ch. 6, 8.

3 C. D'Evelyn and F. A. Foster, 'Saints' legends', in *A Manual of the Writings in Middle English, 1050–1500*, ed. J. B. Severs, II, Hamden, Conn., 1970, pp. 410–57, 553–649. The culmination of the collection of saints' lives (in Latin) was the *Nova Legenda Anglie*, printed by Wynkyn de Worde in 1516: C. Horstman, ed., *Nova Legenda Anglie, as Collected by John of Tynemouth, John Capgrave, and Others, and First Printed, with New Lives, by Wynkyn de Worde, a.d. m d xui*, 2 vols., Oxford, 1901. On the practicality of devotion, e.g. E. Duffy, 'Holy maydens, holy wyfes: the cult of women saints in fifteenth- and sixteenth-century England', *Studies in Church History*, XXVII, 1990, pp. 175–96.

4 J. Catto, 'Religious change under Henry V', in *Henry V, the Practice of Kingship*, ed. G. Harriss, Oxford, 1985, pp. 107–8.

Even though few new English saints were canonised after 1300, continental cults were imported; and numerous unofficial devotions centred on English men (there seem to be none centred on women).[5] *Saints acted as intercessors, and provided miracles; their shrines were the focus of aspirations, and of pilgrimages.*[6] *A key feature of the late Middle Ages in England was also the development of a multiplicity of shrines centred on images of the Virgin, and of a plethora of wayside crosses. Both were foci for offerings, and thus for pilgrimage and miracles. Pilgrimage might also be encouraged by the offering of indulgences and spiritual privileges for those visiting specified locations (below, nos. 28, 36 ii).*

There can be no denying the popularity of pilgrimage in late medieval England. But travel was not restricted to England: continental shrines were also much visited, although it is unlikely that there were many quite as mobile as Margery Kempe, who seems to have gone almost everywhere worth going to.[7] *On the other hand, there was little reason for such travels to be recorded: within England, much of the detailed evidence for pilgrimage derives from financial material generated at the sites themselves. The accounts for the shrine-keepers of Ely and Hereford permit an assessment of the scale of cash offerings, but not of the overall numerical flow of pilgrims. Even so, the relative peaks and troughs throughout the year can be determined.*[8] *In addition to these major offerings, it is also clear that great churches like Ely*

5 The main work on late medieval sainthood on a European scale is A. Vauchez, *La Saintété en occident des derniers siècles du moyen âge, d'après les procès de canonisation et les documents hagiographiques,* Bibliothèque des écoles françaises d'Athènes et de Rome, CCXLI, Rome, 1981; on English sainthood, R. N. Swanson, *Church and Society in Late Medieval England,* Oxford, 1989, pp. 99–101, 287–91; J. R. Bray, 'Concepts of sainthood in fourteenth century England', *Bulletin of the John Rylands University Library of Manchester,* LXVI, 1984, pp. 40–77.

6 The main work on English pilgrimage is now R. C. Finucane, *Miracles and Pilgrims: Popular Beliefs in Medieval England,* London, 1977, although much of the consideration predates 1350 (and the discussion of St Thomas Cantilupe needs revision in the light of the evidence in no. 19 below). For a wider discussion, J. Sumption, *Pilgrimage: an Image of Mediaeval Religion,* London, 1975.

7 C. W. Atkinson, *Mystic and Pilgrim: the Book and the World of Margery Kempe,* Ithaca and London, 1983, pp. 51–8. For extracts from another pilgrimage narrative, D. Englander, D. Norman, R. O'Day and W. R. Owens, eds, *Culture and Belief in Europe, 1450–1600: an Anthology of Sources,* Oxford, 1990, pp. 18–22.

8 For other accounts from major shrines, see E. Venables, 'The shrine and head of St Hugh of Lincoln', *Associated Architectural Societies Reports and Papers,* XXI, 1891–2, pp. 131–51; C. E. Woodruff, 'The financial aspect of the cult of St Thomas of Canterbury, as recorded by a study of the monastic records', *Archaeologia Cantiana,* XLIV, 1932, pp. 13–32. For the possibility of additional sums which by-passed the accounts of the shrine-keeper at Ely, Swanson, *Church and Society,* p. 226.

also had numerous lesser shrines and sources of offerings.[9]

Such lesser sites were also scattered throughout the country: the barely-recorded shrines of obscure saints produced small sums, but these all attest to the popularity of pilgrimage. Many of these shrines were within parish churches: the records of offerings among the parochial accounts of Great Yarmouth and King's Lynn (although these are mainly for Marian images) give some indication of their importance (see nos.14–15).[10]

But money was not the sole means of offering. Many offerings were in kind, which does not appear in the accounts. Wax offerings, not just candles but models of the part of the body or things connected with the offerer's trade, were ubiquitous (their nature being indicated by those discovered at Exeter in the 1940s).[11] *Other donations could be of jewellery, coins (like the nobles and reals affixed to St William's shrine at York), or other possessions, which would be physically attached to the shrine. The description of the shrine of Richard Scrope, the executed archbishop of York (d. 1405), whose tomb became the focus of a cult which made him the northern equivalent of Thomas Becket, indicates the wealth of such offerings.*[12]

9 Swanson, *Church and Society*, p. 227; surviving evidence for the minor offerings at Wells are tabulated in J. C. Colchester, ed., *Wells Cathedral Fabric Accounts, 1390–1600*, Wells, 1983, p. 67. For some of the minor Exeter cults, U. M. Radford, 'The wax images found in Exeter cathedral', *Antiquaries Journal*, XXIX, 1949, pp. 164–8; N. Orme, 'Two saint-bishops of Exeter: James Berkeley and Edmund Lacy', *Analecta Bollandiana*, CIV, 1986, pp. 403–18.

10 For some of these extremely minor cults, N. Orme, 'Saint Walter of Cowick', *Analecta Bollandiana*, CVIII, 1990, pp. 387–93; J. Blair, 'Saint Beornwald of Bampton', *Oxoniensia*, XLIX, 1984, pp. 47-55; J. Blair, 'Saint Beornwald of Bampton: further references', *Oxoniensia*, LIV, 1990, pp. 400–3. In some cases the scale might be considerably larger, if evidence from 1540 on the scale of the cult of St Urith at Chittlehampton (Devon) prior to its suppression can be trusted: J. F. Chanter, 'St Urith of Chittlehampton: a study of an obscure Devon saint', *Report and Transactions of the Devonshire Association for the Advancement of Science, Literature, and Art*, XLVI, 1914, pp. 306–7. For assessment of the Yarmouth material, R. N. Swanson, 'Standards of livings: parochial revenues in pre-Reformation England', in *Religious Belief and Ecclesiastical Careers in Late Medieval England*, ed. C. Harper-Bill, Woodbridge, 1991, pp. 166–7, 169, 188. (I shall be discussing the King's Lynn material in my work on that parish's accounts.)

11 Radford, 'Wax images', pp. 164–7.

12 See also the description of the image of the Virgin in the bridge chapel at Derby, from 1488, in J. C. Cox, *Churchwardens' Accounts from the Fourteenth Century to the Close of the Seventeenth Century*, London, 1913, p. 148. Offerings to images may be encountered in wills and other documents. For Scrope's cult, Swanson, *Church and Society*, pp. 100, 288–9; J. W. McKenna, 'Popular canonization as political propaganda: the case of Archbishop Scrope', *Speculum*, XLV, 1970, pp. 608-23; S. K. Wright, 'The provenance and manuscript tradition of the *Martyrium Ricardi archiepiscopi*', *Manuscripta*, XXVIII, 1984, pp. 92–102; S. K. Wright, 'Paradigmatic ambiguities in monastic historiography: the case of Clement Maidstone's *Martyrium Ricardi archiepiscopi*', *Studia Monastica*, XXVIII, 1986, pp. 311–42.

The scale of pilgrimage is less easily measured. The main testimony is physical, in the pilgrim badges which survive in collections scattered across the country.[13] *Documentary evidence is less common; but the record of the disbursements of Queen Elizabeth of York's representative (vicarious pilgrimage being not uncommon) provide a valid picture of both the distribution of shrines and the concern to visit them. Most of the sites mentioned on her list reflect the proliferation of Marian and cross shrines at this stage; but notable among the 'saints' visited are Henry VI at Windsor and his son Edward at Tewkesbury (this being one of the few indications of the ascription of sanctity to that youth).*[14]

Why people went is less often evident, save in records of miracles, which are clearly not an unbiased source. The acceptance of the miraculous, and what constituted a miracle, is indicated by the proceedings for the canonisations of Osmund of Salisbury and King Henry VI. The collection of miracles associated with the enquiry for the intended canonisation of Henry VI is the lengthiest from England for the late Middle Ages, numbering 174 (although not all survive in full). They present a wide range of interpretations of just what constituted a miracle, spread over several years and a considerable area. The full record is arranged in four books; the entries below are the summaries which precede the full reports of the miracles in the first book. The process for the canonisation of Osmund, bishop of Salisbury, met success only in 1456, although he had died in 1099. Throughout those centuries, a constant succession of miracles had been recorded, of which the two cited here seem to be among the last prior to the success of the canonisation process.

Miracles were also associated with many of the sites which focused on Christ and his mother; material associated with them show some of the tensions in the arrangements. Hailes Abbey in 1512 arranged for details of recent miracles linked with the relic of Christ's blood to be printed up, presumably in the hope of encouraging further visitors.[15] *For the individuals at the centre*

13 B. Spencer, 'Medieval pilgrim badges: some general observations illustrated mainly from English sources', in *Rotterdam Papers: a Contribution to Medieval Archaeology*, ed. J. G. N. Renaud, Rotterdam, 1968, pp. 137–54; B. Spencer, 'King Henry of Windsor and the London pilgrim', in *Collectanea Londiniensia: Studies in London Archaeology and History Presented to Ralph Merrifield*, ed. J. Bird, H. Chapman and J. Clark, London and Middlesex Archaeological Society, Special Papers, II, 1978, pp. 234–64; M. Mitchiner, *Medieval Pilgrim and Secular Badges*, London, 1986.

14 N. Rogers, 'The cult of Prince Edward at Tewkesbury', *Transactions of the Bristol and Gloucestershire Archaeological Society*, CI, 1983, pp. 187–9; K. Mertes, *English Noble Household, 1250–1600: Good Governance and Politic Rule*, Oxford, 1988, p. 148.

15 See J. C. T. Oates, 'Richard Pynson and the Holy Blood of Hailes', *The Library*, 5th ser., XIII, 1958, pp. 269–77. I had originally hoped to include the pamphlet in this collection; but the unique surviving copy has seemingly been mislaid, and I know of no reproductions.

of miraculous events, other concerns and passions might also be allowed to come into play: a miracle associated with the shrine of the Virgin at Ipswich in 1516 gained nation-wide celebrity, but on close examination a number of motivations apart from spirituality may be perceived at play there.[16]

A. Shrines and offerings by pilgrims

18. The ornaments of the shrines in York Minster in the early sixteenth century: lists given in the inventory of the Minster treasures, prepared in 1509–10 [From J. Raine, ed., *The Fabric Rolls of York Minster, with an Appendix of Illustrative Documents*, Surtees Society Publications, XXXV, 1858, pp. 224–6; in Latin and English. The edition has juggled the order of the paragraphs; for the sections here reproduced I have restored the order as in the original document (York Minster Library, M2/2d). The manuscript contains several emendations and additions which are incorporated here without being highlighted]

Around the portable shrine of St William. Five images of gilded silver. Four decorated belts. Two sets of beads [i.e. rosaries] of gilded silver; two sets of coral with gauds [i.e. the larger beads on the rosary] of gilded silver. A set of beads of chalcedon, with gauds of gilded silver; one set of pomander with gauds of gilded silver. Four spoons of gilded silver. One spoon with the handle of coral. Fourteen pieces of coral. Two hearts of gilded silver. Another belt of gilded silver of the gift of the Lady Chymnay. One breast of gilded silver. Three small crucifixes. Four clasps with stones. An image of St Mary in a tabernacle. One pair of shoes of gilded silver. One hand with a sceptre, of gilded silver. Five rings with stones. Three rings without stones. One portable sundial [*chelander*] of gilded silver. One piece of mother of pearl. One gold buckle with 8 stones. One clasp of gilded silver with one stone. One belt of silk interwoven with gold, with an oblong buckle and pendant. Item, 3 reals and 1 old noble. A clasp with 4 stones and 4 pearls.

Around the head of St William. One set of beads of silver, with the gauds gilded. Three sets of beads of coral, with the gauds of gilded silver. One set of beads of white amber, with the gauds of gilded silver. One old noble, and 3 nobles called angels, and 5s. in gold. One belt

16 D. MacCulloch, *Suffolk and the Tudors: Politics and Religion in an English County, 1500–1600*, Oxford, 1986, pp. 143–6.

pendant in Venetian gold, with stones and pearls (light in weight). Item, 11 rings of gilded silver. One ring of silver, enamelled with *Domini fons.* Item, 2 nobles. Item, 5s. in gold. Two gold reals. Item, 1 cruzado in gold. A gold brooch, enamelled. One cross of gold with precious stones of pearls. One set of coral beads with 23 gilded gauds. One set of beads in gold, of great length. One nose in gold. Item, 16 gold rings on one wire. Three rings of gilded silver. Item, 9 lambs of God. Item, 9 St Georges. An image of St Michael. Item, 7 crosses. A pomander of gilded silver. One eagle of silver. A cinquefoil flower, enamelled. A white bear with a ruby in the middle. One bow of silver. One belt decorated with gilded silver for hanging on the head of St William.

Belonging to the tomb of Lord Richard le Scrope. One staff marked with the letter A, on which are two images of men, in silver, large and small; a man's head; a man's heart; two images of bulls, large and small; ten ships of silver. Item, on the staff marked with the letter B, two images of men; a woman's breast and 14 boats in silver. On the staff marked with the letter C, two images of men, one of a woman, and two joined together of a man and a woman, a large man's heart with a gilded chain, another small heart, and ten ships in silver with an anchor of silver. On the staff marked with the letter D, a priest's head, two belts (one green, decorated with branches and birds, the other red with precious stones in the buckle), one large boat and five smaller ones of silver. On the staff marked with the letter E, two images (the larger of a woman, the smaller of a man), half an image of a man, the thigh of a man, two hearts and 12 boats of silver. On the staff marked with the letter F, one belt of black silk with the buckle and pendant gilded, and 6 ships.

For that tomb. Item, 27 oars for boats with one arrow in silver. A set of beads in jet, with six of the gauds in silver. One lamb with the relics of St Stephen (this is not found). An image of St Stephen in gilded silver; to be placed on the shrine of St William. One silver basin with roses and sunbeams in the base, gilded around the rim.

Fixed to the shrine of St William. One heart of gilded silver. A woman's breast of gilded silver. One portable sundial [*chelander*] of gilded silver. Item, 2 shoes of gilded silver with precious stones. A hand with writing in silver gilt. A small belt of purple silk with the buckle and pendant in gold. A belt called a demi-ceint [a narrow girdle of metal plates] of gilded silver. Two pieces of coral decorated at the end with gilded silver. Two pieces of undecorated coral.

This written immediately above is affixed to the portable shrine of St William, although they were around the tomb of the lord Scrope.

For the said tomb of Lord le Scrop. Item, 7 boats of gilded silver, which are affixed to the great shrine of St William. One belt of red silk decorated with gilded silver, which remains not fixed to any shrine so far. Two rings of gold, and two gauds of gold wrapped in red silk, remaining in the ebony box containing many precious stones belonging to that tomb ...

Belonging to the tomb of Lord Scrop, recently found, in the time of Robert Langton, Treasurer of York, 1509. Fixed to the first cloth: Firstly, images of silver on the first cloth, 13. Item, 8 silver crucifixes. Item, 4 silver heads. Item, anchors and hooks, 16, silver. Item, 17 silver buckles. Item, 3 lambs and 2 tables, of silver. Item, 1 silver bow. Item, 7 legs and feet of silver. Item, 4 teeth and 4 hearts of silver. Item, 8 eyes and 2 hands of silver. Item, 2 girdles decorated with silver lettering. Item, 15 pieces of gilt. Item, a gold ring without a stone.

Fixed to the second cloth: Item, images and heads of silver, 6. Item, 4 crucifixes. Item, 4 lambs. Item, 18 anchors and hooks. Item, 2 ships. Item, 7 legs and feet. Item, 4 buckles and pendants. Item, a gold buckle. Item, 10 teeth. Item, a silver chapel. Item, a set of silver beads with gilt gauds. Item, 5 eyes of silver, and 2 of gold. Item, 2 belts decorated with silver. Item, 11 gold rings. Item, an arrow-head in gold. Item, 8 pieces of gold.

Fixed to the third cloth: Item, 8 images and heads. St George on horseback, in silver. A silver horse. Item, 4 hearts. Item, 3 crucifixes. Item, 6 hands and legs. Item, 25 buckles. Item, 4 anchors and hooks. A pap and a tun. Item, 2 pieces of harness for horses' heads. Item, 3 eyes and 2 lambs. A gold brooch, with an angel and a stone in it. A gold heart enamelled with white and green. Item, 2 teeth. Item, a box for a messenger. A tablet of silver. Item, one old noble. One gold ring with a stone. One old decorated girdle, with 3 gold rings on it. A girdle decorated throughout, with knots of silver and gilt.

19. Cash receipts from offerings at Hereford Cathedral, as entered in the clavigers' accounts [Hereford Cathedral Archives; in Latin]

(i) *1478–9* [R369]

Oblations

And [they render account] for 19s. 8d., received from the box of St Thomas on the feast of St Gregory [12 March]; And for 22s. 1d. received from the same box on the eve of Pentecost [9 May]; from pennies received at the head of St Thomas this year, nothing. But they account for 25s. received from that box at the deposition of St Thomas [25 August]; And for £12 17s. 4d. received from that box on the morrow of the octaves of St Thomas; from pennies received for wax sold there, nothing, because with the above total. But they account for 17s. 8d. received at head of St Thomas on that day; And for 5d. received at the relics that day; And for 110s. 1d. received from the box of St Thomas on the morrow of [All] Souls [3 November]; And for 6s. 5d. from pennies received at the head and relics that day.

Total: £22 18s. 8d.

(ii) *1490–1* [R585, f.22r]

Oblations

Firstly, in the box of St Thomas on the day of [All] Souls [2 November]:	£3 6s. 8d.
Item, that day, for wax	11s. 4d.
Item, at the head and relics that day	5s. 2d.
Item, in the box of St Henry on the day of St Silvester [31 December]	3s. 8d.
Item, in the box of St Thomas on the morrow of St Gregory [13 March]	21s. 6d.
Item, at the head and relics that day	18d.
Item, in the box of St Henry that day	18d.
Item, in the box of St Thomas on the eve of Pentecost [21 May]	15s.
Item, in the box of St Henry on the morrow of Corpus Christi [3 June]	3s.
Item, in the box of St Thomas on the day of his deposition [25 August]	16s.
Item, in the box of St Thomas, on the day of St Jerome [30 September]	13s. 4d.
Item, in the box of St Henry on the 14th day of October	6s. 1d.

Item, in the box of St Thomas on the 14th day of October	£7 8d.
Item, for wax sold that day	13s. 4d.
Item, at the head and relics that day	13s. 5½d.
Item, from the price of 1 ox offered to the shrine of St Thomas and sold to *dominus* John Bolt	8s.
Item, from the box of St Thomas on the eve of his Translation [24 October]	3s. 2d.
Item, from broken silver ['and copper' crossed out in MS] sold to Robert Marbyll	6s. 4d.

Total = £17 9s. 8½d.

(iii) *1505–6* [R585, f.1r]

Oblations

Item, in the box of St Thomas on the morrow of All Souls [3 November]	33s. 9d.
Item, that day, at the head of St Thomas	2s.
Item, at the relics that day	13d.
Item, that day, for wax sold	6s. 8d.
Item, in the box of St Thomas, on the day of St Gregory the Pope [12 March]	10s. [...]d.
Item, in the box of St Thomas on the eve of Pentecost [30 May]	13s. 4d.
Item, in that box on the day of St Bartholomew [24 August]	21s. 8d.
Item, at the head and relics that day	10s. [...]d.
Item, in the box of St Thomas on the morrow of St Denys [10 October]	£8 [...]
Item, at the head and relics that day	25s.10d.
Item, that day, for wax sold	16s. 4d.
Item, in the box of King Henry that day	6d.

Total = £15 9s. 8d.

(iv) *1506–7* [R585, f.5r]

Oblations

Item, from the box of St Thomas on the day of St Leonard [6 November]	28s. 3d.
Item, at the head and relics that day	2s. 8d.
Item, for wax sold that day	8s.

Item, from the box of St Thomas on the day of St Gregory the Pope [12 March]	16s. 4d.
Item, from the box on the eve of Pentecost [22 May]	14s. 5d.
Item, from that box on the day of St Bartholomew [24 August]	13s. 7d.
Item, from that box on the morrow of St Denys [10 October]	£6 12s.
Item, at the head and relics that day	22s.
Item, that day, for wax sold	13s. 4d.
Item, from the box of King Henry	2d.
Item, for broken silver sold this year	12d.

Total = £12 11s. 9d.

(v) *1507–8* [R585, f.8v]

Oblations

Item, from the box of St Thomas, the 4th day of November	26s. 4d.
Item, at the head and relics that day	4s. 4d.
Item, for wax sold that day	6s. 9d.
Item, from the box of St Thomas on the day of St Gregory the Pope [12 March]	14s.
Item, from that box on the eve of Pentecost [10 June]	20s. 8d.
Item, from that box on the day of St Bartholomew [24 August]	18s. 6d.
Item, from that box on the morrow of St Denys [10 October]	£5 19s. 2d.
Item, at the head and relics that day	23s.*
Item, for wax sold that day	18s. 4d.
Item, from the box of King Henry that day	5½d.
Item, for broken silver sold this year	4s. 8d.

Total = £12 16s. 2½d.

*corrected from 18s. 4d.

(vi) *1508–9* [R585, f.11r]

Oblations

Item, from the box of St Thomas, the 26th day of November	27s. 9d.
Item, that day, at the head and relics	2s. 3d.
Item, that day, for wax sold	7s. 1d.
Item, from the box of St Thomas on the day of	

St Gregory [12 March]	10s. 4d.
Item, from the box of St Thomas on the eve of Pentecost [26 May]	11s. 7d.
Item, from that box on the day of St Bartholomew [24 August]	33s.
Item, at the head of St Thomas that day	9s. 4d.
Item, at the relics that day	5s. 11d.
Item, from the box of St Thomas on the morrow of St Firminus [26 September]	10s. 8d.
Item, from the box of St Thomas on the morrow of St Denys [10 October]	£8 16s. 8d.
Item, at the head of St Thomas that day	15s. 11d.
Item, at the relics that day	9s. 8d.
Item, that day, for wax sold	20s.
Item, from the box of King Henry	7½d.
Item, for broken silver sold this year	2s. 6d.

Total = £17 3s. 3½d.

(vii) *1509–10* [R585, f.14r]

Oblations

Item, in the box of St Thomas on the morrow of [All] Souls [3 November]	26s.
Item, that day, at the head of St Thomas	4s.
Item, at the relics that day	2s.
Item, that day, for wax sold	4s.
Item, in the box of St Thomas on the day of St Gregory the Pope [12 March]	12s. 8d.
Item, in the box of St Thomas on the day of St Bartholomew [24 August]	28s.
Item, at the head and relics that day	5s. 4d.
Item, in the box of St Thomas on the morrow of Denys [10 October]	£3 13s. 4d.
Item, at the head of St Thomas that day	6s. 8d.
Item, at the relics, that day	3s. 4d.
Item, for wax sold that day	15s. 6d.

Total = £9 0s. 10d.

(viii) *1522–3* [R586]

Oblations

And [they account for] 16s. 2d. received from the box of St Thomas the martyr on the morrow of All Souls [3 November]; And for 2s. 10d. received from that day at the head of St Thomas and the relics; And for 9s. 6d. received for wax sold that day; And for 10s. 2d. received from the said box on the day of St Gregory the Pope [12 March]; And for 19s. 6d. received on the morrow of St Bartholomew the apostle [25 August]; And for 6s. 11d. received at the head and relics that day; And for 71s. received from that box on the morrow of St Denys [10 October]; And for 14s. 9d. received at the head of St Thomas and the relics that day; And for 9s. 1½d. received that day for wax sold; And for 7s. received from broken silver this year; [And for [blank] received from wax sold last year and not yet accounted]. [This last entry crossed out in MS.]

Total: £8 6s. 11½d.

20. Receipts entered in the accounts of the keeper of St Etheldreda's shrine, Ely [Cambridge University Library, Ely Dean and Chapter Records; in Latin. In some of the accounts the repetition of figures for totals of individual headings which appear on the documents has been silently omitted]

(i) *From the 6th weekday in the eve of SS Peter and Paul [28 June], to Michaelmas [29 September], 9 Henry V [1421]* [EDC.5/12/1]

Oblations: And from all oblations deriving to the altar of the relics, with the wax sold to pilgrims at that time: 52s.½d.

Oblations at indulgence time: And from oblations deriving from the shrine and altar of reliquaries for fifteen days at the time of the indulgence: £7 10s.
Sum total of receipts: £10 2s.½d.

(ii) *1421–2* [EDC. 5/12/1]

Oblations with wax sold: And from all oblations deriving from the altar of the reliquaries, with wax sold to pilgrims: £13 5s. 3d.

Sale of wax: And from 64 lb. of wax sold this year, price 4d. per pound: 21s. 4d.

And from £7 6s. 8d. received from oblations deriving from the shrine and relics at the time of the indulgence.

(iii) *1422–3* [EDC. 5/12/2]

Oblations: And from oblations deriving from the altar of reliquaries, with wax sold to pilgrims this year, beyond oblations deriving from the time of dedication for fifteen days: £14 10s. 7½d.

Sale of wax: And from 164 lb. of wax sold this year, price 4d. per pound: 54s. 8d.

Oblations at the time of the indulgence: And from oblations deriving from the shrine and reliquaries at the time of indulgence this year: £6 17d.

(iv) *1423–4* [EDC. 5/12/3]

Oblations: And from oblations deriving from the relics, with wax sold to pilgrims this year, beyond oblations deriving from fifteen days of the time of indulgence: £15 9d.

Sale of wax: And from 174 lb. of wax sold this year, price 4d. per pound: 58s.

Oblations at the time of the indulgence: And from oblations deriving from the shrines and relics in the time of indulgence: £8 8s. 9d.

(v) *1424–5* [EDC. 5/12/4]

Oblations: And from oblations deriving from the altar of reliquaries, with wax sold to pilgrims this year, beyond oblations deriving from the fifteen days of the time of indulgence: £16 18s. 3d.

Oblations at the time of the indulgence: And from oblations deriving from all the shrines and relics at the time of indulgence this year: £7 17s. 6d.

Sale of wax: And from 127 lb. of wax sold this year, price 4d. per pound. Total: 42s. 4d.

(vi) *1425–6* [EDC. 5/12/4]

Oblations: And from oblations deriving from the altar of reliquaries, with wax sold to pilgrims this year, beyond oblations deriving from the time of indulgence for fifteen days: £16 18s. 8½d.

Oblations at the time of the indulgence: And from oblations deriving from all the shrines and relics at the time of indulgence: £6 17s. 6d.

Sale of wax: And from 146 lb. of wax sold this year, price 4d. per pound: 48s. 8d.

(vii) *1426–7* [EDC. 5/12/5]

Oblations: And from oblations deriving from the relics, with wax sold to pilgrims this year, beyond oblations deriving from the fifteen days of the time of indulgence.

Total: £14 14s. 5d.

Sale of wax: And from 138 lb. of wax sold this year, at various prices: 47s. 4d.

Oblations at the time of the indulgence: And from oblations deriving from the shrines and relics at the time of indulgence: £7 12d.

(viii) *1427–8* [EDC. 5/12/5]

Oblations: And from oblations deriving from the altar of reliquaries, with wax sold to pilgrims this year, beyond oblations deriving from the time of indulgence for fifteen days: £14 19s. 3d.

Oblations at the time of the indulgence: And from oblations deriving from all the shrines and relics in the time of indulgence: £6 5s. 4d.

Sale of wax: Item, in 91 lb. of wax sold this year, at various prices: 40s. 8d.

(ix) *1428–9* [damaged] [EDC. 5/12/5]

[*Oblations:*] And from oblations deriving from the altar of reliquaries, with wax sold to pilgrims this year, beyond oblations deriving from the time of indulgence over fifteen days: £11 6½d.

[*Oblations at the time of the indulgence:* And from oblations] deriving from all the shrines and relics in the time of indulgence: £7 12s. 9d.

[*Sale of wax:* And from ?53] lb. of wax sold this year, at various prices: 23s. 1d.

(x) *1464–5* [EDC. 5/12/ unnumbered. The accounts through to no. (xviii) are all contained on the same document]

Receipts of wax and leftover wax

And from 5s. received from oblations at the relics from the feast of Michael [29 September] until the fair, with wax and leftover wax.

And from £6 received from oblations of wax from the feast of Michael in the first quarter until the Lord's Birth [25 December], with the vigil and day of St Etheldreda [16–17 October] at the time of the fair this year, with leftover wax.

And from 3s. 6d. received from oblations at the relics from the feast of the Lord's Birth until the feast of Easter [14 April], with wax and leftover wax.

And from 22s. received from oblations at the relics from the feast of Easter until the feast of the Nativity of St John the Baptist [24 June], with the vigil and day of St Etheldreda [22–3 June] this year, and with wax and leftover wax.

And from 18s. received from oblations of wax and leftover wax from the feast of the Nativity of St John the Baptist until the time of the indulgence.

Total: £8 8s. 6d.

(xi) *1465–6* [EDC. 5/12/ unnumbered]

Receipts of wax and leftover wax

And from 4s. 6d. received from oblations at the relics from the feast of Michael [29 September] until the fair, with wax and leftover wax.

And from 110s. received from oblations of wax from the feast of Michael, the first quarter, until the feast of the Lord's Birth, with the vigil and day of St Etheldreda [16–17 October] at the time of the fair, with wax and leftover wax.

And from 3s. 4d. received from oblations at the shrine from the feast of the Lord's Birth until the feast of Easter [6 April], with wax and leftover wax.

And from 25s. received from oblations at the shrine from the feast of Easter until the feast of the Nativity of St John the Baptist [24 June], with the vigil and day of St Etheldreda [22–3 June] this year, with wax and leftover wax.

And from 16s. received from oblations of wax and leftover wax from the feast of the Nativity of St John the Baptist until the time of the indulgence, this year.

Total: £7 18s. 10d.

(xii) *1466–7* [EDC. 5/12/unnumbered]

Receipts of wax and leftover wax

And from 4s. 10d. received from oblations at the relics from the feast of Michael [29 September] until the fair, with wax and leftover wax.

And from 116s. 10d. received from oblations of wax from the feast of Michael, the first quarter, until the Lord's Birth, with the vigil and day of St Etheldreda [16–17 October] at the time of the fair, this year, with leftover wax.

And from 3s. 8d. received from oblations at the relics from the feast of the Lord's Birth until the feast of Easter [29 March], with wax and leftover wax.

And from 26s. received from oblations at the relics from the feast of Easter until the feast of the Nativity of St John the Baptist [24 June], with the vigil and day of St Etheldreda [22–3 June], with wax and leftover wax.

And from 20s. received from oblations at the relics from the feast of the Nativity of St John the Baptist until the time of the indulgence, with wax and leftover wax.

Total: £8 11s. 4d.

(xiii) *1467–8* [EDC. 5/12/unnumbered]

Receipts of wax with leftover wax
And from 3s. 10d. received from oblations at the relics from the feast of Michael [29 September] until the fair, with wax and leftover wax this year.

And from 113s. 4d. received from oblations of wax at the relics from the feast of Micahel, the first quarter, until the Lord's Birth, with the vigil and day of St Etheldreda [16–17 October] at the time of the fair, with wax and leftover wax.

And from 3s. 8d. received from oblations from the feast of the Lord's Birth until the feast of Easter [17 April], with wax and leftover wax.

And from 20s. 10d. received from oblations from the feast of Easter until the feast of the Nativity of St John the Baptist [24 June], with wax and leftover wax.

And from 18s. 10d. received from oblations of wax from the feast of the Nativity of St John the Baptist until the time of the indulgence, with leftover wax.

Total: £8 6d.

(xiv) *1468–9* [EDC. 5/12/unnumbered]

Receipts of wax with leftover wax
And from 4s. 5½d. received from oblations at the relics from the feast of Michael the Archangel [29 September] until the fair, with wax and leftover wax.

And from £6 received from oblations, with the vigil and day of St Etheldreda [16–17 October] at the time of the fair, until the feast of the Lord's Birth, with wax and leftover wax.

And from 3s. 6d. received from oblations at the relics from the feast of the Lord's Birth until the feast of Easter [2 April], with wax and leftover wax.

And from 26s. 10d. received from oblations from the feast of Easter until the feast of the Nativity of St John the Baptist [24 June], with wax and leftover wax.

And from 18s. 10d. received from oblations from the feast of the Nativity of St John until the time of the indulgence, with wax and leftover wax.

Total: £8 13s. 7½d.

(xv) *1469–70* [EDC. 5/12/unnumbered]

Receipts of wax with leftover wax

And from 3s. 2d. received from oblations of wax at the relics from the feast of Michael [29 September] until the fair, with leftover wax.

And from 100s. received from oblations of wax at the relics with the vigil and day of St Etheldreda [16–17 October] at the time of the fair, until the feast of the Lord's Birth, with leftover wax.

And from 4s. received from oblations of wax from the feast of the Lord's Birth until the feast of Easter [22 April], with leftover wax.

And from 25s. received from oblations of wax from the feast of Easter until the feast of the Nativity of St John the Baptist [24 June], with leftover wax.

And from 18s. 10d. received from oblations of wax from the feast of the Nativity of St John the Baptist until the time of the indulgence, with leftover wax.

Total: £7 11s. 2d. [*sic*]

(xvi) *1471–2* [EDC 5/12/unnumbered]

Receipts of wax with leftover wax

And from 4s. 10d. received from oblations of wax at the relics from the feast of Michael [29 September] until the fair, with wax and leftover wax.

And from £6 received from oblations of wax at the relics with the vigil and day of St Etheldreda [16–17 October] at the time of the fair, until the feast of the Lord's Birth, with leftover wax.

And from 3s. 10d. received from oblations of wax from the feast of the Lord's Birth until the feast of Easter [14 April], with leftover wax.

And from 22s. received from oblations of wax from the feast of Easter until the feast of St John the Baptist [24 June], with leftover wax.

And from 19s. 6d. received from oblations of wax from the feast of St John the Baptist until the time of the indulgence, with leftover wax.

Total: £8 10s. 2d.

(xvii) *1471–2* [EDC. 5/12/ unnumbered]

Receipts of wax with leftover wax
And from 4s. 8d. received from oblations of wax at the relics from the feast of Michael [29 September] until the fair, with leftover wax.

And from 110s. received from oblations of wax at the relics with the vigil and day of St Etheldreda [16–17 October] at the time of the fair, until the feast of the Lord's Birth, with 40s. for leftover wax.

And from 3s. 10d. received from oblations from the feast of the Lord's Birth until the feast of Easter [29 March], with wax and leftover wax.

And from 25s. 6d. received from oblations of wax from the feast of Easter until the feast of St John the Baptist [24 June], with leftover wax.

And from 19s. received from oblations of wax at the relics from the feast of the Nativity of St John the Baptist until the time of the indulgence.

Total: £8 3s.

(xviii) *1472–3* [EDC. 5/12/ unnumbered]

Receipts of wax with leftover wax
And from 4s. 8d. received from oblations of wax at the relics from the feast of Michael [29 September], the first quarter, until the fair, with leftover wax.

And from £7 received from oblations at the relics with the vigil and day of St Etheldreda [16–17 October] at the time of the fair, until the Lord's Birth, with 60s. for wax and leftover wax.

And from 3s. 10d. received from oblations of wax from the feast of the Lord's Birth until Easter [18 April], with leftover wax.

And from 26s. received from oblations of wax from the feast of Easter until the feast of St John [24 June], with leftover wax.

And from 18s. 11d. received from oblations of wax at the relics from the feast of the Nativity of St John until the time of the indulgence, with leftover wax.

Total: £9 13s. 5d.

(xix) *1474–5* [EDC. 5/12/ unnumbered. The accounts through to no (xxi) are all contained on the same document]

Receipts of wax with leftover wax
And from 4s. 11d. received from oblations at the relics from the feast of Michael [29 September] until the fair, with wax and leftover wax.

And from 100s. received from oblations at the relics with the vigil and day of St Etheldreda [16–17 October] at the time of the fair, until the Lord's Birth, with wax and leftover wax.

And from 5s. 6d. received from oblations at the relics from the feast of the Lord's Birth until Easter [26 March], with wax and leftover wax.

And from 29s. received from oblations at the relics from the feast of Easter until the feast of the Nativity of St John [24 June], with wax and leftover wax.

And from 18s. 10d. received from oblations at the relics from the feast of St John until the time of the indulgence, with wax and leftover wax.

Total: £7 18s. 3d.

(xx) *1475–6* [EDC. 5/12/unnumbered]

[*Receipts of wax*] *and leftover wax*
And from 118s. 3d. received from oblations at the relics with wax this year.

And from 79s. from leftover wax sold this year.

And from 7s. 6d. from wax sold this year.

Total: £10 4s. 9d.

(xxi) *1476–7* [EDC. 5/12/unnumbered]

Receipts of wax and leftover wax
And from 5s. 10d. received from oblations at the relics from the feast of Michael [29 September] until the fair, with wax and leftover wax.

And from £7 received from oblations at the relics with the vigil and day of St Etheldreda [16–17 October] at the time of the fair, until the Lord's Birth, with wax and leftover wax [the figure of 60s. here interlineated].

And from 5s. 6d. received from oblations at the relics from the feast of the Lord's Birth until the feast of Easter [6 April], with wax and leftover wax.

And from 30s. received from oblations at the relics from the feast of Easter until the feast of St John [24 June], with wax and leftover wax.

And from 20s. received from oblations at the relics from the feast of the Nativity of St John until the time of the indulgence, with wax and leftover wax.

Total: £10 16d.

Oblations in the time of the indulgence
And from 32s. 11d. received from oblations deriving from all the shrines and relics, with wax sold, in the time of the indulgence.

Total: 32s. 11d.

(xxii) *1491–2* [EDC.5/12/8]

Oblations
And from £7 6s. 1d. from oblations and wax, sold from the feast of St Michael [29 September] until the feast of the indulgence; And from 30s. for 90 lb. of gummed wax sold; And from £12 17s. from leftover wax sold this year; And from 30s. 6d. from oblations at all the shrines and reliquaries, with wax and recovery of wax at the time of the indulgence; And from 6d. for 1½ oz. of jet sold this year.

Total: £23 4s. 1d.

(xxiii) *1497–8* [EDC. 5/12/10]

Oblations
And from 103s. 1½d. from oblations and gummed wax, sold from the feast of St Michael the Archangel [29 September] until the feast of the indulgence; And from £12 2s. from recovery of wax sold this year; And from 64s. 5¾d, from oblations at all the shrines and relquaries, with wax and recovery of wax at the time of the indulgence this year.

Total: £20 9s. 7¼d. [This is a final corrected figure].

(xxiv) *1498–9* [EDC. 5/12/10]

Oblations
And from 100s. 9½d. received from oblations and gummed wax, sold from the feast of St Michael [29 September] until the feast of the indulgence; And from £10 4d. from recovery of wax sold this year;

And from 43s. 1/2d. from oblations at all the shrines and reliquaries, with wax and recovery of wax at the time of the indulgence.

Total: £17 4s. 2d.

21. Small shrines and vicarious pilgrimages: offerings made on behalf of Elizabeth of York, Queen to Henry VII, February–March, 1502
[From N. H. Nicolas, ed., *Privy Purse Expenses of Elizabeth of York; Wardrobe Accounts of Edward the Fourth*, London, 1830, pp. 3–4; in Latin]

Item: delivered to Sir William Barton, priest, for the offerings of the Queen to Our Lady and St George at Windsor, and to the Holy Cross there, 2s. 6d.; to King Henry VI, 2s. 6d.; to Our Lady of Eton, 20d.; to the Child of Grace at Reading, 2s. 6d.; to Our Lady of Caversham, 2s. 6d.; to Our Lady of Cokethorpe, 20d.; to the holy blood of Hailes, 20d.; to Prince Edward, 5s.; to Our Lady of Worcester, 5s.; to the holy rood at Northampton, 5s.; to Our Lady of Grace there, 2s. 6d.; to Our Lady of Walsingham, 6s. 8d.; to Our Lady of Sudbury, 2s. 6d.; to Our Lady of Woolpit, 20d.; to Our Lady of Ipswich, 3s. 4d.; and to Our Lady of Stoke Clare, 20d. Total: 48s. 4d.

Item: to the same Sir William Barton for his costs in going on the said pilgrimage for the Queen over a period of 27 days at 10d. the day: [22s. 6d.]

Item: to Richard Mylmer of Binfield for money to be offered for the Queen to Our Lady of Crowham, 2s. 6d.; to the rood of grace in Kent, 20d.; to St Thomas of Canterbury, 5s.; to Our Lady in the undercroft there, 5s.; to St Adrian, 20d.; to St Augustine, 20d.; to Our Lady of Dover, 20d.; to the rood at the north door of St Paul's, 20d.; to Our Lady of Grace there, 20d.; to St Ignatius, 20d.; to St Dominic, 20d.; to St Peter of Milan, 12d.; to St Francis, 20d.; to St Saviour, 2s. 6d.; to Our Lady of Pew, 2s. 6d.; to Our Lady of Barking, 2s. 6d.; and to Our Lady of Willesden, 2s. 6d. Total: 38s. 6d.

Item: to the same Richard Milner for his costs in going on the said pilgrimages for the Queen over a period of 13 days at 10d. the day: 10s. 10d.

B. Miracles

22. Miracles of St Osmund, *c.*1453 [From A. R. Malden, ed., *The canonization of Saint Osmund, from the Manuscript Records in the Muniment Room of Salisbury Cathedral*, Wiltshire Record Society, II, 1901, pp. 142–3; in Latin and English]

John of Stamford of Thornham in Norfolk, on Maundy Thursday was travelling in a ship of 30 tons bringing sea coals from Newcastle. The ship was sunk, in which were eleven men, of whom the said John and three more were saved, by the grace of God and St Osmund and Our Lady of Doncaster. And the said ship was wrecked 3 miles from the land of the sister churches [i.e. Withernsea and Owthorne, in Yorkshire], and the said John came to land on a flour barrel within an hour and a half, always holding it firmly between his feet and his arms, and by God's disposing the wind from the sea blew towards the land.

Dominus Thomas Lake, vicar of the parish church of Dunton [St Mary] in Bedfordshire, in the diocese of Lincoln, came to the tomb of St Osmund on 20 April, and there offered, telling of a great miracle revealed in the person of John Gregory, a stonemason of Biggleswade, in that diocese, on the left side of his face. From a high scaffold 30 feet in height there fell a rafter 12 feet in length and 4 inches square, being wounded by which he fell to the ground dead, by the judgement of the said curate and all the bystanders; and lay thus for the space of half an hour. Then the said curate besought almighty God and St Mary his mother to demonstrate a miracle of life; afterwards [he prayed] to St Thomas of Canterbury and afterwards to St William, bishop of York, and yet as a dead man he lay as though dead, within the sight of all those standing around. Then St Osmund came into the mind of the said curate, of whose translation he had heard this year; and straight away, by prayers extended to God, to St Mary, and to St Osmund, the said dead man began to vomit, and thus more and more he began to draw breath; and then being led away into the aforesaid parish church, there he said: 'God and Our Lady help [me]; where have I been?' The said curate [then] saying to him thus: 'They assisted you', and the said curate further enquiring of him who had aided him; and he replied, God and his mother and a priest clothed in white. And the said curate was never here before, and for that said reason came here over 100 miles; and the said miracle took place around the feast of the Nativity of St Mary last past, around the eighth hour in the morning.

23. Miracles of Henry VI [From P. Grosjean, ed., *Henrici VI Angliae regis miracula postuma, ex codice Musei Britannici Regio 13.c.VIII*, Subsidia hagiographica, XXII, Brussels, 1935, pp. 12–15; in Latin]

THEMES OF THE MIRACLES IN THE FIRST BOOK

[1] It should be noted therefore, firstly, how a certain boy, being twice in two years submerged in a water mill, was by the invocation of the blessed King Henry VI revived from the dead. In the year of the Lord's incarnation, 1481, which was the twenty-first year of the reign of the most famous King Edward.

[2] How a certain mad woman in the county of Northampton (that is, in the region generally known as Ashby St Leger), the faithful having invoked the blessed King Henry, was miraculously healed. And she was married to a certain Geoffrey Beanston.

[3] How a certain infant girl, languishing almost to death from having swallowed a wheat straw, at invocation of that blessed man was miraculously delivered and healed. In the year of the Lord, 1487.

[4] How a certain forester, having cut the major veins of his right arm with a crossbow bolt, had bled to death, but having invoked the glorious King Henry was most swiftly healed. In the year of the incarnation of the word of God, 1488.

[5] How a most severe bout of pestilence struck down eleven people together in the house of a man named Thomas Symon: but at the invocation of the said blessed King Henry, by an evident miracle it was escaped from. The year given above.

[6] How two horses of the aforesaid Thomas, long sick, having then invoked the blessed Henry, they were marvellously cured.

[7] How three pigs of that Thomas, carried away by theft, at the invocation of the aforesaid blessed king, forty days having already passed, they were suddenly restored.

[8] How Master William Edward, vicar of the parish church of Hollington in the county of Sussex, his eyes being blinded and his tongue totally cut out, by the mental invocation of the before said blessed King both avoided death and suddenly recovered sight and speech. This on the day of the feast of All Saints, in the year 1488.

[9] How the treasure of a certain Thomas att Wode was found, by revelation of the blessed and glorious King Henry, and he was saved

from the peril of death. The first week of the month of February, the year as above.

[10] How a youth, whilst wrestling, was stabbed by his own knife, hanging from his back [and recovered miraculously]. That year, the 1st day of the month of March. His name was John Norman.

[11] How the infant daughter of Ralph Shirley was brought back from the dead, her mother having invoked the blessed King Henry. In the year of the Lord 1489, the 9th day of the month of June. Her name was Beatrice.

[12] How a certain boy, struck by an arrow in the eye, was miraculously healed. The year above stated, the 22nd day of the month of July. His name was Thomas, son of Thomas Fowle.

[13] How a certain man at Barnet, pierced by a lance, after almost twenty-four hours during which he lay despaired of by all and speechless, having invoked the blessed King Henry, he was made healthy. The 17th day of the eighth month, the year of the Lord noted above.

[14] How one David Bukell, at Midhurst, a village of Sussex, was by the merits of the aforesaid man of God graciously delivered of the fits of colic from which he had suffered for a decade. Under the 6th day of February, the year above.

[15] How a certain main, called Thomas Burton, was released from his chains by an apparition of this most blessed King Henry at Colchester, and by his guidance freed from prison. The 11th day of the month and year now abovesaid.

[16] How a certain farmer, called John Steyn, struck down by a bolt of lightning, fell to the ground half dead, and for many days thereafter was burnt up by intolerable heat, and almost consumed; but by the merits of the blessed King Henry was then marvellously restored to his former health, and was not silent about his glory and virtue. The 27th of the month of March, the year 1490 having begun.

[17] How a certain minister of the Lord King in Brittany, languishing almost to death in extraordinary illness, the said man of God, Henry, then being invoked, as though suddenly he was made healthy. Around the time already stated. He is called Robert Warton.

[18] How the small son of the parker of Ashby de la Zouche, in the county of Leicester, William Phillip by name, after he had laid for fully four days immobile and despaired of by all, in an uncommon and unknown illness, was by the merits of the blessed King Henry restored

to his former condition of life. The day before the kalends of April [31 March], in that year of Christ, 1490.

[19] How Miles Branbryke, gentleman, having been extraordinarily troubled for six years by the descent of his intestines into his testicles [i.e., a hernia] was fully restored to health by the blessed King Henry. In the year already stated.

[20] How one John Stevynson of Maidenhead, struck by a crossbow bolt on the head, at the invocation of the oft-mentioned glorious King Henry was most graciously freed from the danger of death. In the year as above.

[21] How someone was killed by a load of great timber falling from a cart, that is, with his head being squashed, but he was resuscitated by the devout invocation of this most blessed man, and immediately walked. The year already noted above.

[22] How one Henry Fromby was stabbed in the chest by a sword, and was preserved from the imminent danger of death by the blessed King Henry, merely by mental invocation. 24 June, year as above.

[23] How Elizabeth, the wife of John Lowe, who had died in an extraordinary manner by the boiling up of her blood, was revived at the invocation of the oft-mentioned blessed King Henry. 8th day of the month of August, in the year as above.

[24] How a certain youth, called Thomas Paynston, whilst he had been taken on for husbandry by the gentle man John Barley, was almost crushed to death by a loaded wagon; but then having prayed most faithfully to King Henry was revived. The same year, the 9th day of August.

[25] How a certain boy of London, struck by a sudden illness, when he had been abandoned by his doctors, he was then made well when his parents had made a vow to visit blessed Henry. The 18th day of the seventh month, in the same year. His name is John Lynkolne.

[26] How Joan, daughter of Robert Barton, a girl of almost 9 years of age, was most graciosly delivered from a horrible kind of death by the merits of blessed Henry. That same month of September, the 27th day, in the same year as above.

[27] How an infant girl, daughter of Thomas Barow, was by devout intercession of the said glorious man restored to her former life from a similar death. Under the 8th day of that same eighth month, the year already oft-mentioned.

[28] How a certain youth John, surnamed Wall, crushed by a loaded carriage, lay for a whole night dead under a bush, and being revived on the following day by invocation of the glorious King Henry, immediately recovered his strength. The 5th day of the month of March, in the year of the lord 1490. And he was a servant of the gentleman Robert Pokapert of White Roothing in Essex.

VIII. Security for the living

The attempt to secure salvation generated a variety of social and other involvements. The doctrine of good works obviously imposed charitable obligations;[1] *the search for assurances of salvation also generated numerous attempts to secure prayers and limit the penalties of sin. While acts of pre-mortem charitable giving are rarely recorded, being by definition personal actions which usually did not require administrative records,*[2] *nevertheless administrative actions and requirements do indicate the recipients of such donations, and the arrangements for collecting. These, as applied also with foundations for the dead (see Section IX), often involved reciprocity in the form of prayers from the recipients of the charity (these would be expected in donations to individuals, as well as to causes).*[3]

Actions before death to secure salvation took several forms, besides making arrangements for commemorations after death (which are dealt with elsewhere).[4] *The participation in prayers and indulgences was the main focus, obtained in several forms. Indulgences, whatever the canonical interpretation, were generally taken to guarantee time off Purgatory in the future; and were widely distributed.*[5] *They might be obtained by visiting a shrine, by membership of a fraternity or by donations to charitable institutions.*[6] *All of*

1 R. N. Swanson, *Church and Society in Late Medieval England*, Oxford, 1989, pp. 299, 301. On ideas of charity, M. Rubin, *Charity and Community in Late Medieval Cambridge*, Cambridge Studies in Medieval Life and Thought, 4th ser., IV, Cambridge, 1987, ch. 3.

2 Personal account books sometimes include such material. Those of the Willougby family from the early sixteenth century have numerous references scattered among them; extracts are in *Historical Manuscripts Commission: Report of the Manuscripts of Lord Middleton Preserved at Wollaton Hall, Nottingham*, London, 1911, pp. 327–87.

3 This is evident in some of the indulgences for worthy causes printed here, in the post-mortem commemorations recorded in Section IX, and in the wills in Section X.

4 See Section IX.

5 Swanson, *Church and Society*, pp. 292–4; W. E. Lunt, *Financial Relations of the Papacy with England, 1327–1534*, Publications of the Mediaeval Academy of America, LXXIV, Cambridge, Mass., 1962, pp. 447–611, passim. See also comments in D. L. D'Avray, 'Papal authority and religious sentiment in the late middle ages', in *The Church and Sovereignty, c.590–1918: Essays in Honour of Michael Wilks*, ed. D. Wood, Studies in Church History, Subsidia IX, Oxford, 1991, pp. 395–8.

6 For lists of indulgences, e.g. J. Raine, ed., *The Fabric Rolls of York Minster, with an Appendix of Illustrative Documents*, Surtees Society Publications, XXXV, 1858, pp. 237–42; A. T. Bannister, ed., *Registrum Caroli Bothe, Episcopi Herefordensis, A.D.*

this reflected personal action, although by participation in a wider institution. The motivations, and comprehension, of such action might also be personal, although often now approachable only by speculation.

The scale of some of this collecting was considerable: the Hospital of St Anthony in London was a nation-wide collecting institution, which farmed out its sale of indulgences. The receipts from those farms, at the standard rate of 4d. per pardon, suggest sales of over 30,000 per annum[7] *– to which have to be added sales figures for all the other national institutions, and the more regional and local ones. The nature of the privileges received also varied; but the benefits conferred on members of the fraternity of St Chad at Lichfield may have been fairly typical of those offered to supporters of a cathedral's fabric. The fabric rolls of other cathedrals, like Wells and Exeter, certainly demonstrate the scale of collecting for such purposes.*[8]

Membership of fraternities also brought privileges. These associations varied considerably in size, and to some extent in intention, but were ubiquitous.[9]

MDXVI–MDXXXV, Canterbury and York Society, XXVIII, 1921, pp. 354–60; see also R. M. Haines, *Ecclesia Anglicana: Studies in the English Church of the Later Middle Ages*, London and Toronto, 1989, pp. 183–91. They were sufficiently widespread to encourage forgery, while Chaucer's Pardoner was also in on the racket: Swanson, *Church and Society*, p. 248.

7 Swanson, *Church and Society*, p. 228. Only the great national institutions paid fees to the diocesan – and probably parochial – authorities: R. N. Swanson, 'Sede vacante administration in the medieval diocese of Carlisle; the accounts of the vacancy of December 1395 to March 1396', *Transactions of the Cumberland and Westmorland Antiquarian and Archaeological Society*, XC, 1990, pp. 185–6.

8 J. C. Colchester, ed., *Wells Cathedral: Fabric Accounts, 1390–1600*, Wells, 1983, pp. 6, 10, 17, 22–3, 29, 36 (see also expenses at pp. 11–12, 18–19, 24–5, 30–1, 38–9); A. M. Erskine, ed., *The Accounts of the Fabric of Exeter Cathedral, 1279–1353*, Devon and Cornwall Record Society, n.s., XXIV, XXVI, 1981–3, ii, p. xi. For what may be a listing of those responding to the quest for the fabric of Lichfield cathedral, see A. J. Kettle, ed., *A List of Families in the Archdeaconry of Stafford, 1532–3*, Collections for a History of Staffordshire, 4th ser., VIII, 1976, esp. pp. ix–xi. These fabric collections were encouraged by touring relics with the collectors. The early-sixteenth-century relic list of York Minster refers to '7 reliquaries of beryl of various shapes, with relics, decorated with silver gilt, set aside for the proctors of the fabric collecting alms from Christ's faithful in the region (of which one has been handed over to the warden of the fabric of St Peter), with the hair of St William, and others': Raine, *Fabric Rolls of York Minster*, p. 221.

9 The main work on English guilds remains H. F. Westlake, *The Parish Guilds of Medieval England*, London, 1919. See also C. M. Barron, 'The parish fraternities of medieval London', in *The Church in Pre-Reformation Society*, ed. C. M. Barron and C. Harper-Bill, Woodbridge, 1985, pp. 13–37; M. Rubin, 'Corpus Christi fraternities and late medieval piety', *Studies in Church History*, XXIII, 1986, pp. 97-109; G. Rosser, 'Communities of parish and guild in late medieval England', in *Parish, Church, and People: Local Studies in Lay Religion, 1350–1750*, ed. S. J. Wright, London, 1988, pp. 32–55; J. J. Scarisbrick, *The Reformation and the English People*, Oxford, 1984, pp. 19–39; Swanson, *Church and Society*, pp. 280–4; J. Mattingly, 'The

Craft guilds in towns generally had a religious aspect, as with the York carpenters, who sought additional spiritual benefits by making arrangements with the friars. The regulations of these fraternities often imposed moral obligations,[10] *as well as making financial demands. Some of the larger fraternities themselves developed into quasi-national institutions, such as the Boston Guild, and the Palmers' Guild of Ludlow, the complex financial administration of which reflects a widespread desire to share in the benefits of membership.*[11]

In all of these instances, individuals might amass considerable collections of memberships and shares in the benefits. Concurrent membership of several fraternities was relatively common; so too was the multiple purchase of indulgences. The Kendalls of Bridgwater in Somerset entered into confraternity with both the Dominicans and the Franciscans (nos. 31 i–ii), and the accounts of the Willoughby family of Sutton Coldfield include several references to payment for pardons and for fraternity memberships.[12]

A. Indulgences

24. Appointment of proctors to collect for a bridge: Bridgwater, 1484–5 [From R. W. Dunning and T. D. Tremlett, eds., *Bridgwater Borough Archives, V, 1468–1485*, Somerset Record Society, LXX, 1971, p. 80; in Latin]

To all of mother Church to whose notice these present letters shall come, Master Richard Croke, bachelor in sacred theology and

medieval parish guilds of Cornwall', *Journal of the Royal Institution of Cornwall*, n.s., X/iii, 1989, pp. 290–329.

10 B. R. McRee, 'Religious guilds and regulation of behaviour in late medieval towns', in *People, Politics, and Community in the Later Middle Ages*, ed. J. T. Rosenthal and C. Richmond, Gloucester, 1987, pp. 108–22. The main printed collection of regulations for late medieval fraternities reflects the responses to the nationwide enquiry of 1389: T. Smith, L. T. Smith and L. Brentano, eds, *English Gilds*, Early English Text Society, original ser., XL, 1870.

11 On the Boston Guild, Lunt, *Financial Relations*, pp. 495–8, 506–7, 509-11; for its printing of indulgences and publicity material, D. E. Rhodes, *Studies in Early European Printing and Book-Collecting*, London, 1983, pp. 14–18. On the Ludlow Palmers, *Victoria County History: Shropshire*, II, Oxford, 1973, pp. 134–40; E. G. H. Kempson, 'A Shropshire guild at work in Wiltshire', *Wiltshire Archaeological and Natural History Magazine*, LVII, 1958–60, pp. 50–5; W. C. Sparrow, 'A register of the Palmers Guild of Ludlow in the reign of Henry VII', *Transactions of the Shropshire Archaeological and Natural History Society*, 1st ser., VII, 1884, pp. 81–126.

12 Swanson, *Church and Society*, p. 228 n. 102; for multiple membership and purchases see pp. 283, 294.

perpetual vicar of the parish church of St Mary the Virgin at Bridgwater, diocese of Bath and Wells, Nicholas Job, mayor of the aforesaid town, and the community thereof, greeting in him from whom flows the health of all to be saved. Know that we, by our unanimous assent and consent in their faithfulness and diligence have ordained and by these present constitute our beloved in Christ Robert Johnson and William Grey as our true and legitimate proctors and special and general envoys to collect and receive alms, gifts and bequests from allsoever who are faithful in Christ and devout to God, in the name of, and to the honour of, God, and all the benefactors, together with the rest of their confreres and consorors whatsoever, towards the chapel of the Holy Cross in that church and the high cross which is in the middle place of the high street there, as well as to the fabric of the bridge of the aforesaid town, which is debilitated and ruinous because many and various carriages from throughout the whole country come and go across it daily, and the ebb and flow of the sea strike at each tide against the said bridge to its grave costs, and to the great danger of the whole people coming and going from the various parts of the realm of England; the which bridge without the alms of Christ's faithful cannot be duly sustained and repaired; for which great indulgences have been granted, as evidently appears from the lord pope in the bull of indulgence. [1484–5]

25. Appointment of proctors to collect for the bridge between Oxford and Abingdon: *c.*1490 [From H. E. Salter, ed., *Snappe's formulary and other records*, Oxford Historical Society, LXXX, 1924, p. 255 – a draft version; in English]

To all people to whom this present writing shall come, Master Richard Hewis, mayor of the town of Oxford, Master William Herward, doctor of divinity and vicar of St Helen's, Abingdon, Master Thomas Say and Thomas Cockys of the same send greeting in Our Lord with due reverence and recommendation as appertains to each person. And for as much as it is meritorious and well rewarded to do deeds of charity and to bear witness to truth in such matters and causes in which the consciences of men might be bruised or blemished by lack of clarity of the truth; therefore we reveal to you by this our present writing that we have appointed and deputed our well-beloved in Christ John Ferrour, now having the status of a hermit, or his sufficient deputy, the bringer of this letter, to receive and collect all the alms and charitable gifts which it may please you and all people of your benevolence and charity to give to the said John Ferrour or his sufficient deputy on his behalf, towards the repairs of the highway, bridge and almost collapsed arches lying between the town of Oxford south towards Abingdon and other places, called the south bridge of Oxford; for which gifts you will doubtless give pleasure to almighty God and also be partners of many good prayers daily said in the town of Oxford, and also of the aforesaid hermit John Ferrour's daily prayers, and of the daily prayers of many others travelling by the aforesaid road in this transitory life and wailing world, from which we shall depart; and at that time such charitable deeds and gifts shall guide you and us to the right way, where there lacks no repair, to endless bliss by the grace of Almighty God, who ever preserve you and all those who hear this our present writing ...

26. Appointment of proctor for sale of indulgences on behalf of St Anthony's Hospital, London: 1479 [Windsor, St George's Chapel archives, XV.37.17; in Latin]

This indenture made between the warden or dean of the college of St George within the castle of Windsor and the canons of that place, appropriators of the house or Hospital of St Antony at London (or 'in England'), on the one part, and Robert Cally, William Turnour, and Walter Machant of the other part, bears witness that the aforesaid warden or dean and canons, appropriators of the aforesaid house or hospital, have transferred, granted and let to farm to the aforesaid Robert, William and Walter, the office of questor, jointly and singly, and all the goods and profits or revenues from whatsoever cause given or to be given, assigned or to be assigned, left or to be left, to God and the said hospital of St Anthony, in whatsoever bodies or things they exist, and howsoever given or granted, or to be given or granted, in and throughout all the bishoprics of Bath and Wells, and Exeter, in exempt places as well as in non-exempt places, together with pigs and other animals within the aforesaid places. And the abovesaid warden or dean and canons or appropriators have ordained and constituted them, Robert, William and Walter, as their legitimate attorneys, proxies and receivers, for, of, and in the aforesaid, giving and granting to them full authority and power of substitution and provision of others as their substitutes in this matter, to have, do and carry out the above without rendering account therefor to the said warden or dean and canons and their successors, from the feast of St Peter ... ad vincula [1 August] next ... until the end and termination of ten years then next following and fully to be completed; paying for this annually to the said warden or dean and canons or their successors, or their true attorney, at London, [£46] ... at the feasts of the Purification of the blessed Virgin Mary [2 February] and St Peter ... ad vincula, in equal portions, or within fifteen days immediately after either of those feasts. [With clause allowing the dean and canons to eject the lessees and re-enter the office if the rent is unpaid, or relet to someone else.] ... Dated at Windsor ... [15 May 1479].

27. Appointment of proctor, to sell indulgences on behalf of St Anthony's Hospital, London: 1536 [Windsor: St George's Chapel archives, XI.F.31; in English]

This indenture made [16 February 1536] ... between the dean and canons of the college of St George within the castle at Windsor, appropriators of the house or Hospital of St Anthony in the city of London or in England, on the one part, and Thomas Mathewe of the city of Winchester, clothier, of the other part, bears witness that the said dean and canons, the day and year abovesaid, have granted, demised, yielded and let to farm to the said Thomas both the office of proctor within the diocese of Canterbury and Chichester and the marches of Calais, Guines and Ham, with the dioceses of Winchester and Rochester, and their tenement with its appurtenances lying in the city of Winchester aforesaid, which the said Thomas now inhabits, together with the Isle of Wight, Jersey and Guernsey, as well as all the profits coming and deriving from the same dioceses, together with the charitable gifts, devotions, legacies and bequests of all well disposed people within the said dioceses, given, bequeathed or assigned to God and St Anthony; to have and to hold the said office of proctor together with the aforesaid tenement with the appurtenances and also the said gifts, devotions, legacies and bequests, to the said Thomas, to his executors and assigns, from [29 September 1536, for] ... the term of five years then next following, and fully to be completed and ended; yielding and paying therefor yearly during the said term to the said dean and canons, to their successors or assigns within the house of St Anthony in London, [£20] ... at two terms in the year, that is to say at the feast of the apostles Philip and James [1 May] and the Nativity of Our Lady [8 September] by equal portions ... [With additional clauses giving the dean and canons rights of re-entry if the rent is unpaid; and promising cancellation of a bond of 40 marks entered into by sureties for Thomas, if he fulfils all the requirements of the contract.]

28. Bristol: a list of indulgences conceded in support of a chapel [presumably either to those visiting and offering alms, or to people contributing towards collections made by questers associated with the Bristol fraternity of St. Anne, whose proctors sealed the document. From R. W. Dunning and T. D. Tremlett, eds., *Bridgwater Borough Archives, V, 1468–1485*, Somerset Record Society, LXX, 1971, p. 76; in English]

In the name of God, Amen. In the year of Our Lord God 1367 a chapel of St Anne was begun [at Brislington], to which our most reverend father in God my lord of Canterbury, our metropolitan, has given 100 days of pardon, my lord archbishop of York 100 days of pardon, my lord of Worcester 40 days of pardon, my lord of Lincoln 40 days of pardon, my lord of Winchester 40 days, my lord of Durham 40 days, my lord of Salisbury 40 days, my lord of Bath 40 days, my lord of Hereford 40 days, my lord of Llandaff 40 days, my lord of Kildare 40 days. [1483–4]

29. Profits of indulgences: the rental of the proctorships for St Anthony's Hospital, London, 1513 [Windsor: St George's Chapel archives, XV.37.29; in Latin]

This indented rental was renewed and made on [1 October 1513] ... of the farms of the proctorships pertaining to the Hospital of St Anthony at London, with the terms and days of payment for those proctorships, as appears in the following:

At the term of St Michael the Archangel [29 September]:

Firstly, for the first payment of the proctorship of the bishopric of Hereford, leased to Thomas Ypurs £9 10s.

And for the first payment of the proctorship of the archdeaconry of Oxford, leased to that Thomas by indenture £5 13s. 4d.

Total: £15 3s. 4d.

And for the first payment of the proctorship of the diocese of Winchester, leased to William Clerk, and paid in hand at the feast of Michaelmas; for if he then should die his assigns ought to collect for this payment until the feast of the Purification of the Blessed Virgin Mary [2 February] £13 10s.

And for the first payment of the proctorship of the diocese of Rochester, deanery of Shoreham, and church of Clyffe, let to the same William £3

And for the first payment of the proctorship of the bishoprics of St Davids and Llandaff, leased to John Vaughan £8 6s. 8d.

Total of aforesaid proctorships: £40

At the term or feast of St Martin in winter [11 November]:

And for the first payment of the proctorship of the diocese of Norwich, for the counties of Suffolk and Norfolk, leased to Walter Smythe £17 10s.

And for the first payment of the proctorship of the diocese of London, leased to the above-named William Clerk £12

Total of the proctorships for this term: £29 10s.

At the term of the Purification of St Mary [2 February]:

And for the second payment of the proctorship of the diocese of Winchester, leased as above to William Clerk, to be paid at the start of the term before he collects £13 10s.

And for the first payment of the proctorship of the diocese and province of York and the Isle of Man, leased to John Egylsfeld and others, etc. £44

And for the first payment of the proctorship of the archdeaconries of Derby, Stafford, Coventry and Salop, leased to John Portte £11.

And for the first payment of the proctorship of the diocese of Chester and Lancaster leased to the same John Portte £5 10s. £16 10s.

And for the first payment of the proctorship of the dioceses of Exeter, Bath and Wells, etc., leased to Henry Lake £25

And for the first payment of the proctorship of the archdeaconries of Northampton, Bedford, Buckingham, together with the jurisdiction of St Albans, leased to Godfrey Tomlynson £15 6s. 8d.

And for the proctorship of the diocese of Worcester, leased to Thomas Morton, paying once in the year £32

And for the first payment of the proctorship of the dioceses of Salisbury, Ely, the archdeaconries of Lincoln, Stowe, Leicester, Huntingdon, and the archdeaconry of Rutland, leased to Fowler and Hulle £70 3s. 4d.

And for the first payment of the proctorship of the dioceses of Canterbury and Chichester, leased to Nicholas Cooper £12

Total of procurations, etc.: £228 10s.

At the term of the Annunciation of St Mary [25 March]:

And for the second payment of the proctorship for the diocese of Rochester, the deaneries of Shoreham, Croydon, and the church of Clyffe, leased as above to William Clerke £3

And for the second payment of the proctorship of the dioceses of St Davids and Llandaff, leased as above to John Vaughan £8 6s. 8d.

And for the payment of the proctorship of the dioceses of Bangor and St Asaph, leased to John Wrexham, paying once in the year £6 13s. 4d.

Total: £18

At the term of the apostles Philip and James [1 May]:

And for the second payment of the proctorship of the bishopric of Hereford, leased as above to Thomas Ypurs £9 10s.

And for the second payment of the proctorship of the archdeaconry of Oxford, leased to the same Thomas, as above £5 13s. 4d. £15 3s. 4d.

And for the second payment of the proctorship of Norfolk and Suffolk, leased as above to Walter Smythe £17 10s.

And for the second payment of the proctorship of the diocese of London, leased to William Clerk as above £12

Total: £44 13s. 4d.

At the term of the Nativity of St John the Baptist [24 June]:

And for the second payment of the proctorship of the province of York and the Isle of Man, leased to John Eglesfeld £44

Total: £44

At the term of St Peter which is said to be 'ad vincula' [1 August]:

And for the second payment of the proctorship of the archdeaconries of Derby, Stafford, Coventry and Salop, leased to John Portte as above £11

And for the second payment of the proctorship of Chester and Lancaster leased to the same John as above £5 10s. £16 10s.

And for the second payment of the proctorship of Exeter, the diocese of Bath and Wells, leased as above to Henry Lake £25

And for the second payment of the proctorship of Northampton, Bedford, Buckingham, as one, and with the jurisdiction of St Albans, leased as above to Godfrey Tomlynson for certain years £15 6s. 8d.

And for the second payment of the proctorship of the dioceses of Salisbury, Ely, archdeaconries of Lincoln, Stowe, Leicester, Huntingdon, as one, and with the archdeaconry of Rutland, leased as above to Fowler, Hulle, and Robert Perys, and others, as above £70 13s. 4d.

And for the second payment of the proctorship of the dioceses of Canterbury and Chichester, leased to Nicholas Cooper £12

Total: £183

Sum total of all the aforesaid proctorships: £543 13s. 4d.

[On the dorse is the list of properties of the hospital in Dagenham, London and Portsmouth, from which the total due in rents is £26 6s. 8d. per year.]

B. Guilds and fraternities

30. Letter of confraternity: from the Franciscans of Bridgwater, 1409/10 [From C. E. Clark-Maxwell, 'Some Further Letters of Confraternity', *Archaeologia*, LXXXIX, 1929, pp. 290–1; in Latin]

To his most dear in Christ William Dyst and Joan his wife, brother William, warden of the friars minor of Bridgwater, greeting, by the merits of this present life to receive joy everlasting. Wishing to compensate with spiritual benefits the devotion which for reverence to God you have towards our order, and especially demonstrated towards our convent by the multiple granting of benefits; by the authority of our father the minister and all the provincial chapter, and by the unanimous assent of our abovesaid convent, I receive you by the tenor of these presents into the totality and singularity of the suffrages of the brothers of the said convent, in life as well as in death, granting to you participation in all the good deeds which should be worked by those brothers as the clemency of the Saviour should see fit; adding further by special grace that when your death should be notified to us, that chapter will do for you as is customarily done for our dead brothers in prayers.

Farewell faithfully in the Lord Jesus Christ and the glorious Virgin his Mother.

Dated at Bridgwater in our local chapter, [10 January 1409/10].

31. Letters of confraternity granted to John Kendale and Maud his wife of Bridgwater [From R. W. Dunning and T. D. Tremlett, eds., *Bridgwater Borough Archives, V, 1468–1485*, Somerset Record Society, LXX, 1971; in Latin]

(i) *From the Franciscans of Bridgwater, 1479* [pp. 35–6]

To the venerable in Christ John Kendale and Matilda his wife, William, and Juliana, from Robert, warden and servant of the convent of the friars minor at Bridgwater, greeting, and by the merits of this present life advancement to the celestial kingdom. Since the most holy father in Christ and lord, the Lord Sixtus IV, by divine providence, Pope, in his apostolic benignity graciously conceded not only to the brothers and sisters of our order, but also to the confreres and consorors thereof who had letters of suffrages, that each of them might choose for himself a suitable confessor who could absolve them and each one of them, from all and singular crimes, excesses and sins, and enjoin a salutary penance (and even once alone this year, to be counted from the publication of the papal letters – that is to say from the 4th day of the month of April – in all cases reserved to the apostolic see; and from others whenever the case shall arise), and benignly by his apostolic letters offered the indulgence that that same or some other confessor could extend to them the plenary remission of all their sins when they are truly on the point of death. Therefore, considering the sincere affection of your devotion, which you have out of reverence for Christ, towards our order, and accepting you, John Kendall, and Matilda his wife, William, and Juliana, as confreres and consorors in all and singular of the suffrages of the brothers of our convent by these presents, I acknowledge that (in life equally as in death) the said apostolic privileges and the benefits of all the spiritual good deeds, according to their form and effect, shall be fully implemented for the health of your souls; adding furthermore out of special grace that when, after your deaths, a showing of these present letters shall be made in our chapter place, there shall be offered for you that recommendation which is there customarily offered for our deceased brothers and sisters. Farewell faithfully in the Lord Jesus Christ, and pray for me. Given in the place mentioned above, the 8th day of ... June, the year of the Lord 1479.

By the authority of almighty God the Father, of his son Our Lord Jesus Christ, and of the blessed Peter and Paul his apostles, and of the whole of Mother Church, and by virtue of this papal bull of indulgence of our most holy father Sixtus, granted to you and committed to me, I absolve you from all your crimes and excesses and sins of which you are truly contrite and which you have confessed to me, and from all the rest of your sins which you would wish to confess if they came into your memory; and if you have had contacts with any excommunicate person, or if you have incurred the sentence of greater or lesser excommunication, by that authority I absolve you, and grant to you plenary remission as far as the keys of the Holy Roman Church extend in that matter, so that you shall be absolved before the tribunal of Our Lord Jesus Christ, and that you should have life eternal and live throughout all ages. Amen.

(ii) *From the Dominicans of Ilchester, 1485* [pp. 80–1]

To the devout and his beloved in Christ, John Kendale and Matilda his wife, brother Stephen Assche, prior of the convent of the order of preachers at Ilchester, greeting and continual grace in the Lord. As is required by the affection of your devotion which you have towards our order and convent, I concede to you by the tenor of these presents special participation in all the masses, prayers and suffrages and other good deeds which the Lord has given to be done by the brothers of our convent, equally in life and in death. Furthermore, since our most holy Lord Innocent VIII, by divine providence Pope, has graciously granted that any confrater or consoror of our order by letters might choose for themselves a suitable regular or secular confessor who could (their confession diligently heard) grant them absolution from all cases reserved to the apostolic see (other than for offences against ecclesiastical liberty, violation of interdict, conspiracy or rebellion in the state of Rome, the killing of priests, the crimes of heresy and simony concerning orders or succession to benefices, personal offences against the bishop or other prelate, imposition of new burdens whether material or personal on churches and ecclesiastical persons, forgery of apostolic letters, to which it applies once only; for others, however, whenever it shall be appropriate), and impose a salutary penance (it being this, though: that each of those confreres or consorors should fast on every sixth weekday throughout the year from the date of these presents; and that if they are neglectful in carrying this out fittingly, in that case the aforesaid confessor would be able to commute that fast into other pious works, as it should seem expedient to him according to God). Therefore I declare you to be participants in this gracious indulgence by these presents. In witness of this the seal of my office is appended to these presents. Given at Ilchester, [1485].

By the authority of the most holy father in Christ and lord, the Lord Pope Innocent VIII, I absolve you from all these sins in so far as the keys of the Church extend to them, and grant you plenary remission of all your sins, in the name of the Father and the Son.

32. Regulations of a trade fraternity: the carpenters of York, 1482
[From M. Sellers, ed., *York Memorandum Book, part II (1388–1493)*, Surtees Society Publications, CXXV, 1914, pp. 278–9; in English]

First, since hitherto there has been for a long time a fraternity established and customary among the occupation and craft [of carpenters] ..., who by long continuity have been accustomed and still yearly are accustomed to find at their own costs a light of several torches on the feast of Corpus Christi, or the morning after, to the honour and worship of God and all saints, and to go in procession with the same torches and the blessed sacrament from the abbey founded for the Holy Trinity in Micklegate in the said city [of York] to the cathedral church of St Peter in the same city; and also have done and performed various other fully good and honourable actions, as hereafter more fully may appear, it is ordained and established by the said mayor, aldermen and all the whole council of the said ... city, by the consent and assent of all those of the said occupation in the said city, that the said fraternity and brotherhood shall be hereafter upheld and continued for ever, as it has been in past times, and that every brother thereof shall pay 6d. annually for its support (that is to say, 3d. at every half year), providing always that every man of the said craft within the said city shall not be compelled nor obliged to be of the said fraternity or brotherhood, or any to belong to it except those who choose of their own free will.

Also, it is ordained and established ... to be kept for ever ... that all the said brethren of the said fraternity shall come together twice in the year, that is to say, the first time on the Sunday next after St Helen's Day, and the second time the Sunday next before or next after the feast of All Hallows, at each of which days each one of the said brethren shall pay 1d. to the use of the said brotherhood; and also the said brotherhood shall cause a trental of masses to be performed at each of the said days by the Austin friars of this city, to the worship of God and all saints, for the souls of all the brothers and sisters previously deceased of the said fraternity and brotherhood, and that every brother who is then absent ... shall pay a pound of wax to the use of the said fraternity, and 6d. to the use of the chamber of this ... city, unless he has a reasonable excuse.

Also, it is ordained that there shall be four wardens of the said fraternity, who shall render their accounts every year either at St Peter's Day or on St Mathias's Day in winter, upon penalty of forfeiture by each warden who fails so to do (unless he has a reasonable excuse) of 3s. 4d. to the use of the chamber of this city and of the said fraternity, to be evenly divided between them.

Also it is ordained that if anyone of the said fraternity shall die, the said brotherhood shall give 5s. for a trental of masses to be performed for his soul by the said Austin friars.

Also, it is ordained that if any of the said brothers die, or any of their wives, that the said torches shall be carried with them to their burial, without their giving anything for that, but only out of devotion; and when any of the said brothers has died, he who has the torches in his keeping shall admonish all the brothers, when anyone has thus died, to come to the burial of their brother on pain of forfeiture of 4d., to be forfeited by the keepers who have failed in this, to the use of the community of this city and of the said fraternity, to be equally divided between them, and the said torch-keepers shall cause the said torches to be carried to the burial of the dead person, and bring them home again at the cost of the brethren, and not of the dead person, if he is buried within the franchise of this city.

Also it is ordained that if any of the said brothers die, any brother of his who is not at his burial shall pay half a pound of wax to the use of the said light, and the value of half a pound of wax to the use of the said community of this said city, unless he has a reasonable excuse (that is to say, that he was not informed, or has other reasonable cause).

Also, it is ordained that if any of the said fraternity shall fall into poverty, so that they may not work, or happen to be blinded, or to lose their possessions by misfortune of this world, then the aforesaid brotherhood shall give them 4d. every week, as long as they live, as alms, provided that he who is so treated shall have truly fulfilled the ordinances above written.

Also, it is ordained that whatever brother is so admitted to receive alms shall be sworn upon a book that he shall truly live upon his alms and his own goods, without waste or giving them away, and whatever he leaves at his death that belongs to himself (his debts being paid and his burial reasonably performed) shall remain to the said fraternity as its own property ...

[The ordinances continue, with further arrangements for members who are out of work, arrangements for meetings and fines for non-attendance, enforcement of fines, and ordinances regarding apprenticeships and working conditions, and quality of workmanship. Among them is an ordinance regarding support for the Corpus Christi play:]

Also it is ordained that all wrights, sawyers, carvers, joiners and cartwrights, and all others who act as masters, or who hereafter shall act as masters in any of the said mysteries, crafts or trades within this said city, and each of them, shall be equally and alike chargeable henceforth annually for the expenses and costs of bringing out and playing the pageant of the wrights on Corpus Christi Day, and for the expense of providing the said light on the morning after Corpus Christi Day, so that no master of the said occupations or crafts shall pay more than another towards the said expenses of the said play or to the said light.

[Some of the other ordinances provide for fines to be divided between the pageant and the light.]

33. Guild membership arrangements: Palmers' Guild of Ludlow [Extract from the 'Riding Book' of 1505–6, detailing payments from members of the fraternity enrolled that year in Salisbury, and their subsequent payments of instalments (indicated by the abbreviations for the names of the stewards, and the numerals for the years of their terms of office) until they had paid sufficient to qualify for registration as full members of the guild Shropshire Record Office, 356/Box 317: Riding Book 1505–6, f.57v; in Latin]

Salisbury, 1st year of Brown and Bragott

Walter Pety, in the parish of St Edmund, glazier 6s. 8d.
Received 4d., 2 Bro.

Thomas A Byrkhed of the same, saddler, and Joanna 13s. 4d.
Received 8d., 3 Bro.; Item, 12d., 2 Bro.; Item, 12d., 1st Ro.; Item, 8d., 2nd Ro.; Item, 12d., 4 Ro.; Item, 8d., 1st Bro.; Item, 12d., 1st Lo.; Item, 12d., 2 Lo.; Item, 8d., 3 Lo.; Item, 12d., 1st Cro.; Item, 12d.,

2 Cro.; Item, 8d., 3 Cro.; Item, 8d., 4 Cro.; Item, 16d., 1st Phe. In full. [Marginal note: 'Paid; to be registered']

Henry Bemond of Closse 6s. 8d.
Received 2d., 2 Bro.; 4d, 3 Bro.

Thomas Brodgard, merchant, and Katherine his wife 13s. 4d.
Received 8d., 2 Bro.; Item, 6d., 3 Bro.; Item, 8d., 1st Ro.; Item, 12d., 2 Ro.; Item, 12d., 3 Ro.; Item, 12d., 4 Ro.; Item, 12d., 2 Lo.; Item, 12d. 3 Lo.; Item, 12d., 1st Cro.; Item, 12d., 3rd Cro.; Item, 12d., 4 Cro.; Item, 12d., 1st Phe.; Item 20d., 2 Phe. In full.
[Marginal note: 'Paid; to be registered']

Robert Solby of the same, blower, and Olive his wife 13s. 4d.
16d., 3 Bro.

Joan, wife of John Newman of the same 6s. 8d.
Received 7s. 4d., 1st Bro. In full.

John Aport in the parish of St Thomas, gentleman 6s. 8d.
Received 8d., 3 Bro.; Item, 8d., 2 Ro.

34. Cumulative totals of guild subscriptions for the Palmers' Guild of Ludlow [Showing the staggered totals of receipts as would-be members paid instalments towards the cost of registration over the years. From the Stewards' account for 25–6 Henry VI, Richard Knyghton and Richard Ryall as stewards. Shropshire Record Office, 356/Box 321; in Latin]

... And of £22 18s. 8d. received from the fines of brethren and sisters admitted this year, whose names appear in the register of this year; And of £10 18s. 4d. received in part payment of fines of brethren and sisters admitted this year whose names appear in the debt list of this year; And of £34 2s. received this year from the two debt lists for the two preceding years drawn up in the time of the said stewards; And for £9 9s. 9d. received this year from various debt lists drawn up in the time of John Hosyer and Richard Dylowe, former stewards of the same guild; And for £4 7s. 8d. received this year from various debt lists drawn up in the time of John Griffith and John Bowdeler, the first of the stewards of the same guild; ... and from 13s. 4d. received this year from the fine of Hugh Cresses, admitted in the time.

35. National membership receipts [Amounts collected by the stewards of the Palmers' Guild of Ludlow in their travels through the country, 1538–9, showing the wide geographical extent of the membership. Shropshire Record Office, 356/Box 321: Stewards' account 1538–9; in Latin]

Memorandum, that the said warden has received from Richard Hore, steward, for his journey made by him to Shrewsbury, Stafford, etc., for which he had not accounted at the said feast in the year last past: 46s.

Memorandum, that the said warden has received from William Phelyppus, steward, for the Lenten journey made by him to Thornbury, Bath, Bristol, Westbury, Keynsham, Wells, Glastonbury, Bruton, Reading, Shaftesbury, Salisbury, Amesbury and Wherwell, collected by him: £6 10s. 2d.

Memorandum, that the said warden has received from Richard Hoore for his Lenten journey to Old Swinford, Birmingham, Coleshill, Atherstone, Nuneaton, Southam, Warwick, Coventry, Banbury, Towcester, Northampton, Leicester, Nottingham, Derby, Ashby, Burton, Lichfield, Wolverhampton, from fines of brothers and sisters collected by him: £12 7s.

Memorandum, that the said warden has received from Richard Hoore, steward, for his second journey made to Llangollen, Oswestry, Wrexham, Ruthin, Denbigh, Holywell, Caernarvon, Chester, from fines of brothers and sisters received by him in this journey, total: £5 11d.

Memorandum, that the said warden has received from Richard Hoore, steward, for his third journey made to Welshpool, Montgomery, Newtown, Machynlleth, Aberystwyth, Hereford, West Tenby, Pysgod [= Tenby], Carmarthen, Kidwelly, Cowbridge, Cardiff, Caerleon, Abergavenny, Brecon, etc., from fines of brothers and sisters received by him and collected in this journey; total: £5 10s. 11d.

Memorandum, that the said warden has received from Richard Hore, steward, for his fourth journey made by him to Shrewsbury, Wem, Whitchurch, Market Drayton, Stafford, Gnosall, Newport, from fines of brothers and sisters collected by him and received in this journey; total: £3 2d.

Memorandum, that William Phelyppus, steward, received in his second journey made by him to Marlborough, Marshfield, Painswick, Bishops Cleeve, Cirencester, Gloucester, Tewkesbury, Pershore, Evesham, Worcester, Hanley, Bodenham, Ross, Monmouth, Newlond,

Chepstow, Hereford, Leominster, Bromyard, etc., from fines of various brothers and sisters collected by him in this journey; total: £7 17s. 11d.

36. Benefits of membership of the fraternity of St Chad, Lichfield; linked to provision for the fabric of Lichfield cathedral

(i) *Total of benefits, as announced by the bishop of Lichfield,* c. *1440.* [From British Library, MS Harley 5179, ff.118–v; in Latin. The date is unclear, the dating clause giving only the day and month, but not the year. The text is somewhat garbled, but is very similar to another equally garbled document (an eighteenth-century transcript) which conveys similar information in Shrewsbury Public Library, MS 2, f.91v (from which it has sometimes been necessary to adopt readings where the phrases are obviously intended to be identical). The Shrewsbury document is dated 1 May 1444, but the precise relationship between the two versions has not yet been clarified]

These are the benefits and indulgences conceded to the brothers and sisters of the fraternity of St Chad in the cathedral church of Lichfield, and their benefactors. Firstly, from the blessed Bishop Chad and others his predecessors and successors as bishops of Lichfield, 4040 days of privilege mercifully remitted in the Lord by this means to benefactors who are truly contrite and confessed for their sins, and, furthermore they have ratified all indulgences justly conceded in this matter and hereafter to be granted. And notwithstanding these, various other Catholic bishops had granted 12000 days of privilege to the aforesaid benefactors; and various pontiffs of the Holy Roman Church had graciously granted 21 years of privilege to those benefactors, and piously relaxed for these benefactors three parts of the enjoined penance for their forgotten sins and for vows negligently unfulfilled, unless such were of the sort which are rightly to be taken to the apostolic see. And furthermore, the abbots and priors and prioresses and persons written below are perpetually bound every year to devoutly celebrate and say (and to cause to be celebrated and said by the ordinance or statutes of the cathedral church of Lichfield rightly and legitimately set out and confirmed together with all the solemnities required in law for the matter) the masses and psalters written below for the aforesaid benefactors: firstly, the abbot of Darley, 100 masses; the abbot of Burton, 100 masses; the abbot of Shrewsbury, 100 masses; the abbot of Beauchief, 100 masses; the abbot of Rocester, 30 masses; the abbot of Croxden, 30 masses; the abbot of Haughmond, 100 masses; the abbot of Lilleshall, 100 masses; the abbot of Dieulacres, 60 masses; the prior of Trentham, 40 masses; the prior of Tutbury, 40 masses; the prior of Stone, 40 masses; the prior of Ronton, 40 masses; the prior of Calwich, 24 masses; the prior of St Thomas [Baswich], 20 masses; the prior of Sandwell, 9 masses; the prior of Canwell, 3 masses; the prior of Lapley, 28 masses; the prior of Cannock, 60 masses; the prioress of Brewood, 42 psalters; the prioress of Derby, 300 psalters; the canons of All Saints, Derby, 100 psalters and 200 masses. Item, it was ordered by the blessed Chad and the aforesaid bishops of Lichfield, and piously confirmed by them, that in the church of Lichfield 4 masses should be celebrated daily for the brothers and sisters and benefactors in perpetuity, 2 for the living, and 2 for the dead; every parish priest within the diocese of Coventry and Lichfield shall also celebrate 30 masses during the year for the brothers and sisters and benefactors of that fraternity. And (provided that those concerned are contrite and confessed) those who, to the detriment of their souls, sinned against their parents by assaulting them, and forgotten penances, and forgotten sins, and the broken vows of the ignorant (whatever the condition of fulfilment) shall, by the mercy of God, be released so that they can be buried in a cemetery like other Christians, if they have entered this fraternity and their names shall be found written among the brothers and sisters of the fraternity of St Chad; on condition that they shall have sent a certain annual sum in alms to this church of Lichfield, whatever the death by which they shall be overtaken, unless they have been excommunicated by name. Moreover, it is enjoined on parish priests by these statutes that, on every Sunday, before the aspersion with holy water, they shall cause the people to pray for those brethren and sisters and benefactors, and that they, with raised hands, shall devoutly say the Lord's Prayer, the priest beginning thus: 'For us, to Saint Chad', with the customary verse of the prayer. Truly, because it would be a matter of great consolation to us if by our provision the due prosperity of our said cathedral church (our spouse, with which in particular we are linked as one body) could be assured, we therefore admonish once, twice, thrice and peremptorily, lest anyone having cure and subject to us should fall under the penalty of the law, that they should allow the questors into the churches which they serve from the first Sunday in Lent until the Sunday on which the office of *Quasimodo genitus* is sung [the first Sunday after Easter] to expound their business by all means; and that at their confessions they should enjoin on their parishioners and effectually induce them to contribute annually towards the concerns of the said fraternity, as the custom is, so that you and yours should each have in this matter what the performance of your devotions might justly be granted by God and men; and that it might similarly work for you for your merits so that you worthily receive what is due to you at the Last Judgement by the intercession of the blessed Chad (our patron) with the Most High. The sum total of masses annually to be celebrated for the brothers and sisters and benefactors of the said fraternity: 2434. The sum total of psalters annually to be said for them: 452. In confirmation of all and singular of these we have caused our common seal to be appended to this. Dated at Lichfield, in our chapter house, 12 kal. April [21 March], the year one thousand ...

(ii) *Further summary of the spiritual privileges linked to membership of St Chad's fraternity* [From Shrewsbury Public Library, MS 2, f.94v; in Latin: an eighteenth-century transcript, the original from which it was copied dating from *c.*1445–50]

PRIVILEGES GRANTED TO THE SAID CHURCH OF LICHFIELD AND THOSE VISITING THE RELICS

Firstly, they are privileged that within the diocese of Lichfield anyone who in person or via a messenger or proctor of the church of Lichfield gives to the church and annually visits the relics, whatever the death by which they shall be overtaken (and even if they should kill themselves) shall freely enjoy ecclesiastical burial, unless excommunicated by name.

Item, if a messenger or proctor of the said church of Lichfield shall come to a church of the said diocese of Lichfield which has had an ecclesiastical interdict imposed on it by the bishop of Lichfield or another in his stead, at least once in the year on the day of his arrival it shall be permitted that divine service may freely be celebrated within it.

Item, if anyone from the diocese of Lichfield shall be enjoined by the bishop or another inferior ecclesiastical judge to undergo public penance or beating around the church or market for his offences, on the arrival of a proctor as set out above at least once in the year, he shall not be bound to undergo the said penance, and he shall be treated as though he had undergone it.

THESE ARE INDULGED BY ALL THE PONTIFFS OF LICHFIELD

PRAYERS OFFERED FOR THE VISITORS, AS ABOVE, ETC.

Firstly, every Sunday throughout the year when there is no double feast occurring to impede it, the whole choir of the cathedral church of Lichfield, in the midst of their procession and before they enter the choir, shall in public hearing devoutly say special prayers to the Most High for the brothers and sisters, both the living who annually visit the said cathedral church and relics, and the dead who had visited them during their lives.

Item, it is ordained and granted that the priest in every parish church throughout the whole diocese of Lichfield before the aspersion with holy water shall enjoin the people to say for them the Lord's Prayer with angelic salutation.

Item, every weekday in Lent, if free of a feast, a mass of requiem shall be sung with solemn music in the church of Lichfield in which solemn mention shall be made of the deceased brothers and sisters of that church who once a year during their lives visited that church and the aforesaid relics, together with the faithful departed.

Item, the masses and psalters which appear written before shall be said in their places for the living and the dead: in the cathedral church of Lichfield and other religious places of the said diocese, 960 each year.

IX. Security for the dead

While there was considerable concern to accumulate spiritual benefits during life, the most important issue was to secure salvation after death. The doctrine of Purgatory required almost everyone destined for Heaven to undergo a period of purging of their sins after death, a process which could be hastened by the living left behind, either through their own prayers or through the maintenance of masses which would be held for the sake of the deceased's soul.[1]

The arrangements for ensuring this were manifold, leading to the funding of a variety of schemes to secure prayers in multiplicity or perpetuity, and preferably both. Numerous short-term bequests to establish prayers are recorded in wills; more elaborate foundations were often arranged before death, or with the details being settled by the executors beyond the confines of the will. Testamentary attempts to erect such prayer institutions cannot always be assumed to have been implemented: executors and heirs were notoriously unreliable.[2]

The post-mortem prayers varied in form, from the trental (a recital of thirty masses, often performed by friars) and the more elaborate St Gregory's trental, to a fully-endowed perpetual chantry, which entailed a daily mass for the soul of the founder (and often other named individuals) in perpetuity. Obits and anniversaries ensured that individuals were remembered at least once a year, in celebrations which ranged from the extremely modest to the extremely extravagant.[3] *The multiplication of foundations, for a family or an individual, was fairly common; but attrition also occurred, as natural*

1 C. Burgess, '"A fond thing vainly invented": an essay on Purgatory and pious provision in the late middle ages', in *Parish, Church and People; Local Studies in Lay Religion, 1350–1750*, ed. S. J. Wright, London, 1988, pp. 56–84. The acquisition of indulgences, and the participation in prayers through post-mortem membership of fraternities, would also fit within this context.

2 Complaints about non-fulfilment of chantry endowments appear in some visitation returns, e.g. K. Wood-Legh, ed., *Kentish Visitations of Archbishop William Warham and his Deputies, 1511–1512*, Kent Records, XXIV, 1984, *passim.*

3 R. W. Pfaff, 'The English devotion of St Gregory's Trental', *Speculum*, XLIX, 1974, pp. 75–90; C. Burgess, 'A service for the dead: the form and function of the medieval anniversary', *Transactions of the Bristol and Gloucestershire Archaeological Society*, CV, 1987, pp. 183–211; K. Wood-Legh, *Perpetual Chantries in Britain*, Cambridge, 1965; A. Kreider, *English Chantries: the Road to Dissolution*, Harvard Historical Studies, XCVII, Cambridge, Mass., and London, 1979; R. N. Swanson, *Church and Society in Late Medieval England*, Oxford, 1989, pp. 296–9, 302–3, 306.

wastage or incompetent management eroded the value of an endowment.[4]

Whether long or short term, chantries often entailed other obligations, especially within a parochial context, and even if not formally recited in the foundation deed.[5] *Several were attached to more wide-ranging charitable foundations, including schools, hospitals and university colleges, and sought the involvement of a wide variety of people in the prayers to be offered: the Hoskyn's chantry deed from Ludlow which is printed here runs through a suitably wide gamut.*[6]

While most evidence of these post-mortem foundations derives from a context which is essentially 'secular' (because the foundations were established as ecclesiastical benefices, or fell under the control of urban authorities), a considerable number were established within monasteries or friaries, involving the religious orders in return for a cash payment.[7] *These, because of the arrangements for their funding and servicing, and perhaps because many of them disappeared with the dissolution of the religious houses (before the general dissolution of the chantries in the 1540s) tend to be rather shadowy.*[8] *Nevertheless, there are sufficient references to them, including documents for their endowment, to indicate the aspirations of their founders.*

4 For the history of one family's foundations, M. Hicks, 'Chantries, obits, and almshouses: the Hungerford foundations', in *The Church in Pre-Reformation Society: Essays in Honour of F. R. H. du Boulay*, ed. C. M. Barron and C. Harper-Bill, Woodbridge, 1985, pp. 123–42.

5 E.g. C. Burgess, '"For the increase of divine service": chantries in the parish in late-medieval Bristol', *Journal of Ecclesiastical History*, XXXVI, 1985, pp. 46–65.

6 The reciprocity of the arrangements for prayers in exchange for charity which is evident in the Hosyer deed is echoed even more bluntly in the declaration issued by the chantry priest of the Wakebridge chantry at Crich (Derbyshire) at the annual distribution of the dole there, *c*1500: 'Neighbours, I would have you aware that on this day (as you know by old custom) the chantry priest of St Nicholas and St Katherine is required to distribute 10s. in pennies or their equivalent, so that anyone ... coming shall have ¼d. in silver, or the equivalent. For this reason I ask that, when the mass is over, you wait to receive your dole, and pray for the founder, William Wakebridge. Also, I ask your youngsters and everyone else to wait within the church, and you will all be served. If you do not, I ask you to consider me excused, for assuredly you will depart without any dole' (A. Saltman, ed., *The Cartulary of the Wakebridge Chantries at Crich*, Derbyshire Archaeological Society, Record Series, VI, 1976, for 1971, no148).

7 Wood-Legh, *Perpetual Chantries*, ch. 6.

8 That many chantries disappeared with the dissolution of the monasteries is part of the received tradition: Hicks, 'Chantries, obits, and almshouses', p. 142; Kreider, *English Chantries*, pp. 128–9. However, it is possible that (as with earlier dissolutions) attempts were in fact made to secure the continuation of such chantries after the religious house had gone. The chantry certificates for Dorset certainly refer to the continaunce of some chantries with endowments from houses recently dissolved: E. A. Fry, 'Dorset chantries', *Proceedings of the Dorset Natural History and Antiquarian Field Club*, XXVII, 1906, pp. 230–1, XXVIII, 1907, pp. 17–18.

A. Obits and Anniversaries

37. Provision of trentals: agreement between the carpenters' fraternity of York and the Augustinian friars of York, 1487 [From J. W. Percy, ed., *York Memorandum Book, BY*, Surtees Society Publications, CLXXXVI, 1973, pp. 254–5; in English]

This present indenture, made at York on the feast of St Mathias the apostle, in the second year of the reign of King Henry the Seventh ... [24 February 1486/7], between brother William Bewyk of the house of the order of Austin friars within the city of York and the covent of the same on the one part, and Richard Bischope and John Couper, searchers of the craft of the carpenters within the said city, James Wynffell, Michael Clerk, William Johnson and Thomas Hunt, wardens of the Holy Fraternity of the Resurrection of Our Lord maintained by the carpenters of the said city on the other part,

Witnesses that the said prior grants to them two trentals of masses to be sung every year for the souls of all the brothers and sisters of the said fraternity, and that the said prior and convent with their full assent and consent grant to them to sing five trentals of masses for every brother of the said fraternity who truly fulfils his obligations, after his death, upon reasonable notification of his decease. And the aforesaid wardens and searchers, with the full assent and consent of themselves and their craft, strictly bind themselves and their successors as searchers and wardens of the said craft of carpenters for the time being, to pay to the said prior and convent and their successors yearly for evermore 10s. of lawful English money, for the singing of the aforesaid two trentals as set out above at two points in the year, that is to say at the feast of the Invention of the Holy Cross [3 May], and of All Hallows [1 November], by equal portions, and for every trental of masses for every deceased brother as detailed above, 5s. of lawful English money, and for the satisfaction and payment of 6s. 8d., part of the said 10s. to be paid yearly as specified above, we, the said searchers and wardens, with the full assent and consent of us and all our said craft, grant and by these presents lease at farm to the said prior and convent two messuages with their appurtenances upon the corner of the landing next to St Leonard's at the River Ouse, adjoining the said house of friars and containing 9 yards in length and 8½ yards in breadth, to have and to hold the said messuages with their appurtenances to the said prior and convent and their successors from the aforesaid feast of St Matthew in the year aforesaid, to the end and termination of 99 years, fully complete. And the aforesaid prior and convent and their successors will repair and maintain the aforesaid two messuages with their appurtenances during the aforesaid term at their own costs and charges. Provided always that if the aforesaid prior and convent and their successors default in the annual singing of the said two trentals as set out above, that then it shall be lawful for the said searchers and wardens and their successors to enter into all the aforesaid two messuages with their appurtenances in their old manner, and to occupy them, notwithstanding these present indentures. In witness whereof the said searchers and wardens have affixed their seals to the one half of these indentures remaining with the aforesaid prior and convent.

Given the day, year and place abovesaid.

38. Obit arrangements: concerning the obit of William Paston, as recorded in a letter from John Bonewell, prior of Norwich, to unnamed addressees, 1486–7 [From N. Davis, ed., *Paston Letters and Papers of the Fifteenth Century*, 2 vols, Oxford, 1971–6, II, no. 926; in English]

... And it is the case that for long and many years there has been hanging a great dispute and grudge between Agnes Paston, deceased, late the wife of William Paston, justice, and William Paston and Clement Paston, deceased, their sons, on the one side, and John Paston, the son of the said William Paston, justice, and ... Agnes his wife, also deceased, and Sir John Paston, knight, deceased, and John Paston still living, sons to the said deceased John, on the other side. And now the said dispute continues between the said William and John who is now living ...

May it please you to know that the said William Paston, justice, during his life was a special lover and friend to our monastery, and for the singular love and trust that he had to be remembered among us after his decease, notwithstanding that he died in London he yet bequeathed his body to be buried (and is buried) in the chapel of Our Lady within our monastery. And the said William Paston, justice, often, and many times in his full life, the said Agnes being present, declared to the prior of our monastery who then was ... and many various others who were of his acquaintance and whom he trusted to declare his intentions to concerning the health of his soul ... that it was truly his last will that out of [certain] ... manors a certain land or annuity should be perpetually amortised, of such value that every monk who sings the last mass in the said chapel where the body of the said William Paston lies buried should have on the day that he sang mass there 4d. to pray for the souls of the said William and of Agnes his wife and for their ancestors, kindred, cousins, affinity and friends, and for all Christian souls; and beyond that a certain sum of money to be paid annually to have the obit of the said William and Agnes kept yearly with *Dirige* and mass in the said chapel.

... it is now 43 years ago that the said William, justice, died. And ... Agnes his wife lived more than 30 winters after her husband, and was particularly trusted by her husband, and one of his executors ... and knew her husband's mind and last will as well as any living creature. She always testified that it was her husband's last will to have this perpetual mass, and called on it all the days of her life, and also at her decease; and she said that it was the will of her husband that the annuity should derive from the ... manor of Swainesthorpe. ... John Paston, deceased, would have had it granted out of the ... manor of Cressingham, and some of the executors would have had the said mass continued only for ... 80 years, and would have drawn up an appropriate deed, but the said Agnes would not agree to that, but always said that it was the last will of her husband to have the mass made perpetual; and the executors declared to us that they would see the will performed. And thereupon the executors by their common agreement left a coffer with a great amount of money from the goods of the said William, justice, to be kept within our monastery, and said and declared to us that the said wealth should never be carried off nor taken out of our place until we were assured of the said annuity. And during all the period that the said coffer with the goods was within our monastery, it was always declared to us that the said annuity would be amortised in perpetuity, and during all the time that the said coffer was in our place we had money given to us annually to pray for his soul in order to keep his obit. And afterwards, by means devised without the knowledge of the said Agnes or any of our brothers, all the wealth that was in the said coffer was carried out of our monastery, and after that was done there was no further money given to us by the said executors, either to keep the said obit or to pray for the soul of the said William, except that the said Agnes during her life gave to us yearly at her own expense to remember the soul; and what has been done since has been done out of our own devotion, and these many years there has been nothing given to us. Notwithstanding, from our own devotion we have recited his name in our bead-roll every Sunday ...

39. Establishment of an obit or anniversary, 1458 [Windsor, St George's Chapel archives, XV.58C.2; in Latin].

To all and singular the faithful in Christ to whom shall come these present tripartite and indented letters, and the contents of those letters, between us, Thomas Mannynge, clerk, dean or warden of the college of royal Chapel of St George within the castle of Windsor and the canons of that place on the first part; and us, Roger Fassenham and Christina his wife, on the second part; and us, Thomas Symnette and Thomas Baker, wardens or masters of the fraternity or guild of the holy and undivided Trinity in the parish church of St John the Baptist at New Windsor on the third part, greeting in the Lord everlasting. Know that we, the above Roger and Christina, by means of a royal licence, have given, granted, and by these presents confirmed to the aforesaid dean and chapter all those lands and tenements, rents and services with their appurtenances which lately belonged to Amoricius Bernard, and formerly to Richard Smyth, in the towns and fields of New Windsor and Old Windsor in the county of Berkshire, to have and to hold those lands and tenements, rents and services with their appurtenances to the said dean and canons and their successors from the capital lords of their fees in perpetuity for the service due therefrom and customary in law, in this manner and condition; that is, that the aforesaid dean and canons and their successors shall annually during the lives of us, the aforesaid Roger and Christina, with the money or sums of money derived from the aforesaid lands, tenements, rents and services, hold and observe the anniversary of Richard Smyth and Alice his wife, the father and mother of me the aforesaid Christina, within the college or Chapel of St George abovesaid, on the 1st day of the month of March, as is fitting, solemnly singing *Placebo* and *Dirige* for the souls of that Richard and Alice, with a mass of requiem in the vigil, according to the manner of an obit or anniversary of any of the canons aforesaid and others as is customary there; for the performance, observance and celebration of which anniversary as set out in each year perpetually in future time successively the aforesaid dean and canons shall pay and offer before the end of the aforesaid mass to the dean, canons, vicars, clerks, choristers and ministers of the said college or chapel as written below who shall be in and present at the annversary and partakers of the sums of money below written, that is:

to the dean of the said college or chapel performing the said obsequies and celebrating the said mass, [2s.] ... and if it is a canon who performs the said obsequies, he shall receive [2s.] ... ; to every other of those canons, [12d.] ... ; to each vicar, [6d.] ... ; to each clerk, [4d.] ... ; to each chorister, [2d.] ... ; and to the verger [6d.] ... if he is present; and also to one of the ministers keeping the vestibule, [3d.] ... , and to two other ministers ringing bells, [4d.] ... for each of them; and also to the precentor there for bread, wine and wax to be provided for the said anniversary, [3s. 4d.] ... ; and that the dean and canons and their successors shall specially pray to God in the said college for the good health of us, the said Roger and Christina, while we live, and after the death or decease of the longer living of either of us, the anniversary of us, the said Roger and Christina, shall similarly be held and observed in the college or chapel aforesaid by the said dean and canons and their successors each year in perpetuity on the day of the obit of the said Roger and Alice his wife, in the manner and form declared and specified above in all things. And if the aforesaid dean and canons or their successors shall neglect or be remiss in holding and observing the aforesaid anniversary, so that it happens that the said anniversary is not held or observed in the form and manner above named on one occasion, then we (the aforesaid Roger and Christina) wish and grant by these presents that the aforesaid lands, tenements rents and services with their appurtenances immediately after this neglect and default by the said dean and canons and their successors shall remain to the aforesaid wardens or masters of the fraternity or guild of the holy and undivided Trinity and their successors, to the intent and effect that they should hold and observe the aforesaid anniversary in all things in the manner and form above expressed within the aforesaid college or chapel. And if those wardens or masters and their successors are similarly negligent or remiss in holding and observing the aforesaid anniversary thus within the said college or chapel, so that that anniversary shall happen not to be held or observed for one occasion in the manner and form prescribed, then we (the aforesaid Roger and Christina) wish and grant by these presents that it shall be well permitted for us and our right heirs to re-enter in, possess and perpetually retain the said lands and tenements, rents and services, notwithstanding in any manner our said grant thereof in the aforesaid form and the seisin delieverd therein. Know, lastly, that we, the said dean and canons of the said college or Chapel of St George aforesaid, gathered together personally and in chapter within our chapter house, solemn discussion and mature deliberation first had and considered among us in this matter, by the tenor of these presents promise and grant and thus have promised and granted the above by our pure, straightforward and free and spontaneous will and with our unanimous consent, that the aforesaid anniversary shall be held, observed and celebrated and all else and singular of the abovesaid in the manner and form above noted shall be done and observed and implemented in all things as set out by us and our successors in the said college or chapel in the manner and form above set out and prescribed. Similarly know that we, the above wardens or masters of the fraternity or guild of the holy and undivided Trinity in the parish church of St John the Baptist, of New Windsor aforesaid, by unanimous assent and consent, and having had mature deliberation amongst us on the above, and their consideration having been carried out, by our simple pure and free and spontaneous will promise and grant by these presents to hold and observe the abovesaid anniversary after the said neglect or defaults of the said dean and canons or their successors in that college or chapel in the manner or form abovewritten and expressed, and the implementation of all and singular of the other things set out in all things, as set out, as soon as the said lands and tenenement, rents and services with their appurtenances shall happen to have devolved to our hands or into our or our successors' possession for the reason aforesaid. ... Dated at Windsor, in the aforesaid castle, in the chapter of the said dean and canons within the college or chapel within the said castle, [25 June, 36 Henry VI].

B. Chantries and almhouses

40. Establishment of a chantry: St James's priory, Bristol, 1400

[From E. W. W. Veale, ed., *The Great Red Book of Bristol*, I, Bristol Record Society, IV, 1933, pp. 243–4; in Latin]

To all the faithful in Christ to whom the present writing shall come, Thomas, by divine permission abbot of the monastery of blessed Mary of Tewkesbury, and the convent of that place, greeting in the Lord. Since lately John Stone, burgess of the town of Bristol, by his certain tripartite writing gave and granted to Richard Wircestre, prior of the church of St James, Bristol, and the priors who shall be there for the time being, two messuages and one shop with their appurtenances in Bristol and the suburbs of that town, to have and to hold to him and the priors who shall be for the time being as is more fully contained in the said tripartite writing, the tenor of which writing follows in these words:

To all the faithful in Christ to whom this present tripartite writing shall come, John Stone, burgess of the towm of Bristol, greeting in the Lord. Know that I, by licence of Henry, by the grace of God, King of England and France and lord of Ireland, dated at Westminster, the eighth day of June in the first year of his reign [1400], have given and granted and by this my present tripartite writing have confirmed to my beloved in Christ Richard Wircestre, prior of the church of St James, Bristol, two messuages and one shop with their appurtenances in Bristol and the suburbs of that town, to have and to hold to him and the priors who shall be there in perpetuity, for finding one monk to celebrate one mass every day at the altar of St Thomas in the parish church of St James at Bristol in perpetuity, so long as that altar shall be fit and worthy in vestments and other due necessities for such celebration. For which gift and grant the said prior grants by these presents for himself and the priors who shall be there for the time being, that for each day when the said mass (as set out) shall not be celebrated (unless reasonable cause shall exist), 40d. shall be payable to the mayor of the town of Bristol and the proctors of the church of St James in that town who shall be for the time being, of which 20d. shall be applied to the use of the said mayor, and the other 20d. shall be disposed and spent for the health of the soul of John Wynchestre at the discretion of the aforesaid proctors and their ordination; provided, however, that if the said messuages and shop by reason of any law or title shall be deraigned or recovered in whole or in part against the abbot of Tewkesbury or the aforesaid prior or priors who shall be there for the time being hereafter, without any collusion on the part of the said abbot or his successors or of the said prior who shall be for the time being, or if they shall be destroyed by the invasion of enemies or other disturbances arising within the realm which are unavoidable by the said prior, so that he could not have the rent or profit thereof to the use of the said prior, that thenceforth the said mass, in whole or *pro rata* for the time according to when it shall be deraigned or recovered or (as set out) destroyed, altogether ceases, and that the prior and the priors who shall be for the time being there, in such case as is aforesaid shall be exonerated from the said mass. And the said prior wishes and grants for himself and for the priors who shall be there for the time being, that if the said mass shall not be duly celebrated according to the form of this ordination and agreement, that then it shall well be allowed for the mayor of Bristol who shall be for the time being to distrain on the said two messuages and shop, and retain the distraints until the aforesaid penalty shall have been paid in the aforesaid manner. And if sufficient distraint cannot be found in the said messuages and shop, then it shall be well allowed for that mayor to distrain on all the lands and tenements of the said priory being within the liberty of the aforesaid town of Bristol, and retain the distraints found thereon until the said penalty shall have been fully paid as set out. ... Dated at Bristol, 14th day of June, the first year of the reign of King Henry, the fourth after the conquest.

We, the aforesaid abbot and convent, approving the aforesaid gift and grant, accept, affirm, and (as far as we can) approve them for us and our successors in perpetuity ... [Tewkesbury, 20 June 1400].

41. Establishment of a chantry in a friary: the Dominican friary at Bristol, 1469 [From E. W. W. Veale, ed., *The Great Red Book of Bristol*, IV, Bristol Record Society, XVIII, 1953, pp. 125–7; in Latin]

To all the sons of Holy Mother Church to whom this present indented writing shall come, William Payn, prior of the house of the Friars Preachers in Bristol, and the convent of that place, greeting in him who is true health. Know that we (on account of the sincere devotion which the noble and our beloved in Christ John Codrynton, Esq., lord of Coddrington in the county of Gloucester, and Alice his wife, display to us and to our order and convent, and for a certain large sum of money by their authority paid and delivered in hand to us by them, for our special benefit and the increase of divine service in our house) by the unanimous assent and consent of all our chapter, have given, conceded, and by this our present writing have confirmed for us and our successors in perpetuity to the aforesaid John Codrynton and Alice his wife, and their heirs, that they shall have a perpetual chantry at the altar of St Peter *de Meleyn*, being in our aforesaid house, in the manner and form following, to be observed from the present date for all time. That is, that one brother of our convent every day at the hours of dawn (that is, in summer time at six, and in winter time at seven) shall celebrate a mass for the good state of them, John and Alice, and for the souls of them, their ancestors, and all the faithful departed; and it shall be called and named in perpetuity *Codryntonesmasse* at the aforesaid altar, so that (that is) the brother who for the time being performs that office before the beginning of his mass, clad in his vestments, shall be held to turn to those standing by and exhort them, out of charity, to pray for the good state of the aforesaid John and Alice while they live, and of the longer living of either of them, and for their souls when they shall have passed from this light, and after their deaths for the good state of the living heir for the time being of that John and Alice (he thus for the time being living and existing) to be specially named by his name and surname in perpetuity, and for the souls of their ancestors and of all the faithful departed, saying to the omnipotent lord these psalms: *Deus misereatur*, etc., with this prayer, *Deus qui est nostra redempcio*, etc., *De profundis*, etc., with this prayer, *Inclina, domine, aurem tuam*, etc.; and each mass thus fully completed and celebrated, this gospel, *Missus est angelus Gabriel*. So that that brother shall celebrate requiem masses weekly on the days when the death shall take place of that John and Alice for that John and Alice, with the ceremonies abovenamed; and each year before the obit of that John and Alice we shall celebrate and hold their exequies in the choir of the church of our aforesaid house, on the day in which the obit of that John shall fall, saying *Placebo* and *Dirige*, with the nine lessons thereof, and on the following day a mass of requiem for the souls of them, their ancestors and of all the faithful departed, and this with chant of the more solemn and more decent manner that we are able. And the aforesaid John and Alice have promised to us, and by their faith are firmly obliged, that their heirs or assigns ought annually to pay to us and our successors on that day during the solemnity of the aforesaid mass 6s. 8d. of the legal money of England to pray for the healthy state of the heir of the aforesaid John and Alice (they, as above set out, being specially named in perpetuity). Wishing all our aforesaid gift and concession to remain always full and unbroken we, the aforesaid prior, and each brother of our aforesaid convent being at the time of the drawing up of this writing in our aforesaid house, holding the most holy gospels of God, have taken a corporal oath for us and our successors to observe them inviolably in perpetuity as set out. And if it happens that we or our successors should infringe the aforesaid donation and concession in any manner afterwards (may that not occur), we wish, and by these presents concede, that we and our successors should be held and reputed faithless and perjured in perpetuity before the mayor of the town of Bristol and all and singular the worthies of that town and whomsoever else, and by the simple denunciation of the aforesaid John and Alice or their heir, or whomsover else from day to day we shall be excommunicated and separated from the communion of all faithful Christians, renouncing concerning all these our privilege of prohibition on whatsoever accusations alleged or to be charged in whatsoever place or court, which we or our successors might put forward concerning the above in any way ... [1 August, 1469].

42. Establishment of a chantry through feoffment to uses: Bridgwater, 1482 [From R. W. Dunning and T. D. Tremlett, eds., *Bridgwater Borough Archives, V, 1468–1485*, Somerset Record Society, LXX, 1971, pp. 53–4; in Latin]

This indenture made between Richard Chokke, knight, one of the justices of common pleas of the lord king, on the one part, and John Wheler, chaplain of the chantry of the blessed Virgin Mary in the parish church of Bridgwater, and John Kendall, John Woder and Robert Cotys, feoffees of and in a messuage or tenement with appurtenances in Bridgwater aforesaid ... to the use of the said chantry of the other part, bears witness that the aforesaid chaplain and feoffees acknowledge that the said Robert Chokke has by his deed released to those same feoffees all his right and title in the said messuage or tenement with its appurtenances, to the use of the said chantry, which is known to be effective and highly useful thereto. Wishing on account of this, as far as in them lies, that that Richard should gain spiritually from the temporal, by their assent and consent they grant to the aforesaid Richard Chokke by these presents that the aforesaid chaplain and his successors among other things shall pray for the good estate of that Richard and Margaret his wife while they live, and for their souls when then have shall have passed on from this world, and for the souls [of other identified persons]... And that in each mass to be celebrated by the chaplain and his successors that chaplain and his successors among other things shall devoutly say among other collects for the good estate of the aforesaid Richard and Margaret, whle they live, this collect, *Deus tuorum*, etc., with the secrets and postulations of that collect, and after their decease *Inclina*, etc., with the secrets and postulations, thereafter throughout time. And the aforesaid chaplain and feoffees, for themselves and their successors, grant by these presents that they and their successors shall annually in perpetuity hold and sustain an obit or anniversary in the aforesaid church for the said Richard and Margaret his wife and the others aforenamed, from when it shall happen that that Richard shall die; so that on the preceding days the exequies of the dead and on the day itself the mass of requiem shall be devoutly said and celebrated in perpetuity by the aforesaid chaplain and his successors for the aforesaid souls with ringing of bells. And the aforesaid feoffees grant for themselves and their successors by these presents that each chaplain of the aforesaid chantry on his admission to the said chantry shall be specially bound to pray, say, celebrate, hold and observe all the aforesaid in the form aforesaid during the time that he shall be chaplain of the chantry ... [5 November, 1482].

43. Regulations for a chantry and almshouses: the foundation deed of Hosyer's charity, Ludlow, 1486 [Shropshire Record Office, 356/Box 315; in English]

To all true Christian people to whom this present tripartite indented writing shall come, Robert Sherman and John Dale, executors of the testament of John Hosyer, late of Ludlow in the county of Shropshire, merchant (now dead), send greeting in Our Lord God. Whereas we, the said Richard Sherman and John Dale, in fulfilling the last will of the said John Hosyer our testator, have given and delivered to the current warden and brethren of the fraternity of St John the Evangelist of Palmers of Ludlow, aforesaid, to the use of the same fraternity, £5 11s. 4d. of lawful money of England, and a cup with a cover of silver, overgilt, weighing 52½ oz. of Troy weight (price the ounce, 5s. 6d.; total £14 8s. 9d.; the sum total thereof is £20); and also whereas we, the foresaid Richard Sherman and John Dale, by our several deeds of enfeoffment sealed with our seals, bearing date the 8th day of December [1486] ... , enfeoffed Walter ap Ricart and Richard Lynton, chaplains, and fully delivered to them seisin of and in certain lands and tenements lying in Ludlow aforesaid, Overton, Hopton, North Cleobery and Ayntree in the said county of Shropshire, the which lands and tenements are of the clear yearly value of £9 13s. 4d., above all charges, and of and in an almshouse with the appurtenances, lately newly built at the cost and charges of the said John Hosyer, set in Ludlow aforesaid; to have and to hold the said lands, tenements and almshouse with their appurtenances to the foresaid Walter ap Ricart and Richard Lynton, and to their heirs for evermore, to the use of the said warden and brethren of the said fraternity who now are and who hereafter shall be, and to the intent to perform therefrom the will of us, the foresaid Robert Sherman and John Dale, hereunder written. Know that we, the same Robert Sherman and John Dale, by these presents declare our will and intent of and upon the said feoffment affecting the said lands and tenements with the appurtenances, in the manner and form following, that is to say:

First, that the said feoffees and either of them, and all others having their estate hereafter, shall fully perform, fulfil and observe our wills and ordinances as ordained by us and hereafter declared; that is to wit, that the said feoffees and either of them, within ten days after they shall have been required to do so by us, the said Robert Sherman and John Dale, or either of us by the advice of our learned counsel, shall make a full estate by their deed, sufficient in law, to twelve such persons as we or either of us shall name, of and in all the foresaid lands and tenements, to have to them and to their heirs and assigns for evermore, to the use and intent to perform therefrom this our present will and ordinance; and that whensoever it shall chance that the said twelve persons so enfeoffed in the said lands or tenements shall be dead or deceased so that the number of them being alive shall be five or six persons, then the same five or six persons so surviving shall enfeof two or three other well-disposed persons in the said lands and tenements, to have to them and their heirs for evermore; and that then those same five or six persons then surviving shall again take an estate to themselves and to other persons to the number of twelve persons in all, of and in the said land and tenements, the same persons to be named by the warden and brethren of the council of the said fraternity, to have and to hold all the said lands and tenements to them and their heirs to the use and intent aforesaid, and thus as often and whenever such a situation shall arise for evermore.

Also we will and ordain by these presents that the said feoffees shall, from the issues and profits of the foresaid lands and tenements, find an honest secular priest such as the warden and his brethren of the council of the said fraternity shall name, being well-disposed and of priestly behaviour, to sing mass daily at the altar of the Holy Trinity in the parochial church of Ludlow aforesaid, from the feast of Easter [15 April] ... in the year ... 1487 for ever thereafter; and that the said priest shall be called by the name of 'the priest of the chantry of John Hosyer', and not by the name of the priest of the said fraternity in any way.

Also, that the same priest shall daily say mass at the said altar immediately after the morrow mass is completed in the said church, and every day, before he begins his said mass, he (standing in his alb and turning his face towards the people) shall say with a loud voice in this manner: 'You shall devoutly pray for the souls of John Hosyer and Alice his wife, at whose cost and charges this mass is established to be said here at this point in the day daily for evermore, and for the souls of all the kinfolk, friends and benefactors of the said John Hosyer and Alice his wife, for whom they are most especially bound to pray. For these souls and for all Christian souls say *Our Father*, etc., and *Hail, Mary*, etc. And then the said priest is to say for all the aforesaid souls this psalm: *Out of the depths I have called*, etc., with the collect, *Fidelium deus omnium creditor*, etc.; and he is then immediately to say mass in a devout manner, with this collect: *Deus, qui proprium minor*, etc., with secret and post-communion. Also, that the said priest shall, every Sunday and other festival day throughout the year, distinctly say evensong and compline at the said altar whilst compline is being sung in the said parish church; and that the said mass be said daily, and the aforesaid evensong and compline every Sunday and other festival day in the year at the said altar by the said chantry priest for the time being in the manner and foresaid for evermore.

Also, that the said feoffees, from the issues and profits of the said lands and tenements, shall yearly pay to the said priest in the name of his salary, 8 marks sterling in equal portions at the feasts of the Nativity of St John the Baptist [24 June], St Michael the Archangel [29 September], the Nativity of Our Lord God [25 December], and Easter; and that the said priest shall have over and as well as his said salary a chamber set aside for him for his habitation in the said almshouse, without yielding or paying anything therefor.

Also, we will and ordain by these presents that if it should happen that the said priest is of vice-ridden behaviour, and will not be reformed by the said warden and brethren for the time being, or else if the same priest be troubled with infirmities and sickness, or take up other occupation, or over-indulge at night, so that he may not fittingly say the said masses, evensongs and complines according to the effect of this our ordinance, then the said priest is to be removed from his said service; and then the said warden and brethren of the council of the said fraternity, and the aforesaid feoffees for the time being, by their general assent, or by the agreement of the greater part of them, shall elect and choose another honest secular priest in his place, who shall say masses, evensongs and complines at the said altar at the times prescribed above, and shall pray for the said souls in the manner and form recited above; and the feoffees shall yearly pay 8 marks sterling from the issues and profits derived from the said lands and tenements to the said priest for his salary at the feasts prescribed above in equal parts, and that the same priest shall have the said chamber for his habitation, without yielding or paying anything therefor; and this shall be done as often as any such situation shall occur, or if any notable crime be proved against the said priest, if he does not amend himself and be reformed in that case after having twice received warning about it from the said warden and brethren of the said council, or from the deputy of the said warden, for evermore.

Moreover, we, the foresaid Robert Sherman and John Dale, will and ordain that at the said feast of Easter the foresaid warden and brethren of the said council and the said feoffees shall choose, elect and name six of the best voiced singing children who are commonly accustomed to sing at the mass of Our Lady St Mary in the said church, and that the same six children shall daily thenceforth sing and help at Our Lady's mass in the said church, and every Sunday and other feast day, immediately after Our Lady's mass is finished, they shall go in their surplices to the tomb of Piers Beaupre, squire, in the said church, and there say for the souls of the same Piers and Agnes his wife the psalm *Out of the depths I have called*, etc., with the collect *Fidelium deus*; and afterwards they shall go immediately from there to the burial place of the said John Hosyer in the said church, and there say for the souls of the same John, and of the foresaid Alice his wife, the same psalm and collect. Also, that as often and whenever the voice or voices of any of the said six children shall happen to change or fail, or else any of the said six children be of evil condition, then and so often the said warden and feoffees shall remove the same child or children, and put other well-voiced, willing to learn song, in his or their place or places; and this ordinance to be kept for evermore. Also we will and ordain that the said feoffees shall, from the same issues and profits, pay 40s. yearly to the said six children for their labours on that account; that is to say, to each of them 6s. 8d. at the aforesaid feasts in equal portions.

Also we will and ordain by these presents that from the issues and profits of the said lands and tenements the said feoffees for the time being shall keep an obit or anniversary annually for evermore on the Thursday next before the feast of the Nativity of St John the Baptist in the said church for the souls of the said John Hosyer and Alice, with *Placebo* and *Dirige* on the eve, and mass of eternal requiem on the morrow, solemnly by note, and that yearly in the same obit 20s. sterling shall be distributed and disposed in the manner and form following; that is to say, to ten priests being present and assisting at every such *Dirige* and mass, 3s. 4d. (that is to say, 4d. to each of them); also in reward for four copes to be used at every such obit, 8d.; and for wax to be used at the same obit, 8d.; also, to two deacons assisting at every such obit, 4d. (that is to say, 2d. to each of them); and 1d. to each of the said six children; also for two knells, 4d.; to the porter of the said fraternity, 6d.; to the bellman proclaiming the obit, 2d.; to every man of the said council of the foresaid fraternity who shall be present at the said obit, 4d.; to the clerk of the said fraternity, 4d.; and that all the residue of the said 20s. remaining over and above the said distributions shall annually be divided equally among the poor people (men and women) of the said almshouse, according to the good discretion of the foresaid warden or his deputy and some of the said feoffees.

Also, we will and ordain that the said warden and his brethren of the said council shall at all times hereafter have the nomination, election and admission of every poor man and poor woman who now or hereafter shall be received into the said almshouse, and also the rule and governance of them after their said admission. And if it happens that any of the said poor men and women should be obstinate, contentious, or of any other evil condition, and will not be reformed in that matter by the said warden or his deputy for the time being, then he or she shall be expelled from the said almshouse, and another be taken into his or her place by the said warden or his deputy for the time being, according to his solemn discretion, as often and whenever such a situation shall occur hereafter for evermore; provided always that no person shall be admitted to the said almshouse other than those persons who, at the time of their said admission therein, are brethren or sisters of the said fraternity who have paid their fine, and have fallen into poverty.

Also we will and ordain that the said feoffees, out of the issues and profits of the said lands and tenements, shall pay 8d. yearly for ever more to the parson or parish priest of the said church, to exhort the people openly in the pulpit every Sunday in the year at the saying of the common bidding, to pray especially for the souls of the said John Hosyer and Alice his wife, their kinfolk and well-wishers. Also, we will that the said feoffees, from the aforesaid issues and profits, well and sufficiently repair the said almshouse and all necessaries thereto belonging, as often and whenever the need occurs, and that they shall annually pay 6s. 8d. to the registrar of the said fraternity for his labour and diligence (both in ensuring that the said almshouse is well repaired in the manner and form aforesaid, and for gathering in the rents of the said lands and tenements and in overseeing that the closures thereof are well kept and closed) so that the same rent collector does the said repairs sufficiently, as often and whenever necessary, and levies the said rents according to his ability, and also annually makes and delivers to the said warden and feoffees a just and true account and reckoning of all the said issues, profits and repairs.

Also we will and ordain that twice every day for evermore (that is to say, at the hour of 8 before noon and the hour of 5 after noon), one of the said almsmen, most solemn and discreet, shall ring the bell of the said almshouse for the duration of a quarter of an hour, and that in that time all the almsfolk of the said house who can walk shall come together in the chapel of the said almshouse; and then the bell shall stop, and he who rang the bell shall say these words in a loud voice: 'We shall devoutly pray to almighty God and to our blessed Lady St Mary, St John the Evangelist, and to the holy company of heaven, for the souls of John Hosyer and Alice his wife, who at their own expense have built this chapel and almshouse, and have established a priest to sing perpetually at the altar of the Blessed Trinity in the parish church of Ludlow, and have established an obit to be kept there annually for ever more in the same church, with a dole of money, besides other good deeds. For these souls and for the souls of all the brethren and sisters of the said fraternity, and of all the kinfolk and benefactors of the said John Hosyer and Alice, and for all Christian souls, say *Our Father*, and *Hail Mary*, with *I believe*, etc.' And that then each of the said almsfolk shall devoutly say, *Our Father*, *Hail Mary*, and *I believe in God*, etc. for the souls listed before. Also we will and ordain that the said feoffees shall pay 2s. yearly from the issues and profits of the said lands and tenements to the said almsman who rings the said bell so, and says the said bidding, for his labour in this matter, at the feasts listed above, in equal portions.

We also, furthermore, will, and by these presents ordain, that if the said warden and brethren and the aforesaid feoffees who now are, or who shall be for the time being hereafter, are remiss, lax, negligent or refuse to keep, observe and carry out this our ordinance or any part thereof, or if there be any default by them so that this our ordinance or any part thereof is not kept, carried out, or fulfilled according to the same for a period of a quarter of a year, that then the prior of the house and conventual church of St John the Baptist, Ludlow, aforesaid, and the brethren of that same place, shall find the said priest and pay him his said salary and repair the aforesaid almshouse, yearly pay the said

40s. to the aforesaid children, and keep the said obit in the manner and form as the said warden, brethren, and feoffees would do if no default were found in them in this matter; and that then all the feoffees of and in the said lands and tenements (such as shall be at the time of the said default), at the request of the said prior and his brethren of the said house then being, shall by their deed sufficient in law enfeof of and in the said lands and tenements such persons (to twenty in number) whom the said prior shall nominate, and shall be compelled to do so by law if they refuse, by a writ *sub poena* at the suit of the said prior; provided always that the same prior shall nominate solemn and well disposed people; and those persons shall have and hold the said lands and tenements to them, their heirs and assigns, to the use and intent that they, with the said prior, shall find the said priest and repair the aforesaid almshouse, pay the said children and keep the aforesaid obit, in a similar manner, form and place as the said warden and feoffees would do if there were no default in them, as set out aforesaid; the said prior and brethren taking and having for their labour annually on that matter all the residue of the issues and profits derived from the said lands and tenements, over and above the said 8 marks paid to the aforesaid priest for his salary, and besides the 40s. which they shall pay yearly to the said children, and 20s. with which to keep the said obit, and above the money which shall be spent on repairs of the said almshouse; and that the said warden and his brethren thereafter shall not be involved further with the said ordinance, lands and tenements, in any manner. And also we will that when the said feoffees who shall chance to be in the said lands and tenements at the nomination of the said prior because of the said default shall have died, and been reduced to the number of five or six, then those same five or six survivors shall enfeof in the said lands and tenements with the appurtenances other solemn, discreet and well-disposed persons (to the number of twenty persons), to have to them and to their heirs and assigns, to the use and intent to do and perform from them (with the said prior) according to the effect of this our present ordinance; and so from feoffees to feoffees for ever more. And we earnestly require and pray the said prior and brethren, and also the said feoffees to be nominated by the same prior, that they keep, observe and carry out this our will and ordinance, if it shall chance that they have an interest in the same as set out aforesaid.

In witness whereof, we, the said Richard Sherman and John Dale, have put our seals to each part of this our present tripartite indented ordinance. And in as much as our said seals are unknown to many men, we therefore have procured that the common seal of the said town of Ludlow has been put to each part of this said deed. And we, John Lane the elder and John Teawe, bailiffs of the same town of Ludlow, at the instances and personal requests of the said Richard Sherman and John Dale, have put the aforesaid common seal of the said town of Ludlow to each part of this present tripartite indented deed, as further testimony and witness to the premisses. Given the said 8th day of December in the year of our Lord, 1486 ...

X. Dispositions by the dying

For reasons already given,[1] *this selection of wills has been deliberately kept brief. The three printed are indicative of the range of bequests and arrangements which a detailed will might contain, without any claim that any of them is in any degree 'representative'. For all three, the caveats issued in the introduction must be re-emphasised; in particular, that these are not necessarily full summaries of the testators' intentions, or trustworthy statements of the eventual disposition of their goods. Particularly important for consideration of 'spirituality' is the residue which, while distributed for the good of the testaor's soul, usually cannot be measured, even though it might be considerable.*[2]

Thomas Kebell, the first testator, was a rising lawyer, whose career can be traced in considerable detail.[3] *The requirements of his will are most obviously notable for the moralistic requirements laid upon his son; with some of the other comments which suggest a real concern for old servants and others being also striking. But there is more to it than that. Here we have a clear indication of the distinction in arrangements for personal property, and for lands: the survival of the separate statement for the disposal of his lands provides information about his chantry arrangements and the provision of an almshouse which are not given in the will proper. Moreover, those arrangements illustrate also the way in which executors retained responsibilities for some time after a death, with his constant concern for his cousin Hotoft's chantry (and the distinction, which has implications for the appearance of chantry evidence in official sources, between the establishment*

1 Above, pp. 30–1.

2 Some indication of the range of discretion available to executors is given in the arrangements for their distribution of the annual payments of 40 marks which were to be made to the executors of Thomas Fyneham in satisfaction of an outstanding debt of over 400 marks, as Fyneham established by his will in 1518: the money was to be 'spent on works of mercy and charitable deeds according to the judgement of my executors, that is to say, to priests to sing for my soul, for the repair and construction of roads, in distribution to poor people where there is need, to prisoners in prison, and in ornaments and jewels to be given to churches, and for the maintenance of poor scholars in their studies.' (J. R. H. Moorman, *The Grey Friars in Cambridge, 1225–1538*, Cambridge, 1952, p. 251).

3 His career is the backbone of E. W. Ives, *The Common Lawyers of Pre-Reformation England*, Cambridge, 1983.

of a non-amortised chantry for Hotoft, and Kebell's concern to secure a mortmain licence).[4]

Jane Strangweys is a rather different case, and seems to offer a better insight into real spirituality, by offering a picture of someone active in a milieu where clerical influence is abundant. The responsibility for souls is a major concern, affecting many of her dispositions – with the key concern being to secure prayers for herself. Her links with the Dominican friars at York are obvious; connections with other religious houses are explicit in several of the bequests.[5] *Some of those hint at major spiritual associations, for the bequests to Richard Methley and John Thornton tie her to the Carthusian priory of Mount Grace (which is mentioned by name in some bequests), and to at least one individual (Methley) who had a very strong reputation for leading a holy life. Mount Grace had been an active centre of spirituality throughout the fifteenth century, with its prior Nicholas Love producing one of that century's 'best sellers' in its early years, and with Richard Methley at its end acquiring almost saintly status.*[6]

In terms of the dispositions, an important aspect is the arrangements made for the provision of the rent-charge to pay for her obit at the Dominicans of York. Here, no property would have been conveyed to the friars; but they would have been given a secure annual payment which would appear to contradict the requirement that they should live solely from insecure revenues. This arrangement parallels the provision for trentals by the carpenters at York from the Augustinian friars, and arrangements elsewhere for friars to provide chantry services (see Section IX).

While the will is redolent with spiritual associations, it would be too simplistic to accept them all at pure face value. Other concerns also come through – the concern for her kin and dependants need not be purely altruistic; and when she insists on bequests to servants being implemented only if they remain in her service, clearly this is not all pure generosity.

The third testator moves forward right to the end of the period. Like Thomas

4 See further, A. Kreider, *English Chantries: the Road to Dissolution*, Harvard Historical Studies, XCVII, Cambridge, Mass., and London, 1979, pp. 73–9.

5 For other considerations of associations with the mendicants at York, R. B. Dobson, 'Mendicant ideal and practice in late medieval York', in *Archaeological Papers from York Presented to M. W. Barley*, ed. P. V. Addyman and V. E. Black, York, 1984, pp. 115–18.

6 J. Hogg, 'Mount Grace Charterhouse and late medieval English spirituality', in *Collectanea Cartusiana, III* (= *Analecta Cartusiana*, LXXXII:iii), Salzburg, 1983, pp. 1–43, esp. 25–39.

Kebell, Sir John Port was a lawyer, who rose to high office.[7] *That took him away from his native roots in Derbyshire; but the recollections of his earlier years clearly are important in his will, or at least in the first version of it. For here we have something relatively rare: a draft, and a later complete revision. Whereas addenda to a will, such as the codicil added to the will of Jane Strangweys, are not uncommon, the survival of two distinctly – and in the present case dramatically – different versions is very unusual.*

The distinctions here are rendered all the more significant because of the time span. The first draft, from 1528, pre-dates the Reformation Parliament of 1529, after whose actions the English church was never to be the same again. The second, and final, will dates from the early 1540s: the changes imposed by the Reformation are strikingly obvious. Yet those changes pose questions: just how much had Sir John Port changed, or was it more the case that the world had changed around him, that the bequests outlined in 1528 had disappeared simply because their intended recipients were no longer there? The change in the preamble of the will, the dedication of the soul, is also a feature: much has been made of such changes in an attempt to chart the progress of the Reformation and the changing of minds; although that is an approach which has been questioned as much as it has been affirmed.[8]

44. The will of Thomas Kebell, 1500 [From E. W. Ives, *The Common Lawyers of Pre-Reformation England*, Cambridge, 1983, pp. 425–31; in English]

In the name of God, Amen. I, Thomas Kebell, the King's Sergeant-at-Law, being whole in mind (thanks be to God), considering the instability of the world, and the certainty and necessity of death, to which I and every living creature am bound, and wishing to provide and arrange for the disposal of such goods as God has permitted me to have here on earth, ordain and make my testament and last will of all my goods and chattels in the form as detailed in the following: First, I bequeath my soul to Almighty God my maker, my redeemer, my preserver from the many dangers to soul and body, and my singular relief, comfort and aid in necessity, adversity, infirmity,

7 J. H. Baker, ed., *The Notebook of Sir John Port*, Selden Society, CII, 1986, pp. xi–xxiii.

8 For discussions of this approach, M. L. Zell, 'The use of religious preambles as a measure of religious belief in the sixteenth century', *Bulletin of the Institute of Historical Research*, L, 1977, pp. 246–9; C. Cross, 'Wills as evidence of popular piety in the reformation period: Leeds and Hull, 1540–1640', in *The End of Strife: Death, Reconciliation, and Expressions of Christian Spirituality*, ed. D. M. Loades, Edinburgh, 1984, pp. 44–51; J. D. Alsop, 'Religious preambles in early modern English wills as formulae', *Journal of Ecclesiastical History*, XL, 1989, pp. 19–27.

poverty and all discomforts, humbly beseeching him to accept it in his mercy and grace; and my simple body to be buried at Humberston, in the chapel where both Margery and Anne, my wives, and my natural cousin Richard Hotoft and my son Edward lie buried, in such manner as my executors shall think appropriate for the rank to which it has pleased God to call me in this world, and to have there a fitting tomb for me and my wives. Also I will that such payments be made for transporting me to Humberston as my executors shall think fitting for the honour of me and my friends, laying aside all vain pomp and glory of this world. Also, I will that there be £20 distributed on my behalf to poor people on the day of my burial, or at other times as shall be thought most fitting by my executors to my status and to God's pleasure. Also I bequeath to my curate such mortuaries as are in agreement with the law; also, to the parson of Rearsby, 20s. for forgotten tithes; also, to the vicar of Humberston, 40s. for the same; also, for the relief of the church of Rearsby, 20s.; also, for the relief of the church of Humberston, 5 marks. Also, I bequeath to the abbey of Leicester, to pray for me, 5 marks; also to the College of Newark [Leicester], to pray for me, 5 marks; also, to the almshouse, to pray for me, 20s.; also, to every house of friars at Leicester, to pray for me, 13s. 4d. Also, I bequeath to the white friars at London, to pray for me, 20s.; also to the prioress and convent of Clerkenwell, to pray for me, 40s.; also to the prioress and convent of Langley, to pray for me, 40s. Also, I will that a thousand masses and as many recitations of *Placebo* and *Dirige* be said for me immediately after my decease, with each priest to have 4d. (the total for this amounts to £26 13s. 4d.); or else as many trentals as amount to 1000 masses, at the discretion of my executors. Also I will that a priest be found for me at Humberston for seven years after my decease, to say daily *Placebo*, *Dirige*, a commendation and mass, for me and for the souls of my said wives, cousin, child, father and mother, and all Christian souls, and three times in the week on different days the seven psalms with litany, and Our Lady's Psalter on the other three days, and every Sunday the psalms of the Passion; and he shall have 7 marks a year. Also I will that John Nichol and Emmitt Lyez, who were formerly servants to my father and mother, and are now old and poor, shall annually have appropriate relief and assistance from my executors while they live, to pray for me and the souls listed beforehand. Also, I heartily beg my executors to satisfy and truly pay my debts to everyone to whom I am indebted; also I beg them to recompense all those people to whom I have done any harm in any way. Also I bequeath to my son Walter Kebell God's blessing and mine, and heartily require and beg him, and by my blessing admonish him, to be good and virtuous, and avoid all vices and misbehaviour, and truly serve God, and duly thank him for the manifold benefits and goodnesses that he has sent to me here on earth, and that he truly maintain his loyalty and always be kind, loving and do his faithful service according to his abilities towards my singular and good lady, Lady Hastings, his godmother, to my lord her son, and to my most especially good lady, Lady Hungerford (his wife) and their children. And that he should be caring towards my soul, his mother's soul, the souls of my father and mother and of my cousin Hotoft and cause us to be prayed for; and that he truly assist in the carrying out of this my will. And that he be kind and loving towards my kinfolk and his, and to me servants and friends and those who love me. ... Also I bequeath to my said son all my books of scripture, of law, of chronicles or histories, and all my other books in Latin, French, or English, with the intention that he shall the better apply himself to virtue and wisdom. Also I give to my said son a gold chain which was my father's (and, after him, my brother's), and a cross which I bought, and also my signet ring and tablets. ... And I will that all the goods, jewels and chattels before designated for my said son shall be retained by my said executors until my said son attains the age of 24 years, with the intention that they may see his disposition and inclinations. And if he is disposed towards virtue and goodness, he is then to receive delivery of them, otherwise they shall be retained until he is so disposed. And if he will not amend and apply himself to virtue, truth and goodness, then he shall have no portion of them, but they shall be used for the buying of properties, and then be disposed of as shall be contained among other things in the will dealing with my properties. Also I will that my said son shall be under the government of my executors; and I humbly and heartily beg and beseech them to take the burden upon them to see him brought up in virtue and good manners, and to gain knowledge, from which virtue and wisdom grow and are nourished. ... Also I will that, until such time as my son shall attain the age of 24 years, my executors shall have and occupy my lease at Stratton, towards the performance of my will ... Also I bequeath to my god-daughter and niece Joyce Kelle, towards her marriage, £10, over and above the £10 in money of hers which I have in keeping out of her father's goods. Also to her sister Elizabeth (who has been satisfied and paid her £10 which I had of her father's goods from the hands of her brother and and others) I bequeath 10 marks to pray for me. Also to my niece Mary Willers towards her marriage, 10 marks. Also, to my godson and cousin, Thomas Cotton, 10 marks. Also, to my godson and cousin, the son of my cousin Thomas Lacy, 10 marks. Also, to my cousin Thomas Broughton of London, to pray for me, 40s. Also, I bequeath to my singular good lady, Lady Hungerford, my gold salt and the book of Froissart, and also 2 pieces of black velvet, each of them containing 19 yards or thereabouts, beseeching her to have me in her remembrance and prayers among her other servants, and to receive this poor bequest with grace. Also I will that such doublet clothes of velvet and other silks that I have be made into vestments and distributed for my soul. Also I bequeath to Mistress Elizabeth Ferrers, to pray for me, 2 cattle, 20 wethers, and 10 marks in money. Also, to my brother Palmer, the grey horse which he now has, and 10 marks out of the £20 in money which he owes to me to be cancelled and remitted to him. Also, to William Smith, one of my horses at the decision of my executors, and 5 marks in money, begging him to be loving towards my soul and my son ... Also, since Thomas Turnour owes me certain money by an obligation, and also in arrears of another account £15 or more, which altogether amounts to more than 50 marks, I bequeath and remit to him all those said debts apart from £20, which £20 I wish my executors to have from him towards the performance of my will (but they are to show him appropriate favour according to their judgement in the payment, so that he may pay it without it being his undoing). ... Also, to Sir John Hamond, 40s., to pray for me. Also I bequeath to the vicar of Thrussington 40s. of the money which he owes to me by an obligation. Also I will that the aforesaid bequests and payments of my debts be implemented and carried out with all my corn and chattels, and with the debts that are due to me for chattels which have been sold; and if they are not sufficient to carry out the same, then the remainder is to be taken from the profits of my lands, tenements, and leases. Also, that my nephew George Wyllers should have from the profits of my lands 40s. yearly during his life, to pray for me and to be loving towards his cousin my son. Also, I will that out of the profits of the said lands, tenements, and leases, there be given 20 marks yearly for the period of twenty years next after my death towards providing for scholars in Arts and Divinity at Oxford and Cambridge, at the discretion and assignment of my executors ... Also I will that a chalice worth 6 marks be purchased for my cousin Hotoft's chantry, which together with a mass book which I have bound in white shall be assigned to that chantry; and also two sets of vestments and altar cloths for the same chantry, one for everyday use, the other for holy days. Also I will that my executors purchase a chalice and a set of vestments for a deacon and subdeacon of rich brocade, and a cope of the same sort, to be given to the church of Humberston to pray for me and for the souls listed before. Also I bequeath to Austyn Flore the *portnos* which was his mother's cloth, to make a gown and hood for him, and 5 marks in money to pray for me. ... And I will that if my son Walter should die before he attains the age of 24 years ... without issue, or if his said issue die before their said ages [of 24 years] ... I will that, of the money previously assigned to the said Walter, my special good lady, Lady Hastings, shall have £20, and the remainder [of the money], debts, jewels, and other things assigned to him before the deaths of him and his issue ... is to be expended for the souls of me, my wives, our children, our ancestors, my cousin Hotoft and other cousins, and for the souls of my good Lord William, late Lord Hastings, and others for whom I am obliged to pray, and for the well-being of my good lady, Lady Hastings, and Lord Hastings and Lady Hungerford and my executors, and for their souls when they have died, in deeds of alms and piety at their discretion, heartily begging them to bear in mind my poor kinfolk and my neighbours, and those places of religion in this region which are poor, or from which I have received fees. ... Also I will that a house be built at Humberston on some suitable plot of mine for the chantry priest who is to serve my cousin Hotoft's chantry in perpetuity ...

This is the last will of me, Thomas Kebell, the King's Sergeant-at-Law, of all my lands, tenements and inheritances, as hereafter follows in order. First, I will that my executors have, receive and take the issues, profits and revenues of all my lands, tenements, inheritances and leases throughout the time that they are carrying out my testament and last will, according to the intentions of them. ... [Until Walter Kebell reaches 24, the executors control the estate, paying an allowance to him.] And the remainder ... for lack of ... issue of my body to be distributed for the souls of me, my wives, children, father and mother, cousin Hotoft and my other ancestors and kinsmen, and for the souls and well-being of those who are set out in my testament to be prayed for, and for all Christian souls. ... [Other arrangements for distribution of the lands, including lands in Humberston.] Provided always that land be set aside in Humberston to build upon for my cousin Hotoft's chantry, and for the chantry and almshouse specified hereafter, at the judgement of my executors, which ground I wish to be exempted from the said gift. ... Moreover, my good cousin Richard Hotoft gave to me and my heirs his lands and tenements in Great Stretton and Little

Stretton and various other places, with the intention that I should keep his obit annually for ever, and also find a priest annually in perpetuity to say divine service daily for his soul in the church of Humberston at the altar in the chapel where he lies buried, and that I should encumber the said land as strictly and securely as I could or might, without amortising it, to ensure the true continuance of the said service and prayers. I heartily entreat and beg my executors, if I shall not have secured this during my life, that, for the well-being of my said cousin's soul, and for the unburdening and well-being of my soul, they will arrange for this to be secured, and assign a reasonable sum out of the said lands in [Great] Stretton and [Little] Stretton aforesaid towards the maintenance of the said priest and keeping the said obit. Furthermore, as I have bought various lands and tenements in [Great] Stretton and [Little] Stretton aforesaid, and also made many enclosures and improvements there, I will that, if I should die without issue of my body, another priest be found to pray perpetually for me, Lady Hungerford, and the soul of my cousin Hotoft, and the souls previously listed in this my will, or in my testament, and also for the souls of those from whom I have received any kind of benefits, and especially for the souls of those whose benefits I have not deserved, with twelve poor men to be maintained perpetually at Humberston to pray daily for me and all the others previously listed. And this chantry and almsmen are both to be amortised, founded and established by a licence from the King, and sufficiently endowed out of all the lands in [Great] Stretton and [Little] Stretton and [various other places] ...

[Humberston, 20 June 1500].

45. Will of Lady Jane Strangweys, 1500 [York, Borthwick Institute of Historical Research, Prob. Reg. 6, fos. 16v–18r; incompletely printed in *Testamenta Eboracensia*, IV, Surtees Society Publications, LIII, 1868, pp. 186–90. English, with some Latin. The will is incorporated within a full notarial instrument, but I have not reproduced those sections; the codicil is entered as a separate document].

In the name of almighty God, the blessed Trinity, the blessed Lady and Virgin St Mary, Amen. The 28th day of October, the year of Our Lord God 1500 ... I, Dame Jane Strangweys, widow, being of full mind and good memory, make this my last will and testament in the manner and to the effect hereafter following. First, I bequeath my soul to almighty God, and to the blessed Lady and Virgin St Mary, and to the whole company of Heaven. Also I will that if it should chance that I should die within the house of the friars preachers at York, where I am now staying, I wish my body to be buried in the choir of those same friars, under the lectern where they read their legend. And if it happens that I should die within 10 miles of York, then I will that my body should be brought to the said friars and be buried within the said choir. And if it should chance that I should die beyond 10 miles of the city of York, I wish my body to be buried within the choir of the parish church where I shall chance to die; and the best garment that I have is to be my mortuary. I wish 10 lb. of wax to be burnt about my body on the day of my burial, and eight torches to be burnt about me on the same day, worth 4 marks. I bequeath 40s. to the four orders of friars within the said city of York, for four trentals of masses to be said, with *Placebo* and *Dirige*, for my soul and for all Christian souls within seven days immediately after the day of my burial, the aforesaid 40s. to be divided equally between them. I wish the prior and the convent of each house of the four orders shall be present around my body on the day of my burial; and that each prior shall have 10s. towards the repair of his house; each priest who is present on the day of my burial shall have 4d.; each parish clerk, 2d.; and each child with a surplice, 1d. Also I bequeath to the cathedral church of St Peter at York, towards their fabric, 26s. 8d. Also I bequeath 7 marks of lawful money of England for a mass to be said daily for my soul, for the space of a year, within the said friary, and that the mass be said by various members of the said convent, and whichever one of them shall say the mass for that day, I wish him to have 2d. for his labour; and the remainder of the said 7 marks is to be given towards the repair of the house, according to the judgement of the prior. Also I bequeath for my grave, wherever my body shall be buried, 10s. Moreover, it is my will to have an honest priest of good name and good reputation to sing for my soul, the souls of my father and mother, and for all Christian souls, for a period of five years, and he is to have 7 marks yearly as his salary, from the hands of my executors. Also, I wish the said priest to be chosen by my executors and Mr Robert Frost, who is chancellor to my lord the Prince [of Wales]. I bequeath to Mount Grace 10 marks, to pray for my soul and the soul of my husband Strangweys, who is buried there; and for the prior, with his brethren, to celebrate an obit for my soul, my husband's soul, and for all Christian souls, in their choir within ten days after their being requested to hold it, with another to be held by them at my twelve-months' day next following. Also, I bequeath to the prior and convent of the abbey of Norton in Cheshire 10 marks, to pray for my soul and for the soul of Roger Dutton, my late husband, and for all Christian souls; the first obit to be celebrated within ten days after they have been informed of my burial, and the second on my twelve-months' day next following. Also, I bequeath and leave to the friars minor of Richmond 10s., to sing a trental of masses for my soul; and 10s. towards the repair of their house and for them to say *Placebo* and *Dirige* and a requiem mass for my soul. Also, I bequeath and leave to the prioress and convent of St Clement at York 10s., to celebrate an obit there with *Placebo* and *Dirige* and a mass of requiem, for my soul and for all Christian souls. Also I bequeath and leave to every person (man and woman) within the four leper houses 1d., to pray for my soul. Also it is my will that my debts be satisfied and paid out of my own goods, as good conscience requires. Also, I bequeath to my son, Laurence Dutton, a gilt piece with a cover, and all such money as he has borrowed from me and received from my hands or via any of my servants, upon this condition: that he will be satisfied to receive it with Christ's blessing and mine, and never trouble my executors with any case or claim against my executors or me, but acquit them, and grant them a general acquittance for all forms of action, real or personal, from the beginning of the world until the making of the said acquittance; then he is to have the aforesaid piece and the money, but in no other manner, and not otherwise. Also I leave to each one of my five god-daughters, for their marriages (that is, Jane Dutton, Jane Aschton, Jane Methope, Jane Ingham and Jane Kyrke), 40s. to each one of them. Also I bequeath and leave to Friar Fraunch of Richmond, 40s. Item, to dan Thurston at Mount Grace, 10s. Item, to dan Richard Metheley, 10s. Also, to Sir Henry Morton, £5. Also, I bequeath to Sir Robert Hochonson, 20s. Also, to Elizabeth Eland, my gentlewoman, 5 marks to pray for my soul, towards her marriage; on condition that she remains in service with me until the hour of my death, and not otherwise. Also I bequeath to Thomas Fleccher 20s., provided that he remains in service with me until the hour of my death. Also, I bequeath to Agnes Nottyngham 11s., provided that she remains in service with me until the hour of my death. Also to Margaret, her daughter, towards her marriage, 6s. 8d. Also, I leave to Prior Maisson of the friars preachers at York, to pray for my soul, 20s. Also I bequeath and leave £20 of lawful money of England to purchase certain lands with an annual value of 20s. for a perpetual obit to be celebrated annually at the friars preachers within the city of York, where I intend (by the grace of God) that my body should be buried; there to pray for my soul, the soul of Mr Robert Frost, the souls of my father and my mother, and for all Christian souls; and this to be arranged and carried out according to the advice and wisdom of the above said Mr Robert Frost and my executors; and if this purchase of 20s. annually can be carried out and done, then I wish that the said yearly rent of 20s. shall be distributed according to this manner and order: First, the prior of the house of the said friars preachers is to have 12d., the subprior 8d., and each priest of the said convent 4d., each professed friar 2d., each novice 1d.; and the remainder of 10s. from the 20s. to be used to increase their pittance for that day, provided that the prior and convent, after they have dined, recite *De profundis* for my soul, and the souls named before, and for all Christian souls. Also I will and bequeath that the other 10s. remaining from the 20s. is to be spent on repairs to the house of the friars, according to the judgement of the prior. And if this purchase of 20s. of rent can be securely established and carried out, I wish it to be done according to the manner and order set out above; if not the said sum of £20 is to be distributed in alms and other deeds of mercy for my soul and the souls named above, and all Christian souls, as shall be thought most meritorious according to the judgement of the said Mr Robert Frost and my executors. Also, it is my will that the remainder of my goods not bequeathed (my debts paid and my will fulfilled) then be given to Sir Henry Mortime, priest, and Richard Maisson, prior of the friars preachers of York, whom I make my executors. They are to dispose of the said goods for the well-being of my soul, according to the judgement of Mr Robert Frost, whom I appoint as overseer, to see that this my last will and testament is carried out and implemented, as my special trust is in him, and to whom I bequeath for his labour 20 marks from the best possessions I have, to be chosen according to his own choice. This is also my will, that the said Mr Robert Frost shall call my executors before him for their accounting, to check the performance of my last will and testament. And I wish the said prior, my executor, to have 10 marks in money for his labour (if it shall turn out that he receives administration of my goods). And the remainder and surplus of all that money which I have set aside in sealed bags to carry out this my will and testament (the which sum appears more clearly in a pair of indentures made between me and the said Sir Henry, bearing date the 2nd day of the month of November, the abovesaid year of our Lord God), I freely give to the said Sir Henry Mortime, my executor, as reward and recompense for his great labours undertaken for me at various times, to pray for my soul and for all Christian souls.

In the name of God, Amen, the 21st day of the month of March, in the year of the Lord 1500 [i.e., 1501]. I, Jane Strangweys, formerly widow of Richard Strangweys, knight, being of sound memory, not changing or diminishing my original testament, drawn up by me prior to the date of this present codicil, but augmenting it, and as far as in me lies, confirming it and its contents, give and bequeath: that is to say, to Friar Richard Maisson, prior of the friars preachers within the city of York, one gilt goblet with a cover belonging to it; also I give to the said prior one pair of fine sheets of three webs in breadth, in order to make a pair of surplices. Also I bequeath and give one vestment of blue satin, with all the things pertaining to it, to the church of St Mary Bishophill, where I lived at some time, to pray for my soul and all Christian souls. Also I bequeath to Elizabeth Eland, my gentlewoman, one feather bed with a bolster, one pair of blankets, one pair of sheets, one coverlet, and one quilt, for the trouble she has taken with me at the time of my illness, and to pray for my soul. Also, I give to Thomas my servant, one mattress, one pair of blankets, one pair of sheets, and one coverlet, to pray for my soul. Also, I give to Agnes Nottyngham one mattress, one pair of blankets, one pair of sheets, and one coverlet, to pray for my soul, provided that she remains in service with me to the hour of my death. Also, I give to my sister Warwycke my best girdle. Also I give to my son's wife, Margaret Dutton, my red velvet bonnet, to pray for my soul. Also, I bequeath and give to Sir Henry Morton, priest, a mass book, one chalice, with other clothing, and everything necessary for the mass, to pray for my soul and all Christian souls. Also I bequeath and give to Mr Robert Frost, the archdeacon, one set of gold beads, to pray for my soul. Also I will that brother James Best, bachelor, shall have one year's salary to sing for my soul and for all Christian souls. Also I will that Sir Thomas, my priest, shall have one year's salary, or two (but it shall be at least one). Also I will that my kinsman, Sir Brian Aschton, shall have two years' salary, to sing for my soul, my father's and my mother's, my husbands', and for all my good friends' souls, if he will agree to it.

46. The wills of Sir John Port, 1528–40

(i) *Original version* [From J. H. Baker, ed., *The Notebook of Sir John Port*, Selden Society Publications, CII, 1986, pp. xlvi–li; in English. This in fact incorporates two drafts. The original is the base text, of January 1528; amendments made in July are incorporated in <>]

In the name of our Lord Jesus Christ, my saviour and creator, Amen. ... [13 January 1528], I, John Port of Etwall, knight, one of the king's justices of his bench, being to my knowledge in reasonable health and memory, as I trust by the mercy and forbearance of Our Lord God, make, ordain and declare my last will and testament ... in the following form:

First, I bequeath my soul to almighty God, three persons in Trinity, humbly beseeching our most blessed Lady St Mary, St John the Evangelist and all the holy company of Heaven, to be intermediaries for me to Our Lord Jesus, so that by the virtue of his blessed passion my soul may be a partaker of everlasting bliss. And my body to be buried in such parish church in the parish which it shall please God that I shall change my life, except that if I die within [Derbyshire] ... I will then that my body be buried in the church of Etwall, under the arch which is between the chancel of the said church and the chapel where I and my wife are usually accustomed to kneel, or in such other place as I or my executors shall then decide. And I will that every priest who is at my burial shall have 4d. to pray for my soul, and every poor man and woman 1d. And all other things appropriate for the same I leave to the will and discretion of my executors, or such persons as shall be present and placed in trust and order for me when I depart from this miserable life. But if I die within the city of London, then I will that my body be buried in the Temple church before the altar in the chapel ... on the south side of the ... church, ... of Our Lady, St John the Evangelist, and St John the Baptist. And I will that my company of the Inner Temple shall have £5 from my executors <and every other place of court 20s., and every place of Chancery 10s.>, humbly beseeching them to pray for my soul <and to be content therewith without any entertainment in food and drink>.

Also I bequeath to the vicar of Etwall, my curate, my best horse as my mortuary, and [*blank*] in money, beyond his other rights, to pray for me, beseeching from him forgiveness and pardon in those things wherein I have not done my duty to God, Holy Church, or to him.

Also I will that <twelve torches be provided at my burial, and six of them with> 13s. 4d. be given to the use of the church and parish of Etwall, and 20s. to be laid out upon repairs to St Ellen's houses, otherwise called the church houses, which I helped to get out of the possession of William Pope, whose soul may our Lord pardon, Amen....

Also I will that my son and heir John Port shall have in money [*blank*], and also plate, household stuff and chattels to the value of [*blank*] at such time as he reaches the age of 24 years; and if he dies before that age so that my daughters become my heirs, that the said money, stuff and chattels shall be disposed of by my executors in repairing and assisting bridges and highways, and partly to Brasennose in Oxford, and on other good deeds of charity. Provided that if my said son dies before the age of 24 years <and after he is 21 years of age>, he shall then have a part of the said premisses <to the value of £100> to be disposed for his soul and other good deeds at his pleasure <which hundred pounds I trust he will discretely dispose … >. …

Also I will that <my heir and executors> shall find and maintain an honest priest for twenty years after my decease to sing and pray at Etwall for my soul, and the soul of my departed wife, the souls of my father and mother, my fathers-in-law, my mothers-in-law, our children, our brothers' and sisters' souls, our ancestors' souls, and all the souls that I or my wives were and are bound to pray for, and all Christian souls, and especially, if I have wronged, hurt or offended any person, for their souls, so that my conscience may be the better discharged thereby; and that the said priest shall have from my lands and rents 7 marks annually during the said term <and if the said honest priest continues after the said twenty years, then if he is so-minded to have the said salary of 7 marks during his life ...>.

Item, after my wife's decease I will that the said honest priest, or another honest priest, be immediately be found at Etwall for the term of [*blank*] years, in order to pray for the souls above written, and to have 7 marks from the profits of my lands, if my goods will not perform the same and accomplish this my will ….

Also I will and bequeath that the persons following, in whom I have found great love and kindness, shall have such things as shall be expressed hereafter, and which I will reveal to my wife and executors, to the intent that they shall remember me after my departure and the better pray for my soul: my brother Sir Thomas Cokayne, knight; my son Germain Pole, esquire; the prior of Repton; my cousin Sir Antony Fitzherbert, one of the king's justices; my cousin, parson of Leek; Richard Rattclyff; the good wife Baker; Henry Aynesworth; my brother Copwood; my sister, his wife; Master Doctor Taylour; my cousin Doctor Pennant; my cousin Thomas Mydulton; the prioress of Nuneaton; Dame Anne Mydulton, nun there.

Also I will that the executors of Master Chauntrell of St Peter in

Cheapside in London be agreed with for £8 10s. that remains left of £10 that my father-in-law John Fitzherbert borrowed from him.

Also I will that for ten years to come <I and> my father in law <John Fitzherbert>, Doctor Odeby, and others be prayed for at Paul's Cross as they have been accustomed to be, at my expense.

Also I will that each of my household servants, men and women, who are hired, shall have a quarter's wages beyond their dues, or a beast or sheep of better value in recompense for the same, to pray for my soul.

Also I will that there be given for the health of my soul to thirty young maids of good reputation towards their marriages, and at the time of their marriage, 10s. to each of them.

Also I will that all such goods as are in my possession which belonged to my uncle Master William Fitzherbert, for whom I was executor, be distributed and sold for the maintenance of two scholars at Brasennose in Oxford for ever, and the £100 of the profits of the reversion of such lands as my father-in-law John Fitzherbert (whom Our Lord pardon) had in Hackney, in ... Middlesex, which Jane Fitzherbert, widow, my mother-in-law, late his wife, has for the term of her life, or such money as the said reversion shall be sold for, so that the money shall be disposed in purchasing lands for the maintenance of the said scholars at Brasennose aforesaid.

Also I bequeath to the prior and convent of ... Beauvale, 20s.; to the abbot and convent of Chester, <10s.>; to the abbots and convents of Burton, <10s.>, and Croxden, <6s. 6d.>; and to the priors of Tutbury, <10s.>, Repton, <10s.> and Trentham, <10s.>, beseeching them to sing or say an obit for my soul and all Christian souls, and to pray for me.

Also I bequeath to the Grey Friars of Lichfield, <40d.>, to the friars of Derby, <6s. 8d.>, and to each house of friars in Chester, <10s.> to each of them, and to the friars of Atherstone, <40d.>.

Also I bequeath towards the repairs of Swarkestone bridge, <40s., *deleted*>, and towards the repair of roads within the lordship of Etwall, <5 marks>, praying my executors and other good folk that the same bridge and roads may be well cared for. ...

Also I will that my son John, after he attains the age of 24 years, shall have all my manors, lands, tenements and farms not given to my wife or otherwise assigned; and in the meantime my executors are to take the profits thereof to distribute as they think best for <performance of

my will> and the health of my soul, and for my son's profit and for the performance of this my will, <except that he shall have yearly for his support as is necessary according to his status, £20, trusting that he will be no waster nor engage in unlawful games; and if he does so, in his need my will is that my feoffees and executors shall help him from my goods. …

Also I bequeath to the prior and convent of ... St Werburgh of Chester, and to their successors for ever, [*blank*] yearly, to be distributed as follows hereafter, upon condition that annually on the Tuesday in the fifth week of Lent, for ever, they devoutly sing and say an obit with *Placebo* and *Dirige* in addition, for my soul and my wife's, our fathers' and mothers', and for such persons' souls as my father, while living, used to have an obit celebrated for annually, and for all our ancestors' souls, and for all Christian souls, with all prayers and suffrages pertaining to the same as they have been accustomed to do for their benefactors. And for that the prior is to have [*blank*] if he is present at the said obit, as part of the same, and the priest who sings or says the mass and does the observance, [*blank*], and every other priest of the said convent who is present at the said obit, [*blank*], and every novice, [*blank*], and the clerk, [*blank*]. And on the Tuesday, [*blank*] to be bestowed in bread and given in alms to poor folk who shall come there to pray for the said souls, and if such do not come, then the bread is to be sent to [*blank*] poor householders. And all of the said [*blank*] that is left over is to be spent on poor men and women. And I will that my feoffees and the heirs of the survivor of them, and my heir, shall yearly pay the said <sum> in the manner before set out from the profits of the messuages, lands and tenements that I or others have to my use in the county of the city of Chester and the franchises of the same. …

(ii) *Final version, dated 6 March 1540* [*ibid.*, p. lvii]

In the name of God amen, the 6th day of March in the thirty first year of the reign of our sovereign Lord King Henry VIII, by the grace of God King of England and France, defender of the faith, lord of Ireland, and on earth the supreme head of the Church of England immediately under God. I, John Port of Etwall in the county of Derby, knight, and one of the king's juctices of his bench of pleas to be held before his highness, being of whole mind and perfect memory, make this my testament and last will in the manner and form following. First, I bequeath my soul to almighty God and my body to be buried in the parish church of Etwall aforesaid. Further, I bequeath to my wife Dame Margery Porte £100 of my moveable goods which are in Lancashire. Also I bequeath to Elizabeth Port, daughter to my son John Port, £100; and to my daughters Barbara Francis and Elyne Bonyng, £20 sterling each. Also I bequeath to Jane Pynderne and Jane Frauncis, towards the marriage of each of them, £40 sterling. Also I bequeath to John Frauncis and William Frauncis, £20 sterling to each of them. And to Jane Carleton £10 sterling. Also I bequeath to my curate, the vicar of the parish church of Etwall, and to Robert Lynnase my old servant, £20 sterling each. Also I bequeath and give to John Compton, clerk, in recompense for certain diligence and pains taken with me in my sickness, and to pray for my soul after my departing, £20 sterling. All and singular of which said sums and goods I will shall be delivered and paid by the hands of my executors, whom I will shall find a priest to sing and pray for my soul in the church of Etwall for the space of a year next after my departing. The residue of all my goods and chattels not given or bequeathed I will that my son John Port, my brother Thomas Gifford and my son John Frauncis, esquires (the debts and funeral paid for and discharged) shall take and dispose of as shall seem best to them for the benefit of my soul according to their wisdom and discretion. The which John Port, Thomas Gifford, and John Frauncis I make, constitute and ordain as my executors to execute and carry out justly and truly this my last will and testament and every part and parcel thereof, according to the trust and confidence I have put in them and every one of them. These being witnesses and present: the said executors, Rauff Fitzherbert, John Compton, clerk, Robert Lynnase, William Hethe, Symond Sterkey, Rauf Holland, and divers others.

The above written testament was proved before the lord [bishop] at London, the 22nd day of the month of March, A.D. 1539 [=1540] by the oath of John Port the executor, sworn on the holy gospels of God in the person of Ralph Hollande, his proxy legitimately appointed for that matter, to well and fully administer and make one etc. full and faithful inventory, as well as to render a full and true account, reserving power, etc., to the other executor.

XI. Complaint and Opposition

The material which can be collected under this heading is voluminous, but no less fragmentary than in the preceding sections. The purpose of the selection is twofold: to indicate the type of complaint being made against contemporary clerics, and to provide some documents about the hunt for heretics which may help towards an assessment of 'Lollardy'. Neither can be adequately achieved within the space available.

The complaint material is highly disparate. The letter regarding the priest at Saltash must be one of the most comprehensive attacks levelled against an individual cleric in this period. It provides evidence of what the laity thought was wrong with some of their priests, and, by inference, what they actually expected from their clergy.[1] *Similar sentiments appear in the extracts from the visitation allegations made in the diocese of Canterbury in 1512. Here, however, the point must be made that these are only allegations: in this instance, we actually have the evidence of the follow-up action, in which the accused often managed to deflect the accusations (although not always). Equally, the authorities were actively responding to the complaints, and where appropriate sought to offer a remedy.*

The complaints offered here are mainly connected with services and their provision; some of the accusations also relate to claims for tithes. There is little – but not a total absence – to suggest widespread disregard for the rules of celibacy, although such accusations do appear in earlier visitation records (such as those for Hereford in 1397), and are frequently encountered in some of the ecclesiastical court material.[2]

To search for evidence of clerical misbehaviour alone is obviously a biased activity. The clergy lived within a context, which might be one of conflict. The disruption at Kennington certainly shows some inhabitants at loggerheads with their vicar; but it may be that the parishioners by their complaints against their disruptive fellows are here actually coming to his defence. The numerous charges levelled against the laity, for a variety of offences, have to

1 R. N. Swanson, 'Problems of the priesthood in pre-reformation England', *English Historical Review*, CV, 1990, pp. 845–69.

2 A. T. Bannister, 'Visitation returns of the diocese of Hereford in 1397', *English Historical Review*, XLIV, 1929, pp. 279–89, 444–53, XLV, 1930, pp. 92–101, 444–63; J. S. Purvis, *A Mediaeval Act Book, with Some Account of Ecclesiastical Jurisdiction at York*, York, n.d. [1943], pp. 14, 20–40, 49–54.

be recalled if not recounted, so that the charges against the clergy can be put into perspective.[3]

The visitation material also provides something of an overlap with considerations of heresy; for the failures to receive communion may convey suggestions of heretical leanings. Suggestions of iconoclastic tendencies, and hostility to clerics which may have bordered on real anticlericalism, certainly appear in the Kennington material (with iconclasm again in another entry, although whether this is of the same calibre as the Kennington statements is open to debate). Yet, again, the fact that the follow-up material survives provides a useful corrective to presuppositions. The entry for Tenterden in the visitation record contains several accusations against people for heresy, and for non-attendance at church. In some cases the heresy accusation seems to have stood, and been held back for further action by the archbishop. Given Tenterden's reputation as a hotbed of Lollardy, the charges of absence from church might also be taken as evidence of heretical inclinations; but here it seems that the people concerned had actually been receiving their communion at another church, sometimes because they were in conflict with the vicar, sometimes by his licence.[4]

With the final few documents, the issues of Lollardy are addressed. The three documents are clearly interconnected, the bishop's mandate giving instructions regarding the visitation of Bury St Edmunds being issued at the start of the campaign which was to incorporate the actions against the individuals whose confessions appear later: there are clear echoes of the monition in some of the statements. The list of identifying features for heretics also has affinities with the confessions; it seems undeniable that a similar list was used to put the charges to the accused, resulting in their somewhat formalised responses.[5] *While the similarities are immediately striking, the differences are also worth noting.*

3 R. N. Swanson, 'Chaucer's Parson and other priests', *Studies in the Age of Chaucer*, XIII, 1991, pp. 78–9.

4 K. Wood-Legh, ed., *Kentish Visitations of Archbishop William Warham and his Deputies, 1511–1512*, Kent Records, XXIV, 1984, no. 174; for Tenterden's reputation, J. A. F. Thomson, *The Later Lollards, 1414–1520*, Oxford, 1965, pp. 173, 175–6, 178, 180, 183, 185, 187–9 (and see p. 190 n. 4).

5 N. P. Tanner, ed., *Heresy Trials in the Diocese of Norwich, 1428–1431*, Camden Society Publications, 4th ser., XX, 1977, pp. 19–20. For the beliefs of this East Anglian group, *ibid.*, pp. 10–22.

A. Anticlericalism?

47. The burgesses of Saltash complain about their vicar, *c.*1406
[Windsor, St George's Chapel archives, XI.K.6; in Latin]

To the venerable men, the dean and college of Windsor: the burgesses and commons of the town of Saltash, your parishioners, send you greetings. The extent to which we were lately said to be against you by the bad and false information on behalf of the present vicar saddens us. And we now have knowledge of the behaviour and mind of that vicar (that is, John Crokhorn), so that we are by no means able to treat him as we ought to treat a spiritual father, for these reasons: He is deaf, and cannot hear confessions except to the scandal of those confessing; he is a discloser of confessions, because he gets drunk and reveals the confessions of parishioners (that is, of John Pyke, and John Genne and others as well); he is a quarreller and general litigator from county to county, and caused some of his parishioners to be outlawed, some to go into exile across the seas, so that the lieges of our lord the king cannot in any way remain in our region because of that John Crokhorn, the vicar, and his brother. Item, the same John Crokhorn, vicar, sells the sacramentals to his parishioners, and refused to minister the last rites to those labouring in the final stages when he was asked, and thus some of the parishioners died without the last rites, that is Gregory Genna and Gilbert Rowe and others. Further, since he was instituted to the benefice he has never expounded the gospel, nor set any other good example to his parishioners by which they could amend their lives, because he carries on like a mere layman, and this is generally known to the populace. These and other worse things he has carried out for six years continuously. On account of these we beg and require you, on behalf of God, and as you would wish to answer to the supreme judge (because the cure of souls is laid upon you for the failing of the vicar) that you should appoint another suitable and literate priest who could instruct us according to the law of God, and also relieve you of this burden. You should know for certain that as far as we can we do not wish to hand over tithes and oblations to him until we have a response from you about this; and the bearer of these presents will inform you further. In testimony of which we have appended our common seal to these presents.

48. Complaints at visitation: Kent, 1511–12 [From K. L. Wood-Legh, ed., *Kentish Visitations of Archbishop William Warham and his LDeputies, 1511–1512*, Kent Records, XXIV, 1984; in both English and Latin]

(i) Church of Sturry [no. 5]

It is alleged: that mass is sung no more than once or twice at most in the week in the said church; we have asked the vicar for masses to be sung more frequently, and he answers: 'Would you have me sing masses when I don't feel like it?'

Item, the said vicar seldom stays within the said parish, regardless of our need for him, and leaves no deputy in his place during his absence.

Item, he frequently rings for the mass at the middle of matins, and sometimes will not permit the ringing for the mass until an hour after matins, on account of which the parishioners have no assurance of the divine service.

Item, the vicar keeps and withholds a piece of woodland adjoining the churchyard, which was given to the parishioners and not to the vicar ...

(ii) *Church of Thanington* [no. 8]

It is alleged: that there is no secular priest in the parish church of Thanington ..., but the prior of St Gregory's [of Canterbury] arranges for one of his canons to serve it during the day, and at night he is in his house, and when they need a priest have to go to search out a priest, on account of which many have died without confession or communion.

(iii) *Church of Swalecliffe* [no. 23]

Item, Sir James, the parish priest, pesters the wife of John Potters, and she cannot be rid of him.

Item, the said Sir James stands listening under people's windows at 10 o'clock at night.

(iv) *Chapel of Hoath in the parish of Reculver* [no. 24]

It is alleged: that the vicar is obliged to find a priest to sing among us on three days each week, which we often do not have.

Item, the chantry priest who is bound to sing there rarely comes there ...

Item, Sir John Michell, chantry priest at Reculver, sows discord between the vicar and his parishioners, and will not distribute holy bread when necessary.

(v) *Church of Barfreston* [no. 39]

It is alleged: that Sir Henry Tankard is full of malice against us, and in his anger denies us holy bread and holy water.

Item, that he uncharitably disturbs his parishioners with writs for keeping the peace, and others of that sort.

Item, that he requires them to look after his tithes for longer than we ought to.

Item, that the parson compels his parishioners to pay the seventh, as with the seventh pig, the seventh lamb, against what is right, and commits many other wrongs.

Item, he would not accept the privy tithes which were offered to him, but out of malice purchased a citation against five of us, and would not let us off until we had reached agreement with him, so that he had for 10d. a noble, and for 3s. 4d., 11s.

Item, that he is so full of malice and demanding towards them that they cannot bear it, but are forced to quit their residences.

(vi) *Church of Waldershare* [no. 42]

It is alleged: that Sir John Hartley, an Irishman, is holding the benefice of Waldershare without having been inducted by my lord of Canterbury.

Item, that the same benefice is not served as it ought to be.

Item, that the aforesaid Sir John serves another cure, and abandons his own.

(vi) *Church of St Mary, Sandwich* [no. 58]

It is alleged: that the chantry priest there does not say his mass daily, as he is required by the foundation, and where he is committed to an hour, he does not keep to it.

Item, that the same chantry priest will not sing the Jesus mass once a week, as others of his predecessors have done before him by an ancient and laudable custom, unless he is given wages for the same.

(viii) *Church of Charlton* [no. 65]

Item, that divine service is not held as it ought to be, nor is the sacrament fittingly administered, to the extent that one Stevynsone of the said parish recently died without confession or communion.

Item, that the parson does not keep residence or hospitality among his parishioners, and comes but rarely among them.

Item, that the parson's barn is in decay, and he cuts down trees in the churchyard.

Item, he retains the documents concerning the lights within our church, on account of which they cannot collect the dues to the church, and when we speak to him about any such matters he is then full of malice, and prepared to fight.

(ix) *Church of Buckland* [no. 74]

Item, that divine service is not maintained as it ought to be, and the sacraments are not administered at the appointed hour and time when they are meant to be.

Item, that there is no curate amongst them, so that when they require the sacraments or a burial, they have to send to wherever they may get one [i.e., a priest].

(x) *Church of St Mary, Dover* [no. 77]

Item, that divine service is not maintained as it ought to be on Wednesdays and Fridays, if there is any memorial service in the town at which our curate might acquire a groat.

(xi) *Church of Wootton* [no. 89]

It is alleged: that matins, mass and divine service are not maintained among them as they ought to be, nor are the sacraments administered at the appropriate time, as they ought to be, to the extent that throughout the Christmas holy days they had neither matins nor mass ...

(xii) *Church of Chilham* [no. 146]

Item, that the parishioners get their heads together to obstruct the right of the parson, and organise a common purse to challenge the said tithes.

Item, the vicar keeps under his control certain lands which ought to support a chantry, which he does not do, but keeps them for his own use.

Item, by a certain agreement the vicar is obliged to provide books and vestments, but he will not.

Item, the vicar puts his horses in the churchyard, which foul it.

Item, that the vicar demands from the parishioners of Chilham certain tithes that no vicar at any time within memory was accustomed to have; that is to say, for horses which are used to ploughing and carting, toiling and working daily, and being pastured within the said parish, 4d. for each one of them; and he compels the said people who have only six lambs or fewer to keep them, without him taking his tithe, until the following year, and in that year, if the said person has a total of seven lambs or above, then he demands two whole tithe lambs, and he would also force them to give the tenth part of great timbers which have been growing for thirty years and more, where they have never been accustomed to give as tithe anything more than a penny for the tenth part (except for young wood alone, of which he has the tenth part).

(xiii) *Church of Bridge* [no. 156]

Item, that they are not fittingly served by a honest priest, but sometimes by a friar, sometimes by no one at all, and that the vicar will not permit a resident priest there.

Item, that the vicar will give no rights [= sacraments] to those who will not satisfy his desires, and if they do not agree with him as he wants.

(xiv) *Church of Kennington* [no. 173]

It is alleged: that Richard Ricard is a man of evil behaviour, and malicious, as is the company he keeps, to the extent that they were minded to have killed the vicar if he had gone to where they were, and this was said by him and his cronies, and he would have done it, because the vicar would not tolerate him in his lewdness ...

Item, that Robert May, Elizabeth May, and Richard Ricard are common slanderers of their neighbours, and back-biters, to the extent that they raised a grievous and unjust defamation against the vicar, of which he was not guilty.

Item, that the said Richard is and has always been in the state that he would not permit any priest to serve amongst them if allowed the choice. He is so determinedly against priests that he is always talking about them, and ready to say the worst against them and their order ...

Item ... that the said Richard owes to the said church 4 marks for the burial of his daughter in the chapel of St Nicholas. ...

Item, that Thomas Ambrose of the same parish does not come to his parish church at Easter as a Christian man ought to do.

Item, that ... Thomas Fuller leaves the church at the time for preaching, and sits in the church porch talking and discussing the words of the sermon unfittingly at alehouses.

Item, that Robert May, Thomas Monson and John Pend assaulted the vicar, and drove him into the said parish churchyard, so that because of them the vicar dares not stay in his vicarage or his cure.

Item, that Thomas Fuller, Richard Ricard and Robert May behave badly in the alehouse, and the said Robert May rants against preachers, saying that they will roast eggs *with the statues of the saints.*

Item, that the said Richard Ricard and his companions rebuke those who help the vicar to sing mass, to the extent that often when he would have sung the mass he could get no one to help him, and this all by his [Ricard's] incitement.

Item, he will not allow the vicar to use the churchyard in the manner to which he was accustomed.

Item, that Robert May said that it was as good to roast meat with the images in the church as with any other wood, they all being of the same matter.

Item, when holy water and holy bread are distributed, he leaves the church.

Item, that M. John May has broken an obit which has been observed for a long time, for which he has leased two cows to observe the said obit. He is also one of those who supports his son against the vicar. ...

Item, Thomas Ambrose was not confessed and did not communicate in his parish church at Easter last; nor is it known where he received [those sacraments].

(xv) *Church of Rolvenden* [no. 175]

It is alleged: that one John Baylis's wife went on Relic Sunday on pilgrimage to the relics, and when she came home he asked her where she had been. And she answered: 'On pilgrimage to the relics, for the parson declared and announced that for every foot that a man or woman journeyed towards the relics he would receive great pardon.' The said John answered and said, 'He said so because he wants to get people's money.' 'No; for the parson said', she said, 'that when the church was burnt the silk with the relics closed up, and the fire had no power over them.' Then the said John said, 'When I see them in front of me, placed between two burning faggots, and they are not destroyed, then I will believe that they are holy relics.' ...

(xvi) *Church of Ospring* [no. 190]

Item, that the vicar does not sing the services at the set hours, and keeps to no order. For one time he sings at one hour, at another at another, as he sees fit; and sometimes will complete all the services by 8 o'clock, and sometimes by 11 o'clock; and thus services are maintained at no good and set times.

B. Heresy and Lollardy

49. The hunt for heretics: mandate of the bishop of Norwich for inquisition into questionable activity in Bury St Edmunds, 1428 [British Library, MS Add. 14848, f.109r; in Latin]

William, by divine permission bishop of Norwich, to the venerable and religious men, the abbot and convent of the monastery of St Edmund at Bury in our diocese, greeting, grace and benediction. There having been committed to us the care of the government over which, by the lord's permission, we preside, it behoves us to extend our strengths against the enemies of the faith for the extermination of heretical depravity ... [He has heard of heretical activity within Bury, which is subject to his authority in this matter regardless of claims to exemption.] Therefore ... we order you to cite or cause to be forewarned six priests and six laymen of the more notable living within your jurisdiction who are not suspected of heretical depravity, that they should appear (and each of them to appear) before us or our commissaries in the parish church of St James within the precinct of your [monastery] on the Monday ... the fourth ... of October concerning heretics and their believers, receivers and supporters and defenders, as well as [*vel*] anyone celebrating private conventicles or making conventicles away from the common gathering of the faithful, and on festival days withdrawing themselves from churches or the general converse of men, or holding exceptional views on the faith or sacred matters, and possessing or learning from books in our vulgar English tongue, and those who are suspected, known or reported of the above or any one of them, if they know of them, who they are to disclose and depose ... about in that matter to us or our commissaries by virtue of the oath which we or our commissaries intend to extract from them and each of them, and furthermore to do and carry out ... what justice and the nature of this business demand and require ... [3 September 1428].

50. The definition of 'Lollardy': a questionnaire developed by the ecclesiastical authorities for identification of suspected heretics [From A. Hudson, *Lollards and Their Books*, London and Ronceverte, 1986, pp. 133–4; in Latin].

ARTICLES ON WHICH HERETICS OR LOLLARDS SHOULD BE EXAMINED, DRAWN UP BY A LAWYER

1. Firstly, whether after consecration the true body of Christ is on the altar, and not bread and wine in material substance.
2. Item, whether a priest has the power to make the body of Christ.
3. Item, whether a bishop or priest, being in mortal sin, can ordain, consecrate, transform [*conficit*], or baptise.
4. Item, whether it is established in the gospel that Christ ordained the mass.
5. Item, in a case where a man is contrite, whether an external confessor is then necessary for him.
6. Item, whether it is necessary for salvation to confess to a priest.
7. Item, whether a child born of a Christian woman needs to be baptised in water, or whether baptism in water celebrated according to the custom of the Church is necessary for the salvation of the soul.
8. Item, whether after Urban VI anyone should be accepted as pope, and whether the pope is truly Christ's vicar on earth.
9. Item, whether it is contrary to holy writ that men of the Church should have possessions [i.e. landed property].
10. Item, whether any prelate ought to excommunicate anyone unless he first knows him to have been excommunicated by God.
11. Item, whether anyone ought to give up preaching or hearing the word of God on account of excommunication by men.
12. Item, whether it is permitted for any deacon or priest to preach the word of God without the authorisation of the apostolic see or a Catholic bishop, and whether it is permitted to everyone indifferently to preach the word of God.
13. Item, whether temporal lords can take away temporal goods from the Church and ecclesiastical men according to their will.
14. Item, whether the people are able, or whether it is permitted to them, to correct delinquent lords according to their judgement.

15. Item, whether tithes should be given to ecclesiastical persons, or whether they are pure alms; and if the parishioners can withdraw them according to their will on account of the sins of their prelates.
16. Item, if anyone entering a private religion [= religious order] of any sort, whether of the possessioners [= monks or canons] or the mendicants, should be considered more fitting and more apt for the observance of God's mandates.
17. Item, if the friars are bound to acquire their food by their manual labour and not by begging.
18. Item, if the religious living in private religions are of the religion of Christ.
19. Item, whether it is licit for anyone to accept a salary from temporal goods to pray for the dead.
20. Item, whether excommunication by the pope or any prelate should be feared.
21. Item, whether it is necessary to believe that the Roman Church is supreme among other churches.
22. Item, whether the confirmation of youngsters, the ordination of clerics and the consecration of places are necessary or licit.
23. Item, whether Augustine, Benedict and Bernard did well in that they had possessions and instituted private religions.
24. Item, whether Lent was ordained by God, and whether it is necessary to fast then and abstain from meat and milk products.
25. Item, if the fasts established by the Church advance the health of the soul, or whether they are to be observed by Christ's faithful.
26. Item, whether venerations of the cross and images should be performed.
27. Item, whether offerings made at images in churches in honour of those saints whom the images represent are meritorious.
28. Item, whether pilgrimages to holy places are necessary or meritorious for the health of souls.
29. Item, whether prayers should be made to any saints.
30. Item, whether prayers ought to be directed only to God.
31. Item, whether it is permitted to anyone to bless himself with the sign of the cross.

32. Item, if the pope or bishops can make constitutions.

33. Item, whether decrees, decretals or papal, synodal, or provincial constitutions are to be observed.

34. Item, whether it is permitted to swear on the book [= gospels].

35. Item, whether oaths taken in either court (that is, ecclesiastical or temporal) in customary cases and according to the usual manner, are licit.

36. Item, whether the genuflections, bowings, censings, kissings, raising of lights and scattering of blessed water customarily done in church are licit and meritorious.

37. Item, whether all things should be in common.

38. Item, whether sabbaths and principal feasts should necessarily be observed and sanctified, or if it should be done according to will.

39. Item, whether it is permitted for a priest to have a wife.

40. Item, whether the evil are part of the Catholic Church.

51. Lollard confessions: from the trials in the diocese of Norwich in 1430 [From N. P. Tanner, ed., *Heresy Trials in the Diocese of Norwich, 1428–31*, Camden Society Publications, 4th ser., XX, 1977; in English, unless otherwise stated]

(i) *Hawisia Moone, wife of Thomas Moone of Loddon* [pp. 140–3]

In the name of God, before you, the worshipful father in Christ William, by the grace of God bishop of Norwich, I, Hawise Moone, the wife of Thomas Moone of Loddon within your diocese, your subject, knowing, aware and understanding that prior to this time I have been very friendly and secretive with many heretics, knowing them to be heretics, and have received and lodged them in our house, and have concealed, comforted, supported, maintained and favoured them with all my ability. The which heretics' names are these: Sir William White, Sir William Caleys, Sir Hugh Pye, Sir Thomas Pert, priests; John Waddon, John Fowlyn ... and many others, who have often maintained, held, and continued schools of heresy in private chambers and private places of ours, in which schools I have heard, conceived, learned and repeated the errors and heresies which are written and contained in these indentures. That is to say,

First, that the sacrament of baptism carried out in water in the manner customary within the church is but a trifle, and of no weight, for all Christian people are sufficiently baptised in the blood of Christ, and so Christian people need no other baptism.

Also, that the sacrament of confirmation performed by a bishop is of no value nor necessarily to be received, since when a child has gained discretion and can and will understand the word of God it is sufficiently confirmed by the Holy Spirit, and needs no other confirmation.

Also, that confession should be made only to God, and to no other priest, because no priest has the power to remit sins, nor to absolve a man of any sins.

Also, that no one is obliged to do any penance which a priest enjoins on him for the sins which he has confessed to the priest, since it is sufficient penance for all types of sin for every person to abstain from lying, speaking ill of people, and evil acts, and no one is obliged to do any other penance.

Also, that no priest has the power to make Christ's true body in the form of bread, but that after the sacramental words are said at mass by the priest material bread alone remains.

Also, that the pope of Rome is the father of Antichrist, and false in all his activities, and has no greater power from God than any other unlearned person, unless he is of holier life; nor does the pope have any power to create bishops, priests or any other orders; and he whom the people call the pope of Rome is no pope, but a false extortioner and deceiver of the people.

Also, that he alone who is the most holy and most perfect in his manner of living on earth is the true pope; and these mass-singers who are called priests are no priests, but lecherous and covetous men, and false deceivers of the people, and with their subtle teaching and preaching, singing and reading, they despicably despoil the people of their possessions, and with them uphold their pride, their lechery, their laziness and all other vices; and they are always making new laws and new ordinances to curse and cruelly kill all those other people who attack their living in vice.

Also, that consent of love between a man and a woman, without any contract by words, and without solemnisation in church, and without calling of banns, is itself sufficient for the sacrament of matrimony.

Also, that it is but a trifle to anoint a sick man with material oil consecrated by a bishop; for at his last end it is sufficient for every one to have God alone in his thoughts.

Also, that everyone may lawfully withdraw and withhold tithes and offerings from priests and curates, and give them to the poor people, and that is more pleasing to God.

Also, that the secular lords and secular men may lawfully take all possessions and temporal goods from all men of Holy Church, and from all bishops and prelates – both horses and harness – and give their goods to poor people; and that the secular people are obliged to do this on penalty of deadly sin.

Also, that it is no sin for anyone to act contrary to the precepts of Holy Church.

Also, that every man and woman who leads a good life, out of sin, is a good priest, and has as much power from God in all things as any ordained priest, even if he is pope or bishop.

Also, that the censures of Holy Church, judgements and cursings, or suspensions, imposed by prelates or ordinaries, are not to be dreaded or feared, for God blesses [to counter] the cursings of the bishops and ordinaries.

Also, that it is not lawful to swear in any cause, nor is it lawful to plead about anything.

Also, that it is not lawful to kill a man for any reason, nor to condemn any traitor or anyone to death by legal process for any treason or felony, nor to put anyone to death for any reason; but everyone should remit all vengeance to the judgement of God alone.

Also, that no one is obliged to fast in Lent, on Ember Days, Fridays, or vigils of saints; but at all those days and times it is lawful for all Christ's people to eat meat, and all kinds of food without worrying, according to their own desire as often as they are hungry, just as much as on other days which are not proclaimed to be fast days.

Also, that no pilgrimages ought to be undertaken or performed, for all going on pilgrimages serves no purpose but to give possessions to priests who are too rich, and to make innkeepers happy and ostelers proud.

Also, that no worship or reverence ought to be offered to any images of the crucifix, of Our Lady, or of any other saints, for all such images are nothing but idols, and made by the activity of human hands; but worship and reverence ought to be paid to the image of God, which is man alone.

Also, that all prayer ought to be offered to God alone, and to no other saints; for it is questionable whether there are any saints in heaven such as these mass-singers approve of and have commanded to be worshipped and prayed to here on earth.

Because of which, and many other errors and heresies, I am summoned before you, worshipful father, who have care over my soul. And being fully informed by you that my said affirmations, beliefs and holdings are overt errors and heresies, and contrary to the determinations of the church of Rome, on that account I, wishing to follow and seek the teaching of Holy Church, and leave off all kinds of error and heresy, and turn with a good will and heart to the unity of the Church, and considering that Holy Church does not bar her bosom to him who will return, and that God does not desire the death of a sinner, but rather that he be converted and live, with a pure heart I confess, detest and despise my said errors and heresies, and I confess the said opinions to be heretical and erroneous, and repugnant to the faith of the Church of Rome and all of the Holy Universal Church. And in so far as that by the said things which I so held, believed and affirmed, I revealed myself corrupt and unfaithful, I promise that from henceforth I shall show myself to be uncorrupt and faithful, and truly maintain the faith and doctrine of Holy Church. And I abjure and forswear all manner of error and heresy, doctrine and opinion against the faith of Holy Church and the determination of the Church of Rome (and particularly the opinions recited before); and swear by these gospels, physically touched by me, that from henceforth I shall never hold any error or heresy or false doctrine against the faith of Holy Church and the determination of the Church of Rome; nor shall I obstinately defend any such things; nor shall I obstinately defend any person holding or teaching such kind of thing, by me or any other person, whether secretly or openly; nor shall I ever trust in them; nor shall I knowingly maintain fellowship with them, or be friendly with them, or give them advice, gifts, succour, favour or comfort. If I know any heretics, or any person suspect of heresy, or their supporters, encouragers or defenders, or of any people holding private conventicles or assemblies, or holding any different or individual opinions divergent from the common doctrine of the Church, I shall let you, worshipful father (or your vicar general in your absence, or the diocesans of such persons) have speedy and swift knowledge. So help me God at the holy judgement, and these holy gospels.

In witness of all these things I subscribe here with my own hand a cross, +; and set my signet to this indented part, to remain in your registry. And I accept the other indented part, under your seal, to stay with me until my life's end. Given at Norwich, in the chapel of your palace ... [4 August 1430].

(ii) *John Skylan of Bergh Apton* [pp. 146–51]

In the name of God, before you, the worshipful father in Christ William, by the grace of God bishop of Norwich, I, John Skylan, the son of Wat Skylan of Bergh within your diocese, your subject, aware and understanding that prior to this time I have mingled greatly and been friendly with many and varied heretics, knowing them to be heretics (that is to say Sir William White, Sir Hugh Pye, Sir Thomas Peert and Sir William Caleys, priests, John Waddon, John Fowlyn, ... and many others), whose schools I have long continued in and attended (first with Sir William White at Bergh, and since then at Colchester with John Werkewode and many others, and after that at London with various people); in which schools I have heard, conceived, learned and repeated all the errors and heresies which are contained in these following articles, which I have held, believed and affirmed. That is to say:

First, that the sacrament of baptism carried out in water in the manner customary within the church is empty, and not necessarily to be carried out or received, because all Christ's people are sufficiently baptised in the blood of Christ, and require no other baptism.

Also, that the sacrament of confirmation performed by a bishop is of no value, in as much as when a child has discretion, and can and will understand the word of God, he is sufficiently confirmed by the Holy Spirit, and requires no other confirmation.

Also, that confession should be made only to God, and to no earthly priest, because no priest has the power to absolve himself or any other man of the sins confessed to him, even if he be the pope's penitentiary.

Also that no man or woman is obliged to carry out any penance which the priest enjoins on him to be done for sins which he has confessed to the priest; but sufficient penance for all types of sin is to abstain from lying, speaking ill of people, and evil actions.

Also, that no priest has the power to make Christ's true body at the mass in the form of bread; but that after the sacramental words have been said by the priest in any mass, there is left pure material bread alone.

Also, that there never was any pope after the death of Peter. And he who is called the pope of Rome is the father of Antichrist, false and accursed in all his actions, falsely and subtly (under an appearance of holiness) deceiving the people to acquire possessions. And he has no greater power from God than any other ordinary person, unless he is more holy in his living. And he has no power to make bishops; and bishops have no power to grant ordination, nor perform any other sacraments, nor to make priests. But all the parsons of the Church, from the highest to the lowest, and all their teaching and preaching, and all their enshacklements, are false and accursed and untrue, and established by these priests only to beguile and deceive the people, to acquire possessions in order to maintain their pride, their laziness and their lechery.

Also, that the accused Caiaphases, bishops and their proud priests, each year make new laws and new ordinances to kill and burn all Christ's true people who would teach and preach the true law of Christ, which they are aware of, and keep hidden from the knowledge of God's people.

Also, that the true pope is that person who is the holiest on earth.

Also, that every good man and good woman is a priest.

Also, that consent of love between a man and a woman is alone sufficient for the sacrament of matrimony, even though the man and woman never speak and are never solemnised in church.

Also, that it is but a trifle to anoint a sick man with material oil consecrated by a bishop, for it is enough that everyone at their last end should have God alone in their thoughts.

Also, that it is lawful for everyone to withdraw and withhold offerings and tithes from priests and churches.

Also, that all secular lords and all secular men are bound on pain of mortal sin to take all possessions and all temporal goods, horses, harness and jewels, from the greedy bishops and proud prelates of the church, and give those goods to the poor people, and force them to sustain themselves by the labour of their own hands.

Also, that it is no sin to act contrary to the precepts of Holy Church.

Also, that the censures of Holy Church, cursings and suspensions, enacted by bishops or ordinaries, are not to be feared, for when bishops or ordinaries curse anyone, God blesses that same person.

Also, that it is not lawful to swear in any cause, nor to plead for any right or wrong.

Also, it is not lawful to kill a man in any cause, not to condemn anyone to death by legal process for felony, treason or any other reason; but everyone should remit all vengeance to the judgement of God alone.

Also, that no one is obliged to fast in Lent, on Ember Days, Fridays, or the vigils of saints which are proclaimed by the Church to be fasted on; but on such days and times it is lawful for the people to eat meat and all other food without worrying, at all hours and times when they have the desire and appetite to eat; for on all such days and times I have eaten meat as often as I desired, when I could obtain it.

Also, that no pilgrimages should be carried out to the lady of Falsingham, the lady of Foulpit, and to Thomas of Cankerbury [i.e. Our Lady of Walsingham, Our Lady of Woolpit, and Thomas Becket at Canterbury], nor to any other saints or images.

Also, that no worship or reverence ought to be offered to any images of Our Lady or of any other saints; nor ought greater reverence be paid to the images of the cross than ought to be paid to the gallows which men are hanged upon, for all such images are nothing but idols, and the makers of them are accursed.

Also, that the four doctors – Augustine, Ambrose, Gregory and Jerome – whom the church of Rome has approved as saints, were heretics, and their teachings, which Christ's people call a doctor's draught, are overt heresies.

Also, that as soon as any man is dead, his soul goes immediately to Heaven or to Hell, because there is no place called Purgatory, but this world alone.

Also, that the chastity of secular and regular priests is not to be commended, or meritorious; but it is more meritorious, lawful and to be commended that all priests should take wives for themselves, and all nuns take husbands for themselves and bring forth the fruit of their bodies.

[He abjures in English, in the form of words used for Hawisia Moone; and subscribes in the same manner, in the chapel of the bishop's palace at Norwich, 4 August 1430. The entry then continues in Latin, recounting the procedure of the abjuration, and that Hardy swore to undergo penance and was then absolved from excommunication. The document of absolution is also recited, noting that the bishop intended to assign penance at a later time.]

[Afterwards, on 7 August 1430] ... the said father, sitting judicially in the chapel of the palace of Norwich, enjoined on the said John Skylan ... the following penance for his offences written above: that is, that he should fast on bread and water on each vigil of St Mary over seven years continually; and that on every Friday for three years he should abstain from fish and milky things; and that on three Sundays he should walk around the cemetery of the church of Bergh in their solemn procession, with bare neck, head and feet, his body clothed only in a shirt and breeches, in the manner of the penitent, carrying a candle of one pound in weight, which on the final Sunday he should offer to the high altar after the gospel in the high mass there; and that in a similar manner he should walk around the market place at Loddon on three market days, with another candle of the said weight, which candle he should offer to the high altar of Loddon on the final market day, after he had carried out his penance; and that on each Ash Wednesday and each Maundy Thursday in the forthcoming three years he shall personally present himself with the other penitents before the said father, or his deputy in this matter, in the cathedral church of Norwich, to undergo solemn penance for his offences ...

(iii) *William Hardy of Mundham, tailor* [pp. 152–6]

In the name of God, before you, the worshipful father in Christ William, by the grace of God bishop of Norwich, I, William Hardy of Mundham within your diocese, aware and understanding that prior to this time I have mingled with and been familiar and friendly with heretics (and especially with one called Sir William Caleys, priest, and another called Hygon, and with others besides) in the house of John Abraham, cordwainer, of Colchester, maintaining and holding schools in heresy; from whom I have heard, understood and repeated the errors and heresies which are written and contained in this indenture, the which errors and heresies I have held, believed and affirmed within your diocese:

First, that the sacrament of baptism carried out in water in the manner customary within the Church is not necessary, or of any profit to be received, for the faith of every person and child of Christian faith is sufficiently baptised in the Passion of Christ, and requires no other baptism.

Also, that the sacrament of confirmation performed by a bishop in the form customary within the Church is but a trifle, for as soon as any child has discretion, and can understand the word and the law of God, he is sufficiently confirmed.

Also, that confession ought to be made only to God, and to no other priest, because no priest has the power to absolve a man of any sins.

Also that every good Christian man who lacks ordination is a good priest, and has as much power to carry out and administer all of the sacraments of the Church as any other ordained priest.

Also, that no priest has the power to make Christ's true body in the sacrament at the altar in the form of bread.

Also, that consent of love between a man and a woman is alone sufficient for the sacrament of perfect matrimony, without any contract by words or solemnisation in church; for such solemnisation is no more than vainglory, introduced by the covetousness of the priests to get money from the people.

Also, that it is but a pointless trick to anoint a sick man threatened by death with material oil consecrated by a bishop.

Also, that it is not lawful to swear in any cause.

Also, it is not lawful in any cause to put anyone to death, nor to condemn a thief or a traitor by legal process.

Also, that no one is obliged to hold Sundays or any other feast days as holy, but it is lawful for everyone to do all other physical actions except sin on all those Sundays and all other feast days which the priests of the church command should be considered holy; for the priests appointed all holy days out of covetousness to receive offerings and tithes from the people.

Also, that it is meritorious and charitable of everyone to withdraw and withhold from the priests and curates all offerings and tithes, because offerings and tithes make priests proud and lecherous and subject to vice; and on this account it would be more meritorious to spend such goods to other purposes.

Also, that censures and cursings laid by bishops and ordinaries on the people are not to be feared, since their cursings are as good as their blessings.

Also, that no Christian person is obliged to fast in Lent, or on Ember Days, Fridays or the vigils of saints on which priests of the Church command there should be fasts; but everyone may lawfully on all such days and times eat flesh and all kinds of food without worrying, according to their own desires as often as they wish, provided that a person fasts from sin.

Also, all kinds of prayer ought to be offered only to God, and to no other saints; because all saints are created by the ordinances of popes and other prelates and priests of the Church, and for this reason it may be doubted whether it is pleasing to God that prayers are said to any saints or not.

Also, that no pilgrimages ought to be made to any saints or locations, but only to poor people.

Also, that no worship or reverence ought to be offered to any images of the crucifix, of Our Lady St Mary, or to any other saints; for the sign of the cross is the sign of Antichrist, and no greater worship or reverence ought to be paid to the cross than ought to be paid to the gallows which men are hanged upon.

Also, there is no Church, but Heaven alone.

Also, that holy bread and holy water are none the better for all the conjurations and charms which priests say and sing over them.

[He abjures in English, in the form of words used for Hawisia Moone; and subscribes in the same manner, in the chapel of the bishop's palace at Norwich, 4 August 1430. The entry then continues in Latin, recounting the procedure of the abjuration, and that Hardy swore to undergo penance and was then absolved from excommunication.] And the bishop reserved to himself the imposition of penance for the offences at a later time. And thereafter the said father declared to that William the danger in recidivism, if he should contravene his above-written abjuration: that is, that then he should rightly be handed over to the secular power for burning ...

[7 August 1430] ... the said father, sitting judicially in the chapel of the palace of Norwich, enjoined on the said William Hardy ... the following penance for his offences written above: that is, that on three Sundays he should walk around the cemetery of the church of St Peter at Mundham in their solemn procession, with bare head and feet, his body clothed only in a shirt, carrying a candle of one pound in weight, which on the final Sunday he should offer to the high altar of the said church of Mundham after he had carried out his penance there; and that he should walk around the market place at Loddon, clothed in the aforesaid manner, on three market days of that town, with another candle of the said weight, which candle he should humbly and devoutly offer to the high altar of the church of Loddon on the final market day, after he had carried out his penance around the said market place; and that on each Ash Wednesday and each Maundy Thursday in the forthcoming three years he shall personally present himself with the other penitents before the said father, or his deputy in this matter, in the cathedral church of Norwich, to undergo solemn penance for his offences …

Bibliography of printed works cited

J. Alexander and P. Binski, eds, *The Age of Chivalry: Art in Plantagenet England, 1200–1400*, London, 1987.

J. A. Alford, 'Richard Rolle and related works', in *Middle English Prose: a Critical Guide to Major Authors and Genres*, ed. A. S. G. Edwards, New Brunswick, N.J., 1984, pp. 35–60.

H. E. Allen, *Writings Ascribed to Richard Rolle, Hermit of Hampole, and Materials for his Biography*, Modern Language Association of America, Monograph Series, III, New York and London, 1927.

J. D. Alsop, 'Religious preambles in early modern English wills as formulae', *Journal of Ecclesiastical History*, XL, 1989, pp. 19–27.

C. A. J. Armstong, *England, France, and Burgundy in the Fifteenth Century*, London, 1983.

M. Aston, *Lollards and Reformers: Images and Literacy in Late Medieval England*, London, 1984.

C. W. Atkinson, *Mystic and Pilgrim: the Book and the World of Margery Kempe*, Ithaca and London, 1983.

R. F. Atkinson, *Knowledge and Explanation in History: an Introduction to the Philosophy of History*, London and Basingstoke, 1978.

J. H. Baker, ed., *The Notebook of Sir John Port*, Selden Society, CII, 1986.

A. T. Bannister, ed., *Registrum Caroli Bothe, Episcopi Herefordensis, A.D. MDXVI–MDXXXV*, Canterbury and York Society, XXVIII, 1921.

A. T. Bannister, 'Visitation returns of the diocese of Hereford in 1397', *English Historical Review*, XLIV, 1929, pp. 279–89, 444–53, XLV, 1930, pp. 92–101, 444–63.

P. H. Barnum, ed., *Dives and Pauper*, Early English Text Society, original ser., CCLXXV, CCLXXX, 1976–80.

A. Barratt, 'Works of religious instruction', in *Middle English Prose: a Critical Guide to Major Authors and Genres*, ed. A. S. G. Edwards, New Brunswick, N.J., 1984, pp. 412–32.

C. M. Barron, 'The parish fraternities of medieval London', in *The Church in Pre-Reformation Society*, ed. C. M. Barron and C. Harper-Bill, Woodbridge, 1985, pp. 13–37.

N. L. Beaty, *The Craft of Dying: a Study in the Literary Tradition of the Ars moriendi in England*, Yale Studies in English, CLXXV, New Haven, 1970.

C. Beaune, *The Birth of an Ideology: Myths and Symbols of Nation in Late-Medieval France*, Berkeley, Los Angeles and Oxford, 1991.

S. Beckwith, 'A very material mysticism: the medieval mysticism of Margery Kempe', in *Medieval Literature: Criticism, Ideology, and History*, ed. D. Aers, New York, 1986, pp. 34–57.

S. G. Bell, 'Medieval women book owners: arbiters of lay piety and ambassadors of culture', in *Sisters and Workers in the Middle Ages*, ed. J. M. Bennett et al., Chicago and London, 1989, pp. 135–61 (also in *Women and Power in the Middle Ages*, ed. M. Erler and M. Kowaleski, Athens, Ga., and London, 1988, pp. 149–87).

H. S. Bennett, *English Books and Readers, 1475 to 1557*, 2nd ed., Cambridge, 1969.

N. H. Bennett, 'Blunham rectory accounts, 1520–39', in *Hundreds, Manors, Parishes, and Churches: a Selection of Early Documents for Bedfordshire*, ed. J. S. Thompson, Publications of the Bedfordshire Historical Record Society, LXIX, 1990, pp. 124–69.

T. H. Bestul, 'Chaucer's Parson's Tale and the late-medieval tradition of religious meditation', *Speculum*, LXIV, 1989, pp. 600–19.

P. Biller, 'Words and the medieval notion of "religion"', *Journal of Ecclesiastical History*, XXXVI, 1985, pp. 351–69.

J. Blair, 'Saint Beornwald of Bampton', *Oxoniensia*, XLIX, 1984, pp. 47–55.

J. Blair, 'Saint Beornwald of Bampton: further references', *Oxoniensia*, LIV, 1990, pp. 400–3.

N. F. Blake, ed., *Middle English Religious Prose*, London, 1972.

N. F. Blake, *The English Language in Medieval Literature*, London and New York, 1977.

N .F. Blake, 'Vernon manuscript: contents and organisation', in *Studies in the Vernon Manuscript*, ed. D. Pearsall, Woodbridge, 1990, pp. 45–59.

J. Bossy, 'The mass as a social institution', *Past and Present*, C, August 1983, pp. 29–61.

J. Bossy, 'Prayers', *Transactions of the Royal Historical Society*, 6th ser., I, 1991, pp. 137–48.

R. Bowers, 'Obligation, agency, and *laissez-faire*: the promotion of polyphonic composition for the church in fifteenth-century England', in *Music in Medieval and Early Modern Europe: Patronage, Sources, and Texts*, ed. I. Fenlon, Cambridge, 1981, pp. 1–19.

L. E. Boyle, 'The Fourth Lateran Council and manuals of popular theology', in *The Popular Literature of Medieval England*, ed. T. J. Heffernan, Tennessee Studies in Literature, XXVIII, Knoxville, Tenn., 1985, pp. 30–44.

M. T. Brady, 'The pore caitif: an introductory study', *Traditio*, X, 1954, 529–48.

J. R. Bray, 'Concepts of sainthood in fourteenth century England', *Bulletin of the John Rylands University Library of Manchester*, LXVI, 1984, pp. 40–77.

S. Brigden, *London and the Reformation*, Oxford, 1989.

M. G. Briscoe, 'Preaching and medieval English drama', in *Contexts for Early English Drama*, ed. M. G. Briscoe and J. C. Coldewey, Bloomington and Indianapolis, 1989, pp. 151–72.

C. Burgess, '"For the increase of divine service": chantries in the parish in late-medieval Bristol', *Journal of Ecclesiastical History*, XXXVI, 1985, pp. 46–65.

C. Burgess, '"By quick and by dead": wills and pious provision in late medieval Bristol', *English Historical Review*, CII, 1987, pp. 837–58.

C. Burgess. 'A service for the dead: the form and function of the anniversary in late medieval Bristol', *Transactions of the Bristol and Gloucestershire Archaeological Society*, CV, 1987, pp. 183–211.

C. Burgess, '"A fond thing vainly invented": an essay on Purgatory and pious motive in late medieval England', in *Parish, Church, and People: Local Studies in Lay Religion, 1350–1750*, ed. S. J. Wright, London, 1988, pp. 56–84.

C. Burgess, 'Strategies for eternity: perpetual chantries in late medieval Bristol', in *Religious Belief and Ecclesiastical Careers in Late Medieval England*, ed. C. Harper-Bill, Woodbridge, 1991, pp. 1–32.

C. Burgess, 'Late medieval wills and pious convention: testamentary evidence reconsidered', in *Profit, Piety, and the Professions in Later Medieval England*, ed. M. A. Hicks, Gloucester, 1990, pp. 14–33.

C. Butler, *Western Mysticism: the Teaching of Augustine, Gregory, and Bernard on Contemplation and the Contemplative Life*, 3rd ed., London, 1967.

Cambridge University Library MS Ff.2.38, introduction by F. McSparran and P. R. Robinson, London, 1979.

C. Carpenter, 'The religion of the gentry of fifteenth-century England', in *England in the Fifteenth Century: Proceedings of the 1986 Harlaxton Symposium*, ed. D. Williams, Woodbridge, 1987, pp. 53–74.

M. J. Carruthers, *The Book of Memory: a Study of Memory in Medieval Culture*, Cambridge Studies in Medieval Literature, X, Cambridge, 1990.

J. Catto, 'Religious change under Henry V', in *Henry V, the Practice of Kingship*, ed. G. Harriss, Oxford, 1985, pp. 97–115.

J. F. Chanter, 'St Urith of Chittlehampton: a study of an obscure Devon saint', *Report and Transactions of the Devonshire Association for the Advancement of Science, Literature, and Art*, XLVI, 1914, pp. 290–308.

F. Cheetham, *English Medieval Alabasters*, Oxford, 1984.

G. Cigman, 'The preacher as performer: Lollard sermons as imaginative discourse', *Journal of Literature and Theology*, II, 1988, pp. 69–82.

G. Cigman, 'Luceat lux vestra: the Lollard preacher as truth and light', *Review of English Studies*, XL, 1989, pp. 479–96.

G. Cigman, ed., *Lollard Sermons*, Early English Text Society, original ser. CCXCVI, 1989.

A. Clark, ed., *Lincoln Diocese Documents, 1450–1544*, Early English Text Society, original ser. CXLIX, 1914.

C. E. Clark-Maxwell, 'Some further letters of confraternity', *Archaeologia*, LXXIX, 1929, pp. 179–216.

B. Coe, *Stained Glass in England, 1150–1500*, London, 1981.

J. C. Colchester, ed., *Wells Cathedral Fabric Accounts, 1390–1600*, Wells, 1983.

J. Coleman, *English Literature in History, 1350–1400: Medieval Readers and Writers*, London, 1981.

M. Collins, 'A little known "Art of Dying" by a Brigittine of Syon: *A daily exercise and experience of death* by Richard Whytford', in *Dies illa: Death in the Middle Ages. Proceedings of the 1983 Manchester Colloquium*, ed. J. H. M. Taylor, Vinaver Studies in French, I, Liverpool, 1984, pp. 179–93.

F. M. M. Comper, ed., *The Book of the Craft of Dying, and Other Early English Tracts Concerning Death*, London, 1917.

J .C. Cox, *Churchwardens' Accounts from the Fourteenth Century to the Close of the Seventeenth Century*, London, 1913.

A. Craiger-Smith, *English Medieval Mural Paintings*, Oxford, 1963.

C. Cross, 'Religious and social protest among Lollards in early Tudor England', in *The Church in a Changing Society*, Publications of the Swedish Society of Church History, XXX, Uppsala, 1978, pp. 71–5.

C. Cross, '"Great reasoners in scripture": the activities of women lollards, 1380–1530', in *Medieval Women*, ed. D. Baker, Studies in Church History, Subsidia I, Oxford, 1978, pp. 359–80.

C. Cross, 'Wills as evidence of popular piety in the reformation period: Leeds and Hull, 1540–1640', in *The End of Strife: Death, Reconciliation, and Expressions of Christian Spirituality*, ed. D. M. Loades, Edinburgh, 1984, pp. 44–51.

R. G. Davies, 'Lollardy and locality', *Transactions of the Royal Historical Society*, 6th ser., I, 1991, pp. 191–212.

J. F. Davis, 'Lollardy and the Reformation in England', *Archiv für Reformationsgeschichte*, LXXIII, 1982, pp. 217–36.

N. Davis, ed., *Paston Letters and Papers of the Fifteenth Century*, 2 vols., Oxford, 1970.

V. Davis, 'The rule of Saint Paul, the first hermit, in late medieval England', *Studies in Church History*, XXII, 1985, pp. 203–14.

D. L. D'Avray, 'Papal authority and religious sentiment in the late middle ages', in *The Church and Sovereignty, c. 590–1918: Essays in Honour of Michael Wilks*, ed. D. Wood, Studies in Church History, Subsidia IX, Oxford, 1991, pp. 393–408.

M. Deanesly, *The Lollard Bible and Other Medieval Biblical Versions*, Cambridge, 1920.

M. Denley, 'Elementary teaching techniques and Middle English religious didactic writings', in *Langland, the Mystics, and the Medieval English Religious Tradition: Essays in Honour of S. S. Hussey*, ed. H. Phillips, Woodbridge, 1990, pp. 223–41.

C. D'Evelyn and F. A. Foster, 'Saints' legends', in *A Manual of the Writings in Middle English, 1050–1500*, ed. J. B. Severs, II, Hamden, Conn., 1970, pp. 410–57, 553–649.

A. G. Dickens, 'The shape of anticlericalism and the English Reformation', in *Politics and Society in Reformation Europe: Essays for Sir Geoffrey Elton on his Sixty Fifth Birthday*, ed. E. I. Kouni and T. Scott, Basingstoke and London, 1987, pp. 379–410.

A. G. Dickens, *The English Reformation*, 2nd ed., London, 1989.

R. B. Dobson, 'Mendicant ideal and practice in late medieval York', in *Archaeological Papers from York presented to M. W. Barley*, ed. P. V. Addyman and V. E. Black, York, 1984, pp. 109–22.

C. Dodgson, 'English devotional woodcuts of the late fifteenth century, with special reference to those in the Bodleian library', *Walpole Society*, XVII, 1928–9, pp. 95–108.

A. I. Doyle, 'Reflections of some manuscripts of Nicholas Love's *Myrrour of the blessed lyf of Jesu Christ*', *Leeds Studies in English*, n.s. XIV, 1983, pp. 82–93.

A. I. Doyle, 'Publication by members of the religious orders', in *Book Production and Publishing in Britain, 1375–1475*, ed. J. Griffiths and D. Pearsall, Cambridge, 1989, pp. 109–23.

M. W. Driver, 'Pictures in print: late fifteenth- and early sixteenth-century English religious books for lay readers', in *De Cella in Seculum: Religious and Secular Life and Devotion in Late Medieval England*, ed. M. G. Sargent, Woodbridge, 1989, pp. 229–44.

F. R. H. du Boulay, 'The quarrel between the Carmelite friars and the secular clergy of London, 1464–1468', *Journal of Ecclesiastical History*, VI, 1955, pp. 156–74.

E. Duffy, 'Devotion to the crucifix and related images in England on the eve of the Reformation', in *Bilder und Bildersturm im Spätmittelalter und in der früher Neuzeit*, ed. R. Scribner, Wolfenbütteler Forschungen, XLVI, Wiesbaden, 1990, pp. 21–36.

E. Duffy, 'Holy maydens, holy wyfes: the cult of women saints in fifteenth- and sixteenth-century England', *Studies in Church History*, XXVII, 1990, pp. 175–96.

R. W. Dunning and T. D. Tremlett, eds., *Bridgwater Borough Archives, V: 1468–1485*, Somerset Record Society, LXX, 1971.

G. R. Elton, *England, 1200–1640*, London, 1969.

D. Englander, D. Norman, R. O'Day and W. R. Owens, eds, *Culture and Belief in Europe, 1450–1600: an Anthology of Sources*, Oxford, 1990.

T. Erbe, ed., *Mirk's Festial: a Collection of Homilies by Johannes Mirkus (John Mirk)*, Early English Text Society, extra ser., XCVI, 1905.

A. M. Erskine, ed., *The Accounts of the Fabric of Exeter Cathedral, 1279–1353*, Devon and Cornwall Record Society, n.s., XXIV, XXVI, 1981–3.

R. C. Finucane, *Miracles and Pilgrims: Popular Beliefs in Medieval England*, London, 1977.

P. W. Fleming, 'Charity, faith, and the gentry of Kent, 1422–1529', in *Property and Politics: Essays in Later Medieval English History*, ed. T. Pollard, Gloucester, 1984, pp. 36–57.

A. J. Fletcher, 'Unnoticed sermons from John Mirk's *Festial*', *Speculum*, LV, 1980, pp. 514–22.

A.J. Fletcher, 'John Mirk and the Lollards', *Medium Ævum*, LVI, 1987, pp. 217–24.

S. Forde, 'Nicholas Hereford's Ascension Day sermon, 1382', *Mediaeval Studies*, LI, 1989, pp. 205–41.

J. Forshall and F. Madden, eds, *The New Testament in English, According to the Version by John Wycliffe, about A.D. 1380, and Revised by John Purvey about A.D. 1388*, Oxford, 1879.

D. B. Foss, 'John Mirk's *Instructions for parish priests*', *Studies in Church History*, XXVI, 1989, pp. 131–40.

W. H. Frere, 'York service books', in *Walter Howard Frere: a Collection of his Papers on Liturgical and Historical Subjects*, ed. J. H. Arnold and E. G. P. Wyatt, Alcuin Club Collections, XXXV, 1940, pp. 159–69 .

E. A. Fry, 'Dorset chantries', *Proceedings of the Dorset Natural History and Antiquarian Field Club*, XXVII, 1906, pp. 214–33, XXVIII, 1907, pp. 12–29.

A. Gash, 'Carnival against Lent: the ambivalence of medieval drama', in *Medieval Literature: Criticism, Ideology, and History*, ed. D. Aers, New York, 1986, pp. 74–98.

G. McM. Gibson, *The Theater of Devotion: East Anglian Drama and Society in the Late Middle Ages*, Chicago and London, 1989.

V. Gillespie, 'Vernacular books of religion', in *Book Production and Publishing in Britain, 1375–1475*, ed. J. Griffiths and D. Pearsall, Cambridge, 1989, pp. 317–44.

S. L. Greenslade, 'English versions of the Bible, 1525–1611', in *The Cambridge History of the Bible* [vol. III]: *The World from the Reformation to the Present Day*, ed. S. L. Greenslade, Cambridge, 1963, pp. 141–74.

P. Grosjean, ed., *Henrici VI Angliae regis miracula postuma, ex Codice Musei Britannici Regio 13.C.VIII*, Subsidia Hagiographica, XXII, Brussels, 1935.

P. Gwyn, *The King's Cardinal: the Rise and Fall of Thomas Wolsey*, London, 1990.

C. Haigh, 'Introduction', in *The English Reformation Revised*, ed. C. Haigh, Cambridge, 1987, pp. 1–17.

C. Haigh, 'Anticlericalism in the English Reformation', in *The English Reformation Revised*, ed. C. Haigh, Cambridge, 1987, pp. 56–74.

R. M. Haines, *Ecclesia Anglicana: Studies in the English Church of the Later Middle Ages*, London and Toronto, 1989.

B. Hamilton, *Religion in the Medieval West*, London, 1986.

C. Harper-Bill, 'Dean Colet's convocation sermon and the pre-Reformation church in England', *History*, LXXIII, 1988, pp. 191–210.

C. Harper-Bill, *The Pre-Reformation Church in England, 1400–1530*, London and New York, 1989.

F. Ll. Harrison, *Music in Medieval Britain*, 4th ed., London, 1980.

P. Heath, *The English Parish Clergy on the Eve of the Reformation*, London and Toronto, 1960.

P. Heath, *Medieval Clerical Accounts*, St Anthony's Hall Publications, XXVI, York, 1964.

P. Heath, 'Urban piety in the later middle ages: the evidence of Hull wills', in *The Church, Politics, and Patronage in the Fifteenth Century*, ed. R. B. Dobson, Gloucester, 1984, pp. 209–34.

T. J. Heffernan, 'Sermon literature', in *Middle English Prose: a Critical Guide to Major Authors and Genres*, ed. A. S. G. Edwards, Brunswick, NJ, 1984, pp. 177–207.

M. Hicks, 'Chantries, obits, and almshouses: the Hungerford foundations', in *The Church in Pre-Reformation Society: Essays in Honour of F. R. H. du Boulay*, ed. C. M. Barron and C. Harper-Bill, Woodbridge, 1985, pp. 123–42.

M. A. Hicks, 'The piety of Margaret, Lady Hungerford (d.1478)', *Journal of Ecclesiastical History*, XXXVIII, 1987, pp. 19–38.

Walter Hilton, *The Scale of Perfection*, trans. G. Sitwell, London, 1953.

J. C. Hirsh, 'Prayer and meditation in late medieval England: MS Bodley 789', *Medium Ævum*, XLVIII, 1979, pp. 55–66.

J. C. Hirsh, 'Margery Kempe', in *Middle English Prose: a Critical Guide to Major Authors and Genres*, ed. A. S. G. Edwards, New Brunswick, N.J., 1984, pp. 109–19.

J. C. Hirsh, *The Revelations of Margery Kempe: Paramystical Practices in Late Medieval England*, Medieval and Renaissance Authors, X, Leiden, 1989.

Historical Manuscripts Commission: Report of the Manuscripts of Lord Middleton Preserved at Wollaton Hall, Nottingham, London, 1911.

P. Hodgson, '*Ignorancia sacerdotum*: a fifteenth century discourse on the Lambeth constitutions', *Review of English Studies*, XXIV, 1948, pp. 1–11.

J. Hogg, 'Mount Grace Charterhouse and late medieval English spirituality', in *Collectanea Cartusiana, III* (= *Analecta Cartusiana*, LXXXII: iii), Salzburg, 1983, pp. 1–43.

S. E. Holbrook, 'Margery Kempe and Wynkyn de Worde', in *The Medieval Mystical Tradition in England: Exeter Symposium IV. Papers read at Dartington Hall, July 1987*, ed. M. Glasscoe, Woodbridge, 1987, pp. 27–46.

A. Hope, 'Lollardy: the stone the builders rejected?', in *Protestantism and the National Church in Sixteenth Century England*, ed. P. Lake and M. Dowling, London, New York, and Sydney, 1987, pp. 1–35.

C. Horstman, ed., *Yorkshire Writers: Richard Rolle of Hampole and his Followers*, 2 vols, London, 1895–6.

C. Horstman, ed., *Nova Legenda Anglie, as Collected by John of Tynemouth, John Capgrave, and Others, and First Printed, with New Lives, by Wynkyn de Worde, a.d. m d xui*, 2 vols, Oxford, 1901.

A. Hudson, 'Wycliffite prose', in *Middle English Prose: a Critical Guide to Major Authors and Genres*, ed. A. S. G. Edwards, New Brunswick, N.J., 1984, pp. 249–70.

A. Hudson, 'A new look at the *Lay folks' catechism*', *Viator*, XVI, 1985, pp. 243–58.

A. Hudson, *Lollards and their Books*, London and Ronceverte, 1986.

A. Hudson, *The Premature Reformation: Wycliffite Texts and Lollard History*, Oxford, 1988.

A. Hudson, 'Lollard book production', in *Book Production and Publishing in Britain, 1375–1475*, ed. J. Griffiths and D. Pearsall, Cambridge, 1989, pp. 125–42.

A. Hudson and P. Gradon, eds, *English Wycliffite Sermons*, Oxford, 1983–.

J. Huizinga, *The Waning of the Middle Ages*, London, 1968.

R. F. Hunnisett, 'The reliability of inquisitions as historical evidence', in *The Study of Medieval Records: Essays in Honour of Kathleen Major*, ed. D. A. Bullough and R. L. Storey, Oxford, 1971, pp. 206–35.

R. Hutton, 'The local impact of the Tudor Reformations', in *The English Reformation Revised*, ed. C. Haigh, Cambridge, 1987, pp. 114–38.

The Interpretacyon and Sygnyfycacyon of the Masse, London, 1532.

E. W. Ives, *The Common Lawyers of Pre-Reformation England*, Cambridge, 1983.

G. M. Jantzen, *Julian of Norwich: Mystic and Theologian*, London, 1987.

P. S. Jolliffe, *A Check-List of Middle English Prose Writings of Spiritual Guidance*, Pontifical Institute of Mediaeval Studies, Subsidia Mediaevalia, II, Toronto, 1974.

M. K. Jones and M. G. Underwood, *The King's Mother: Lady Margaret Beaufort, Countess of Richmond and Derby*, Cambridge, 1992.

E. G. H. Kempson, 'A Shropshire guild at work in Wiltshire', *Wiltshire Archaeological and Natural History Magazine*, LVII, 1958–60, pp. 50–5.

D. G. Kennedy, *Incarnational Element in Hilton's Spirituality*, Salzburg Studies in English Literature: Elizabethan and Renaissance Studies, XCII: iii, Salzburg, 1982.

A. J. Kettle, ed., *A List of Families in the Archdeaconry of Stafford, 1532–3*, Collections for a history of Staffordshire, 4th ser., VIII, 1976.

A. A. King, *Liturgies of the Past*, London, 1959.

P. King, 'The English cadaver tomb in the late fifteenth century: some indications of a Lancastrian connection', in *Dies Illa: Death in the Middle Ages. Proceedings of the 1983 Manchester Colloquium*, ed. J. H. M. Taylor, Vinaver Studies in French, I, Liverpool, 1984, pp. 45–57.

J. L. Kirby, ed., *Calendar of Inquisitions Post Mortem and Other Analogous Documents Preserved in the Public Record Office; vol. XVIII, 1–6 Henry IV, 1399–1405*, London, 1987.

D. Knowles, *The Religious Orders in England*, 3 vols, Cambridge, 1948–61.

D. Knowles, *The English Mystical Tradition*, London, 1961.

A. Kreider, *English Chantries: the Road to Dissolution*, Harvard Historical Studies, XCVII, Cambridge, Mass., and London, 1979.

G. Kristensson, ed., *John Mirk's Instructions for Parish Priests, Edited from MS Cotton Claudius A II and Six Other Manuscripts, with Introduction, Notes, and Glossary*, Lund Studies in English, XLIX, Lund, 1974.

D. Kunzle, *The Early Comic Strip: Narrative Strips and Picture Stories in the European Broadsheet from c.1450 to 1825*, Berkeley, Los Angeles and London, 1973.

V. M. Lagorio and R. Bradley, *The Fourteenth Century English Mystics: a Comprehensive Annotated Bibliography*, New York and London, 1981.

G. I. Langmuir, *History, Religion, and Antisemitism*, Berkeley, Los Angeles, and Oxford, 1990.

N. A. H. Lawrance, ed., *Fasti Parochiales, vol. 3: Deanery of Dickering*, Yorkshire Archaeological Society Record Series, CXXIX, 1967.

J. W. Legg, ed., *The Processional of the Nuns of Chester*, Henry Bradshaw Society, XVIII, 1899.

J. W. Legg, ed., *Tracts on the Mass*, Henry Bradshaw Society, XXVII, London, 1904.

L. Lepow, *Enacting the Sacrament: Counter-Lollardy in the Towneley cycle*, London and Toronto, 1990.

C. Lindberg, ed., *The Middle English Bible: The Book of Judges*, Oslo, 1989.

H. Littlehales, ed., *The Prymer, or Lay Folks' Prayer Book*, part 1, Early English Text Society, original ser. CV, 1895.

H. Littlehales, *English Fragments from Latin Medieval Service-Books*, Early English Text Society, extra ser., XC, 1903.

W. E. Lunt, *Financial Relations of the Papacy with England, 1327–1534*, Publications of the Mediaeval Academy of America, LXXIV, Cambridge, Mass., 1962.

J. H. Lupton, *A Life of John Colet, D.D., Dean of St Paul's and Founder of St Paul's School*, London, 1887.

D. MacCulloch, *Suffolk and the Tudors: Politics and Religion in an English County, 1500–1600*, Oxford, 1986, pp. 143–6.

J. W. McKenna, 'Popular canonization as political propaganda: the case of Archbishop Scrope', *Speculum*, XLV, 1970, pp. 608–23.

P. McNiven, *Heresy and Politics in the Reign of Henry IV: the Burning of John Badby*, Woodbridge, 1987.

B. R. McRee, 'Religious guilds and regulation of behaviour in late medieval towns', in *People, Politics, and Community in the Later Middle Ages*, ed. J.T. Rosenthal and C. Richmond, Gloucester, 1987, pp. 108–22.

A. R. Malden, ed., *The Canonization of Saint Osmund, from the Manuscript Records in the Muniment Room of Salisbury Cathedral*, Wiltshire Record Society, II, 1901.

C. A. Martin, 'Middle English manuals of religious instruction', in *So Meny People, Longages, and Tonges: Philological Essays in Scots and Mediaeval English Presented to Angus McIntosh*, ed. M. Benskin and M. L. Samuels, Edinburgh, 1981, pp. 283–98.

J. Mattingly, 'The medieval parish guilds of Cornwall', *Journal of the Royal Institution of Cornwall*, n.s., X: iii, 1989, pp. 290–329.

J. E. B. Mayor, ed., *The English Works of John Fisher, Bishop of Rochester*, Early English Text Society, extra ser., XXVII, 1876.

S. B. Meech, 'John Drury and his English writings', *Speculum*, IX, 1934, pp. 70–83.

H. Mellick, 'In defence of a fifteenth-century manuscript', *Parergon*, VIII, April, 1974, pp. 20–4.

K. Mertes, *The English Noble Household, 1250–1600: Good Governance and Politic Rule*, Oxford, 1988.

R. G. K. A. Mertes, 'The household as a religious community', in *People, Politics, and Community in the Fifteenth Century*, ed. J. T. Rosenthal and C. Richmond, Gloucester, 1987, pp. 123–39.

A. Minnis, 'The *Cloud of Unknowing* and Walter Hilton's *Scale of Perfection*', in *Middle English Prose: a Critical Guide to Major Authors and Genres*, ed. A. S. G. Edwards, New Brunswick, N.J., 1984, pp. 61–81.

M. Mitchiner, *Medieval Pilgrim and Secular Badges*, London, 1986.

J. R. H. Moorman, *The Grey Friars in Cambridge, 1225–1538*, Cambridge, 1952.

J. A. H. Moran, *The Growth of English Schooling, 1340–1538: Learning, Literacy, and Laicization in Pre-Reformation York Diocese*, Princeton, N.J., 1985.

A. R. Myers, ed., *English Historical Documents, 1327–1485*, London, 1969.

The New English Bible, Oxford and Cambridge, 1970.

N. H. Nicholas, ed., *Privy Purse Expenses of Elizabeth of York; Wardrobe Accounts of Edward the Fourth*, London, 1830.

J. C. T. Oates, 'Richard Pynson and the Holy Blood of Hailes', *The Library*, 5th ser., XIII, 1958, pp. 269–77.

M. C. O'Connor, *The Art of Dying Well: the Development of the Ars Moriendi*, New York, 1942.

R. O'Day, *The Debate on the English Reformation*, London, 1986.

S. J. Ogilvie-Thomson, ed., *Walter Hilton's Mixed Life, Edited from Lambeth Palace MS 472*, Salzburg Studies in English Literature: Elizabethan and Renaissance Studies, XCII: xv, Salzburg, 1986.

N. Orme, 'Two saint-bishops of Exeter: James Berkeley and Edmund Lacy', *Analecta Bollandiana*, CIV, 1986, pp. 403–18.

N. Orme, 'Saint Walter of Cowick', *Analecta Bollandiana*, CVIII, 1990, pp. 387–93.

D. M. Owen, *The Records of the Established Church in England, Excluding Parochial Records*, British Records Association: Archives and the User, no. I, 1970.

D. M. Owen, 'Bacon and eggs: Bishop Buckingham and superstition in Lincolnshire', *Studies in Church History*, VIII, 1972, pp. 139–42.

G. R. Owst, *Preaching in Medieval England: an Introduction to Sermon Manuscripts of the Period c.1350–1450*, Cambridge, 1926.

G. R. Owst, *Literature and Pulpit in Medieval England: a Neglected Chapter in the History of English Letters and of the English People*, 2nd ed., Oxford, 1961.

W. A. Pantin, 'Instructions for a devout and literate layman', in *Medieval Learning and Literature: Essays Presented to Richard William Hunt*, ed. J. J. G. Alexander and M. T. Gibson, Oxford, 1976, pp. 398–422.

D. Pearsall, ed., *Studies in the Vernon Manuscript*, Woodbridge, 1990.

J. W. Percy, ed., *York Memorandum Book BY*, Surtees Society Publications, CLXXXVI, 1973.

R. W. Pfaff, *New Liturgical Feasts in Later Medieval England*, Oxford, 1970.

R. W. Pfaff, 'The English devotion of St Gregory's Trental', *Speculum*, XLIX, 1974, pp. 75–90.

O. S. Pickering, 'Brotherton Collection MS. 501: a Middle English anthology reconsidered', *Leeds Studies in English*, n.s. XXI, 1990, pp. 141–65.

S. Powell, ed., *The Advent and Nativity Sermons from a Fifteenth-Century Revision of John Mirk's Festial*, Middle English Texts, XIII, Heidelberg, 1981.

S. Powell, 'A new dating of John Mirk's *Festial*', *Notes and Queries*, CCXXVII, 1982, pp. 487–9.

S. Powell, 'Lollards and Lombards: late medieval bogeymen', *Medium Ævum*, LIX, 1990, pp. 133–9.

J. S. Purvis, *A Mediaeval Act Book, with Some Account of Ecclesiastical Jurisdiction at York*, York, n.d. [1943].

U. M. Radford, 'The wax images found in Exeter cathedral', *Antiquaries Journal*, XXIX, 1949, pp. 164–8.

J. Raine, ed., *The Fabric Rolls of York Minster, with an Appendix of Illustrative Documents*, Surtees Society Publications, XXXV, 1858.

The Records of the Northern Convocation, Surtees Society Publications, CXIII, 1907.

G. Redworth, *In Defence of the Church Catholic: the Life of Stephen Gardiner*, Oxford, 1990.

V. Reinburg, 'Note on John Bossy, "Prayers"', *Transactions of the Royal Historical Society*, 6th ser., I, 1991, pp. 148–50.

R. Rex, 'The English campaign against Luther in the 1520s', *Transactions of the Royal Historical Society*, 5th ser., XXXIX, 1989, pp. 85–106.

S. Reynolds, 'Social mentalities and the case of medieval scepticism', *Transactions of the Royal Historical Society*, 6th ser., I, 1991, pp. 21–41.

D. E. Rhodes, *Studies in Early European Printing and Book-Collecting*, London, 1983.

C. Richmond, 'Religion and the fifteenth-century English gentleman', in *The Church, Politics, and Patronage in the Fifteenth Century*, ed. R. B. Dobson, Gloucester, 1984, pp. 193–208.

C. Richmond, 'The English gentry and religion, c.1500', in *Religious Belief and Ecclesiastical Careers in Late Medieval England*, ed. C. Harper–Bill, Woodbridge, 1991, pp. 121–50.

J. Ridgard, ed., *Medieval Framlingham, Select Documents, 1270–1524*, Suffolk Record Society, XXVII, 1985.

W. Riehle, *The Middle English Mystics*, London, Boston, and Henley, 1981.

R. H. Robbins, 'Popular prayers in middle English verse', *Modern Philology*, XXXVI, 1938–9, pp. 337–50.

R. H. Robbins, 'Private prayers in middle English verse', *Studies in Philology*, XXXVI, 1939, pp. 466–75.

N. Rogers, 'The cult of Prince Edward at Tewkesbury', *Transactions of the Bristol and Gloucestershire Archaeological Society*, CI, 1983, pp. 187–9.

G. Rosser, 'Communities of parish and guild in late medieval England', in *Parish, Church, and People: Local Studies in Lay Religion, 1350–1750*, ed. S. J. Wright, London, 1988, pp. 32–55.

G. Rosser, 'Parochial conformity and popular religion in late medieval England', *Transactions of the Royal Historical Society*, 6th ser., I, 1991, pp. 173–89.

M. Rubin, 'Corpus Christi fraternities and late medieval piety', *Studies in Church History*, XXIII, 1986, pp. 97–109.

M. Rubin, *Charity and Community in Late Medieval Cambridge*, Cambridge Studies in Medieval Life and Thought, 4th ser., IV, Cambridge, 1987.

M. Rubin, *Corpus Christi: the Eucharist in Late Medieval Culture*, Cambridge, 1991.

G. H. Russell, 'Vernacular instruction of the laity in the later middle ages in England: some texts and notes', *Journal of Religious History*, II, 1962, pp. 98–119.

H. E. Salter, ed., *Snappe's Formulary and Other Records*, Oxford Historical Society, LXXX, 1924.

A. Saltman, ed., *The Cartulary of the Wakebridge Chantries at Crich*, Derbyshire Archaeological Society, Record Series, VI, 1976, for 1971.

M. G. Sargent, 'Minor devotional writings', in *Middle English Prose: a Critical Guide to Major Authors and Genres*, ed. A. S. G. Edwards, New Brunswick, N.J., 1984, pp. 147–75.

J. J. Scarisbrick, *The Reformation and the English People*, Oxford, 1984.

M. Sellers, ed., *York Memorandum Book, Part II (1388–1493)*, Surtees Society Publications, CXXV, 1914.

J. Shaw, 'The influence of canonical and episcopal reform on popular books of instruction', in *The Popular Literature of Medieval England*, ed. T. J. Heffernan,

Tennessee Studies in Literature, XXVIII, Knoxville, Tenn., 1985, pp. 44–60.

P. Sheingorn, 'Appropriating the Holy Kinship: gender and family history', in *Interpreting Cultural Symbols: Saint Anne in Late Medieval Society*, ed. K. Ashley and P. Sheingorn, Athens, Ga., and London, 1990, pp. 169–98.

P. Sheldrake, *Spirituality and History: Questions of Interpretation and Method*, London, 1991.

T. F. Simmons, ed., *The Lay Folks' Mass Book*, Early English Text Society, original ser., LXXI, 1879.

T. Smith, L. T. Smith and L. Brentano, eds, *English Gilds*, Early English Text Society, original ser., XL, 1870.

C. A. Sneyd, ed., *A Relation, or Rather a True Account, of the Island of England, with Sundry Particulars of these People and of the Royal Revenues under King Henry the Seventh, about the Year 1500*, Camden Society Publications, 1st ser., XXVII, 1847.

W. C. Sparrow, 'A register of the Palmers Guild of Ludlow in the reign of Henry VII', *Transactions of the Shropshire Archaeological and Natural History Society*, 1st ser., VII, 1884, pp. 81–126.

B. Spencer, 'Medieval pilgrim badges: some general observations illustrated mainly from English sources', in *Rotterdam Papers: a Contribution to Medieval Archaeology*, ed. J. G. N. Renaud, Rotterdam, 1968, pp. 137–54.

B. Spencer, 'King Henry of Windsor and the London pilgrim', in *Collectanea Londiniensia: Studies in London Archaeology and History Presented to Ralph Merrifield*, ed. J. Bird, H. Chapman and J. Clark, London and Middlesex Archaeological Society, Special Papers, II, 1978, pp. 234–64.

U. Stargardt, 'The beguines of Belgium, the Dominican nuns of Germany, and Margery Kempe', in *The Popular Literature of Medieval England*, ed. T. J. Heffernan, Tennessee Studies in Literature, XXVIII, Knoxville, Tenn., 1985, pp. 277–313.

B. Stock, *The Implications of Literacy: Written Language and Models of Interpretation in the Eleventh and Twelfth Centuries*, Princeton, N.J., 1983.

B. Stock, *Listening for the Text: on the Uses of the Past*, Baltimore and London, 1990.

J. Sumption, *Pilgrimage: an Image of Mediaeval Religion*, London, 1975.

R. N. Swanson, *Church and Society in Late Medieval England*, Oxford, 1989.

R. N. Swanson, 'Sede vacante administration in the medieval diocese of Carlisle: the accounts of the vacancy of December 1395 to March 1396', *Transactions of the Cumberland and Westmorland Antiquarian and Archaeological Society*, XC, 1990, pp. 183–94.

R. N. Swanson, 'Problems of the priesthood in pre-Reformation England', *English Historical Review*, CV, 1990, pp. 845–69.

R. N. Swanson, 'Standards of livings: parochial revenues in pre-Reformation England', in *Religious Belief and Ecclesiastical Careers in Late Medieval England*, ed. C. Harper-Bill, Woodbridge, 1991, pp. 151–96.

R. N. Swanson, 'Chaucer's parson and other priests', *Studies in the Age of Chaucer*, XIII, 1991, pp. 41–80.

R. N. Swanson, 'Medieval liturgy as theatre: the props', *Studies in Church History*, XXIX, 1992, pp. 239–53.

N. P. Tanner, ed., *Heresy Trials in the Diocese of Norwich, 1428–31*, Camden Society Publications, 4th ser., XX, 1977.

Testamenta Eboracensia, III, Surtees Society Publications, XLV, 1865.

Testamenta Eboracensia, IV, Surtees Society Publications, LIII, 1868.

J. A. F. Thomson, *The Later Lollards, 1414–1520*, Oxford, 1965.

J. A. F. Thomson, *The Transformation of Medieval England, 1370–1529*, London, 1983.

J. A. F. Thomson, 'Orthodox religion and the origins of Lollardy', *History*, LXXIV, 1989, pp. 39–55.

The Thornton Manuscript, Lincoln Cathedral MS. 91, introduction by D. S. Brewer and A. E. B. Owen, London, 1975.

R. G. Twombly, 'Remembering death and dismembering the self; 1418, 1440 and after', *Journal of Literature and Theology*, II, 1989, pp. 189–210.

M. G. A. Vale, *Piety, Charity, and Literacy among the Yorkshire Gentry, 1370–1480*, Borthwick Papers, L, York, 1976.

A. Vauchez, *La sainteté en occident des derniers siècles du moyen âge, d'après les procès de canonisation et les documents hagiographiques*, Bibliothèque des écoles françaises d'Athènes et de Rome, CCXLI, Rome, 1981.

E. W. W. Veale, ed., *The Great Red Book of Bristol, I*, Bristol Record Society, IV, 1933.

E. W. W. Veale, ed., *The Great Red Book of Bristol, IV*, Bristol Record Society, XVIII, 1953.

E. Venables, 'The shrine and head of St Hugh of Lincoln', *Associated Architectural Societies Reports and Papers*, XXI, 1891–2, pp. 131–51.

The Vernon Manuscript; a Facsimile of Bodleian Library, Oxford, MS. Eng. Poet.a.1, introduction by A. I. Doyle, Cambridge, 1987.

Victoria County History: Shropshire, II, Oxford, 1973.

M. F. Wakelin, 'A note on preaching "roodes and othyr ymages" in mediaeval England', *Downside Review*, CIII, 1985, pp. 76–86.

S. S. Walker, 'Proof of age of feudal heirs in medieval England', *Mediaeval Studies*, XXXV, 1973, pp. 306–23.

J. Walsh, *Pre-Reformation English Spirituality*, London, n.d.

A. K. Warren, *Anchorites and their Patrons in Medieval England*, Berkeley, Los Angeles and London, 1988.

F. E. Warren, ed., *The Sarum Missal in English*, Alcuin Club Collections, XI, 2 vols, London, 1913.

R. Weber, ed., *Biblia Sacra iuxtra Vulgatam versionem*, 2 vols, Stuttgart, 1969.

S. Wenzel, *Preachers, Poets, and the Early English Lyric*, Princeton, N.J., 1986.

H. F. Westlake, *The Parish Guilds of Medieval England*, London, 1919.

R. Whiting, *The Blind Devotion of the People: Popular Religion and the English Reformation*, Cambridge, 1989.

R. S. Wieck, *Time Sanctified: the Book of Hours in Medieval Art and Life*, New York, 1988.

M. Wilks, 'Misleading manuscripts: Wyclif and the non-Wycliffite Bible', *Studies in Church History*, XI, 1975, pp. 147–61.

C. H. Williams, ed., *English Historical Documents, 1485–1558*, London, 1963.

B. L. Windeatt, ed., *The Book of Margery Kempe*, Harmondsworth, 1985.

C. Wolters, ed., *Julian of Norwich, Revelations of Divine Love*, Harmondsworth, 1966.

M. Wood, *The English Mediaeval House*, London, 1981.

K. Wood-Legh, *Perpetual Chantries in Britain*, Cambridge, 1965.

K. L. Wood-Legh, *Kentish Visitations of Archbishop William Warham and his Deputies, 1511–1512*, Kent Records, XXIV, 1984.

C. E. Woodruff, 'The financial aspect of the cult of St Thomas of Canterbury, as recorded by a study of the monastic records', *Archaeologia Cantiana*, XLIV, 1932, pp. 13–32.

C. Wordsworth, ed., *Ordinale Sarum, sive directorium sacerdotum*, Henry Bradshaw Society, XX, XXII, 1901.

D. P. Wright, ed., *The Register of Thomas Langton, Bishop of Salisbury, 1485–93*, Canterbury and York Society, LXXIV, 1985.

S. K. Wright, 'The provenance and manuscript tradition of the *Martyrium Ricardi archiepiscopi*', *Manuscripta*, XXVIII, 1984, pp. 92–102.

S. K. Wright, 'Paradigmatic ambiguities in monastic historiography: the case of Clement Maidstone's *Martyrium Ricardi archiepiscopi*', *Studia Monastica*, XXVIII, 1986, pp. 311–42.

M. L. Zell, 'The use of religious preambles as a measure of religious belief in the sixteenth century', *Bulletin of the Institute of Historical Research*, L, 1977, pp. 246–9.

C. Zika, 'Hosts, processions, and pilgrimages in fifteenth-century Germany', *Past and Present*, CXVIII, Feb. 1988, pp. 25–64.

Index

This is not intended to be a full index: the Table of Contents offers an initial breakdown of the material. The function of this index is supplementary, for purposes of cross-reference, and to give more detail for matters not immediately evident from the Contents. The Introduction and preliminary comments to each Section have been fully indexed, including names and places. The documents have not been so treated: for them this is only a subject index, the depth varying according to the nature of the document under consideration.

Abbey of the Holy Ghost, 17-18, 92-3
abjuration, 273, 276, 279
absolution, 80, 84, 146, 212-13, 271, 274, 278
accounts, churchwardens', 26-8
  rectorial, 28-9, 150-65
  shrine-keepers', *see* shrines, accounts of
alabasters, 5
Alcock, John, bishop of Ely, 92
alms, 25, 59, 214, 219-20, 252
almshouses, 234, 238-9, 242, 248-9
anchorites, 165
angels, 68, 99, 138, 146-7
  guardian, 21, 138
animals, leasing of, 27
Anne, St, 9
anniversary, offering at 150-6; *see also* obit
anticlericalism, 32-4, 260
apocrypha, 12, 52
archives, 7-8, 26-7, 30, 164
audiences, 21-4
Augustine, St, 93, 269
Ave Maria, 9, 16, 20, 84, 87, 89, 91, 123, 175, 221, 236, 239

bankruptcy, 31
baptism, 29, 56, 268, 270-1, 274, 277
bead-roll, 227, 238
Beaufort, Lady Margaret, 40-1, 94, 166
bequests, 25, 30-1, 204, 206, 222
  to churches, 157, 159-63, 245, 247, 253-4
  for marriages, 246, 251, 256-7, 258
  to religious houses, 245, 248, 250-1, 256; *see also* friars
  for vestments, 247
Bible, access to, 9-12
  citation of 92
  translation of, 10-11
Blunham, accounts of, 29n
Book of the Craft of Dying, 17, 19-20, 92-5
books, 245, 267
Books of Hours, 20, 175
Boston guild, 203
boxes, oblations in, 157-9, 161-3
bread, holy, 160-1, 262-3, 266, 279
bridges, 165, 204, 255-6
Brigittines, 18
burial, 55, 219-20, 225, 245, 250, 254, 254, 258, 265; *see also* funerals
Bury St Edmunds, 37

Carthusians, 18, 243
catechising, 20
cathedrals, shrines in, 176
celibacy, clerical, 259
censures, ecclesiastical, *see* excommunication
chantries, 26-8, 30, 39, 222-3, 235-43, 245, 247-9, 255, 258, 262-4, 269
chapels, bridge, 161-2, 167, 172
  parochial, 152, 155, 159-63, 171, 172-3, 204
  private, 164-5
  see also images; shrines
chaplains, payments to, 28; *see also* priests, salaries of
charity, 46, 54, 71, 76, 87, 90, 97-9, 106-10, 115-16, 119, 131-2, 136, 201, 204-6, 223, 242n, 248, 255

works of, 55-6, 105
chastity, vows of, 42, 166
Chaucer, Geoffrey, *Parson's Tale*, 17
children, obligations of, 246
choristers, 237, 240
Christ, devotion to, 39, 120-1, 175
and Eucharist, 78-82, 88-9, 101, 268, 271, 274, 278
as model, 59, 109, 137
Passion of, 80-1, 101, 111, 120, 124, 130, 134-7, 139, 144-5, 254, 277
as personification of Church, 111-12
prayers to, 21, 86-7, 89, 91, 138, 142-5
visions of, 116
Church, ages of, 65-6, 68
definition of, 1, 7, 111
patriarchy in, 9
records of, 3; *see also* archives; courts, ecclesiastical; visitation
churches, activity within, 27-30
building and maintenance, 27-8, 101
gifts to, 161
shrines in, 177
churchwardens 230
accounts of, *see* accounts, churchwardens'
clergy, 10, 14, 61, 66, 69-70, 74-5, 108, 110, 268, 270, 275
attitudes to, 25, 32-4, 40, 259-60
theology provided by, 34
Colet, John, 14, 34
commonplace books, 16, 21
'common profit' books, 94
communion, 78n, 91, 260, 262-3; *see also* mass
confession, 53, 73, 78, 81, 84, 91, 130, 140, 213-14, 262-3, 268, 271, 274, 277
confessors, appointment of, 211-13
confirmation, 56-7, 269, 271, 274, 277
contemplation, 97, 107-8
Corpus Christi, 78, 213, 215
Courtenay, William, archbishop of Canterbury, 31
courts, ecclesiastical, records of, 33-4, 36-7
Creed, 9, 15, 20, 51n, 56, 84, 86-9, 91, 128-9, 135, 239
Crich, chantry at, 223n

death, 19-20, 60, 73, 94-5
debts, 245, 247, 251
cancellation of, 247
despair, 129-31
devil, 76, 98-9, 103-4, 113, 128-30, 132-3
devotion, 2, 39, 101-2, 120, 123-4, 142
'devotional theatre', 23
Dives and Pauper, 25, 51n
doles, 25, 243n; *see also* alms
Drury, John, 15-16, 51

England, linguistic divisions in, 7n
spirituality in, 7-8, 31-2, 42-3
English, linguistic development of, 23-4
excommunication, 141, 212, 219-20, 232, 268-9, 272, 275, 278
executors, 31, 40, 222, 226, 234-42, 245-9, 251-2, 254, 256-8
exempla, 60-4, 68-9, 111-12
Exeter cathedral, 202

faith, articles of, *see* Creed
fasting, 105, 212, 269, 272, 275, 277-8
fashion, 25-6
feasts, liturgical, 32, 175, 270, 272, 275, 278
feoffees to uses, transfers between, 235, 240
Fish, Simon, 33-4
Fisher, John, 41
fraternities, 201-3, 227-8, 234-9; *see also* guilds
fraud, 74
friars, 160, 213-14, 222, 243, 265, 269
bequests to, 25, 243, 245, 250-1, 256
preaching by, 12-14
friaries, burial in, 250
chantries in, 223
obits within, 251-2
funerals, 25, 28-9, 150, 214, 250, 254
offerings at, 151-6
Fyneham, Thomas, will of, 242n

gentry, spirituality of, 41
Gerson, Jean, 93
godchildren, 247, 251
godparents, 9, 246
Gregory, St, 92
trental of, 222
guilds, 30, 39, 150, 152-4, 158, 161-3
craft, 203, 224-5
see also fraternities

Hail Mary *see* Ave Maria
Hailes, holy blood of, 175, 178, 195
Henry VI, cult of, 150, 158-9, 182-5, 195
  miracles of, 178
Hereford, Nicholas, 13
heresy, 13-14, 22, 34-8, 128, 135, 212, 260
hermits, 165-6, 174, 204-5
hierarchy, 16
Hilton, Walter, 93
  Epistle of the Mixed Life, 17-19, 92-3
  Scale of Perfection, 93
Hornsea, accounts of, 29
household, 8-9, 24, 164
Hull, 27
Hungerford, Margaret Lady, 40-1

iconoclasm, 260, 266
iconography, 6, 9, 12, 16
idolatry, 74, 272, 276
Ignorantia sacerdotum, 15
images, 17, 37, 142, 164, 179-81, 195, 269, 272, 276, 279
  offerings to, 157-63, 269
Imitation of Christ, 40
imprisonment, false, 75
indulgences, 16, 20n, 30, 39, 160, 176, 186-8, 194-5, 201-3, 218
interdict, 220
inventories, 165
Ipswich, 179

Jesus, *see* Christ
jubilation, 99
Judgement, Last, 55-6, 64-6

Kebell, Thomas, 165, 242-3
Kempe, Margery, 22-4, 166, 176
  Book of, 4, 13, 23, 41-2
King's Lynn, 13, 42
  accounts of, 28-9, 150
  shrines at, 150, 176

laity, and clergy, *see* clergy, attitudes to
  offences by, 59, 259-60, 265-6
  spirituality of, 17-18, 21
Langmuir, Gavin, 1-2, 7n, 8n, 30n
Latin, 10-12, 23, 51, 78
law, canon, 270, 275
Layfolks' Catechism, 15
Layfolks' Mass Book, 79

leper houses, bequests to, 251
letters, 3
Lichfield cathedral, 202
lights, provision of, 213, 215, 264
literacy, lay, 10, 21
liturgy, 5, 21n, 32, 78
Lollardy, 7, 9-11, 21n, 33, 35-8, 51-3, 56, 260
London, St Anthony's hospital, 202
  St Paul's Cross, 13
Love, Nicholas, 16, 243
Ludlow, Palmers guild of, 203
Luther, Martin, 40
lyrics, 12n

marriage, 29, 57, 59, 271, 275, 278
  bequests for, 245, 251, 256
  payments at, 25, 28, 150
Mary, Virgin, 9, 39, 120-1, 138, 145, 175, 195-6,
  chapels for, 157-63
  see also images; prayers; saints
mass, 20, 29, 39, 57, 101, 218-21, 237, 253, 268, 271, 274, 278
  lay action at, 78-9
  payments for, 28, 78, 150, 157, 159-61
  for souls, 157-63, 212, 221-2, 226, 232, 242n, 245, 251
  votive, 78
meditation, 17, 93, 101-2, 111-12, 122-3
memory, 9, 11, 13, 15-16, 21
Methley, Richard, 243
Michael, St, 144
miracles, 178-9
Mirk, John. *Festial*, 51-2
  Instructions for Parish Priests, 14-15, 95
mnemonics, use of, 15-16
monasteries, chantries in, 223
  obits in, 225-6
  oversight of chantries by, 239-40
monks, 269
mortmain, 226-7, 230, 242-3, 249
mortuary, 25, 150, 157-62, 245, 250, 254
Mount Grace, 243
music, 5-6; *see also* choristers
mysticism, 4, 17, 22
nationalism, 175
Norwich, Julian of, 9, 95
nunneries, bequests to, 245
nuns, spirituality of, 21

oaths, 270, 272, 276, 278

obits, 150, 222, 232-3, 237-8, 240, 243, 249-52, 256-7, 266
offerings at, 151-7
oblations, 25, 28, 150-63, 261, 278
offerings, *see* oblations
oratories, within nunnery, 169
see also chapels, private
ordination of clergy, 57, 269, 275
Osmund, St, miracles of, 178
Our Father, 9, 16, 20, 84-91, 123, 219, 221, 236, 239
Oxford, parishes within, 29n

papacy, indulgences offered by, 211
offences reserved to for absolution, 212
parish, 7
financial records of, *see* accounts, church-wardens'; accounts, rectorial
Paston, Margaret, 164
Paul, St, Rule of, 166
Peasants' Revolt, 35
Pecham, John, archbishop of Canterbury, 15
penance, 53, 72, 78, 99-100, 105, 211-12, 218, 220, 271, 274, 277, 279-80
pilgrim badges, 178
pilgrimage, 29, 39, 42, 150, 175-8, 186-8, 201, 269, 272, 276, 279
plague, 150, 159
plays, 5, 12, 27, 39, 78, 215
politics, 25
poor, donations to, 25, 97, 242n, 248, 254, 257
pope, 268, 271, 274
Pore Caitif, 51n, 94n
Port, Sir John, 244
poverty, 14
prayer, 17, 80, 99, 119, 137, 273
prayers, 20-1, 84-91, 95, 124, 137-9, 141-7, 196, 201, 205, 212, 221-3, 232-3, 236-8, 245-53, 269, 279
preaching, 12, 24, 65-6, 268; *see also* sermons
priests, 9, 22, 24, 80, 271, 274, 276, 278
financial accounts of, *see* accounts, rectorial
quality of, 236-7
salaries of, 26, 236-7, 250, 253, 255, 269
see also clergy
printing, 3-4, 32, 39, 52, 92, 94
processions, 5, 213, 221
proofs of age, 29
psalms, 20, 236-7, 245, 252
Psalter, 10n, 11
recitation of, 123, 218-20
Purgatory, 20, 66, 78, 89, 95, 132, 201, 222, 276
purification, 29
payments at, 28, 150-63

questors, 205-6, 219-20

rationality, 6-7
rectories, appropriated, 28
financial accounts of, *see* accounts, rectorial
reform, 34, 43
Reformation, 6, 14, 26, 33, 38, 43, 244
relics, 155, 164, 182-94, 202n, 220, 266
religion, definition of, 1-2
popular and elite, 8, 24
'religiosity', 1-2, 30n, 37
rent charges, for masses, 226
for obits, 158-9
for trentals, 224-5
restitution, 136
roads, 165, 205, 242n, 255-6
Robin Hood, 43
Rolle, Richard, 3, 18-19, 92
Rosary, 20, 179-80, 253

sacraments, 16, 56-7, 278; *see also under individual sacraments*
saints, 29, 32, 37, 39, 65, 67, 120-1, 138-9, 157, 161-3, 175-6, 196, 269, 273, 276, 279; *see also* prayers
Saltash, 33-4, 259
Sarum, Use of, 32
Scarborough, accounts of, 28-9, 150
scholars, support of, 242n, 247, 256
schools and colleges, bequests to, 255
chantries and, 223
sectarianism, 36-7
sermons, 11, 12-14, 30, 39, 42-3, 51-3
shrines, 176-8
accounts of, 176
domestic, 20n
donations to, 43, 150, 176
simony, 75
sin, 15, 53-4, 58-9, 62-3, 69, 75-7, 82, 96,

105, 113, 116, 119, 121, 130-1, 133, 135-8, 140-1, 143-6, 201, 272, 275
plenary remission of, 211-13
see also absolution; confession
spirituality, appreciations of, 6-7, 22-3, 25, 30-2, 38-9
changes in, 40
continuity in, 8
definition of, 1-3
domestic, 164
localism of, 7, 27-9, 31-2, 34, 42
motivations and, 25, 31, 166, 175, 179, 202
social status and, 25, 40-2
status, social, 25, 115
Strangweys, Jane, 243
suicide, 220

Ten Commandments, 15, 51n, 53-4
Tenterden, 260
texts, approaches to, 4, 6, 12-13, 16, 22, 40, 52, 92, 94-5
compilations of, 4, 15-16, 51n, 94
devotional and instructional, 3, 7-8, 11-13, 15-22, 51n, 78-9, 92-5, 164
printed, 4, 19
publication of, 16
reception of, 21-2, 24, 38, 92
textual community, 21
theology, vocabulary of, 11, 23-4
three estates, doctrine of, 53, 61, 72-4
tithes, 25, 157-9, 245, 261-5, 269, 272, 275, 278
personal, 150, 157-63
tombs, 25, 245
towns, 7, 14
translation, into English, 19, 40, 79, 92, 95
trental, 213-14, 222, 243, 245, 250-1

unction, extreme, 57, 261, 271-2, 275, 278

vestments, 247-8, 253
virtues, 57-8, 96-105, 120
visions, 23
visitation, records of, 33-4, 259-60
vows, 218-19

wall paintings, 5
water, holy, 142; *see also* bread, holy
wax, 27, 151-60, 177, 182-95, 211, 250
Wells cathedral, 202
Whytford, Richard, 8
wills, 8, 25, 27, 30-1, 41, 139-40, 222, 242-4
women, and transmission of religion, 9, 138
woodcuts, 20n, 39n, 164
Wycliffe, John, 35

Yarmouth, Great, accounts of, 28-9, 150, 177
York, Cicely, duchess of, 40
York Minster, 202n
relics at, 202n